COMPILER DESIGN

By

Dr. O.G. KAKDE

M.Tech. (Comp. Sc.) IIT Bombay, Ph.D.
DIRECTOR, VJTI, Mumbai
Maharashtra

UNIVERSITY SCIENCE PRESS

(An Imprint of Laxmi Publications Pvt. Ltd.)
An ISO 9001:2008 Company

BENGALURU • CHENNAI • COCHIN • GUWAHATI • HYDERABAD
JALANDHAR • KOLKATA • LUCKNOW • MUMBAI • RANCHI • NEW DELHI
INDIA • USA • GHANA • KENYA

COMPILER DESIGN

Printed and bound in India

Typeset at : Goswami Associates, Delhi

Third Edition : 2005, *Reprint* : 2007, *Fourth Edition* : 2008, *Reprint* : 2009, 2010, 2011, 2014

ISBN : 978-81-318-0564-0

PUBLISHED IN INDIA BY

UNIVERSITY SCIENCE PRESS

(An Imprint of Laxmi Publications Pvt. Ltd.)

An ISO 9001:2008 Company

113, GOLDEN HOUSE, DARYAGANJ, NEW DELHI-110002, INDIA

Telephone : 91-11-4353 2500, 4353 2501

Fax : 91-11-2325 2572, 4353 2528

www.laxmipublications.com info@laxmipublications.com

Branches

✆ **Bengaluru**	080-26 75 69 30
✆ **Chennai**	044-24 34 47 26
✆ **Cochin**	0484-237 70 04, 405 13 03
✆ **Guwahati**	0361-254 36 69, 251 38 81
✆ **Hyderabad**	040-27 55 53 83, 27 55 53 93
✆ **Jalandhar**	0181-222 12 72
✆ **Kolkata**	033-22 27 43 84
✆ **Lucknow**	0522-220 99 16
✆ **Mumbai**	022-24 91 54 15, 24 92 78 69
✆ **Ranchi**	0651-220 44 64

C—9820/015/02

Printed at : Sanjeev Offset Printes, Delhi.

COMPILER DESIGN

PREFACE TO THE FOURTH EDITION

This book on algorithms for compiler design covers the various aspects of designing a language translator in depth. The book is intended to be a basic reading material in compiler design.

Enough examples and algorithms have been used to effectively explain various tools of compiler design. The first chapter gives a brief introduction of the compiler and is thus important for the rest of the book.

Other issues like context free grammar, parsing techniques, syntax directed definitions, symbol table, code optimization and more are explain in various chapters of the book.

The final chapter has some exercises for the readers for practice.

ACKNOWLEDGMENTS

The author wishes to thank all of the colleagues in the Department of Electronics and Computer Science Engineering at Visvesvaraya Regional College of Engineering Nagpur, whose constant encouragement and timely help have resulted in the completion of this book. Special thanks go to Dr. C. S. Moghe, with whom the author had long technical discussions, which found their place in this book. Thanks are due to the institution for providing all of the infrastructural facilities and tools for a timely completion of this book. The author would particularly like to acknowledge Mr. P. S. Deshpande and Mr. A. S. Mokhade for their invaluable help and support from time to time. Finally, the author wishes to thank all of his students.

CONTENTS

1 INTRODUCTION

1.1 PROGRAM AND PROGRAMMING LANGUAGE

Program

A program is a specification of what data computer is required to process, by using what operations, and by going in what sequence.

Programming Language

A programming language is a notation used to specify the data operations/ instructions and sequence, and which is available on a computer or understandable to the computer.

Every computer is designed to understand one language, which is called as machine language of that computer, and it is a language whose alphabet contains only two symbols 0 and 1. An **alphabet** of a language is a finite set of symbols used to form every valid word of that language. For example alphabet of English contains a to z and A to Z. Machine language of a computer allows us to specify data, instructions, and sequence, which are the three basic elements of any program. Hence it is a programming language. A machine language program is made of sequence of statements each having opcode field and operand field. The opcode field is used to specify the operation, whereas the operand field is used to specify the data to be operated on. And the order in which the statements are written decides the sequence in which these operations are carried out.

When we use machine language the program is directly understandable to the computer and hence can be directly loaded and executed on the computer. But the cost of program development is very high. (That means the cost of preparing the specification of what data computer should process, by using what operations, and by going in what sequence is very high). The reason for this is poor support for abstractions. While solving a problem, programmer generally thinks of a solution to the problem in terms of abstractions. For example while solving a particular problem a programmer may encounter a situation of selecting one of the two alternatives. The most natural construct that comes to mind to deal with this situation is **if-then-else**, which is an abstraction of control. Another example is if a programmer wants to manipulate **n** data items that are identical, and related in some way. (For example they are all marks scored by students of a particular class in a particular subject). The most natural structure that comes to mind for representing these data is a **list**, which is an abstraction of data. Now if the programming language to be used supports these abstractions, then programming becomes natural, easier and less time consuming. But unfortunately machine language does not support these abstractions. Therefore implementation of those abstractions becomes the responsibility of programmer while writing program, thereby making the program development less natural, and hence time consuming.

Therefore to make the process of program development efficient such a notation is required to be used as a programming language, that provides reasonably good support of those abstractions that programmer uses while solving problem. The high-level language notations fulfils this requirement, and hence the use of high-level language notation makes the program development more natural, easier and efficient.

But when a high-level language notation is used, the program written is not directly understandable to the computer or machine on which we want to get the task done. Therefore a need arises to make high-level language that we want to use understandable to the computer or machine. This is done by writing down a system program called as compiler or by writing a system program called as interpreter. Both compiler and interpreter serves the same purpose, i.e., making a high-level language notation understandable to computer. But the approaches used are different. Compiler uses an approach of translation, whereas an interpreter uses an approach of software simulation.

When a program written in a high-level language is given as input to the compiler of that language, then the compiler analyzes it to check for is validity, and then interprets it to come to know what operations are specified, and generates either assembly language or machine language or some intermediate language code, for getting those operations carried. If the generated code is machine code then it can be linked and loaded directly for execution on target computer. When we use an interpreter then it also analyzes and interprets the source code to come to know what operations are specified, but instead of generating code to get those operations carried out, it executes itself carrying out those operations. Hence, simulating the execution of high-level language program on target computer. Therefore when an interpreter is used source program is run directly, no object code is generated. Whereas when a compiler is used, the object is generated, to be executed later, to get operations specified in the source code carried out. Therefore no object file is generated when an interpreter is used.

1.2 WHAT IS A COMPILER?

A compiler is a program that translates a high-level language program into a functionally equivalent low-level language program. So, a compiler is basically a translator whose source language (i.e., language to be translated) is the high-level language, and the target language is a low-level language; that is, a compiler is used to implement a high-level language on a computer.

1.3 WHAT IS A CROSS-COMPILER?

A cross-compiler is a compiler that runs on one machine and produces object code for another machine. The cross-compiler is used to implement the compiler, which is characterized by three languages:

1. The source language,
2. The object language, and
3. The language in which it is written.

If a compiler has been implemented in its own language, then this arrangement is called a "bootstrap" arrangement. The implementation of a compiler in its own language can be done as follows.

Implementing a Bootstrap Compiler

Suppose we have a new language, L, that we want to make available on machines A and B. As a first step, we can write a small compiler: ${}^{S}C_{A}{}^{A}$, which will translate an S subset of L to the object code for machine A, written in a language available on A. We then write a compiler ${}^{S}C_{S}^{A}$, which is compiled in language L and generates object code written in an S subset of L for machine A. But this will not be able to execute unless and until it is translated by ${}^{S}C_{A}^{A}$; therefore, ${}^{S}C_{S}^{A}$ is an input into ${}^{S}C_{A}^{A}$, as shown below, producing a compiler for L that will run on machine A and self-generate code for machine A: ${}^{S}C_{A}^{A}$.

$${}^{S}C_{S}^{A} \rightarrow {}^{S}C_{A}^{A} \rightarrow {}^{L}C_{A}^{A}$$

Now, if we want to produce another compiler to run on and produce code for machine B, the compiler can be written, itself, in L and made available on machine B by using the following steps:

$${}^{L}C_{L}^{B} \rightarrow {}^{L}C_{A}^{A} \rightarrow {}^{L}C_{A}^{B}$$
$${}^{L}C_{L}^{B} \rightarrow {}^{L}C_{A}^{B} \rightarrow {}^{L}C_{B}^{B}$$

1.4 COMPILATION

Compilation refers to the compiler's process of translating a high-level language program into a low-level language program. This process is very complex; hence, from the logical as well as an implementation point of view, it is customary to partition the compilation process into several phases, which are nothing more than logically cohesive operations that input one representation of a source program and output another representation.

A typical compilation, broken down into phases, is shown in Figure 1.1.

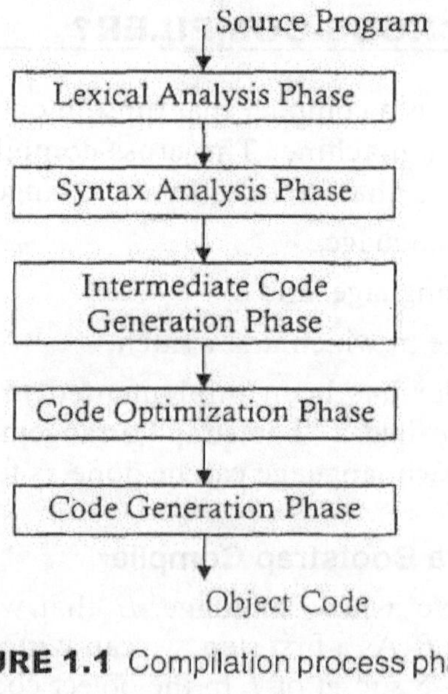

FIGURE 1.1 Compilation process phases.

The initial process phases analyze the source program. The lexical analysis phase reads the characters in the source program and groups them into streams of tokens; each token represents a logically cohesive sequence of characters, such as identifiers, operators, and keywords. The character sequence that forms a token is called a "lexeme." Certain tokens are augmented by the lexical value; that is, when an identifier like *xyz* is found, the lexical analyzer not only returns id, but it also enters the lexeme *xyz* into the symbol table if it does not already exist there. It returns a pointer to this symbol table entry as a lexical value associated with this occurrence of the token id. Therefore, when internally representing a statement like $X := Y + Z$, after the lexical analysis will be $\text{id}_1 := \text{id}_2 + \text{id}_3$.

The subscripts 1, 2, and 3 are used for convenience; the actual token is id. The syntax analysis phase imposes a hierarchical structure on the token string, as shown in Figure 1.2.

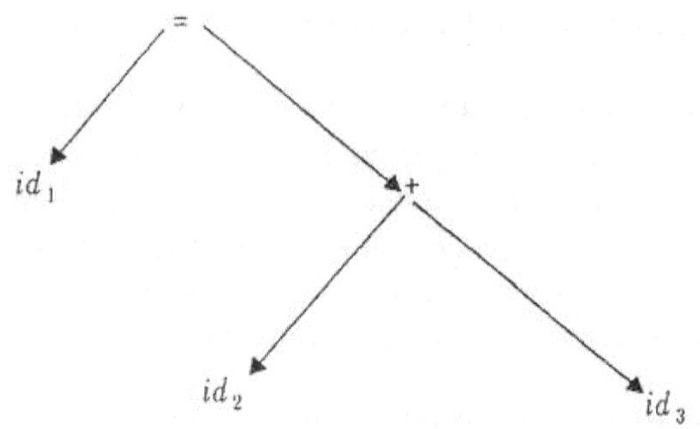

FIGURE 1.2 Syntax analysis imposes a structure hierarchy on the token string.

Intermediate Code Generation

Some compilers generate an explicit intermediate code representation of the source program. The intermediate code can have a variety of forms. For example, a three-address code (TAC) representation for the tree shown in Figure 1.2 will be:

$$T_1 := \text{id}_2 + \text{id}_3$$
$$\text{id}_1 := T_2$$

where T_1 and T_2 are compiler-generated temporaries.

Code Optimization

In the optimization phase, the compiler performs various transformations in order to improve the intermediate code. These transformations will result in faster-running machine code.

Code Generation

The final phase in the compilation process is the generation of target code. This process involves selecting memory locations for each variable used by the program. Then, each intermediate instruction is translated into a sequence of machine instructions that performs the same task.

Compiler Phase Organization

This is the logical organization of compiler. It reveals that certain phases of the compiler are heavily dependent on the source language and are independent of the code requirements of the target machine. All such phases, when grouped together, constitute the front end of the compiler; whereas those phases that are dependent on the target machine constitute the back end of the compiler. Grouping the compilation phases in the front and back ends facilitates the re-targeting of the code; implementation of the same source language on different machines can be done by rewriting only the back end.

NOTE

Different languages can also implemented on the same machine by rewriting the front end and using the same back end. But to do this, all of the front ends are required to produce the same intermediate code; and this is difficult, because the front end depends on the source language, and different languages are designed with different viewpoints. Therefore, it becomes difficult to write the front ends for different languages by using a common intermediate code.

Having relatively few passes is desirable from the point of view of reducing the compilation time. To reduce the number of passes, it is required to group several phases in one pass. For some of the phases, being grouped into one pass is not a major problem. For example, the lexical analyzer and syntax analyzer can easily be grouped into one pass, because the interface between them is a single token; that is, the processing required by the token is independent of other tokens. Therefore, these phases can be easily grouped together, with the lexical analyzer working as a subroutine of the syntax analyzer, which is charge of the entire analysis activity.

Conversely, grouping some of the phases into one pass is not that easy. Grouping intermediate and object code-generation phases is difficult, because it is often very hard to perform object code generation until a sufficient number of intermediate code statements have been generated. Here, the interface between the two is not based on only one intermediate instruction-certain languages permit the use of a variable before it is declared. Similarly, many languages also permit forward jumps. Therefore, it is not possible to generate object code for a construct until sufficient intermediate code statements have been generated. To overcome this problem and enable the merging of intermediate and object code generation into one pass, the technique called "back-patching" is used; the object code is generated by leaving 'statement holes,' which will be filled later when the information becomes available.

1.4.1 Lexical Analysis Phase

In the lexical analysis phase, the compiler scans the characters of the source program, one character at a time. Whenever it gets a sufficient number of characters to constitute a token of the specified language, it outputs that token. In order to perform this task, the lexical analyzer must know the keywords, identifiers, operators, delimiters, and punctuation symbols of the language to be implemented. So, when it scans the source program, it will be able to return a suitable token whenever it encounters a token lexeme. (Lexeme refers to the sequence of characters in the source program that is matched by language's character patterns that specify identifiers, operators, keywords, delimiters, punctuation symbols, and so forth.) Therefore, the lexical analyzer design must:

1. Specify the token of the language, and
2. Suitably recognize the tokens.

We cannot specify the language tokens by enumerating each and every identifier, operator, keyword, delimiter, and punctuation symbol; our specification would end up spanning several pages—and perhaps never end, especially for those languages that do not limit the number of characters that an identifier can have. Therefore, token specification should be generated by specifying the rules that govern the way that the language's alphabet symbols can be combined, so that the result of the combination will be a token of that language's identifiers, operators, and keywords. This requires the use of suitable language-specific notation.

Regular Expression Notation

Regular expression notation can be used for specification of tokens because tokens constitute a regular set. It is compact, precise, and contains a deterministic finite automata (DFA) that accepts the language specified by the regular expression. The DFA is used to recognize the language specified by the regular expression notation, making the automatic construction of recognizer of tokens possible. Therefore, the study of regular expression notation and finite automata becomes necessary. Some definitions of the various terms used are described below.

1.5 REGULAR EXPRESSION NOTATION/FINITE AUTOMATA DEFINITIONS

String

A string is a finite sequence of symbols. We use a letter, such as w, to denote a string. If w is the string, then the length of string is denoted as $| w |$, and it is a count of number of symbols of w. For example, if $w = xyz$, $| w | = 3$. If $| w | = 0$, then the string is called an "empty" string, and we use $\in$ to denote the empty string.

Prefix

A string's prefix is the string formed by taking any number of leading symbols of string. For example, if $w = abc$, then $\in$, a, ab, and abc are the prefixes of w. Any prefix of a string other than the string itself is called a "proper" prefix of the string.

Suffix

A string's suffix is formed by taking any number of trailing symbols of a string. For example, if $w = abc$, then $\in$, c, bc, and abc are the suffixes of the w. Similar to prefixes, any suffix of a string other than the string itself is called a "proper" suffix of the string.

Concatenation

If w_1 and w_2 are two strings, then the concatenation of w_1 and w_2 is denoted as $w_1.w_2$—simply, a string obtained by writing w_1 followed by w_2 without any space in between (i.e., a juxtaposition of w_1 and w_2). For example, if $w_1 = xyz$, and $w_2 = abc$, then $w_1.w_2 = xyzabc$. If w is a string, then $w.\in = w$, and $\in.w = w$. Therefore, we conclude that $\in$ (empty string) is a concatenation identity.

Alphabet

An alphabet is a finite set of symbols denoted by the symbol Σ.

Language

A language is a set of strings formed by using the symbols belonging to some previously chosen alphabet. For example, if $\Sigma = \{ 0, 1 \}$, then one of the languages that can be defined over this Σ will be $L = \{ \in, 0, 00, 000, 1, 11, 111, \dots \}$.

Set

A set is a collection of objects. It is denoted by the following methods:

1. We can enumerate the members by placing them within curly brackets ({ }). For example, the set A is defined by: $A = \{ 0, 1, 2 \}$.
2. We can use a predetermined notation in which the set is denoted as: $A = \{ x \mid P(x) \}$. This means that A is a set of all those elements x for which the predicate $P(x)$ is true. For example, a set of all integers divisible by three will be denoted as: $A = \{ x \mid x \text{ is an integer and } x \bmod 3 = 0\}$.

Set Operations

- *Union*: If A and B are the two sets, then the union of A and B is denoted as: $A \cup B = \{ x \mid x \text{ in } A \text{ or } x \text{ is in } B \}$.
- *Intersection*: If A and B are the two sets, then the intersection of A and B is denoted as: $A \cap B = \{ x \mid x \text{ is in } A \text{ and } x \text{ is in } B \}$.
- *Set difference*: If A and B are the two sets, then the difference of A and B is denoted as: $A - B = \{ x \mid x \text{ is in } A \text{ but not in } B \}$.
- *Cartesian product*: If A and B are the two sets, then the Cartesian product of A and B is denoted as: $A \times B = \{ (a, b) \mid a \text{ is in } A \text{ and } b \text{ is in } B \}$.
- *Power set:* If A is the set, then the power set of A is denoted as : $2^A = P \mid P \text{ is a subset of } A \}$ (i.e., the set contains of all possible subsets of A.) For example:

  $A = \{ 0, 1 \}$

  $2^A = \{ \Phi, \{0\}, \{1\}, \{0, 1\} \}$
- *Concatenation*: If A and B are the two sets, then the concatenation of A and B is denoted as: $AB = \{ ab \mid a \text{ is in } A \text{ and } b \text{ is in } B \}$. For example, if $A = \{ 0, 1 \}$ and $B = \{ 1, 2 \}$, then $AB = \{ 01, 02, 11, 12 \}$.
- *Closure*: If A is a set, then closure of A is denoted as: $A^* = A^0 \cup A^1 \cup A^2 \cup \ldots \cup A^\infty$, where A^i is the i th power of set A, defined as $A^i = A.A.A \ldots i$ times.

  $A^0 = \{ \in \}$

  (i.e., the set of all possible combination of members of A of length 0)

  $A^1 = A$

  (i.e., the set of all possible combination of members of A of length 1)

$A^2 = A.A$

(i.e., the set of all possible combinations of members of A of length 2)

Therefore A^* is the set of all possible combinations of the members of A. For example, if $\Sigma = \{ 0,1)$, then Σ^* will be the set of all possible combinations of zeros and ones, which is one of the languages defined over Σ.

1.6 RELATIONS

Let A and B be the two sets; then the relationship R between A and B is nothing more than a set of ordered pairs (a, b) such that a is in A and b is in B, and a is related to b by relation R. That is:

$R = \{ (a, b) \mid a \text{ is in } A \text{ and } b \text{ is in } B, \text{ and } a \text{ is related to } b \text{ by } R \}$

For example, if $A = \{ 0, 1 \}$ and $B = \{ 1, 2 \}$, then we can define a relation of 'less than,' denoted by $<$ as follows:

$$< \; = \{ (0, 1), (0, 2), (1, 2) \}$$

A pair (1, 1) will not belong to the $<$ relation, because one is not less than one. Therefore, we conclude that a relation R between sets A and B is the subset of $A \times B$.

If a pair (a, b) is in R, then aRb is true; otherwise, aRb is false.

A is called a "domain" of the relation, and B is called a "range" of the relation. If the domain of a relation R is a set A, and the range is also a set A, then R is called as a relation on set A rather than calling a relation between sets A and B. For example, if $A = \{ 0, 1, 2 \}$, then $a <$ relation defined on A will result in: $< \; = \{ (0, 1), (0, 2), (1, 2) \}$.

1.6.1 Properties of the Relation

Let R be some relation defined on a set A. Therefore:

1. R is said to be reflexive if aRa is true for every a in A; that is, if every element of A is related with itself by relation R, then R is called as a reflexive relation.
2. If every aRb implies bRa (i.e., when a is related to b by R, and if b is also related to a by the same relation R), then a relation R will be a symmetric relation.
3. If every aRb and bRc implies aRc, then the relation R is said to be transitive; that is, when a is related to b by R, and b is related to c by R, and if a is also related to c by relation R, then R is a transitive relation.

If R is reflexive and transitive, as well as symmetric, then R is an equivalence relation.

Property Closure of a Relation

Let R be a relation defined on a set A, and if P is a set of properties, then the property closure of a relation R, denoted as P-closure, is the smallest relation, R', which has the properties mentioned in P. It is obtained by adding every pair (a, b) in R to R', and then adding those pairs of the members of A that will make relation R have the properties in P. If P contains only transitivity properties, then the P-closure will be called as a transitive closure of the relation, and we denote the transitive closure of relation R by R^+; whereas when P contains transitive as well as reflexive properties, then the P-closure is called as a reflexive-transitive closure of relation R, and we denote it by R^*. R^+ can be obtained from R as follows:

$R^+_{old} = \Phi$
$R^+_{new} = R$
While $(R^+_{old} \neq R^+_{new})$
{
$R^+_{old} = R^+_{new}$
for (every pair (a, b) and (b, c) in R^+_{old}) do
add pair (a, c) to R^+_{new} if not already present
}
$R^+ = R^+_{new}$

For example, if:

$R = \{ (0, 1), (1, 2), (3, 4) \}$ then
$R^+ = \{ (0, 1), (1, 2), (3, 4), (0, 2) \}$
$R^* = \{ (0, 1), (1, 2), (3, 4), (0, 2), (0, 0),$
$(1, 1), (2, 2), (3, 3), (4, 4) \}$
$R^* = R^+ \cup \{ (a, a) \mid \text{for every } a \text{ in } A \}$

EXERCISE

1. What is the difference between a compiler and an interpreter?
2. Explain how use of backpatching allows reduction in the number of passes of a compiler?
3. Explain with suitable example, what is bootstrapping?

4. Explain with suitable examples, the concept of r-value and l-value of an expression.
5. What is the advantage of dividing the design of a compiler into front-end design and back-end design?
6. "Code optimization is an optional phase of compilation process". Comment.

2 FINITE AUTOMATA AND REGULAR EXPRESSIONS

2.1 FINITE AUTOMATA

A finite automata consists of a finite number of states and a finite number of transitions, and these transitions are defined on certain, specific symbols called input symbols. One of the states of the finite automata is identified as the initial state the state in which the automata always starts. Similarly, certain states are identified as final states. Therefore, a finite automata is specified as using five things:

1. The states of the finite automata;
2. The input symbols on which transitions are made;
3. The transitions specifying from which state on which input symbol where the transition goes;
4. The initial state; and
5. The set of final states.

Therefore formally a finite automata is a five-tuple:

$$M = (Q, \Sigma, \delta, q_0, F)$$

where:

- Q is a set of states of the finite automata,
- Σ is a set of input symbols, and
- δ specifies the transitions in the automata.

If from a state p there exists a transition going to state q on an input symbol a, then we write $\delta(p, a) = q$. Hence, δ is a function whose domain is a set of ordered pairs, (p, a), where p is a state and a is an input symbol, and the range is a set of states.

Therefore, we conclude that δ defines a mapping whose domain will be a set of ordered pairs of the form (p, a) and whose range will be a set of states. That is, δ defines a mapping from

$$Q \times \Sigma \text{ to } Q,$$

q_0 is the initial state, and

F is a set of final sates of the automata. For example:

$$M = (\{q_0, q_1\}, \{0, 1\}, \delta, q_0, \{q_1\})$$

where

$$\delta(q_0, 0) = q_1, \delta\ (q_0, 1) = q_0$$
$$\delta(q_1, 0) = q_1, \delta\ (q_1, 1) = q_0$$

A directed graph exists that can be associated with finite automata. This graph is called a "transition diagram of finite automata." To associate a graph with finite automata, the vertices of the graph correspond to the states of the automata, and the edges in the transition diagram are determined as follows.

If $\delta\ (p, a) = q$, then put an edge from the vertex, which corresponds to state p, to the vertex that corresponds to state q, labeled by a. To indicate the initial state, we place an arrow with its head pointing to the vertex that corresponds to the initial state of the automata, and we label that arrow "start." We then encircle those vertices twice, that correspond to the final states of the automata. Therefore, the transition diagram for the described finite automata will resemble Figure 2.1.

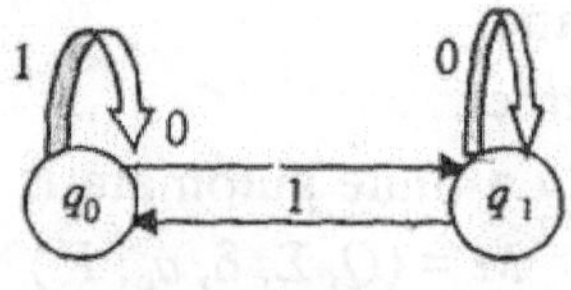

FIGURE 2.1 Transition diagram for finite automata δ (p, a) = q.

A tabular representation can also be used to specify the finite automata. A table whose number of rows is equal to the number of states, and whose number of columns equals the numoer of input symbols, is used to specify the transitions in the automata. The first row specifies the transitions from the initial state; the rows specifying the transitions from the final states are marked as *. For example, the automata above can be specified as follows:

	0	1
q_0	q_1	q_0
$*q_1$	q_1	q_0

A finite automata can be used to accept some particular set of strings. If x is a string made of symbols belonging to Σ of the finite automata, then x is accepted by the finite automata if a path corresponding to x in a finite automata starts in an initial state and ends in one of the final states of the automata; that is, there must exist a sequence of moves for x in the finite automata that takes the transitions from the initial state to one of the final states of the automata. Since x is a member of Σ^*, we define a new transition function, δ_1, which defines a mapping from $Q \times \Sigma^*$ to Q. And if $\delta_1(q_0, x)$ = a member of F, then x is accepted by the finite automata. If x is written as wa, where a is the last symbol of x, and w is a string of the of remaining symbols of x, then:

$\delta_1(q_0, x) = \delta\{\delta_1(q_0, w), a\}$, Since δ_1 defines a mapping from $Q \times \Sigma^*$ to Q

$\delta_1(q_0, a) = \delta(q_0, a)$

For example:

$M = (\{q_0, q_1\}, \{0, 1\}, \delta, q_0, \{q_1\})$,

where

$\delta(q_0, 0) = q_1, \delta(q_0, 0) = q_0$

$\delta(q_1, 0) = q_1, \delta(q_1, 1) = q_0$

Let x be 010. To find out if x is accepted by the automata or not, we proceed as follows:

$\delta_1(q_0, 0) = \delta(q_0, 0) = q_1$

Therefore, $\delta_1(q_0, 01) = \delta\{\delta_1(q_0, 0), 1\} = q_0$

Therefore, $\delta_1(q_0, 010) = \delta\{\delta_1(q_0, 0\,1), 0\} = q_1$

Since q_1 is a member of F, $x = 010$ is accepted by the automata.

If $x = 0101$, then $\delta_1(q_0, 0101) = \delta\{\delta_1(q_0, 010), 1\} = q_0$

Since q_0 is not a member of F, x is not accepted by the above automata.

Therefore, if M is the finite automata, then the language accepted by the finite automata is denoted as $L(M) = \{x \mid \delta_1(q_0, x) = \text{member of } F\}$.

In the finite automata discussed above, since δ defines mapping from $Q \times \Sigma$ to Q, there exists exactly one transition from a state on an input symbol; and therefore, this finite automata is called as a deterministic finite automata (DFA).

Therefore, we define the DFA as the finite automata:

$M = (Q, \Sigma, \delta, q_0, F)$, such that there exists exactly one transition from a state on a input symbol.

2.2 NON-DETERMINISTIC FINITE AUTOMATA

If the basic finite automata model is modified in such a way that from a state on an input symbol zero, one or more transitions are permitted, then the corresponding finite automata is called a "non-deterministic finite automata" (NFA). Therefore, an NFA is a finite automata in which there may exist more than one paths corresponding to x in Σ^* (because zero, one, or more transitions are permitted from a state on an input symbol). Whereas in a DFA, there exists exactly one path corresponding to x in Σ^*. Hence, an NFA is nothing more than a finite automata:

$$M = (Q, \Sigma, \delta, q_0, F)$$

in which δ defines mapping from $Q \times \Sigma$ to 2^Q (to take care of zero, one, or more transitions). For example, consider the finite automata shown below:

$$M = (\{q_0, q_1, q_2, q_3\}, \{0, 1\}, \delta, q_0, \{q_3\})$$

where:

$$\delta(q_0, 0) = \{q_1\}, \quad \delta(q_0, 1) = \Phi$$
$$\delta(q_1, 0) = \{q_1\}, \quad \delta(q_1, 1) = \{q_1, q_2\}$$
$$\delta(q_2, 0) = \Phi, \quad \delta(q_2, 1) = \{q_3\}$$
$$\delta(q_3, 0) = \{q_3\}, \quad \delta(q_3, 1) = \{q_3\}$$

The transition diagram of this automata is:

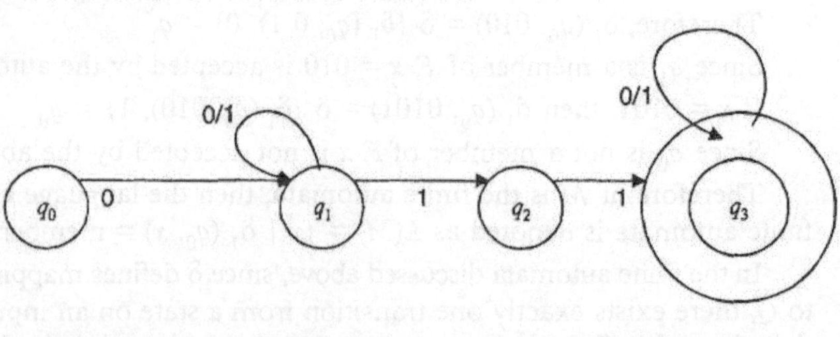

FIGURE 2.2 Transition diagram for finite automata that handles several transitions.

2.2.1 Acceptance of Strings by Non-deterministic Finite Automata

Since an NFA is a finite automata in which there may exist more than one path corresponding to x in Σ^*, and if this is, indeed, the case, then we are required to test the multiple paths corresponding to x in order to decide whether or not x is accepted by the NFA, because, for the NFA to accept x, at least one path corresponding to x is required in the NFA. This path should start in the initial state and end in one of the final states. Whereas in a DFA, since there exists exactly one path corresponding to x in Σ^*, it is enough to test whether or not that path starts in the initial state and ends in one of the final states in order to decide whether x is accepted by the DFA or not.

Therefore, if x is a string made of symbols in Σ of the NFA (*i.e.*, x is in Σ^*), then x is accepted by the NFA if at least one path exists that corresponds to x in the NFA, which starts in an initial state and ends in one of the final states of the NFA. Since x is a member of Σ^* and there may exist zero, one, or more transitions from a state on an input symbol, we define a new transition function, δ_1, which defines a mapping from $2^Q \times \Sigma^*$ to 2^Q; and if $\delta_1(\{q_0\}, x) = P$, where P is a set containing at least one member of F, then x is accepted by the NFA. If x is written as wa, where a is the last symbol of x, and w is a string made of the remaining symbols of x then:

$\delta_1(\{q_0\}, x) = \delta_1(\delta_1(\{q_0\}, w), a)$ since δ_1 defines a mapping from $2^Q \times \Sigma^*$ to 2^Q

$$\delta_1(p, a) = \cup_{\text{for every } q \text{ in } P}\, \delta(q, a)$$

For example, consider the finite automata shown below:

$$M = (\{q_0, q_1, q_2, q_3\}, \{0, 1\}, \delta, q_0, \{q_3\})$$

where:

$$\begin{aligned}
&\delta(q_0, 0) = \{q_1\}, && \delta(q_0, 1) = \Phi\\
&\delta(q_1, 0) = \{q_1\}, && \delta(q_1, 1) = \{q_1, q_2\}\\
&\delta(q_2, 0) = \Phi, && \delta(q_2, 1) = \{q_3\}\\
&\delta(q_3, 0) = \{q_3\}, && \delta(q_3, 1) = \{q_3\}
\end{aligned}$$

If $x = 0111$, then to find out whether or not x is accepted by the *NFA*, we proceed as follows:

$$\delta_1(\{q_0\}, 0) = \delta(q_0, 0) = \{q_1\}$$

$$\begin{aligned}
\text{Therefore } \delta_1(\{q_0\}, 01) &= \delta_1(\delta_1(\{q_0\}, 0), 1)\\
&= \delta_1(\{q_1\}, 1) = \delta(q_1, 1)\\
&= \{q_1, q_2\}\\
\text{Therefore } \delta_1(\{q_0\}, 011) &= \delta_1(\delta_1(\{q_0\}, 01), 1)\\
&= \delta_1(\{q_1, q_2\}, 1)\\
&= \delta(q_1, 1) \cup \delta(q_2, 1)
\end{aligned}$$

$$= \{q_1, q_2\} \cup \{q_3\}$$
$$= \{q_1, q_2, q_3\}$$

Therefore $\delta_1 (\{q_0\}, 0111) = \delta_1 (\delta_1 (\{q_0\}, 011), 1)$
$$= \delta_1 (\{q_1, q_2, q_3\}, 1)$$
$$= \delta (q_1, 1) \cup \delta (q_2, 1) \cup \delta (q_3, 1)$$
$$= \{q_1, q_2\} \cup \{q_3\} \cup \{q_3\}$$
$$= \{q_1, q_2, q_3\}$$

Since $\delta_1 (\{q_0\}, 0111) = \{q_1, q_2, q_3\}$, which contains q_3, a member of F of the NFA—, hence, $x = 0111$ is accepted by the NFA.

Therefore, if M is a NFA, then the language accepted by NFA is defined as:

$L(M) = \{x \mid \delta_1 (\{q_0\} x) = P$, where P contains at least one member of $F\}$.

2.3 TRANSFORMING NFA TO DFA

For every non-deterministic finite automata, there exists an equivalent deterministic finite automata. The equivalence between the two is defined in terms of language acceptance. Since an NFA is a nothing more than a finite automata in which zero, one, or more transitions on an input symbol is permitted, we can always construct a finite automata that will simulate all the moves of the NFA on a particular input symbol in parallel. We then get a finite automata in which there will be exactly one transition on an input symbol; hence, it will be a DFA equivalent to the NFA.

Since the DFA equivalent of the NFA simulates (parallels) the moves of the NFA, every state of a DFA will be a combination of zero one or more states of the NFA. Hence, every state of a DFA will be represented by some subset of the set of states of the NFA; and therefore, the transformation from NFA to DFA is normally called the subset construction. Therefore, if a given NFA has n states, then the equivalent DFA will have 2^n number of states, with the initial state corresponding to the subset $\{q_0\}$. Therefore, the transformation from NFA to DFA involves finding all possible subsets of the set of states of the NFA, considering each subset to be a state of a DFA, and then finding the transition from it on every input symbol. But all the states of a DFA obtained in this way might not be reachable from the initial state; and if a state is not reachable from the initial state on any possible input sequence, then such a state does not play role in deciding what language is accepted by the DFA. (Such states are those states of the DFA that have outgoing transitions on the input symbols—but either no incoming transitions, or they only have incoming transitions from other unreachable states.) Hence, the amount of work involved in transforming an NFA to a DFA can be reduced if we attempt to generate only reachable states of a DFA. This can be done by proceeding as follows:

Let $M = (Q, \Sigma, \delta, q_0, F)$ be an NFA to be transformed into a DFA.

Let Q_1 be the set states of equivalent DFA.

```
begin:
    Q1old = Φ
    Q1new = {q0}

    While (Q1old ≠ Q1new)
    {
        Temp = Q1new - Q1old
        Q1 = Q1new
        for every subset P in Temp do
                for every a in Σ do
                        If transition from P on a goes to new subset S of Q
                        then
                        (transition from P on a is obtained by finding out
                        the transitions from every member of P on a in a given
                        NFA
                        and then taking the union of all such transitions)
                Q1 new = Q1 new ∪ S
    }
    Q1 = Q1 new
    end
```

A subset P in Q_1 will be a final state of the DFA if P contains at least one member of F of the NFA. For example, consider the following finite automata:

$$M = (\{q_0, q_1, q_2, q_3\}, \{0, 1\}, \delta, q_0, \{q_3\})$$

where:

$\delta(q_0, 0) = \{q_1\}$, $\delta(q_0, 1) = \Phi$

$\delta(q_1, 0) = \{q_1\}$, $\delta(q_1, 1) = \{q_1, q_2\}$

$\delta(q_2, 0) = \Phi$, $\delta(q_2, 1) = \{q_3\}$

$\delta(q_3, 0) = \{q_3\}$, $\delta(q_3, 1) = \{q_3\}$

The DFA equivalent of this NFA can be obtained as follows:

	0	1
$\{q_0\}$	$\{q_1\}$	Φ
$\{q_1\}$	$\{q_1\}$	$\{q_1, q_2\}$
$\{q_1, q_2\}$	$\{q_1\}$	$\{q_1, q_2, q_3\}$
$*\{q_1, q_2, q_3\}$	$\{q_1, q_3\}$	$\{q_1, q_2, q_3\}$
$*\{q_1, q_3\}$	$\{q_1, q_3\}$	$\{q_1, q_2, q_3\}$
Φ	Φ	Φ

The transition diagram associated with this DFA is shown in Figure 2.3.

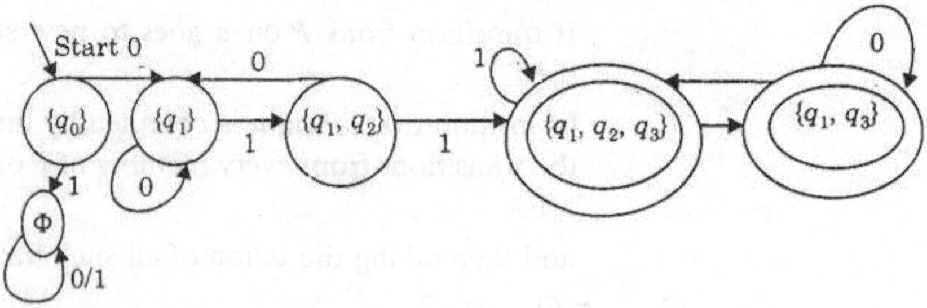

FIGURE 2.3 Transition diagram for $M = (\{q_0, q_1, q_2, q_3\}, \{0, 1\} \delta, q_0, \{q_3\})$.

2.4 THE NFA WITH ∈-MOVES

If a finite automata is modified to permit transitions without input symbols, along with zero, one, or more transitions on the input symbols, then we get an NFA with '∈-moves,' because the *transitions* made without symbols are called "∈-transitions."

Consider the NFA shown in Figure 2.4.

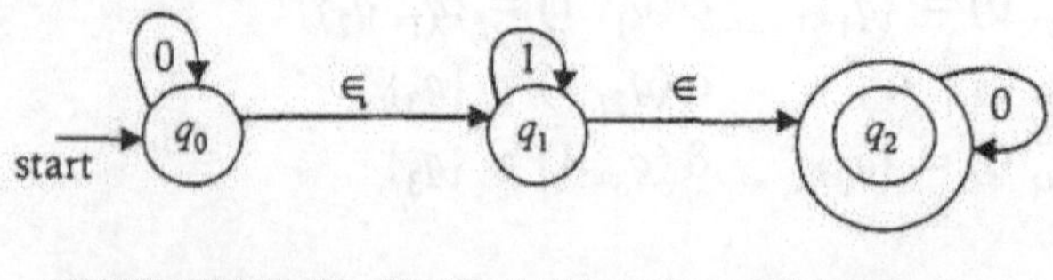

FIGURE 2.4 Finite automata with ∈-moves.

This is an NFA with $\in$-moves because it is possible to make transition from state q_0 to q_1 without consuming any of the input symbols. Similarly, we can also make transition from state q_1 to q_2 without consuming any input symbols. Since it is a finite automata, an NFA with $\in$-moves is also denoted as a five-tuple:

$$M = (Q, \Sigma, \delta, q_0, F)$$

where Q, Σ, q_0, and F have the usual meanings, and δ defines a mapping from

$$Q \times (\Sigma \cup \in) \text{ to } 2^Q$$

(to take care of the $\in$-transitions as well as the non $\in$-transitions).

Acceptance of a String by the NFA with $\in$-Moves

A string x in Σ^* will be accepted by the NFA, if at least one path exists that corresponds to x and starts in an initial state and ends in one of the final states. But since this path may be formed by $\in$-transitions as well as non-$\in$-transitions, to find out whether x is accepted or not by the NFA with -$\in$-moves, we must define a function, $\in$-closure(q), where q is a state of the automata.

The function $\in$-closure(q) is defined follows:

$\in$-closure(q)= set of all those states of the automata that can be reached from q on a path labeled by $\in$.

For example, in the NFA with $\in$-moves given above:

$\in$-closure(q_0) = $\{ q_0, q_1, q_2\}$

$\in$-closure(q_1) = $\{ q_1, q_2\}$

$\in$-closure(q_2) = $\{ q_2\}$

The function

$\in$-closure (q) will never be an empty set, because q is always reachable from itself, without dependence on any input symbol; that is, on a path labeled by $\in$, q will always exist in $\in$-closure(q).

If P is a set of states, then the $\in$-closure function can be extended to find $\in$-closure(P), as follows:

$$\in\text{-closure}(P) = \cup_{\text{for every } q \text{ in } P} \in\text{-closure}(q)$$

2.4.1 Algorithm for Finding $\in$-Closure(q)

Let T be the set that will comprise $\in$-closure(q). We begin by adding q to T, and then initialize the stack by pushing q onto stack:

```
while (stack not empty) do
{
  p = pop (stack)
  R = δ (p, ∈)
  for every member of R do
   if it is not present in T then
   {
      add that member to T
      push member of R on stack
   }
}
```

Since x is a member of Σ^*, and there may exist zero, one, or more transitions from a state on an input symbol, we define a new transition function, δ_1, which defines a mapping from $2^Q \times \Sigma^*$ to 2^Q. If x is written as wa, where a is the last symbol of x and w is a string made of remaining symbols of x then:

$$\delta_1 (\{q_0\}, x) = \delta_1 (\delta_1 (\{q_0\}, w), a)$$

since δ_1 defines a mapping from $2^Q \times \Sigma^*$ to 2^Q.

A string x will be accepted by the NFA with $\in$-moves if:

$$\in\text{-closure}(\delta_1 (\in\text{-closure } (q_0), x) = P$$

such that P contains at least one member of F and:

$$\in\text{-closure}(\delta_1 (\in\text{-closure } (q_0), x)$$
$$= \in\text{-closure } (\in\text{-closure } (\delta_1 (\in\text{-closure } (q_0), w)), a)$$

For example, in the NFA with $\in$-moves, given above, if $x = 01$, then to find out whether x is accepted by the automata or not, we proceed as follows:

$$\begin{aligned}
\delta_1 (\in\text{-closure } (q_0), 0) &= \delta_1 (\{q_0, q_1, q_2\}), 0) \\
&= \delta (q_0, 0) \cup \delta (q_1, 0) \cup \delta (q_2, 0) \\
&= \{q_0\} \cup \phi \cup \{q_2\} = \{q_0, q_2\} \\
\delta_1 (\in\text{-closure } (q_0), 01) &= \delta_1 (\in\text{-closure } (\delta_1 (\in\text{-closure } (q_0), 0)), 1) \\
&= \delta_1 (\in\text{-closure } (\{q_0, q_2\}), 1) \\
&= \delta_1 (\{q_0, q_1, q_2\}), 1) \\
&= \delta (q_0, 1) \cup \delta (q_1, 1) \cup \delta (q_2, 1) \\
&= \phi \cup \{q_1\} \cup \phi \\
&= \{q_1\}
\end{aligned}$$

Therefore:

$\in$-closure(δ_1 ($\in$-closure (q_0), 01) = $\in$-closure($\{q_1\}$) = $\{q_1, q_2\}$

Since q_2 is a final state, $x = 01$ is accepted by the automata.

Equivalence of NFA with ∈-Moves and NFA Without ∈-Moves

For every NFA with ∈-moves, there exists an equivalent NFA without ∈-moves that accepts the same language. To obtain an equivalent NFA without ∈-moves, given an NFA with ∈-moves, what is required is elimination of ∈-transitions from a given automata. But simply eliminating the ∈-transitions from a given NFA with ∈-moves will change the language accepted by the automata. Hence, for every ∈-transition to be eliminated, we have to add some non-∈-transitions as substitutes in order to maintain the language's acceptance by the automata. Therefore, transforming an NFA with ∈-moves to and NFA without ∈-moves involves finding the non-∈-transitions that must be added to the automata for every ∈-transition to be eliminated.

Consider the NFA with ∈-moves shown in Figure 2.5.

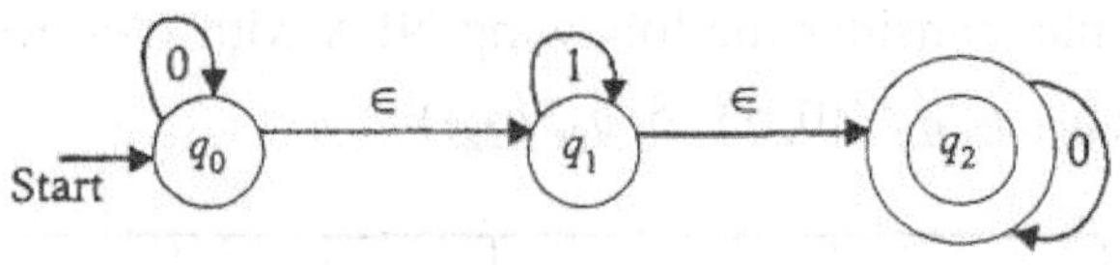

FIGURE 2.5 NFA with∈-moves.

There are ∈-transitions from state q_0 to q_1 and from state q_1 to q_2. To eliminate these ∈-transitions, we must add a transition on 0 from q_0 to q_1, as well as from state q_0 to q_2. Similarly, a transition must be added on 1 from q_0 to q_1, as well as from state q_0 to q_2, because the presence of these ∈-transitions in a given automata makes it possible to reach from q_0 to q_1 on consuming only 0, and it is possible to reach from q_0 to q_2 on consuming only 0. Similarly, it is possible to reach from q_0 to q_1 on consuming only 1, and it is possible to reach from q_0 to q_2 on consuming only 1. It is also possible to reach from q_1 to q_2 on consuming 0 as well as 1; and therefore, a transition from q_1 to q_2 on 0 and 1 is also required to be added. Since ∈ is also accepted by the given NFA ∈-moves, to accept ∈, and initial state of the NFA without ∈-moves is required to be marked as one of the final states. Therefore, by adding these non-∈-transitions, and by making the initial state one of the final states, we get the automata shown in Figure 2.6.

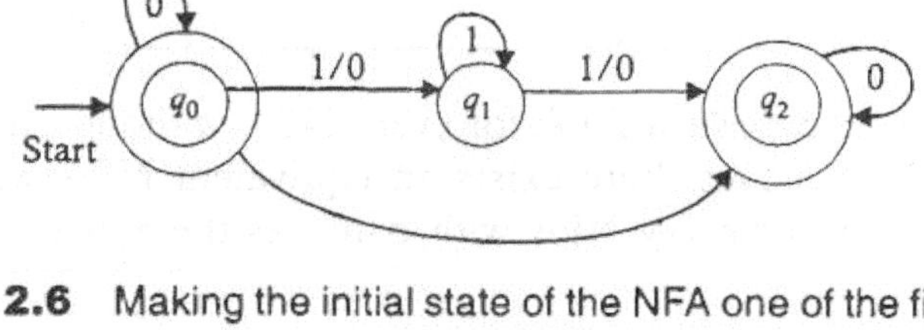

FIGURE 2.6 Making the initial state of the NFA one of the final states.

Therefore, when transforming an NFA with $\in$-moves into an NFA without $\in$-moves, only the transitions are required to be changed; the states are not required to be changed. But if a given NFA with q_0 and $\in$-moves accepts $\in$ (*i.e.*, if the $\in$-closure (q_0) contains a member of F), then q_0 is also required to be marked as one of the final states if it is not already a member of F. Hence:

If $M = (Q, \Sigma, \delta, q_0, F)$ is an NFA with $\in$-moves, then its equivalent NFA without $\in$-moves will be $M_1 = (Q, \Sigma, \delta_1, q_0, F_1)$
where $\delta_1 (q, a) = \in\text{-closure}(\delta (\in\text{-closure}(q), a))$
and

$F_1 = F \cup (q_0)$ if $\in$-closure (q_0) contains a member of F

$F_1 = F$ otherwise

For example, consider the following NFA with $\in$-moves:

$M = (\{q_0, q_1\, q_2\} \{0, 1\}, \delta, q_0, \{q_2\})$

where

δ	0	1	$\in$
q_0	$\{q_0\}$	ϕ	$\{q_1\}$
q_1	ϕ	$\{q_1\}$	$\{q_2\}$
q_2	ϕ	$\{q_2\}$	ϕ

Its equivalent NFA without $\in$-moves will be:

$$M_1 = (\{q_0, q_1, q_2\} \{0, 1\}, \delta_1, q_0, \{q_0, q_2\})$$

where

δ_1	0	1
q_0	$\{q_0, q_1, q_2\}$	$\{q_1, q_2\}$
q_1	ϕ	$\{q_1, q_2\}$
q_2	ϕ	$\{q_2\}$

Since there exists a DFA for every NFA without $\in$-moves, and for every NFA with $\in$-moves there exists an equivalent NFA without $\in$-moves, we conclude that for every NFA with $\in$-moves there exists a DFA.

2.5 THE NFA WITH ∈-MOVES TO THE DFA

There always exists a DFA equivalent to an NFA with ∈-moves which can be obtained as follows:

Let $M = (Q, \Sigma, \delta, q_0, F)$ be an NFA with ∈-moves.

A DFA equivalent to this NFA will be:

$M_1 = (Q_1, \Sigma, \delta_1, q_1, F_1)$, where Q_1 is a subset of 2^Q; that is, every state of a DFA corresponds to a subset of Q.

$q_1 = \in$-closure(q_0), and it is the initial state of the DFA. We initially add q_1 to Q_1, and then we find the transition from q_1 as follows:

$$\delta_1 (q_1, a) = \in\text{-closure } (\delta \text{ (subset representation of } q_1, a))$$

If this transition generates a new subset of Q, then it will be added to Q_1; and next time transitions from it are found, we continue in this way until we cannot add any new states to Q_1. After this, we identify those states of the DFA whose subset representations contain at least one member of F. The act of such states of A constitute F_1.

Consider the following NFA with ∈-moves:

$$M = (\{q_0, q_1, q_2\}, \{0, 1\}, \delta, q_0, \{q_2\})$$

where

δ	0	1	$\in$
q_0	$\{q_0\}$	ϕ	$\{q_1\}$
q_1	ϕ	$\{q_1\}$	$\{q_2\}$
q_2	ϕ	$\{q_2\}$	ϕ

A DFA equivalent to this will be:

$$M_1 = (\{\{q_0, q_1, q_2\}, \{q_1, q_2\}, \phi,\} \{0, 1\}, \delta_1, \{q_0, q_1, q_2\}, \{\{q_0, q_1, q_2\}, \{q_1, q_2\}\})$$

where

δ_1	0	1
$\{q_0, q_1, q_2\}$	$\{q_0, q_1, q_2\}$	$\{q_1, q_2\}$
$\{q_1, q_2\}$	ϕ	$\{q_1, q_2\}$
ϕ	ϕ	ϕ

If we identify the subsets $\{q_0, q_1, q_2\}$, $\{q_0, q_1, q_2\}$ and ϕ as A, B, and C, respectively, then the automata will be:

$$M_1 = (\{A, B, C\}, \{0,1\}, \delta_1, A, \{A, B\})$$

where

δ_1	0	1
A	A	B
B	C	B
C	C	C

EXAMPLE 2.1: Obtain a DFA equivalent to the NFA shown in Figure 2.7.

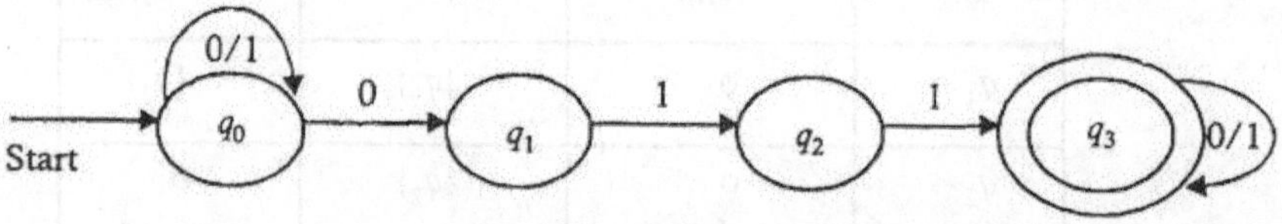

FIGURE 2.7 Example 2.1 NFA.

A DFA equivalent to NFA in Figure 2.7 will be:

	0	1
$\{q_0\}$	$\{q_0, q_1\}$	$\{q_0\}$
$\{q_0, q_1\}$	$\{q_0, q_1\}$	$\{q_0, q_2\}$
$\{q_0, q_2\}$	$\{q_0, q_1\}$	$\{q_0, q_3\}$
$\{q_0, q_2, q_3\}$*	$\{q_0, q_1, q_3\}$	$\{q_0, q_3\}$
$\{q_0, q_1, q_3\}$*	$\{q_0, q_3\}$	$\{q_0, q_2, q_3\}$
$\{q_0, q_3\}$*	$\{q_0, q_1, q_3\}$	$\{q_0, q_3\}$

where $\{q_0\}$ corresponds to the initial state of the automata, and the states marked as * are final states. If we rename the states as follows:

$\{q_0\}$	*A*
$\{q_0, q_1\}$	*B*
$\{q_0, q_2\}$	*C*
$\{q_0, q_2, q_3\}$	*D*
$\{q_0, q_1, q_3\}$	*E*
$\{q_0, q_3\}$	*F*

then the transition table will be:

	0	1
A	*B*	*A*
B	*B*	*C*
C	*B*	*F*
*D**	*E*	*F*
*E**	*F*	*D*
*F**	*E*	*F*

EXAMPLE 2.2: Obtain a DFA equivalent to the NFA illustrated in Figure 2.8.

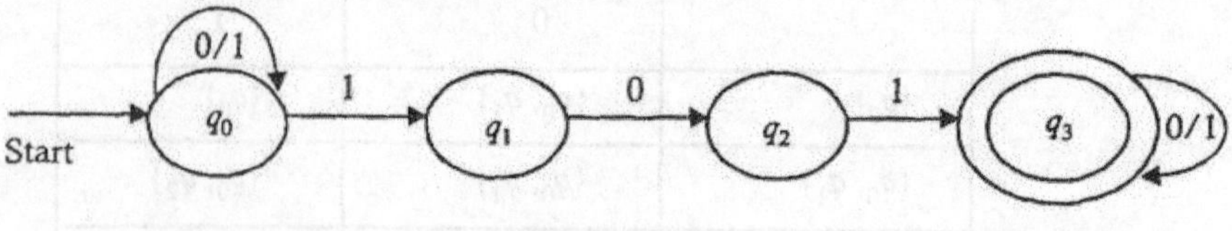

FIGURE 2.8 Example 2.2 DFA equivalent to an NFA.

A DFA equivalent to the NFA shown in Figure 2.8 will be:

	0	1
$\{q_0\}$	$\{q_0\}$	$\{q_0, q_1\}$
$\{q_0, q_1\}$	$\{q_0, q_2\}$	$\{q_0, q_1\}$
$\{q_0, q_2\}$	$\{q_0\}$	$\{q_0, q_1, q_3\}$
$\{q_0, q_1, q_3\}$*	$\{q_0, q_2, q_3\}$	$\{q_0, q_1, q_3\}$
$\{q_0, q_2, q_3\}$*	$\{q_0, q_3\}$	$\{q_0, q_1, q_3\}$
$\{q_0, q_3\}$*	$\{q_0, q_3\}$	$\{q_0, q_1, q_3\}$

where $\{q_0\}$ corresponds to the initial state of the automata, and the states marked as * are final states. If we rename the states as follows:

$\{q_0\}$	A
$\{q_0, q_1\}$	B
$\{q_0, q_2\}$	C
$\{q_0, q_2, q_3\}$	D
$\{q_0, q_1, q_3\}$	E
$\{q_0, q_3\}$	F

then the transition table will be:

	0	1
A	*A*	*B*
B	*C*	*B*
C	*A*	*E*
*D**	*F*	*E*
*E**	*D*	*E*
*F**	*F*	*E*

2.6 MINIMIZATION/OPTIMIZATION OF A DFA

Minimization/optimization of a deterministic finite automata refers to detecting those states of a DFA whose presence or absence in a DFA does not affect the language accepted by the automata. Hence, these states can be eliminated from the automata without affecting the language accepted by the automata. Such states are:

- ***Unreachable States:*** Unreachable states of a DFA are not reachable from the initial state of DFA on any possible input sequence.
- ***Dead States:*** A dead state is a nonfinal state of a DFA whose transitions on every input symbol terminates on itself. For example, q is a dead state if q is in $Q\text{-}F$, and $\delta(q, a) = q$ for every a in Σ.
- ***Nondistinguishable States:*** Nondistinguishable states are those states of a DFA for which there exist no distinguishing strings; hence, they cannot be distinguished from one another.

Therefore, optimization entails:

1. Detection of unreachable states and eliminating them from DFA;
2. Identification of nondistinguishable states, and merging them together; and
3. Detecting dead states and eliminating them from the DFA.

2.6.1 Algorithm to Detect Unreachable States

Input $M = (Q, \Sigma, \delta, q_0, F)$

Output = Set U (which is set of unreachable states)

{Let R be the set of reachable states of DFA. We take two R's, R_{new}, and R_{old} so that we will be able to perform iterations in the process of detecting unreachable states.}

```
begin
    R_old = ϕ
    R_new = {q0}
    while (R_old # R_new) do
    begin
    temp1 = R_new − R_old
    R_old = R_new
    temp2 = ϕ
        for every a in Σ do
    temp2 = temp2 ∪ δ( temp1, a)
    R_new = R_new ∪ temp2
    end
U = Q − R_new
end
```

If p and q are the two states of a DFA, then p and q are said to be 'distinguishable' states if a distinguishing string w exists that distinguishes p and q.

A string w is a distinguishing string for states p and q if transitions from p on w go to a nonfinal state, whereas transitions from q on w go to a final state, or vice versa.

Therefore, to find nondistinguishable states of a DFA, we must find out whether some distinguishing string w, which distinguishes the states, exists. If no such string exists, then the states are nondistinguishable and can be merged together.

The technique that we use to find nondistinguishable states is the method of successive partitioning. We start with two groups/partitions: one contains all nonfinal states, and other contains all the final state. This is because if every final state is known to be distinguishable from a nonfinal state, then we find transitions from members of a partition on every input symbol. If on a particular input symbol a we find that transitions from some of the members of a partition goes to one place, whereas transitions from other members of a partition go to an other place, then we conclude that the members whose transitions go to one place are distinguishable from members whose transitions goes to another place. Therefore, we divide the partition in two; and we continue this partitioning until we get partitions that cannot be partitioned further. This happens when either a partition contains only one state, or when a partition contains more than one state, but they are not distinguishable from one another. If we get such a partition, we merge all of the states of this partition into a single state. For example, consider the transition diagram in Figure 2.9.

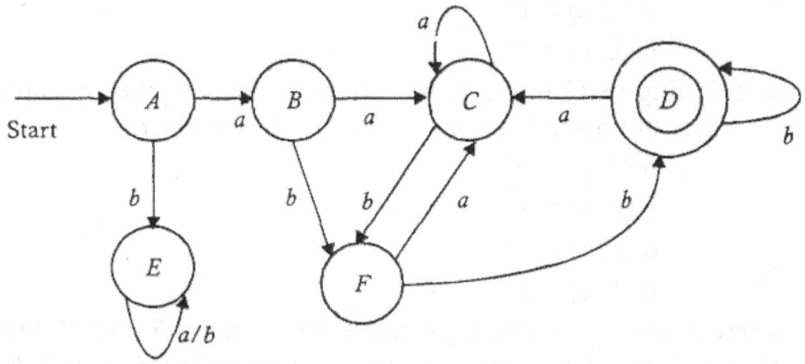

FIGURE 2.9 Transition diagram of a *DFA*.

Initially, we have two groups, as shown below:

A, B, C, E, F	*D*
Group I	Group II

Since $\delta\,(A, a) = B$
$\delta\,(B, a) = C$
$\delta\,(C, a) = C$
$\delta\,(E, a) = E$
$\delta\,(F, a) = C$

Partitioning of Group I is not possible, because the transitions from all the members of Group I go only to Group I. But since

$\delta\,(A, b) = E$
$\delta\,(B, b) = F$
$\delta\,(C, b) = F$
$\delta\,(E, b) = E$
$\delta\,(F, b) = D$

state F is distinguishable from the rest of the members of Group I. Hence, we divide Group I into two groups: one containing A, B, C, E, and the other containing F, as shown below:

A, B, C, E	F	D
Group I	Group II	Group III

Since $\delta(A, a) = B$
$\delta(B, a) = C$
$\delta(C, a) = C$
$\delta(E, a) = E$

partitioning of Group I is not possible, because the transitions from all the members of Group I go only to Group I. But since

$\delta(A, b) = E$
$\delta(B, b) = F$
$\delta(C, b) = F$
$\delta(E, b) = E$

states A and E are distinguishable from states B and C. Hence, we further divide Group I into two groups: one containing A and E, and the other containing B and C, as shown below:

A, E	B, C	F	D
Group I	Group II	Group III	Group IV

Since $\delta(A, a) = B$
$\delta(E, a) = E$

state A is distinguishable from state E. Hence, we divide Group I into two groups: one containing A and the other containing E, as shown below:

A	E	B, C	F	D
Group I	Group II	Group III	Group IV	Group V

Since $\delta(B, a) = C$
$\delta(C, a) = C$

partitioning of Group III is not possible, because the transitions from all the members of Group III on a go to group III only. Similarly,

$\delta(B, b) = F$
$\delta(C, b) = F$

partitioning of Group III is not possible, because the transitions from all the members of Group III on b also only go to Group III.

Hence, B and C are nondistinguishable states; therefore, we merge B and C to form a single state, B_1, as shown in Figure 2.10.

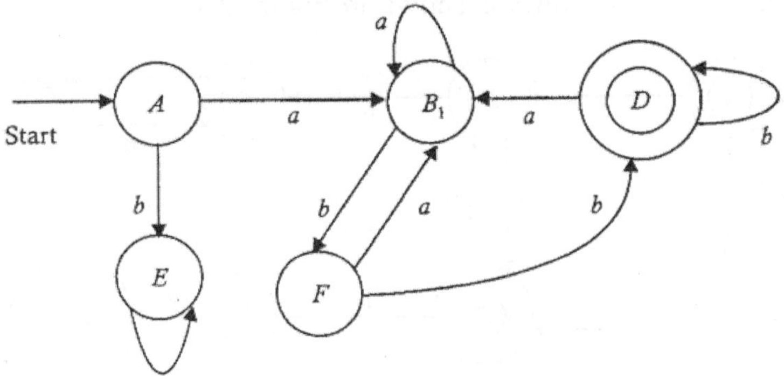

FIGURE 2.10 Merging nondistinguishable states B and C into a single state B_1.

2.6.2 Algorithm for Detection of Dead States

Input $M = (Q, \Sigma, \delta, q_0, F)$
Output = Set X (which is a set of dead states)

```
{
X = φ
for every q in (Q – F) do
{
    flag = true;
    for every a in Σ do
            if (δ (q, a) # q) then
                    {
                    flag = false
                    break
                    }
    if flag = true then
X = X ∪ {q}
}
}
```

2.7 EXAMPLES OF FINITE AUTOMATA CONSTRUCTION

EXAMPLE 2.3: Construct a finite automata accepting the set of all strings of zeros and ones, with at most one pair of consecutive zeros and at most one pair of consecutive ones.

A transition diagram of the finite automata accepting the set of all strings of zeros and ones, with at most one pair of consecutive zeros and at most one pair of consecutive ones is shown in Figure 2.11.

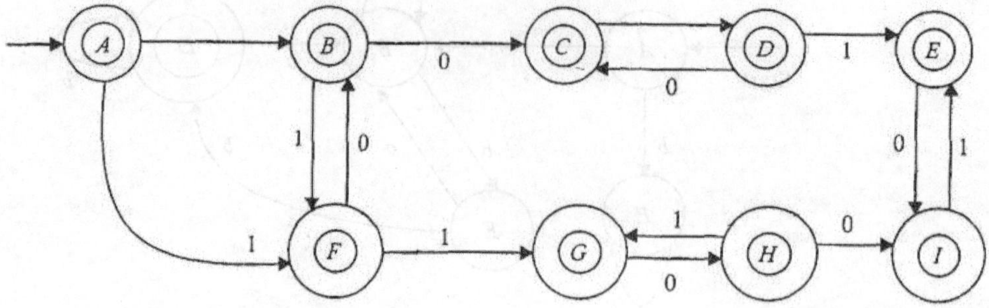

FIGURE 2.11 Transition diagram for Example 2.3 finite automata.

EXAMPLE 2.4: Construct a finite automata that will accept strings of zeros and ones that contain even numbers of zeros and odd numbers of ones.

A transition diagram of the finite automata that accepts the set of all strings of zeros and ones that contains even numbers of zeros and odd numbers of ones is shown in Figure 2.12.

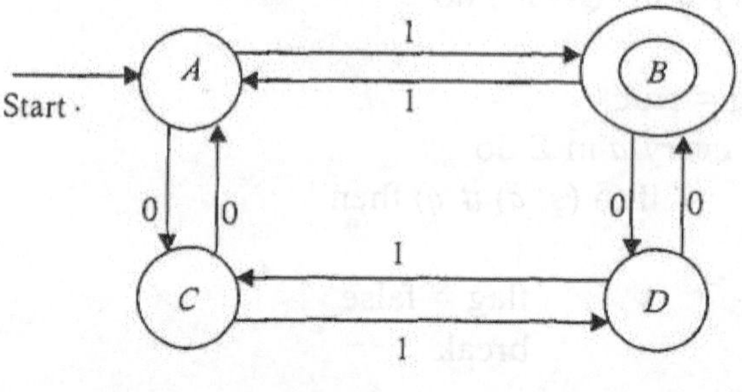

FIGURE 2.12 Finite automata accepting strings over {0, 1}, containing even number of zeros and odd number of ones.

EXAMPLE 2.5: Construct a finite automata that will accept a string of zeros and ones that contains an odd number of zeros and an even number of ones.

A transition diagram of finite automata accepting the set of all strings of zeros and ones that contains an odd number of zeros and an even number of ones is shown in Figure 2.13.

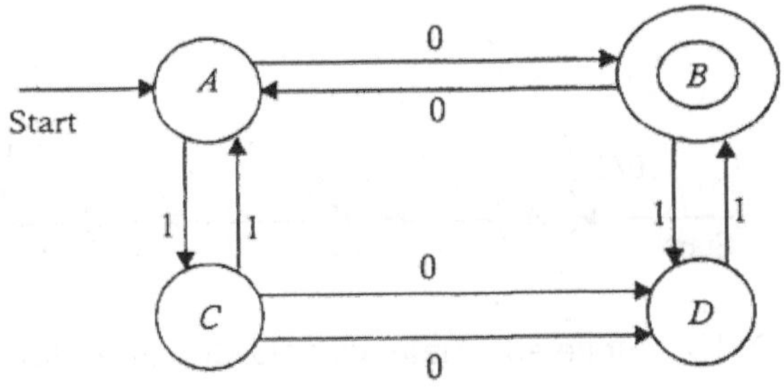

FIGURE 2.13 Finite automata accepting strings over {0, 1}, containing odd number of zeros and even number of ones.

EXAMPLE 2.6: Construct the finite automata for accepting strings of zeros and ones that contain equal numbers of zeros and ones, and no prefix of the string should contain two more zeros than ones or two more ones than zeros.

A transition diagram of the finite automata that will accept the set of all strings of zeros and ones, contain equal numbers of zeros and ones, and contain no string prefixes of two more zeros than ones or two more ones than zeros is shown in Figure 2.14.

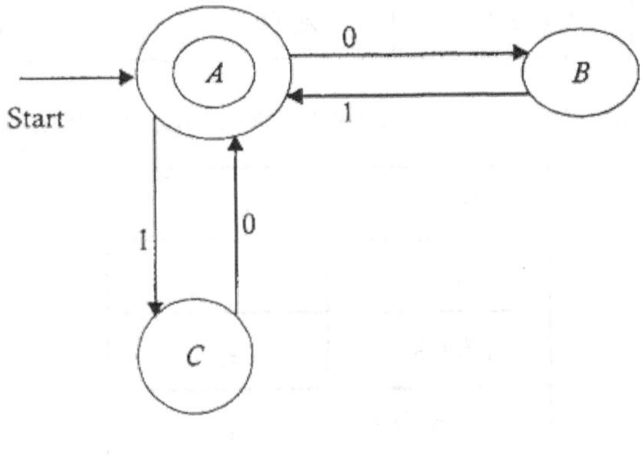

FIGURE 2.14 Finite automata for example 2.6.

EXAMPLE 2.7: Construct a finite automata for accepting all possible strings of zeros and ones that do not contain 101 as a substring.

Figure 2.15 shows a transition diagram of the finite automata that accepts the strings containing 101 as a substring.

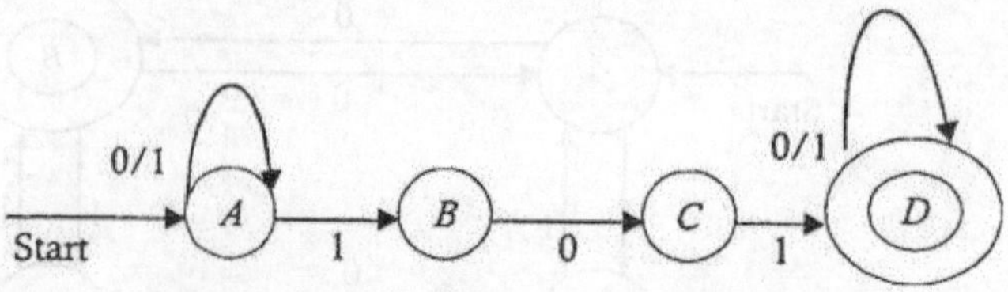

FIGURE 2.15 Finite automata accepts strings containing the substring 101.

A DFA equivalent to this NFA will be:

	0	1
{A}	{A}	{A, B}
{A, B}	{A, C}	{A, B}
{A, C}	{A}	{A, B, D}
{A, B, D}*	{A, C, D}	{A, B, D}
{A, C, D}*	{A, D}	{A, B, D}
{A, C, D}*	{A, D}	{A, B, D}

Let us identify the states of this DFA using the names given below:

{A}	q_0
{A, B}	q_1
{A, C}	q_2
{A, B, D}	q_3
{A, C, D}	q_4
{A, D}	q_5

The transition diagram of this automata is shown in Figure 2.16.

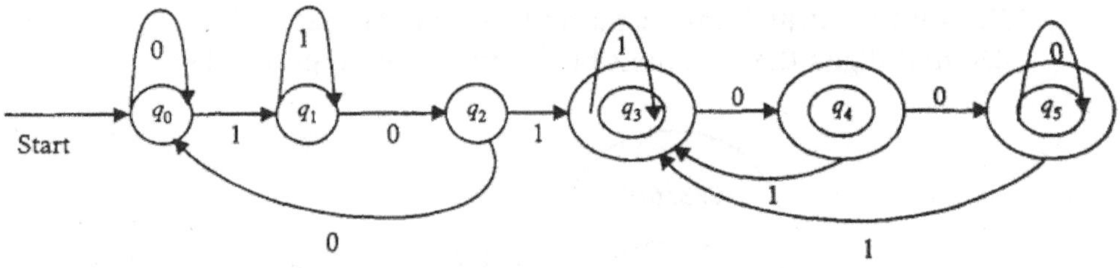

FIGURE 2.16 DFA equivalent to NFA of Figure 2.15.

The complement of the automata in Figure 2.16 is shown in Figure 2.17.

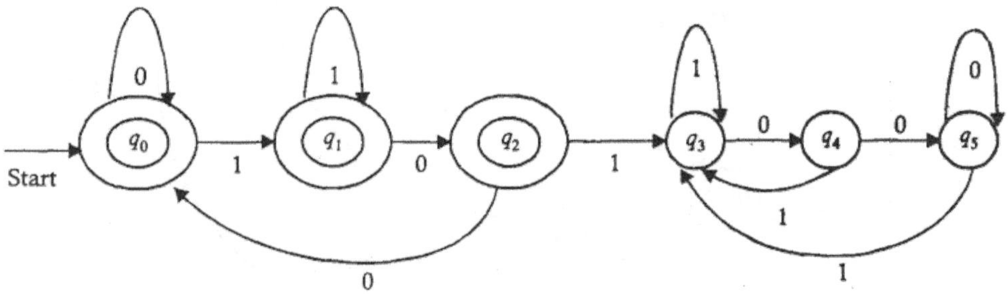

FIGURE 2.17 Complement of DFA of Figure 2.16 automata.

After minimization, we get the DFA shown in Figure 2.18, because states q_3, q_4, and q_5 are nondistinguishable states. Hence, they get combined, and this combination becomes a dead state and, can be eliminated.

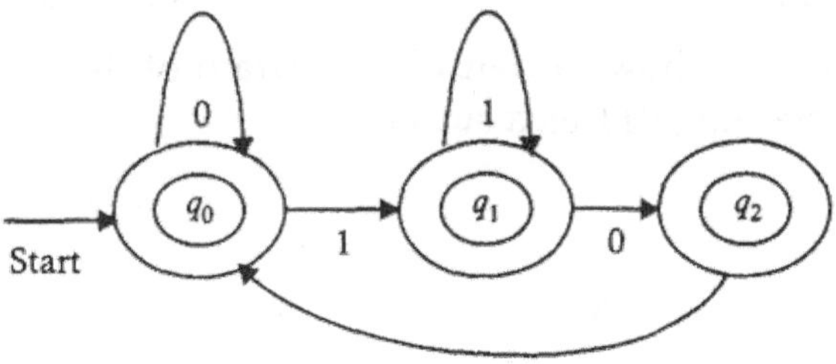

FIGURE 2.18 DFA after minimization.

EXAMPLE 2.8: Construct a finite automata that will accept those strings of decimal digits that are divisible by three (see Figure 2.19).

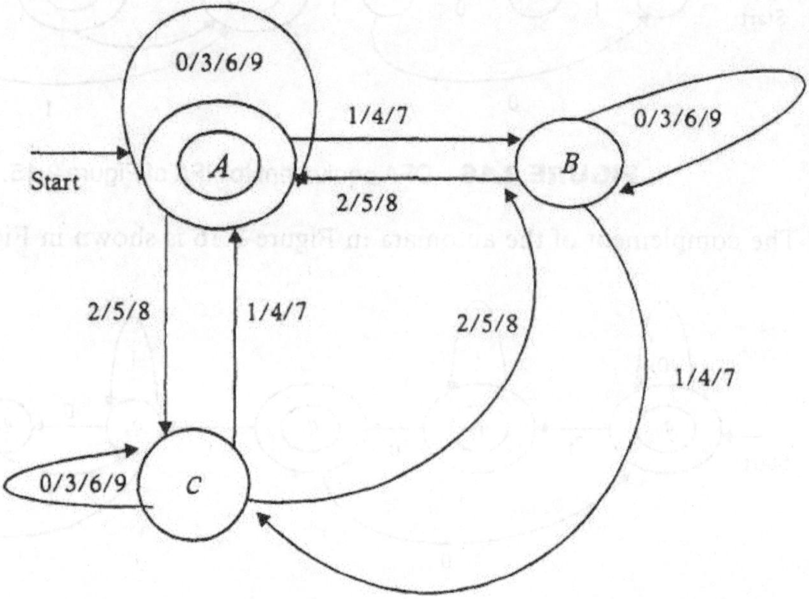

FIGURE 2.19 Finite automata that accepts string of decimal digits that are divisible by three.

EXAMPLE 2.9: Construct a finite automata that accepts all possible strings of zeros and ones that do not contain 011 as a substring.

Figure 2.20 shows a transition diagram of the automata that accepts the strings containing 011 as a substring.

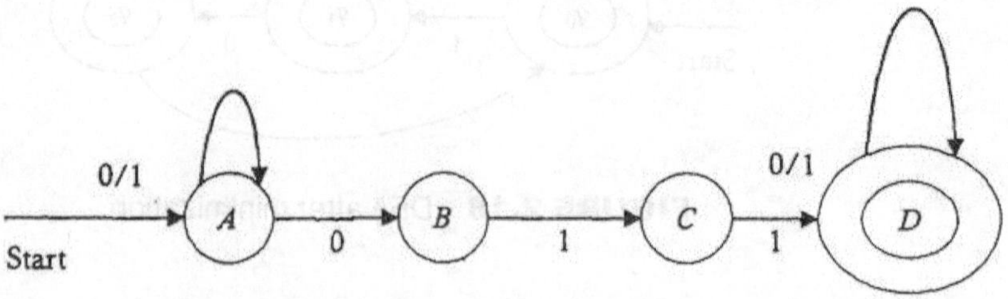

FIGURE 2.20 Finite automata accepts strings containing 011 as substituting.

A DFA equivalent to this NFA will be:

	0	1
$\{A\}$	$\{A, B\}$	$\{A\}$
$\{A, B\}$	$\{A, B\}$	$\{A, C\}$
$\{A, C\}$	$\{A, B\}$	$\{A, D\}$
$\{A, D\}$*	$\{A, B, D\}$	$\{A, D\}$
$\{A, B, D\}$*	$\{A, B, D\}$	$\{A, C, D\}$
$\{A, C, D\}$*	$\{A, B, D\}$	$\{A, D\}$

Let us identify the states of this DFA using the names given below:

$\{A\}$	q_0
$\{A, B\}$	q_1
$\{A, C\}$	q_2
$\{A, D\}$	q_3
$\{A, B, D\}$	q_4
$\{A, C, D\}$	q_5

The transition diagram of this automata is shown in Figure 2.21.

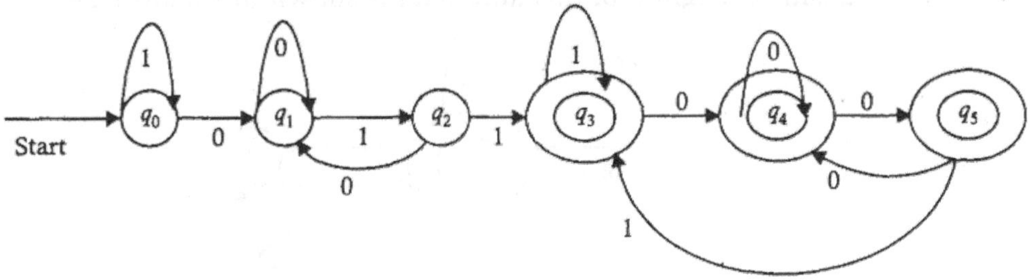

FIGURE 2.21 DFA equivalent to NFA of Figure 2.20.

The complement of automata shown in Figure 2.21 is illustrated in Figure 2.22.-

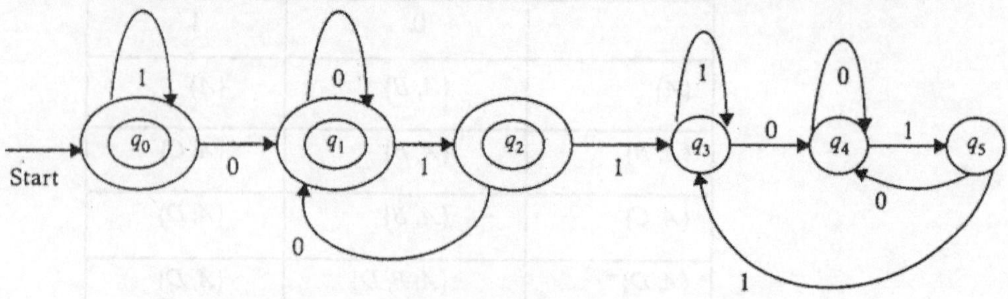

FIGURE 2.22 Complement of DFA of Figure 2.21 automata.

After minimization, we get the DFA shown in Figure 2.23, because the states q_3, q_4, and q_5 are nondistinguishable states. Hence, they get combined, and this combination becomes a dead state that can be eliminated.

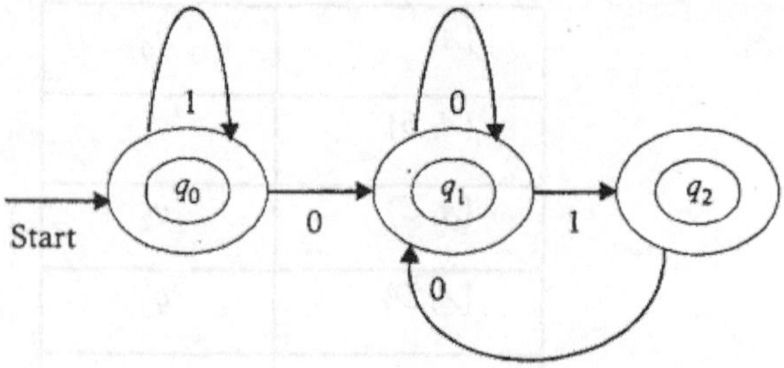

FIGURE 2.23 Minimal states DFA.

EXAMPLE 2.10: Construct a finite automata that will accept those strings of a binary number that are divisible by three.

The transition diagram of this automata is shown in Figure 2.24.

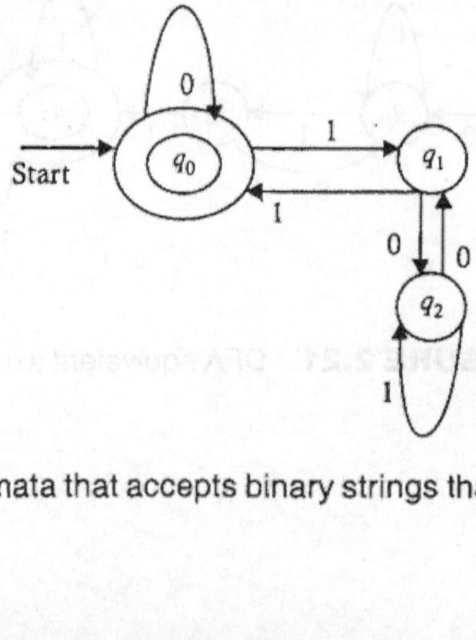

FIGURE 2.24 Automata that accepts binary strings that are divisible by three.

2.8 REGULAR SETS AND REGULAR EXPRESSIONS

2.8.1 Regular Sets

A regular set is a set of strings for which there exists some finite automata accepting that set. That is, if R is a regular set, then $R = L(M)$ for some finite automata M. Similarly, if M is a finite automata, then $L(M)$ is always a regular set.

2.8.2 Regular Expression

A regular expression is a notation to specify a regular set. Hence, for every regular expression, there exists a finite automata that accepts the language specified by the regular expression. Similarly, for every finite automata M, there exists a regular expression notation specifying $L(M)$. Regular expressions and the regular sets they specify are shown in the following table.

Regular expression	Regular Set	Finite automata
ϕ	{ }	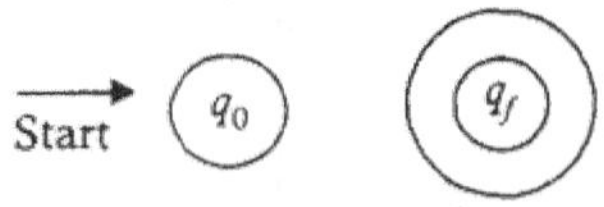
$\in$	$\{ \in \}$	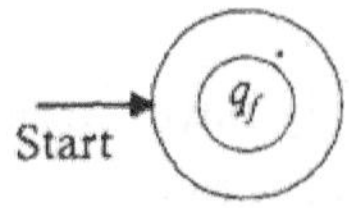
Every a in Σ is a regular expression	$\{a\}$	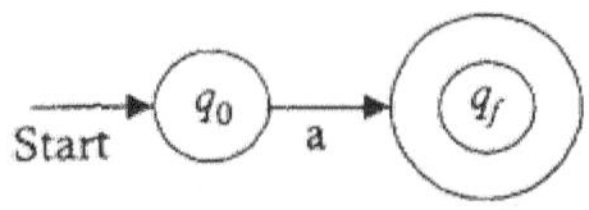

$r_1 + r_2$ or $r_1 \mid r_2$ is a regular expression,	$R_1 \cup R_2$ (Where R_1 and R_2 are regular sets corresponding to r_1 and r_2, respectively)	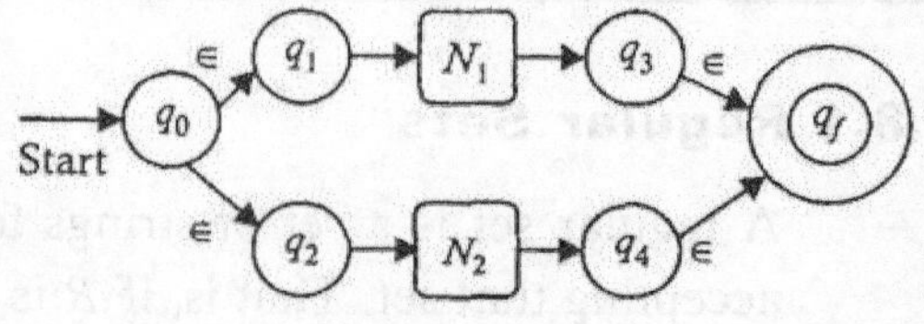 where N_1 is a finite automata accepting R_1, and N_2 is a finite automata accepting R_2
$r_1 . r_2$ is a regular expression,	$R_1.R_2$ (Where R_1 and R_2 are regular sets corresponding to r_1 and r_2, respectively)	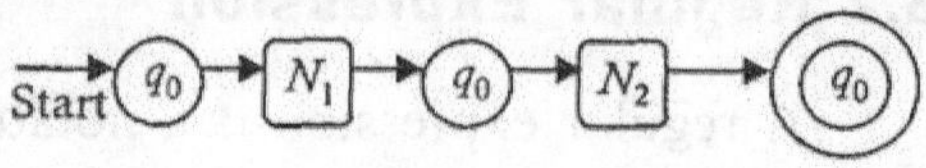 where N_1 is a finite automata accepting R_1, and N_2 is finite automata accepting R_2
r^* is a regular expression,	R^* (where R is a regular set corresponding to r)	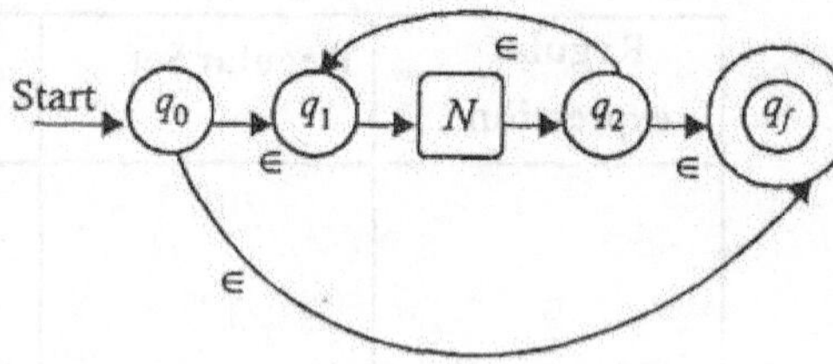 where N is a finite automata accepting R.

Hence, we only have three regular-expression operators: | or + to denote union operations,. for concatenation operations, and * for closure operations. The precedence of the operators in the decreasing order is: *, followed by., followed by |. For example, consider the following regular expression:

$$a. (a + b)^*. b.b$$

To construct a finite automata for this regular expression, we proceed as follows: the basic regular expressions involved are a and b, and we start with automata for a and automata for b. Since brackets are evaluated first, we initially construct the automata for $a + b$ using the automata for a and the automata for b, as shown in Figure 2.25.

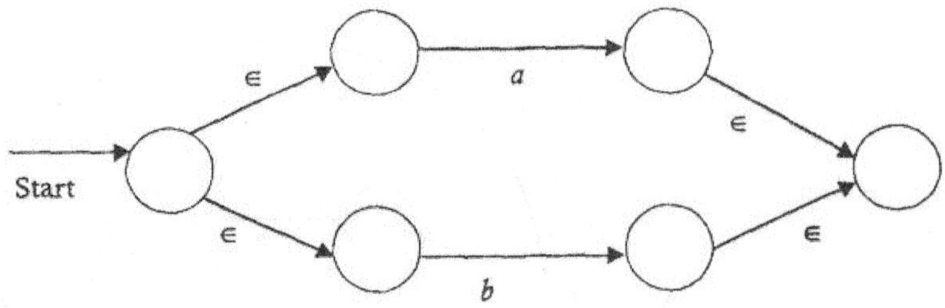

FIGURE 2.25 Transition diagram for $(a + b)$.

Since closure is required next, we construct the automata for $(a + b)^*$, using the automata for $a + b$, as shown in Figure 2.26.

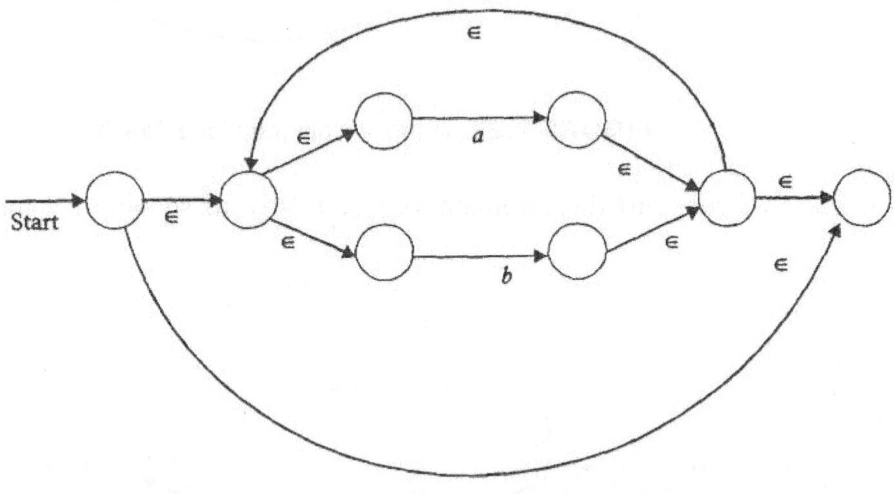

FIGURE 2.26 Transition diagram for $(a + b)^*$.

The next step is concatenation. We construct the automata for $a. (a + b)^*$ using the automata for $(a + b)^*$ and a, as shown in Figure 2.27.

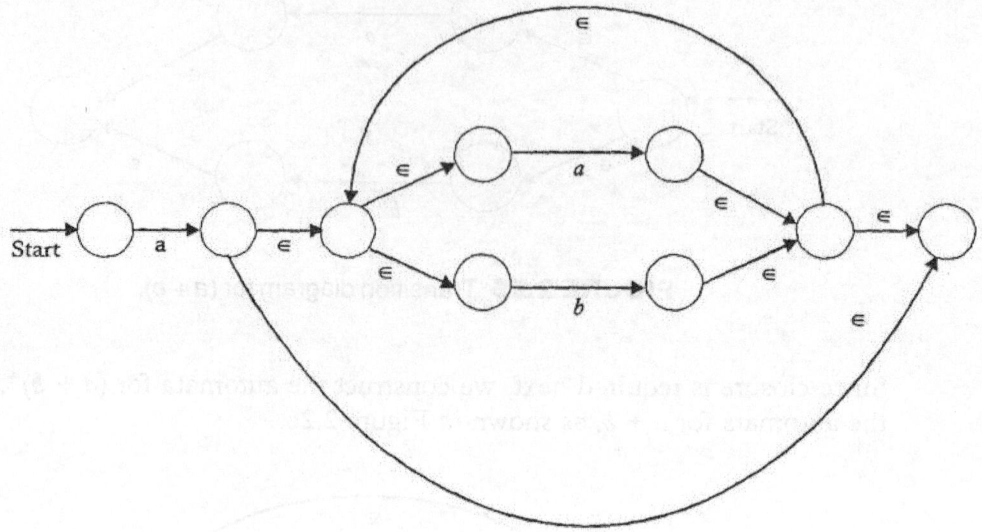

FIGURE 2.27 Transition diagram for $a.(a + b)^*$.

Next we construct the automata for $a.(a + b)^*.b$, as shown in Figure 2.28.

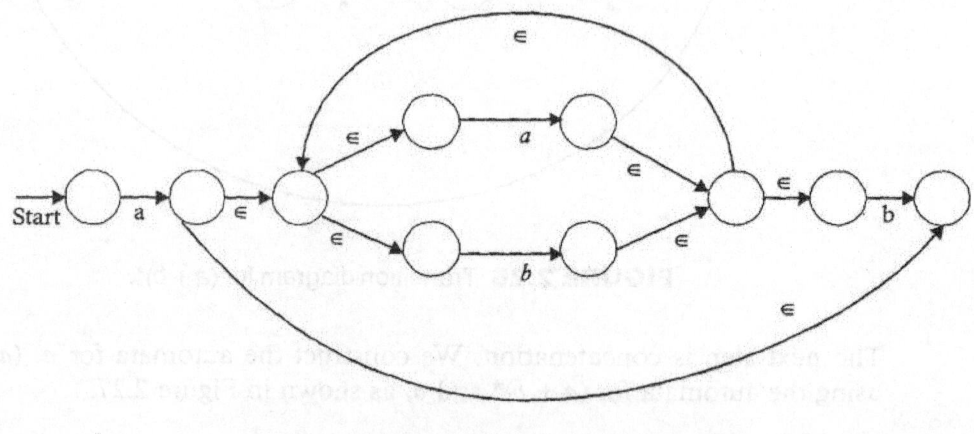

FIGURE 2.28 Automata for $a.(a + b)^* .b$.

Finally, we construct the automata for $a.(a + b)^*.b.b$ (Figure 2.29).

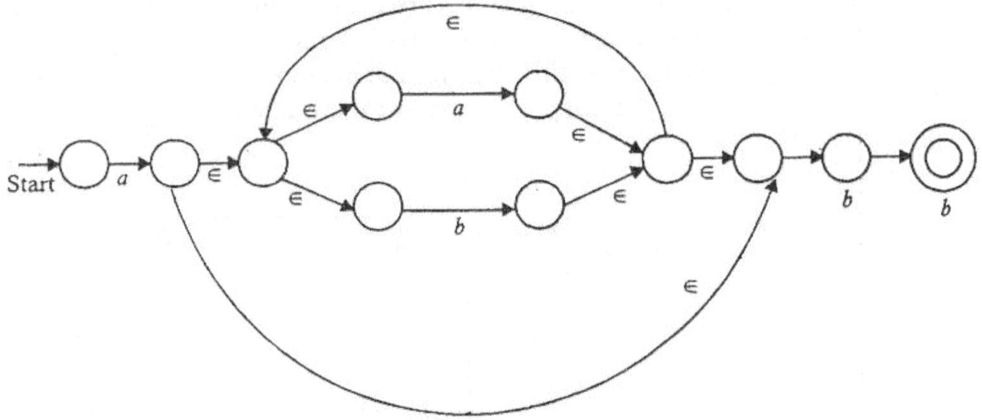

FIGURE 2.29 Automata for $a.(a + b)^*.b.b.$

This is an NFA with ∈-moves, but an algorithm exists to transform the NFA to a DFA. So, we can obtain a DFA from this NFA.

2.9 OBTAINING THE REGULAR EXPRESSION FROM THE FINITE AUTOMATA

Given a finite automata, to obtain a regular expression that specifies the regular set accepted by the given finite automata, the following steps are necessary:

1. Associate suitable variables (e.g., A, B, C, etc.) with the states of finite automata.
2. Form a set of equations using the following rules:
   a. If there exists a transition from a state associated with variable A to a state associated with variable B on an input symbol a, then add the equation

      $A = aB$ to the set of equation.

   b. If the state associated with variable A is a final state, add $A = \in$ to the set of equations.
   c. If we have the two equations $A = ab$ and $A = bc$, then they can be combined as $A = aB \mid bc$.
3. Solve these equations to get the value of the variable associated with the starting state of the automata. In order to solve these equations, it is necessary to bring the equation in the following form:

$$S = aS \mid b$$

where S is a variable, and a and b are expressions that do not contain S. The solution to this equation is $S = a^*b$. (Here, the concatenation operator is between a^* and b, and is not explicitly shown.) For example, consider the finite automata whose transition diagram is shown in Figure 2.30.

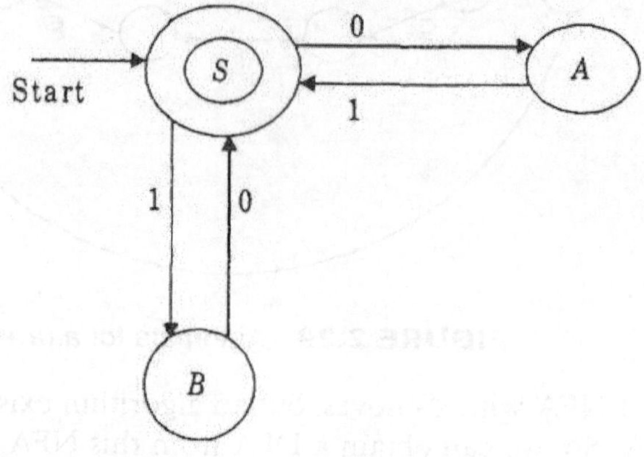

FIGURE 2.30 Transition diagram of DFA.

We use the names of the states of the automata as the variable names associated with the states.

The set of equations obtained by the application of the rules are:

$$S = 0A \mid 1B \mid \in \quad \text{(I)}$$

$$A = 1S \quad \text{(II)}$$

$$B = 0S \quad \text{(III)}$$

To solve these equations, we do the substitution of (II) and (III) in (I), to obtain:

$$S = 01S \mid 10S \mid \in$$

$$S = (01 \mid 10)S \mid \in$$

Therefore, the value of variable S comes out be:

$$S = (01 \mid 10)^* \in$$

$$= (01 \mid 10)^* \text{ (because } \in \text{ is a concatenation identity).}$$

Therefore, the regular expression specifying the regular set accepted by the given finite automata is

$$(01 \mid 10)^*.$$

2.10 LEXICAL ANALYZER DESIGN

Since the function of the lexical analyzer is to scan the source program and produce a stream of tokens as output, the issues involved in the design of lexical analyzer are:

1. Identifying the tokens of the language for which the lexical analyzer is to be built, and to specify these tokens by using suitable notation, and
2. Constructing a suitable recognizer for these tokens.

Therefore, the first thing that is required is to identify what the keywords are, what the operators are, and what the delimiters are. These are the tokens of the language. After identifying the tokens of the language, we must use suitable notation to specify these tokens. This notation, should be compact, precise, and easy to understand. Regular expressions can be used to specify a set of strings, and a set of strings that can be specified by using regular-expression notation is called a "regular set." The tokens of a programming language constitutes a regular set. Hence, this regular set can be specified by using regular-expression notation. Therefore, we write regular expressions for things like operators, keywords, and identifiers. For example, the regular expressions specifying the subset of tokens of typical programming language are as follows:

operators = +| -| * |/ | mod|div
keywords = if|while|do|then
letter = $a|b|c|d|....|z|A|B|C|....|Z$
digit = 0|1|2|3|4|5|6|7|8|9
identifier = letter (letter|digit)*

The advantage of using regular-expression notation for specifying tokens is that when regular expressions are used, the recognizer for the tokens ends up being a DFA. Therefore, the next step is the construction of a DFA from the regular expression that specifies the tokens of the language. But the DFA is a flow-chart (graphical) representation of the lexical analyzer. Therefore, after constructing the DFA, the next step is to write a program in suitable programming language that will simulate the DFA. This program acts as a token recognizer or lexical analyzer. Therefore, we find that by using regular expressions for specifying the tokens, designing a lexical analyzer becomes a simple mechanical process that involves transforming regular expressions into finite automata and generating the program for simulating the finite automata.

Therefore, it is possible to automate the procedure of obtaining the lexical analyzer from the regular expressions specifying the tokens—and this is what precisely the tool LEX is used to do. LEX is a compiler-writing tool that facilitates writing the lexical analyzer, and hence a compiler. It's inputs are the regular expression specifying the token to be recognized and generates a C program as output that acts as a lexical analyzer for the tokens specified by the inputted regular expressions.

2.10.1 Format of the Input or Source File of LEX

The LEX source file contains two things:

1. Auxiliary definitions having the format: name = regular expression.

   The purpose of the auxiliary definitions is to identify the larger regular expressions by using suitable names.

   LEX makes use of the auxiliary definitions to replace the names used for specifying the patterns of corresponding regular expressions.

2. The translation rules having the format:

   pattern {action}.

   The 'pattern' specification is a regular expression that specifies the tokens, and '{action}' is a program fragment written in C to specify the action to be taken by the lexical analyzer generated by LEX when it encounters a string matching the pattern. Normally, the action taken by the lexical analyzer is to return a pair to the parser or syntax analyzer. The first member of the pair is a token, and the second member is the value or attribute of the token. For example, if the token is an identifier, then the value of the token is a pointer to the symbol-table record that contains the corresponding name of the identifier. Hence, the action taken by the lexical analyzer is to install the name in the symbol table and return the token as an id, and to set the value of the token as a pointer to the symbol table record where the name is installed. Consider the following sample source program:

```
letter                      [ a-z, A-Z ]
digit                       [ 0-9 ]
%%
begin                       { return ("BEGIN")}
end                         { return ("END")}
if                          {return ("IF")}
letter ( letter|digit)*     { install ( );
                              return ("identifier")
                            }
<                           { return ("LT")}
< =                         { return ("LE")}
%%
definition of install()
```

In the above specification, we find that the keyword 'begin' can be matched against two patterns one specifying the keyword and the other specifying identifiers. In this case, pattern-matching is done against whichever pattern comes first in the physical order of the specification. Hence, 'begin' will be recognized as a keyword and not as an identifier. Therefore, patterns that specify keywords of the language are required to be listed before a pattern-specifying identifier; otherwise, every keyword will get recognized as identifier. A lexical analyzer generated by LEX always tries to recognize the longest prefix of the input as a token. Hence, if < = is read, it will be recognized as a token "*LE*" *not* "*LT*"

2.11 PROPERTIES OF REGULAR SETS

Since the union of two regular sets is always a regular set, regular sets are closed under the union operation. Similarly, regular sets are closed under concatenation and closure operations, because the concatenation of a regular sets is also a regular set, and the closure of a regular set is also a regular set.

Regular sets are also closed under the complement operation, because if $L(M)$ is a language accepted by a finite automata M, then the complement of $L(M)$ is $\Sigma^* - L(M)$. If we make all final states of M nonfinal, and we make all nonfinal states of M final, then the automata accepts $\Sigma^* - L(M)$; hence, we conclude that the complement of $L(M)$ is also a regular set. For example, consider the transition diagram in Figure 2.31.

NOTE *The finite automata M must be deterministic.*

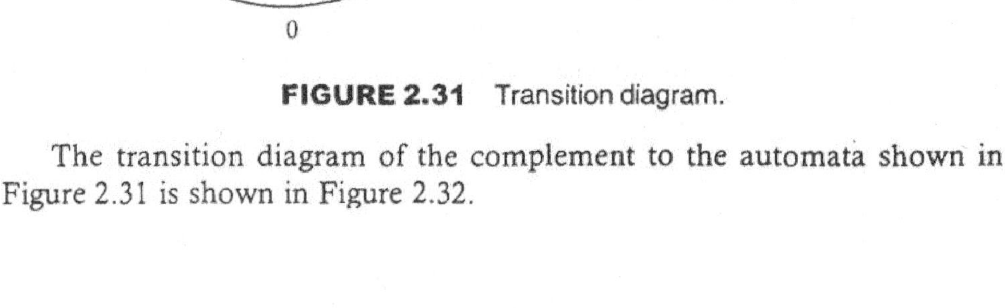

FIGURE 2.31 Transition diagram.

The transition diagram of the complement to the automata shown in Figure 2.31 is shown in Figure 2.32.

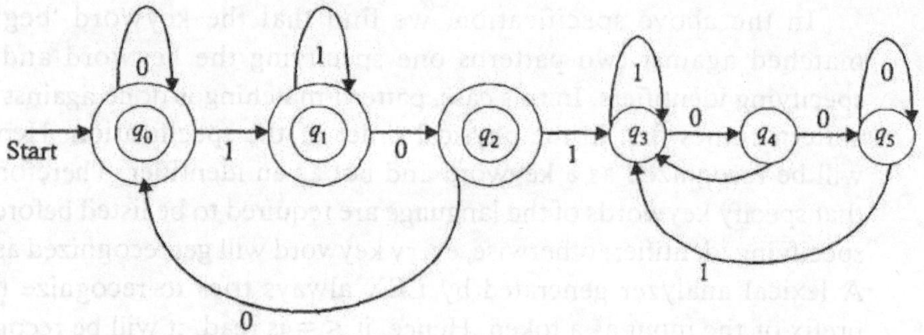

FIGURE 2.32 Complement to transition diagram in Figure 2.31.

Since the regular sets are closed under complement as well as union operations, they are closed under intersection operations also, because intersection can be expressed in terms of both union and complement operations, as shown below:

$$L_1 \cap L_2 = \overline{\overline{L_1} \cup \overline{L_2}}$$

where $\overline{L_1}$ denotes the complement of L_1.

An automata for accepting $L_1 \cap L_2$ is required in order to simulate the moves of an automata that accepts L_1 as well as the moves of an automata that accepts L_2 on the input string x. Hence, every state of the automata that accepts $L_1 \cap L_2$ will be an ordered pair $[p, q]$, where p is a state of the automata accepting L_1 and q is a state of the automata accepting L_2.

Therefore, if $M_1 = (Q_1, \Sigma, \delta_1, q_1, F_1)$ is an automata accepting L_1, and if $M_2 = (Q_2, \Sigma, \delta_2, q_2, F_2)$ is an automata accepting L_2, then the automata accepting $L_1 \cap L_2$ will be: $M = (Q_1 \times Q_2, \Sigma, \delta, [q_1, q_2], F_1 \times F_2)$ where $\delta([p, q], a) = [\delta_1(p, a), \delta_2(q, a)]$. But all the members of $Q_1 \times Q_2$ may not necessarily represent reachable states of M. Hence, to reduce the amount of work, we start with a pair $[q_1, q_2]$ and find transitions on every member of Σ from $[q_1, q_2]$. If some transitions go to a new pair, then we only generate that pair, because it will then represent a reachable state of M.

We next consider the newly generated pairs to find out the transitions from them. We continue this until no new pairs can be generated.

Let $M_1 = (Q_1, \Sigma, \delta_1, q_1, F_1)$ be a automata accepting L_1, and let $M_2 = (Q_2, \Sigma, \delta_2, q_2, F_2)$ be a automata accepting L_2. $M = (Q, \Sigma, \delta, q_0, F)$ will be an automata accepting $L_1 \cap L_2$.

```
begin
        Q_old = Φ
        Q_new = { [ q1, q2 ] }
        While ( Q_old ≠ Q_new )
        {
                Temp = Q_new − Q_old
                Q_old = Q_new
                for every pair [p, q] in Temp do
                        for every a in Σ do
                                Q_new = Q_new ∪ δ ([p, q ], a)
        }
        Q = Q_new
end
```

Consider the automatas and their transition diagrams shown in Figure 2.33 and Figure 2.34.

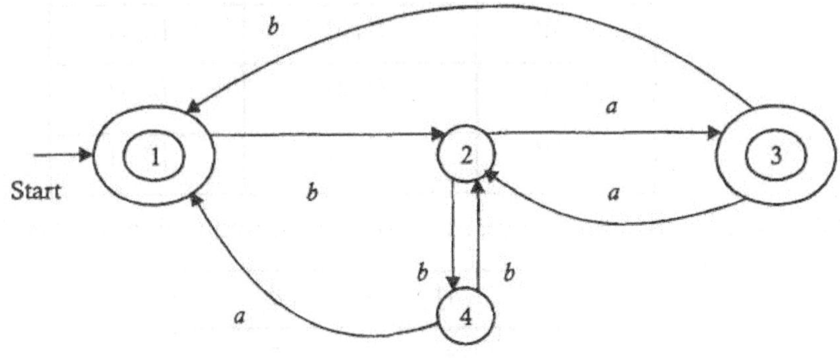

FIGURE 2.33 Transition diagram of automata M_1.

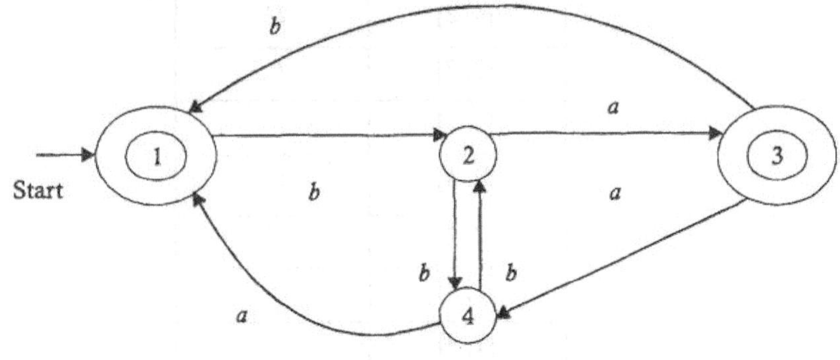

FIGURE 2.34 Transition diagram of automata M_2.

The transition table for the automata accepting $L(M_1) \cap L(M_2)$ is:

δ	*A*	*b*
[1, 1]	[1, 1]	[2, 4]
[2, 4]	[3, 3]	[4, 2]
[3, 3]	[2, 2]	[1, 1]
[4, 2]	[1, 1]	[2, 4]
[2, 2]	[3, 1]	[4, 4]
[3, 1]	[2, 1]	[1, 4]
[4, 4]	[1, 3]	[2, 2]
[2, 1]	[3, 1]	[4, 4]
[1, 4]*	[1, 3]	[2, 2]
[1, 3]	[1, 2]	[2, 1]
[1, 2]*	[1, 1]	[2, 4]

We associate the names with states of the automata obtained, as shown below:

[1, 1]	*A*
[2, 4]	*B*
[3, 3]	*C*
[4, 2]	*D*
[2, 2]	*E*
[3, 1]	*F*
[4, 4]	*G*
[2, 1]	*H*
[1, 4]	*I*
[1, 3]	*J*
[1, 2]	*K*

The transition table of the automata using the names associated above is:

δ	*a*	*B*
A	*A*	*B*
B	*C*	*D*
C	*E*	*A*
D	*A*	*B*
E	*F*	*G*
F	*H*	*I*
G	*J*	*E*
H	*F*	*G*
*I**	*J*	*E*
J	*K*	*H*
*K**	*A*	*B*

2.12 EQUIVALENCE OF TWO AUTOMATAS

Automatas M_1 and M_2 are said to be equivalent if they accept the same language; that is, $L(M_1) = L(M_2)$. It is possible to test whether the automatas M_1 and M_2 accept the same language—and hence, whether they are equivalent or not. One method of doing this is to minimize both M_1 and M_2, and if the minimal state automatas obtained from M_1 and M_2 are identical, then M_1 is equivalent to M_2.

Another method to test whether or not M_1 is equivalent to M_2 is to find out if:

$$(L(M_1) \cap \overline{L(M_2)}) \cup (\overline{L(M_1)} \cap L(M_2)) = \phi$$

For this, complement M_2, and construct an automata that accepts both the intersection of language accepted by M_1 and the complement of M_2. If this automata accepts an empty set, then it means that there is no string acceptable to M_1 that is not acceptable to M_2. Similarly, construct an automata that accepts the intersection of language accepted by M_2 and the complement of M_1. If this automata accepts an empty set, then it means that there is no string acceptable to M_2 that is not acceptable to M_1. Hence, the language accepted by M_1 is same as the language accepted by M_2.

EXERCISE

1. What do you mean by token and value of token? Explain with suitable examples.
2. The language like 'C' allows the use of same name for two different variables. Is it possible for lexical analyzer to distinguish between such variables?
3. Consider the following program:

```
main()
    {
        int x,y,z;
        z = x + y;
    }
```

   List down the lexemes, tokens and the attributes of the tokens, at the end of the lexical analysis of the above program.
4. Construct a finite automata for recognizing identifier token. Where an identifier token is formed by a sequence that starts with letter or underscore followed by letter or digit and maximum upto eight characters.
5. Construct DFA accepting the strings of binary digits which are even numbers.
6. Construct DFA accepting the reserved words **int** and **if** of 'C'.
7. Construct a minimal state DFA for the following regular expression:
   (a|b)* | (ab)*b | a*(bb)*

8. Identify dead state in the following DFA:

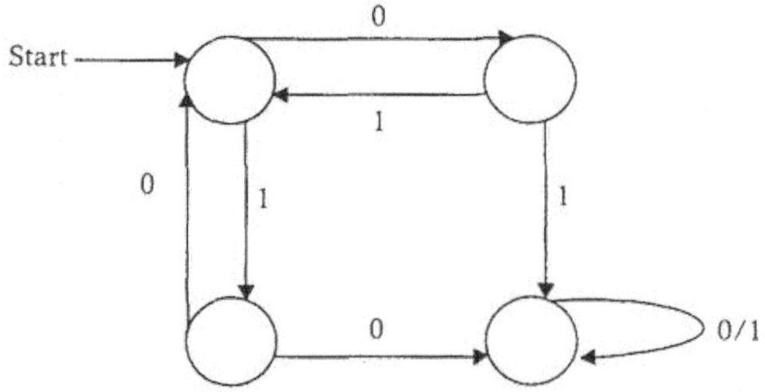

9. Obtain regular expression equivalent to the following finite automata:

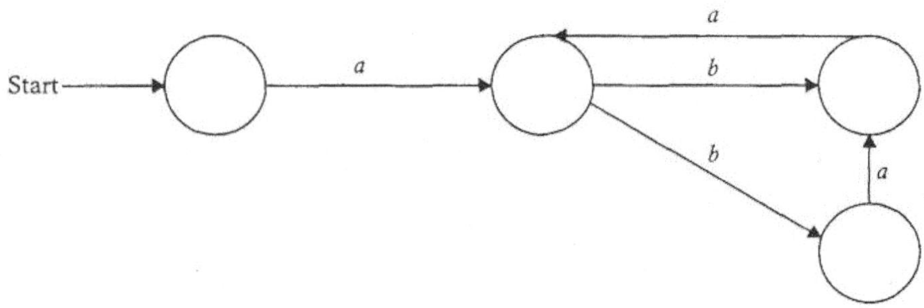

3 CONTEXT-FREE GRAMMAR AND SYNTAX ANALYSIS

3.1 SYNTAX ANALYSIS

In the syntax-analysis phase, a compiler verifies whether or not the tokens generated by the lexical analyzer are grouped according to the syntactic rules of the language. If the tokens in a string are grouped according to the language's rules of syntax, then the string of tokens generated by the lexical analyzer is accepted as a valid construct of the language; otherwise, an error handler is called. Hence, two issues are involved when designing the syntax-analysis phase of a compilation process:

1. All valid constructs of a programming language must be specified. That is, we form a specification of what tokens the lexical analyzer will return, and we specify in what manner these tokens are to be grouped so that the result of the grouping will be a valid construct of the language.
2. A suitable recognizer is required to be designed to recognize whether a string of tokens generated by the lexical analyzer is a valid construct or not.

Therefore, suitable notation must be used to specify the constructs of a language. The notation for the construct specifications should be compact, precise, and easy to understand. The syntax-structure specification for the programming language (i.e., the valid constructs of the language) uses context-free grammar (CFG), because for this class of grammar, we can automatically construct an efficient parser or recognizer that determines if a source program is syntactically correct. Hence, CFG notation is required topic for study.

3.2 CONTEXT-FREE GRAMMAR

CFG notation specifies a context-free language that consists of terminals, nonterminals, a start symbol, and productions. The terminals are nothing more than tokens of the language, used to form the language constructs. Nonterminals are the variables that denote a set of strings. For example, *S* and *E* are nonterminals that denote statement strings and expression strings, respectively, in a typical programming language. The nonterminals define the sets of strings that are used to define the language generated by the grammar.

They also impose a hierarchical structure on the language, which is useful for both syntax analysis and translation. Grammar productions specify the manner in which the terminals and string sets, defined by the nonterminals, can be combined to form a set of strings defined by a particular nonterminal. For example, consider the production $S \rightarrow aSb$. This production specifies that the set of strings defined by the nonterminal *S* are obtained by concatenating terminal *a* with any string belonging to the set of strings defined by nonterminal *S*, and then with terminal *b*. Each production consists of a nonterminal on the left-hand side, and a string of terminals and nonterminals on the right-hand side. The left-hand side of a production is separated from the right-hand side using the "$\rightarrow$" symbol, which is used to identify a relation on a set $(V \cup T)^*$ Therefore context-free grammar is a four-tuple denoted as:

$$G = (V, T, P, S)$$

where:

1. *V* is a finite set of symbols called as nonterminals or variables,
2. *T* is a set a symbols that are called as terminals,
3. *P* is a set of productions, and
4. *S* is a member of *V*, called as start symbol.

For example:

$G = (\{S\}, \{a, b\}, P, S)$ where *P* contains:

$$P = \{ S \rightarrow asa,$$
$$S \rightarrow bsb,$$
$$S \rightarrow \in$$
$$\}$$

3.2.1 Derivation

Derivation refers to replacing an instance of a nonterminal in a given string's nonterminal, by the right-hand side of the production rule, whose left-hand side contains the nonterminal to be replaced. Derivation produces a new string from a given string; therefore, derivation can be used repeatedly to obtain a new string from a given string. If the string obtained as a result of the derivation contains only terminal symbols, then no further derivations are possible. For example, consider the following grammar for a string S:

$$G = (\{S\}, \{a, b\}, P, S)$$

where P contains the following productions:

$$P = \{ S \rightarrow aSa,$$
$$S \rightarrow bSb,$$
$$S \rightarrow \in$$
$$\}$$

It is possible to replace the nonterminal S by a string aSa. Therefore, we obtain aSa from S by deriving S to aSa. It is possible to replace S in aSa by $\in$, to obtain a string aa, which cannot be further derived.

If α_1 and α_2 are the two strings, and if α_2 can be obtained from α_1, then we say α_1 is related to α_2 by "derives to relation," which is denoted by "$\rightarrow$." Hence, we write $\alpha_1 \rightarrow \alpha_2$, which translates to: α_1 derives to α_2. The symbol $\rightarrow$ denotes a derive to relation that relates the two strings α_1 and α_2 such that α_2 is a direct derivative of α_1 (if α_2 can be obtained from α_1 by a derivation of only one step). Therefore, $\overset{+}{\rightarrow}$ will denote the transitive closure of derives to relation, and if we have the two strings α_1 and α_2 such that α_2 can be obtained from α_1 by derivation, but α_2 may not be a direct derivative of α_1, then we write $\alpha_1 \overset{+}{\rightarrow} \alpha_2$, which translates to: α_1 derives to α_2 through one or more derivations.

Similarly, $\overset{*}{\rightarrow}$ denotes the reflexive transitive closure of derives to relation; and if we have two strings α_1 and α_2 such that α_1 derives to α_2 in zero, one, or more derivations, then we write $\alpha_1 \overset{*}{\rightarrow} \alpha_2$. For example, in the grammar above, we find that $S \rightarrow aSa \rightarrow abSba \rightarrow abba$. Therefore, we can write $S \overset{*}{\rightarrow} abba$.

The language defined by a CFG is nothing but the set of strings of terminals that, can be generated from S as a result of derivations using productions of the grammar. Hence, it is defined as the set of those strings of terminals that are derivable from the grammar's start symbol. Therefore, if $G = (V, T, P, S)$ is a grammar, then the language generated by the grammar is denoted as $L(G)$ and defined as:

$$L(G) = \{ \omega \mid \omega \text{ is in } T^* \text{ and } S \overset{*}{\rightarrow} \omega \}$$

the above grammar can generate the string $\in$, *aa*, *bb*, *abba*, ..., but not *aba*.

3.2.2 Standard Notation

1. The capital letters toward the start of the alphabet are used to denote nonterminals (e.g., *A*, *B*, *C*, etc.).
2. Lowercase letters toward the start of the alphabet are used to denote terminals (e.g., *a*, *b*, *c*, etc.).
3. *S* is used to denote the start symbol.
4. Lowercase letters toward the end of the alphabet (e.g., *u*, *v*, *w*, etc.) are used to denote strings of terminals.
5. The symbols α, β, γ, and so forth are used to denote strings of terminals as well as *strings* of nonterminals.
6. The capital letters toward the end of alphabet (e.g., *X*, *Y*, and *Z*) are used to denote grammar symbols, and they may be terminals or nonterminals.

The benefit of using these notations is that it is not required to explicitly specify all four grammar components. A grammar can be specified by only giving the list of productions; and from this list, we can easily get information about the terminals, nonterminals, and start symbols of the grammar.

3.2.3 Derivation Tree or Parse Tree

When deriving a string *w* from *S*, if every derivation is considered to be a step in the tree construction, then we get the graphical display of the derivation of string *w* as a tree. This is called a "derivation tree" or a "parse tree" of string *w*. Therefore, a derivation tree or parse tree is the display of the derivations as a tree. Note that a tree is a derivation tree if it satisfies the following requirements:

1. All the leaf nodes of the tree are labeled by terminals of the grammar.
2. The root node of the tree is labeled by the start symbol of the grammar.
3. The interior nodes are labeled by the nonterminals.
4. If an interior node has a label *A*, and it has *n* descendents with labels X_1, X_2, ..., X_n from left to right, then the production rule $A \rightarrow X_1\, X_2\, X_3 \ldots\ldots X_n$ must exist in the grammar.

For example, consider a grammar whose list of productions is:

$E \rightarrow E + E$

$E \rightarrow E * E$

$E \rightarrow \text{id}$

The tree shown in Figure 3.1 is a derivation tree for a string id + id * id.

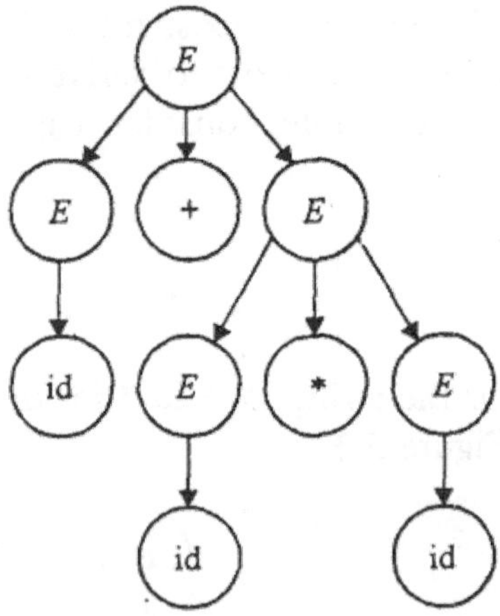

FIGURE 3.1 Derivation tree for the string id + id * id.

Given a parse (derivation) tree, a string whose derivation is represented by the given tree is obtained by concatenating the labels of the leaf nodes of the parse tree in a left-to-right order.

Consider the parse tree shown in Figure 3.2. A string whose derivation is represented by this parse tree is *abba*.

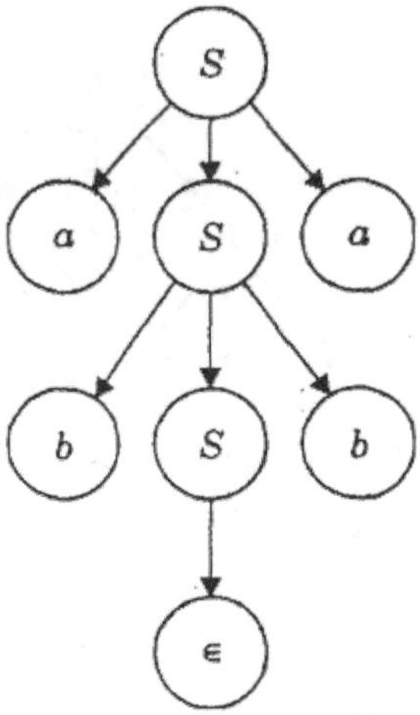

FIGURE 3.2 Parse tree for the string abba.

Since a parse tree displays derivations as a tree, given a grammar $G = (V, T, P, S)$ for every w in T^*, and which is derivable from S, there exists a parse tree displaying the derivation of w as a tree. Therefore, we can define the language generated by the grammar as:

$$L(G) = \{ w \mid w \text{ is in } T^* \text{ and there exists at least one parse tree for } w \}$$

For some w in $L(G)$, there may exist more than one parse tree. This means that more than one way may exist to derive w from S, using the productions of the grammar. For example, consider a grammar having the productions listed below:

$E \rightarrow E + E$

$E \rightarrow E * E$

$E \rightarrow \text{id}$

We find that for the string id + id * id, there exists more than one parse tree, as shown in Figure 3.3.

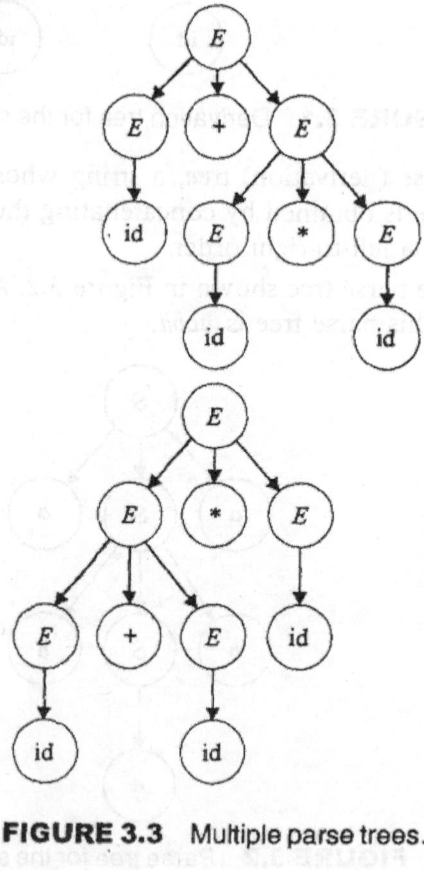

FIGURE 3.3 Multiple parse trees.

If more than one parse tree exists for some w in $L(G)$, then G is said to be an "ambiguous" grammar. Therefore, the grammar having the productions $E \rightarrow E + E \mid E * E \mid \text{id}$ is an ambiguous grammar, because there exists more than one parse tree for the string id + id * id in $L(G)$ of this grammar.

Consider a grammar having the following productions:

$$S \rightarrow aSbS \mid bSaS \mid \in$$

This grammar is also an ambiguous grammar, because more than one parse tree exists for a string *abab* in $L(G)$, as shown in Figure 3.4.

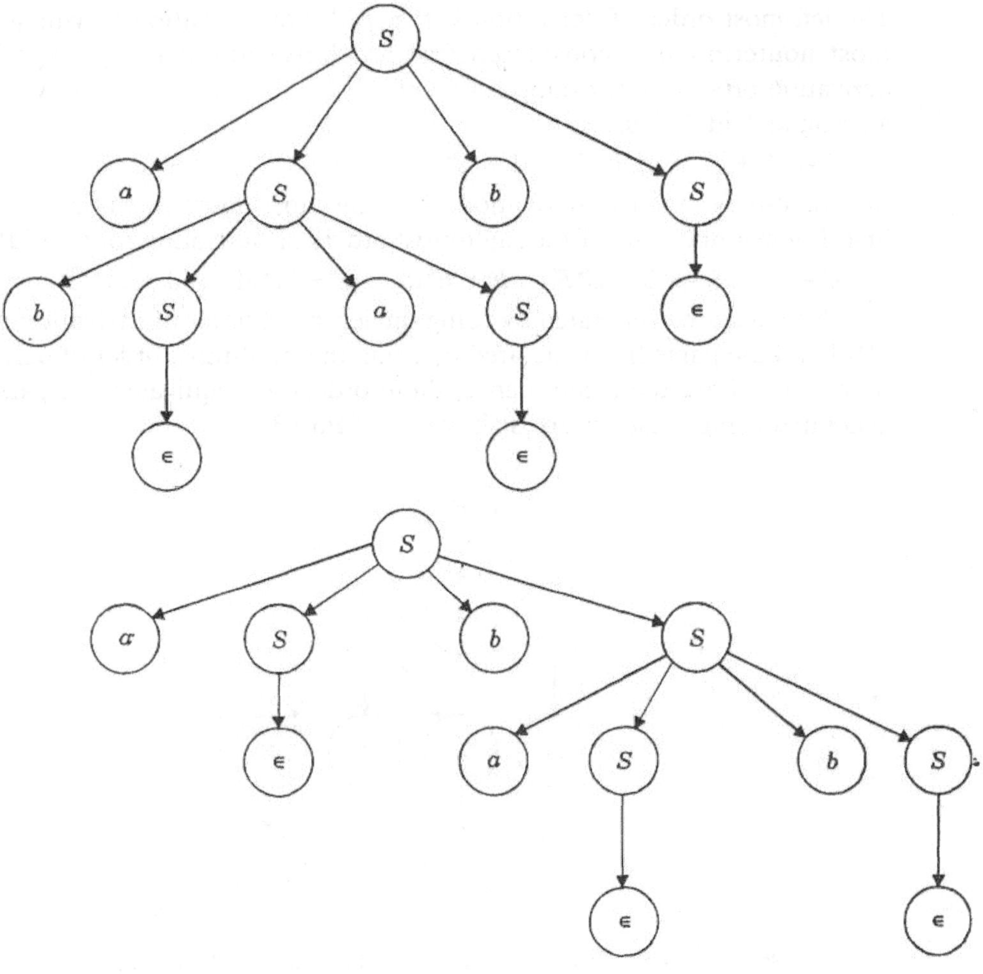

FIGURE 3.4 Multiple parse trees for the string abab.

The parse tree construction process is such that the order in which the nonterminals are considered for replacement does not matter. That is, given a string *w*, the parse tree for that string (if it exists) can be constructed by considering the nonterminals for derivation in any order. The two specific orders of derivation, which are important from the point of view of parsing, are:

1. Left-most order of derivation
2. Right-most order of derivation

The left-most order of derivation is that order of derivation in which a left-most nonterminal is considered first for derivation at every stage in the derivation process. For example, one of the left-most orders of derivation for a string id + id * id is:

$$E \rightarrow E + E \rightarrow \text{id} + E \rightarrow \text{id} + E^*E \rightarrow \text{id} + \text{id}^*E \rightarrow \text{id} + \text{id}^*\text{id}$$

In a right-most order of derivation, the right-most nonterminal is considered first. For example, one of the right-most orders of derivation for id + id* id is:

$$E \rightarrow E + E \rightarrow E + E^*E \rightarrow E + E^*\text{id} \rightarrow E + \text{id}^*\text{id} \rightarrow \text{id} + \text{id}^*\text{id}$$

The parse tree generated by using the left-most order of derivation of id + id*id and the parse tree generated by using the right-most order of derivation of id + id*id are the same; hence, these orders are equivalent. A parse tree generated using these orders is shown in Figure 3.5.

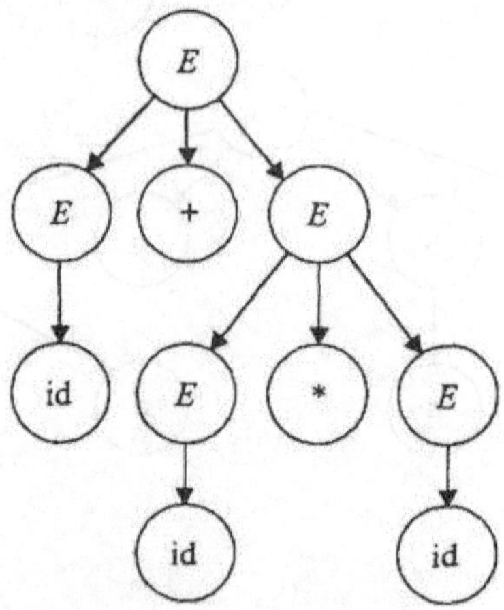

FIGURE 3.5 Parse tree generated by using both the right- and left-most derivation orders.

Another left-most order of derivation of id + id* id is given below:

$$E \rightarrow E^* E \rightarrow E + E^* E \rightarrow \text{id} + E^* E \rightarrow \text{id} + \text{id}^* E \rightarrow \text{id} + \text{id}^* \text{id}$$

And here is another right-most order of derivation of id + id*id:

$E \rightarrow E^* E \rightarrow E^*$ id $\rightarrow E + E^*$ id $\rightarrow E$ + id* id $\rightarrow$ id + id* id

The parse tree generated by using the left-most order of derivation of id + id* id and the parse tree generated using the right-most order of derivation of id + id* id are the same. Hence, these orders are equivalent. A parse tree generated using these orders is shown in Figure 3.6.

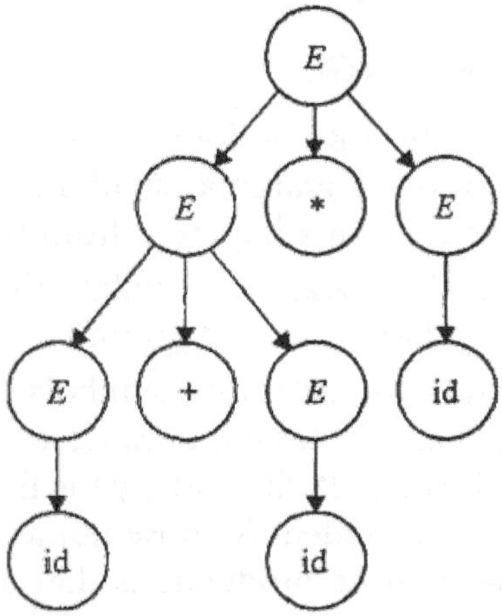

FIGURE 3.6 Parse tree generated from both the left- and right-most orders of derivation.

Therefore, we conclude that for every left-most order of derivation of a string w, there exists an equivalent right-most order of derivation of w, generating the same parse tree.

NOTE *If a grammar G is unambiguous, then for every w in L(G), there exists exactly one parse tree. Hence, there exists exactly one left-most order of derivation and (equivalently) one right-most order of derivation for every w in L(G). But if grammar G is ambiguous, then for some w in L(G), there exists more than one parse tree. Therefore, there is more than one left-most order of derivation; and equivalently, there is more than one right-most order of derivation.*

3.2.4 Reduction of Grammar

Reduction of a grammar refers to the identification of those grammar symbols (called "useless grammar symbols"), and hence those productions, that do not play any role in the derivation of any w in $L(G)$, and which we eliminate from the grammar. This has no effect on the language generated by the grammar. For example, a grammar symbol X is useful if and only if:

1. It derives to a string of terminals, and
2. It is used in the derivation of at least one w in $L(G)$.

Thus, X is useful if and only if:

1. $X \overset{*}{\rightarrow} w$, where w is in T^*, and
2. $S \overset{*}{\rightarrow} \alpha X \beta \overset{*}{\rightarrow} w$ in $L(G)$.

Therefore, reduction of a given grammar G, involves:

1. Identification of those grammar symbols that are not capable of deriving to a w in T^* and eliminating them from the grammar; and
2. Identification of those grammar symbols that are not used in any derivation and eliminating them from the grammar.

When identifying the grammar symbols that do not derive a w in T^*, only nonterminals need be tested, because every terminal member of T will also be in T^*; and by default, they satisfy the first condition. A simple, iterative algorithm can be used to identify those nonterminals that do not derive to w in T^*: we start with those productions that are of the form $A \rightarrow w$ that is, those productions whose right side is w in T^*. We mark as nonterminal every A on the left side of every production that is capable of deriving to w in T^*, and then we consider every production of the form $A \rightarrow X_1 X_2 \ldots X_n$, where A is not yet marked. If every X_i (for $1 <= i <= n$) is either a terminal or a nonterminal that is already marked, then we mark A (nonterminal on the left side of the production).

We repeat this process until no new nonterminals can be marked. The nonterminals that are not marked are those not deriving to w in T^*. After identifying the nonterminals that do not derive to w in T^*, we eliminate all productions containing these nonterminals in order to obtain a grammar that does not contain any nonterminals that do not derive in T^*. The algorithm for identifying as well as eliminating the nonterminals that do not derive to w in T^* is given below:

Input: $G = (V, T, P, S)$

Output: $G_1 = (V_1, T, P_1, S)$

{ where V_1 is the set of nonterminals deriving to w in T^*, we maintain $V_{1\ old}$ and $V_{1\ new}$ to continue iterations, and P_1 is the set of productions that do not contain nonterminals that do not derive to w in T^* }

Let U be the set of nonterminals that are not capable of deriving to w in T^*. Then,

```
begin
    V_1old = φ
    V_1new = φ
    for every production of the form A → w do
        V_1new = V_1new ∪ { A }
        while (V_1old ≠ V_1new) do
            begin
                temp = V − V_1new
                V_1old = V_1new
                For every A in temp do
                for every A-production of the form A → X_1 X_2 ... X_n in P do
                if each Xi is either in T or in V_1old, then
                    begin
                        V_1new = V_1new ∪ { A }
                        break;
                    end
            end
        V_1 = V_1new
        U = V − V_1
        for every production in P do
        if it does not contain a member of U then
        add the production to P_1
end
```

If S is itself a useless nonterminal, then the reduced grammar is a 'null' grammar.

When identifying the grammar symbols that are not used in the derivation of any w in $L(G)$, terminals as well as nonterminals must be tested. A simple, iterative algorithm can be used to identify those grammar symbols that are not used in the derivation of any w in $L(G)$: we start with S-productions and mark every grammar symbol X on the right side of every S-production. We then consider every production of the form $A \rightarrow X_1 X_2 \ldots X_n$, where A is an already-marked nonterminal; and we mark every X on the right side of these productions. We repeat this process until no new nonterminals can be marked. We do not mark any terminals or nonterminals not used in the derivation of any w in $L(G)$. After identifying the terminals and nonterminals not used in the derivation of any w in $L(G)$, we eliminate all productions containing them; thus, we obtain a grammar that does not contain any useless symbols-hence, a reduced grammar.

The algorithm for identifying as well as eliminating grammar symbols that are not used in the derivation of any w in $L(G)$ is given below:

Input: $G_1 = (V_1, T, P_1, S)$

{ The grammar obtained after elimination of the nonterminals not deriving to w in T^* }

Output: $G_2 = (V_2, T_2, P_2, S)$

{ where V_2 is the set of nonterminals used in derivation of some w in $L(G)$, and T_2 is set of terminals used in the derivation of some w in $L(G)$, and P_2 is set of productions containing the members of V_2 and T_2 only. We maintain $V_{2\ old}$ and $V_{2\ new}$ to continue iterations }

```
begin
  T2 = φ
  V2 old = φ
  P2 = φ
  V2 new = { S }
  While (V2 old # V2 new) do
  begin
      temp = V2 new - V2 old
      V2 old = V2 new
      for every A in temp do
      for every A-production of the form A → X1 X2 ... Xn in P1 do
      for each Xi (1 <= i <= n) do
      begin
          if (Xi is in V1) then
          V2 new = V2 new ∪ { Xi }
          if (X1 is in T) then
          T2 = T2 ∪ { Xi }
      end
  end
          V2 = V2 new
          temp1 = V1 - V2
```

temp$_2$ = $T_1 - T_2$
for every production in P_1 do add the production to P_2 if it does not contain a member of temp$_1$ as well as temp$_2$
$G_2 = (V_2, T_2, P_2, S)$

end

EXAMPLE 3.1: Find the reduced grammar equivalent to CFG

$G = (\{S, A, B, C\} \{a, b, d\} S, P)$

where P contains

$S \rightarrow AC \mid SB$

$A \rightarrow bASC \mid a$

$B \rightarrow aSB \mid bbC$

$C \rightarrow Bc \mid ad$

Since the productions $A \rightarrow a$ and $C \rightarrow ad$ exist in form $A \rightarrow w$, nonterminals A and C are derivable to w in T^*, The production $S \rightarrow AC$ also exists, the right side of which contains the nonterminals A and C, which are derivable to w in T^*. Hence, S is also derivable to w in T^*. But since the right side of both of the B-productions contain B, the nonterminal B is not derivable to w in T^*. Hence, B can be eliminated from the grammar, and the following grammar is obtained:

$G_1 = (\{S, A, C\} \{a, b, d\} S, P_1)$

where P_1 contains

$S \rightarrow AC$

$A \rightarrow bASC \mid a$

$C \rightarrow ad$

Since the right side of the S-production of this grammar contains the nonterminals A and C, A and C will be used in the derivation of some w in $L(G)$. Similarly, the right side of the A-production contains $bASC$ and a; hence, the terminals a and b will be used. The right side of the C-production contains ad, so terminal d will also be useful. Therefore, every terminal, as well as the nonterminal in $G1$, is useful. So the reduced grammar is:

$G_1 = (\{S, A, C\} \{a, b, d\} S, P_1)$

where P_1 contains

$S \rightarrow AC$

$A \rightarrow bASC \mid a$

$C \rightarrow ad$

3.2.5 Useless Grammar Symbols

A grammar symbol is a useless grammar symbol if it does not satisfy either of the following conditions:

$X \overset{*}{\rightarrow} w$, where w is in T^*

$S \overset{*}{\rightarrow} \alpha X \beta \overset{*}{\rightarrow} w$, w is in $L(G)$

That is, a grammar symbol X is useless if it does not derive to terminal strings. And even if it does derive to a string of terminals, X is a useless grammar symbol if it does not occur in a derivation sequence of any w in $L(G)$. For example, consider the following grammar:

$S \rightarrow aB \mid bX$

$A \rightarrow BAd \mid bSX \mid q$

$B \rightarrow aSB \mid bBX$

$X \rightarrow SBD \mid aBx \mid ad$

First, we find those nonterminals that do not derive to the string of terminals so that they can be separated out. The nonterminals A and X directly derive to the string of terminals because the production $A \rightarrow q$ and $X \rightarrow ad$ exist in a grammar. There also exists a production $S \rightarrow bX$, where b is a terminal and X is a nonterminal, which is already known to derive to a string of terminals. Therefore, S also derives to string of terminals, and the nonterminals that are capable of deriving to a string of terminals are: S, A, and X. B ends up being a useless nonterminal; and therefore, the productions containing B can be eliminated from the given grammar to obtain the grammar given below:

$S \rightarrow bX$

$A \rightarrow bSX \mid q$

$X \rightarrow ad$

We next find in the grammar obtained those terminals and nonterminals that occur in the derivation sequence of some w in $L(G)$. Since every derivation sequence starts with S, S will always occur in the derivation sequence of every w in $L(G)$. We then consider those productions whose left-hand side is S, such as $S \rightarrow bX$, since the right side of this production contains a terminal b and a nonterminal X. We conclude that the terminal b will occur in the derivation sequence, and a nonterminal X will also occur in the derivation sequence. Therefore, we next consider those productions whose left-hand side is a nonterminal X. The production is $X \rightarrow ad$. Since the right side of this production contains terminals a and d, these terminals will occur in the derivation sequence. But since no new nonterminal is found, we conclude that the nonterminals S and X, and the terminals a, b, and d are the grammar symbols that can occur in the derivation sequence. Therefore, we conclude that the nonterminal A will be a useless nonterminal, even though it derives to the string of terminals. So we eliminate the productions containing A to obtain a reduced grammar, given below:

$$S \rightarrow bX$$
$$X \rightarrow ad$$

EXAMPLE 3.2: Consider the following grammar, and obtain an equivalent grammar containing no useless grammar symbols.

$$A \rightarrow xyz \mid Xyzz$$
$$X \rightarrow Xz \mid xYx$$
$$Y \rightarrow yYy \mid XZ$$
$$Z \rightarrow Zy \mid z$$

Since $A \rightarrow xyz$ and $Z \rightarrow z$ are the productions of the form $A \rightarrow w$, where w is in T^*, nonterminals A and Z are capable of deriving to w in T^*. There are two X-productions: $X \rightarrow Xz$ and $X \rightarrow xYx$. The right side of these productions contain nonterminals X and Y, respectively. Similarly, there are two Y-productions: $Y \rightarrow yYy$ and $Y \rightarrow XZ$. The right side of these productions contain nonterminals Y and X, respectively. Hence, both X and Y are not capable of deriving to w in T^*. Therefore, by eliminating the productions containing X and Y, we get:

$$A \rightarrow xyz$$
$$Z \rightarrow Zy \mid z$$

Since A is a start symbol, it will always be used in the derivation of every w in $L(G)$. And since $A \rightarrow xyz$ is a production in the grammar, the terminals x, y, and z will also be used in the derivation. But no nonterminal Z occurs on the right side of the A-production, so Z will not be used in the derivation of any w in $L(G)$. Hence, by eliminating the productions containing nonterminal Z, we get:

$$A \rightarrow xyz$$

which is a grammar containing no useless grammar symbols.

EXAMPLE 3.3: Find the reduced grammar that is equivalent to the CFG given below:

$$S \rightarrow aC \mid SB$$
$$A \rightarrow bSCa$$

$B \rightarrow aSB \mid bBC$

$C \rightarrow aBC \mid ad$

Since $C \rightarrow ad$ is the production of the form $A \rightarrow w$, where w is in T^*, nonterminal C is capable of deriving to w in T^*. The production $S \rightarrow aC$ contains a terminal a on the right side as well as a nonterminal C that is known to be capable of deriving to w in T^*.

Hence, nonterminal S is also capable of deriving to w in T^*. The right side of the production $A \rightarrow bSCa$ contains the nonterminals S and C, which are known to be capable of deriving to w in T^*. Hence, nonterminal A is also capable of deriving to w in T^*. There are two B-productions: $B \rightarrow aSB$ and $B \rightarrow bBC$. The right side of these productions contain the nonterminals S, B, and C; and even though S and C are known to be capable of deriving to w in T^*, nonterminal B is not. Hence, by eliminating the productions containing B, we get:

$S \rightarrow aC$

$A \rightarrow bSCa$

$C \rightarrow ad$

Since S is a start symbol, it will always be used in the derivation of every w in $L(G)$. And since $S \rightarrow aC$ is a production in the grammar, terminal a as well as nonterminal C will also be used in the derivation. But since a nonterminal C occurs on the right side of the S-production, and $C \rightarrow ad$ is a production, terminal d will be used along with terminal a in the derivation. A nonterminal A occurs nowhere in the right side of either the S-production or the C-production; it will not be used in the derivation of any w in $L(G)$. Hence, by eliminating the productions containing nonterminal A, we get:

$S \rightarrow aC$

$C \rightarrow ad$

which is a reduced grammar equivalent to the given grammar, but it contains no useless grammar symbols.

EXAMPLE 3.4: Find the useless symbols in the following grammar, and modify the grammar so that it has no useless symbols.

$S \rightarrow 0 \mid A$

$A \rightarrow AB$

$B \rightarrow 1$

Since $S \rightarrow 0$ and $B \rightarrow 1$ are productions of the form $A \rightarrow w$, where w is in T^*, the nonterminals S and B are capable of deriving to w in T^*. The production $A \rightarrow AB$ contains the nonterminals A and B on the right side; and even though B is known to be capable of deriving to w in T^*, nonterminal A is not capable of deriving to w in T^*. Therefore, by eliminating the productions containing A, we get:

$S \rightarrow 0$

$B \rightarrow 1$

Since S is a start symbol, it will always be used in the derivation of any w in $L(G)$. And because $S \rightarrow 0$ is a production in the grammar, terminal 0 will also be used in the derivation. But nonterminal B does not occur anywhere in the right side of the S-production, it will not be used in the derivation of any w in $L(G)$. Hence, by eliminating the productions containing nonterminal B, we get:

$S \rightarrow 0$

which is a grammar equivalent to the given grammar and contains no useless grammar symbols.

EXAMPLE 3.5: Find the useless symbols in the following grammar, and modify the grammar to obtain one that has no useless symbols.

$S \rightarrow AB \mid CA$

$B \rightarrow BC \mid AB$

$A \rightarrow a$

$C \rightarrow aB \mid b$

Since $A \rightarrow a$ and $C \rightarrow b$ are productions of the form $A \rightarrow w$, where w is in T^*, the nonterminals A and C are capable of deriving to w in T^*. The right side of the production $S \rightarrow CA$ contains nonterminals C and A, both of which are known to be derivable to w in T^*.

Hence, S is also capable of deriving to w in T^*. There are two B-productions, $B \rightarrow BC$ and $B \rightarrow AB$. The right side of these productions contain the nonterminals A, B, and C. Even though A and C are known to be capable of deriving to w in T^*, nonterminal B is not capable of deriving to w in T^*. Therefore, by eliminating the productions containing B, we get:

$S \rightarrow CA$

$A \rightarrow a$

$C \rightarrow b$

Since S is a start symbol, it will always be used in the derivation of every w in $L(G)$. And since $S \rightarrow CA$ is a production in the grammar, nonterminals C and A will both be used in the derivation. For the productions $A \rightarrow a$ and $C \rightarrow b$, the terminals a and b will also be used in the derivation. Hence, every grammar symbol in the above grammar is useful. Therefore, a grammar equivalent to the given grammar that contains no useless grammar symbols is:

$S \rightarrow CA$
$A \rightarrow a$
$C \rightarrow b$

3.2.6 ∈-Productions and Nullable Nonterminals

A production of the form $A \rightarrow \in$ is called a "∈-production." If A is a nonterminal, and if $A \xrightarrow{*} \in$ (i.e., if A derives to an empty string in zero, one, or more derivations), then A is called a "nullable nonterminal."

Algorithm for Identifying Nullable Nonterminals

Input: $G = (V, T, P, S)$

Output: Set N (i.e., the set of nullable nonterminals)
{ we maintain N_{old} and N_{new} to continue iterations }

```
begin
  N_old = φ
  N_new = φ
  for every production of the form A → ∈ do
  N_new = N_new ∪ { A }
  while (N_old ≠ N_new) do
  begin
    temp = V − N_new
    N_old = N_new
    For every A in temp do
    for every A-production of the form A → X1 X2 ...Xn in P do
    if each X1 is in N_old then
    N_new = N_new ∪ { A }
  end
  N = N_new
end
```

EXAMPLE 3.6: Consider the following grammar and identify the nullable nonterminals.

$S \rightarrow ACB \mid CbB \mid Ba$
$A \rightarrow da \mid BC$
$B \rightarrow gC \mid \in$
$C \rightarrow ha \mid \in$

By applying the above algorithm, the results after each iteration are shown below:

Initially:

$N_{old} = \phi$

$N_{new} = \phi$

After the execution of the first *for* loop:

$N_{old} = \phi$

$N_{new} = \{ B, C \}$

After the first iteration of the *while* loop:

$N_{old} = \{ B, C \}$

$N_{new} = \{ B, C, A \}$

After the second iteration of the *while* loop:

$N_{old} = \{ B, C, A \}$

$N_{new} = \{ B, C, A, S \}$

After the third iteration of the *while* loop:

$N_{old} = \{ B, C, A, S \}$

$N_{new} = \{ B, C, A, S \}$

Therefore, $N = \{ S, A, B, C \}$; and hence, all the nonterminals of the grammar are nullable.

3.2.7 Eliminating ∈-Productions

Given a grammar G that contains ∈-productions, if $L(G)$ does not contain ∈, then it is possible to eliminate all ∈-productions in the given grammar G. Whereas, if $L(G)$ contains ∈, then elimination of all ∈-productions from G gives a grammar G_1 for which $L(G_1) = L(G) - \{ \in \}$. To eliminate the ∈-productions from a grammar, we use the following technique.

If $A \rightarrow \in$ is an ∈-production to be eliminated, then we look for all those productions in the grammar whose right side contains A, and we replace each occurrence of A in these productions by ∈. Thus, we obtain the non-∈-productions to be added to the grammar so that the language's generation remains the same. For example, consider the following grammar:

$S \rightarrow aA$

$A \rightarrow b \mid \in$

To eliminate $A \rightarrow \in$ form the above grammar, we replace A on the right side of the production $S \rightarrow aA$ and obtain a non-∈-production, $S \rightarrow a$, which is added to the grammar as a substitute in order to keep the language generated by the grammar the same. Therefore, the ∈-free grammar equivalent to the given grammar is:

$S \rightarrow aA \mid a$

$A \rightarrow b$

EXAMPLE 3.7: Consider the following grammar, and eliminate all the ∈-productions from the grammar without changing the language generated by the grammar.

$S \rightarrow ABAC$

$A \rightarrow aA \mid \epsilon$

$B \rightarrow bB \mid \epsilon$

$C \rightarrow c$

To eliminate $A \rightarrow \epsilon$ from this grammar, the non-∈-productions to be added are obtained as follows: the list of the productions containing A on the right-hand side is:

$S \rightarrow ABAC$

$A \rightarrow aA$

Replace each occurrence of A in each of these productions in order to obtain the non-∈-productions to be added to the grammar. The list of these productions is:

$S \rightarrow BAC \mid ABC \mid BC$

$A \rightarrow a$

Add these productions to the grammar, and eliminate $A \rightarrow \epsilon$ from the grammar. This gives us the following grammar:

$S \rightarrow ABAC \mid BAC \mid ABC \mid BC$

$A \rightarrow aA \mid a$

$B \rightarrow bB \mid \epsilon$

$C \rightarrow c$

To eliminate $B \rightarrow \epsilon$ from the grammar, the non-∈-productions to be added are obtained as follows. The productions containing B on the right-hand side are:

$S \rightarrow ABAC \mid BAC \mid ABC \mid BC$

$B \rightarrow bB$

Replace each occurrence of B in these productions in order to obtain the non-∈-productions to be added to the grammar. The list of these productions is:

$S \rightarrow AAC$

$S \rightarrow AC$

$S \to C$

$B \to b$

Add these productions to the grammar, and eliminate $A \to \epsilon$ from the grammar in order to obtain the following:

$S \to ABAC \mid BAC \mid ABC \mid BC \mid AAC \mid AC \mid C$

$A \to aA \mid a$

$B \to bB \mid b$

$C \to c$

EXAMPLE 3.8: Consider the following grammar and eliminate all the ϵ-productions without changing the language generated by the grammar.

$S \to AaA$

$A \to Sb \mid bCC \mid \epsilon$

$C \to CC \mid abb$

To eliminate $A \to \epsilon$ from the grammar, the non-ϵ-productions to be added are obtained as follows: the list of productions containing A on right is:

$S \to AaA$

Replace each occurrence of A in this production to obtain the non-ϵ-productions to be added to the grammar. This are:

$S \to aA \mid Aa \mid a$

Add these productions to the grammar, and eliminate $A \to \epsilon$ from the grammar to obtain the following:

$S \to AaA \mid aA \mid Aa \mid a$

$A \to Sb \mid bCC$

$C \to CC \mid abb$

3.2.8 Eliminating Unit Productions

A production of the form $A \to B$, where A and B are both nonterminals, is called a "unit production." Unit productions in the grammar increase the cost of derivations. The following algorithm can be used to eliminate unit productions from the grammar:

```
While there exist a unit production A → B in the grammar do
  {
    select a unit production A → B such that there exists
    at least one nonunit production
    B → α
```

for every nonunit production $B \rightarrow \alpha$ do
add production $A \rightarrow \alpha$ to the grammar
eliminate $A \rightarrow B$ from the grammar
}

EXAMPLE 3.9: Given the grammar shown below, eliminate all the unit productions from the grammar.

$S \rightarrow AB$
$A \rightarrow a$
$B \rightarrow C \mid b$
$C \rightarrow D$
$D \rightarrow E$
$E \rightarrow a$

The given grammar contains the productions:

$B \rightarrow C$
$C \rightarrow D$
$D \rightarrow E$

which are the unit productions. To eliminate these productions from the given grammar, we first select the unit production $B \rightarrow C$. But since no nonunit *C*-productions exist in the grammar, we then select $C \rightarrow D$. But since no nonunit *D*-productions exist in the grammar, we next select $D \rightarrow E$. There *does* exist a nonunit *E*-production: $E \rightarrow a$. Hence, we add $D \rightarrow a$ to the grammar and eliminate $D \rightarrow E$. But since $B \rightarrow C$ and $C \rightarrow D$ are still there, we once again select unit production $B \rightarrow C$. Since no nonunit *C*-production exists in the grammar, we select $C \rightarrow D$. Now there exists a nonunit production $D \rightarrow a$ in the grammar. Hence, we add $C \rightarrow a$ to the grammar and eliminate $C \rightarrow D$. But since $B \rightarrow C$ is still there in the grammar, we once again select unit production $B \rightarrow C$. Now there exists a nonunit production $C \rightarrow a$ in the grammar, so we add $B \rightarrow a$ to the grammar and eliminate $B \rightarrow C$. Now no unit productions exist in the grammar. Therefore, the grammar that we get that does not contain unit productions is:

$S \rightarrow AB$
$A \rightarrow a$
$B \rightarrow a \mid b$
$C \rightarrow a$
$D \rightarrow a$
$E \rightarrow a$

But we see that the grammar symbols C, D, and E become useless as a result of the elimination of unit productions, because they will not be used in the derivation of any w in $L(G)$. Hence, we can eliminate them from the grammar to obtain:

$$S \rightarrow AB$$
$$A \rightarrow a$$
$$B \rightarrow a \mid b$$

Therefore, we conclude that to obtain the grammar in the most simplified form, we have to eliminate unit productions first. We then eliminate the useless grammar symbols.

3.2.9 Eliminating Left Recursion

If a grammar contains a pair of productions of the form $A \rightarrow A\alpha \mid \beta$, then the grammar is a "left-recursive grammar." If left-recursive grammar is used for specification of the language, then the top-down parser designed for the grammar's language may enter into an infinite loop during the parsing process on some erroneous input. This is because a top-down parser attempts to obtain the left-most derivation of the input string w; hence, the parser may see the same nonterminal A every time as the left-most nonterminal. And every time, it may do the derivation using $A \rightarrow A\alpha$. Therefore, for top-down parsing, nonleft-recursive grammar should be used. Left-recursion can be eliminated from the grammar by replacing $A \rightarrow A\alpha \mid \beta$ with the productions $A \rightarrow \beta B$ and $B \rightarrow \alpha\beta \mid \epsilon$. In general, if a grammar contain productions:

$$A \rightarrow A\alpha_1 \mid A\alpha_2 \mid \ldots \mid A\alpha_m \mid \beta_1 \mid \beta_2 \mid \ldots \mid \beta_n$$

then the left-recursion can be eliminated by adding the following productions in place of the ones above.

$$A \rightarrow \beta_1 B \mid \beta_2 B \mid \ldots \mid \beta_n B$$
$$B \rightarrow \alpha_1 B \mid \alpha_2 B \mid \ldots \mid \alpha_m B \mid \epsilon$$

EXAMPLE 3.10: Consider the following grammar:

$$S \rightarrow aBDh$$
$$B \rightarrow Bb \mid c$$
$$D \rightarrow EF$$
$$E \rightarrow g \mid \epsilon$$
$$F \rightarrow f \mid \epsilon$$

The grammar is left-recursive because it contains a pair of productions, $B \rightarrow Bb \mid c$. To eliminate the left-recursion from the grammar, replace this pair of productions with the following productions:

$B \rightarrow cC$
$C \rightarrow bC \mid \in$

Therefore, the grammar that we get after the elimination of left-recursion is:

$S \rightarrow aBDh$
$B \rightarrow cC$
$C \rightarrow bC \mid \in$
$D \rightarrow EF$
$E \rightarrow g \mid \in$
$F \rightarrow f \mid \in$

EXAMPLE 3.11: Consider the following grammar:

$S \rightarrow A$
$A \rightarrow Ad \mid Ae \mid aB \mid aC$
$B \rightarrow bBC \mid f$
$C \rightarrow g$

The grammar is left-recursive because it contains the productions $A \rightarrow Ad \mid Ae \mid aB \mid aC$. To eliminate the left-recursion from the grammar, replace these productions by the following productions:

$A \rightarrow aBD \mid aCD$
$D \rightarrow dD \mid eD \mid \in$

Therefore, the resulting grammar after the elimination of left-recursion is:

$S \rightarrow A$
$A \rightarrow aBD \mid aCD$
$D \rightarrow dD \mid eD \mid \in$
$B \rightarrow bBc \mid f$
$C \rightarrow g$

EXAMPLE 3.12: Consider the following grammar:

$S \rightarrow (L) \mid a$
$L \rightarrow L, S \mid S$

The grammar is left-recursive because it contains the productions $L \rightarrow L, S \mid S$. To eliminate the left-recursion from the grammar, replace these productions by the following productions:

$L \rightarrow SA$
$A \rightarrow SA \mid \in$

Therefore, after the elimination of left-recursion, we get:

$S \rightarrow (L) \mid a$

$L \rightarrow SA$

$A \rightarrow SA \mid \epsilon$

3.3 REGULAR GRAMMAR

Regular grammar is a context-free grammar in which every production is restricted to one of the following forms:

1. $A \rightarrow aB$, or
2. $A \rightarrow w$, where A and B are the nonterminals, a is a terminal symbol, and w is in T^*.

The ϵ-productions are permitted as a special case when $L(G)$ contains ϵ. This grammar is called "regular grammar," because if the format of every production in CFG is restricted to $A \rightarrow aB$ or $A \rightarrow a$, then the grammar can specify only regular sets. Hence, a finite automata exists that accepts $L(G)$, if G is regular grammar. Given a regular grammar G, a finite automata accepting $L(G)$ can be obtained as follows:

1. The number of states of the automata will be equal to the number of nonterminals of the grammar plus one; that is, there will be a state corresponding to every nonterminal of the grammar. And one more state will be there, which will be the final state of the automata. The state corresponding to the start symbol of the grammar will be the initial state of the automata. If $L(G)$ contains ϵ, then make the start state also the final state.
2. The transitions in the automata can be obtained as follows:

   for every production $A \rightarrow aB$ do

   make $\delta(A, a) = B$

   for every production of the form $A \rightarrow a$ do

   make $\delta(A, a) =$ final state

EXAMPLE 3.13: Consider the regular grammar shown below and the transition diagram of the automata, shown in Figure 3.7, that accepts the language generated by the grammar.

$S \rightarrow 0A \mid 1B \mid 0 \mid 1$

$A \rightarrow 0S \mid 1B \mid 1$

$B \rightarrow 0A \mid 1S$

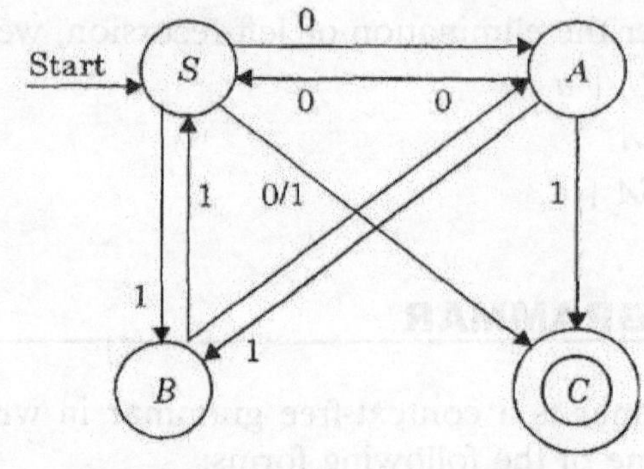

FIGURE 3.7 Transition diagram for automata that accepts the regular grammar of Example 3.13.

This is a non-deterministic automata. Its deterministic equivalent can be obtained as follows:

	0	1
{ S }	{ A, C }	{ B, C }
*{ A, C }	{ S }	{ B, C }
*{ B, C }	{ A }	{ S }
{ A }	{ S }	{ B, C }

The transition diagram of the automata is shown in Figure 3.8.

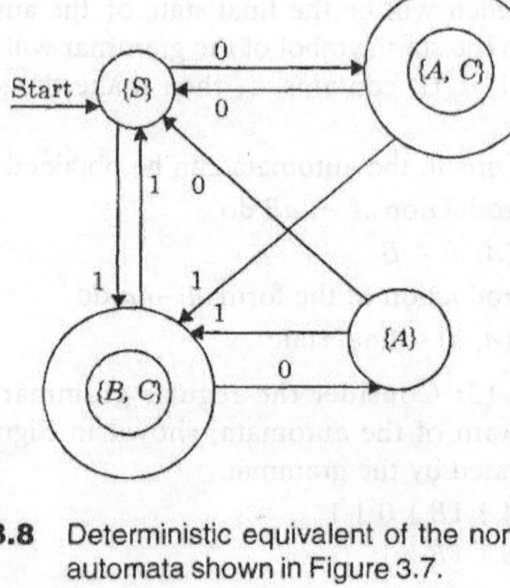

FIGURE 3.8 Deterministic equivalent of the non-deterministic automata shown in Figure 3.7.

Consider the following grammar:

$S \rightarrow 0S \mid 1A \mid 1$

$A \rightarrow 0A \mid 1A \mid 0 \mid 1$

The transition diagram of the finite automata that accepts the language generated by the above grammar is shown in Figure 3.9.

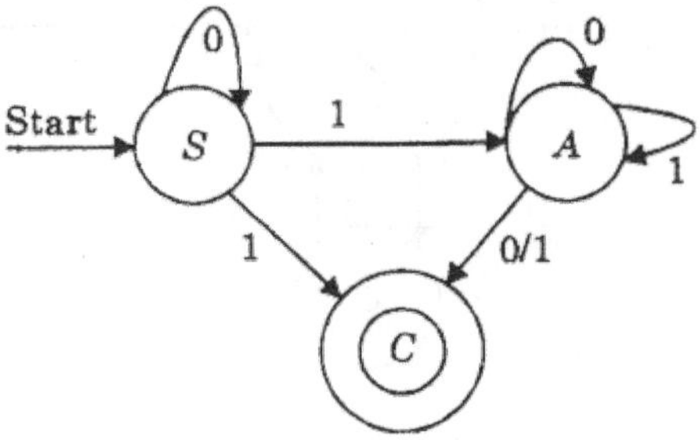

FIGURE 3.9 Non-deterministic automata.

This is a non-deterministic automata. Its deterministic equivalent can be obtained as follows, and the transition diagram is shown in Figure 3.10.

	0	1
{ *S* }	{ *S* }	{ *A*, *C* }
*{ *A*, *C* }	{ *A*, *C* }	{ *A*, *C* }

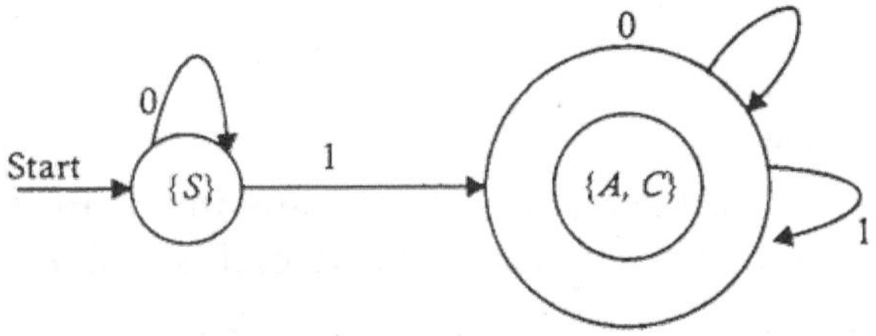

FIGURE 3.10 Transition diagram for deterministic automata equivalent shown in Figure 3.9.

Given a finite automata *M*, a regular grammar *G* that generates *L*(*M*) can be obtained as follows:

1. Associate suitable variables like A, B, C, etc, with the states of the automata. The labels of the states can also be used as variable names.
2. Obtain the productions of the grammar as follows. If $\delta(A, a) = B$, then add a production $A \rightarrow aB$ to the list of productions of the grammar. If *B* is a final state, then add either $A \rightarrow a$ or $B \rightarrow \in$, to the grammar's list of productions.

3. The variable associated with the initial state of the automata is the start symbol of the grammar.

   For example consider the automata shown in Figure 3.11.

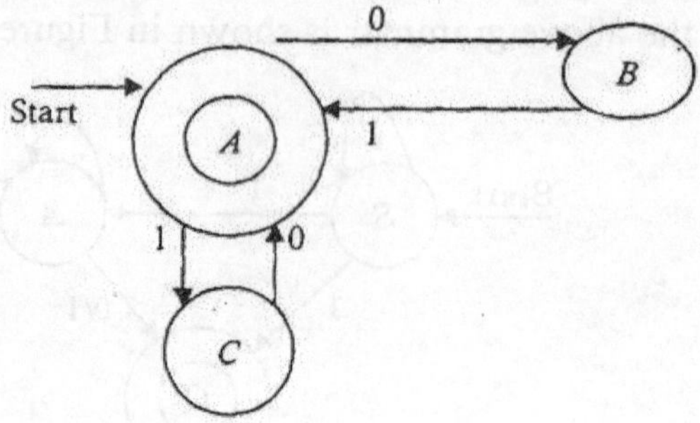

FIGURE 3.11 Regular-grammar automata.

The regular grammar that generates the language accepted by the automata shown in Figure 3.11 will have the following productions:

$A \rightarrow 0B \mid 1C \mid \epsilon$

$B \rightarrow 1A$

$C \rightarrow 0A$

or

$A \rightarrow 0B \mid 1C$

$B \rightarrow 1A \mid 1$

$C \rightarrow 0A \mid 0$

where A is the start symbol. Both the grammars are same, but the first one contains ϵ-productions, whereas the second is ϵ-free.

EXAMPLE 3.14: Find out whether the following grammar generates the same language.

G_1:

$A \rightarrow 0B \mid 1E$

$B \rightarrow 0A \mid 1F \mid \epsilon$

$C \rightarrow 0C \mid 1A$

$D \rightarrow 0A \mid 1D \mid \epsilon$

$E \rightarrow 0C\ 1A$

$F \rightarrow 0A \mid 1B \mid \epsilon$

where A is a start symbol

G_2:

$X \to 0Y \mid 0 \mid 1Z$
$Y \to 0X \mid 1Y \mid 1$
$Z \to 0Z \mid 1X$
where X is a start symbol

Since the grammars G_1 and G_2 are the regular grammars, $L(G_1) = L(G_2)$ if the minimal state automata accepting $L(G_1)$, and the minimal state automata accepting $L(G_2)$ are identical. The transition diagram of the automata accepting $L(G_1)$ is shown in Figure 3.12.

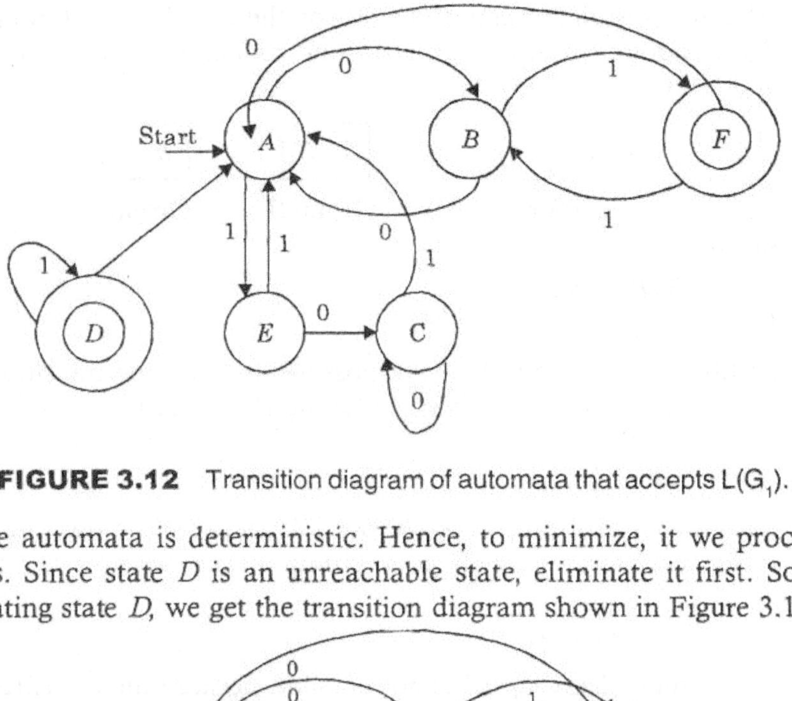

FIGURE 3.12 Transition diagram of automata that accepts $L(G_1)$.

The automata is deterministic. Hence, to minimize, it we proceed as follows. Since state D is an unreachable state, eliminate it first. So, after eliminating state D, we get the transition diagram shown in Figure 3.13.

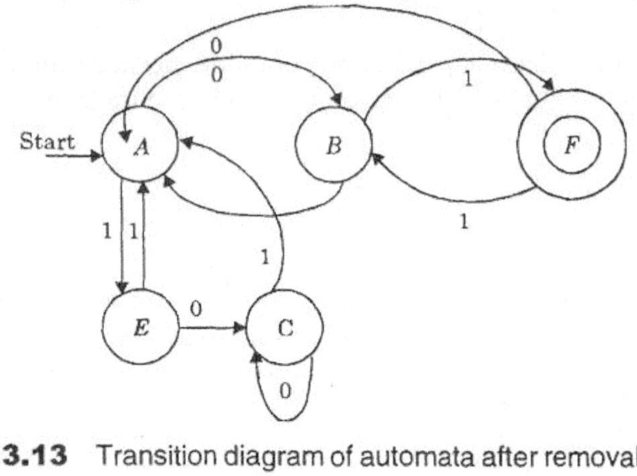

FIGURE 3.13 Transition diagram of automata after removal of state D.

We then identify the nondistinguishable states of the automata shown in Figure 3.13, as follows. Initially, we have two groups:

A, E, C	B, F
Group I	Group II

Since

$\delta(A, 0) = B$

$\delta(E, 0) = C$

$\delta(C, 0) = C$

state *B* is distinguishable from rest of the members of Group I. Hence, we divide Group I into two groups—one containing *A*, and other containing *E* and *C*, as shown below:

A	E, C	B, F
Group I	Group II	Group III

Since

$\delta(E, 0) = C$

$\delta(C, 0) = C$

partitioning of Group II is not possible, because the transitions from all the members of Group II only go to Group II. Similarly:

$\delta(E, 1) = A$

$\delta(C, 1) = A$

Partitioning of Group II is not possible, because the transitions from all the members of Group II only go to Group I. And since:

$\delta(B, 0) = A$

$\delta(F, 0) = A$

partitioning of Group III is not possible, because the transitions from all the members of Group III only go to Group I. Similarly:

$\delta(B, 1) = F$

$\delta(F, 1) = B$

Partitioning of Group III is not possible, because the transitions from all the members of Group III only go to Group III. Hence, states *E* and *C* are nondistinguishable states. States *B* and *F* are also nondistinguishable states. Therefore, if we merge *E* and *C* to form a state E_1, and we merge *B* and *F* to form B_1, we get the automata shown in Figure 3.14.

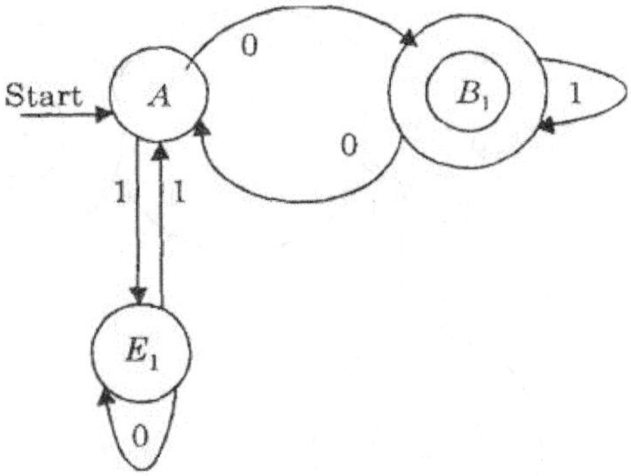

FIGURE 3.14 Transition diagram for the automata that results from merged states.

Since no dead states exist in the automata shown in Figure 3.14, it is a minimal state automata that accepts $L(G_1)$. The transition diagram of the non-deterministic automata that accepts $L(G_2)$ is shown in Figure 3.15.

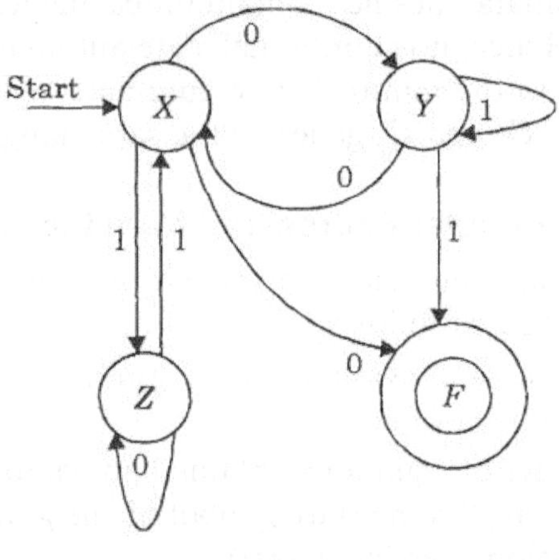

FIGURE 3.15 Non-deterministic automata that accepts $L(G_2)$.

Its equivalent deterministic automata is as follows, and the transition diagram is shown in Figure 3.16.

	0	1
{ X }	{ Y, F }	{ Z }
*{ Y, F }	{ X }	{ Y, F }
{ Z }	{ Z }	{ X }

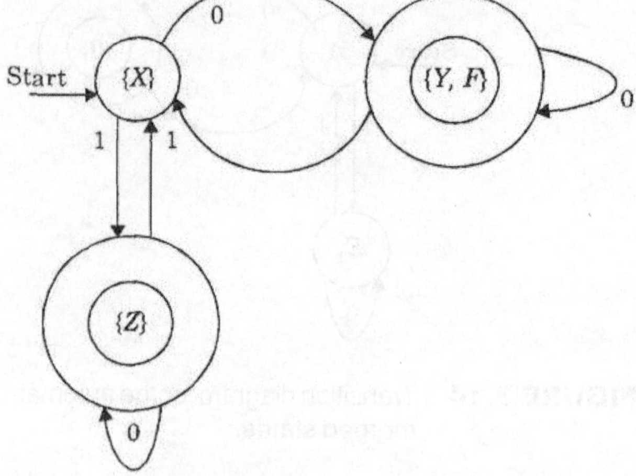

FIGURE 3.16 Transition diagram of the equivalent deterministic automata for Figure 3.15.

This automata does not contain unreachable, nondistinguishable states or dead states. Hence, it is a minimal state automata accepting $L(G_2)$, and since it is identical to the minimal state automata accepting $L(G_1)$, $L(G_2) = L(G_2)$; and therefore, G_1 and G_2 generate the same language.

Obtaining a Regular Expression from the Regular Grammar

Given a regular grammar G, a regular expression that specifies $L(G)$ can be directly obtained as follows:

1. Replace the "→" symbols in the grammar's productions with "=" symbols to get a set of equations.
2. Solve the set of equations obtained above to obtain the value of the variable S, where S is the start symbol of the grammar. The result is the regular expression specifying $L(G)$.

For example consider the following regular grammar:

$S \rightarrow 0A \mid 0 \mid 1B$

$A \rightarrow 1A \mid 1$

$B \rightarrow 0B \mid 1S$

3. Replacing the "→" symbol in the productions of the grammar with the "=" symbol, we get the following set of equations:

$S = 0A \mid 0 \mid 1B$ (I)

$A = 1A \mid 1$ (II)

$B = 0B \mid 1S$ (III)

From equation (III) we get:

$$B = 0^*1S$$

because equation (III) is of the form $A = aA \mid b$, where a and b are the expressions that do not contain variable A, and the solution of this is $A = a^*b$. Similarly, from equation (II) we get:

$$A = 1^*1$$

Substituting the values of A in (I) gives:

$$S = 01^*1 \mid 0 \mid 10^*1S$$

$$S = (10^*1)S \mid (01^*1 \mid 0)$$

Therefore, $S = (10^*1)^*(01^*1 \mid 0)$.

Hence, the required regular expression is:

$$(10^*1)^*(01^*1 \mid 0)$$

3.4 RIGHT LINEAR AND LEFT LINEAR GRAMMAR

3.4.1 Right Linear Grammar

Right linear grammar is a context-free grammar in which every production is restricted to one of the following forms:

1. $A \rightarrow wB$
2. $A \rightarrow w$, where A and B are the nonterminals, and w is in T^*

Since w is in T^*, w can also be a single terminal; hence, every regular grammar, by default, satisfies this requirement of a right linear grammar. Therefore every regular grammar is a right linear grammar. Similarly, when $|w| > 1$, productions containing w on the right side can be split into more than one production. Each contains only one terminal and only one nonterminal on the right side by using additional nonterminals, because w can be written as ay, where a is the first terminal symbol of w and y is string made of the remaining symbols of w. Therefore, a production $A \rightarrow wB$ can be split into the productions $A \rightarrow aB_1$ and $B_1 \rightarrow yB$ without affecting the language generated by the grammar. The production $B_1 \rightarrow yB$ can be further split in a similar manner. And this can continue until $|y|$ becomes one. A production $A \rightarrow w$ can also be split into the productions $A \rightarrow aB_1$ and $B_1 \rightarrow y$ without affecting the language generated by the grammar. The production $B_1 \rightarrow y$ can be further split in a similar manner, and this can continue until $|y|$ becomes one, bringing the productions into the form required by the regular grammar. Therefore, we conclude that every right linear grammar can be rewritten in a such a manner that every production of the grammar will satisfy the requirement of the regular grammar. For example, consider the following grammar:

$$S \rightarrow aaB \mid ab$$
$$B \rightarrow bB \mid bb$$

The grammar is a right linear grammar; the production $S \rightarrow aaB$ can be split into the productions $S \rightarrow aC$ and $C \rightarrow aB$ without affecting what is derived from S. Similarly, the production $S \rightarrow ab$ can be split into the productions $S \rightarrow aD$ and $D \rightarrow a$. The production $B \rightarrow bb$ can also be split into the productions $B \rightarrow bE$ and $E \rightarrow b$. Therefore, the above grammar can be rewritten as:

$$S \rightarrow aC$$
$$C \rightarrow aB$$
$$S \rightarrow aD$$
$$D \rightarrow a$$
$$B \rightarrow bB$$
$$B \rightarrow bE$$
$$E \rightarrow b$$

which is a regular grammar.

3.4.2 Left Linear Grammar

Left linear grammar is a context-free grammar in which every production is restricted to one of the following forms:

1. $A \rightarrow Bw$
2. $A \rightarrow w$, where A and B are the nonterminals, and w is in T^*

For every left linear grammar, there exists an equivalent right linear grammar that generates the same language, and vice versa. Hence, we conclude that every linear grammar (left or right) is a regular grammar. Given a right linear grammar, an equivalent left linear grammar can be obtained as follows:

1. Obtain a regular expression for the language generated by the given grammar.
2. Reverse the regular expression obtained in step 1, above.
3. Obtain the regular or right linear grammar for the regular expression obtained in step 2.
4. Reverse the right side of every production of the grammar obtained in step 3. The resulting grammar will be an equivalent left linear grammar.

For example consider the right linear grammar given below:

$$S \rightarrow 01B \mid 0$$
$$B \rightarrow 1B \mid 11$$

The regular expression for the above grammar is obtained as follows. Replace the $\rightarrow$ by = in the above productions to obtain the equations:

$$S = 01B \mid 0 \qquad \text{(I)}$$

$$B = 1B \mid 11 \qquad \text{(II)}$$

Solving equation (II) gives:

$B = 1^*(11)$

By substituting the value of B in (I), we get:

$S = 011^*11 \mid 0$

Therefore, the required regular expression is:

$(011^*11 \mid 0)$

And the reverse regular expression is:

$(0 \mid 111^*10)$

The finite automata accepting the language specified by the above regular expression is shown in Figure 3.17.

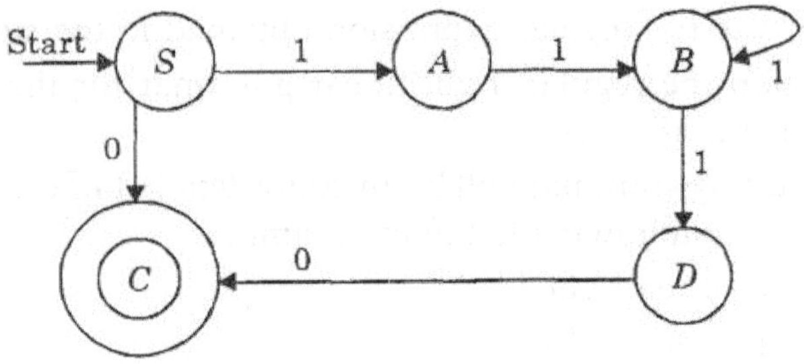

FIGURE 3.17 Finite automata accepting the right linear grammar for a regular expression.

Therefore, the right linear grammar that generates the language accepted by the automata in Figure 3.17 is:

$S \rightarrow 1A \mid 0C \mid 0$

$A \rightarrow 1B$

$B \rightarrow 1D \mid 1B$

$D \rightarrow 0C \mid 0$

Since C is not useful, eliminating C gives:

$S \rightarrow 1A \mid 0$

$A \rightarrow 1B$

$B \rightarrow 1D \mid 1B$

$D \rightarrow 0$

which can be further simplified by replacing D in $B \to 1D$, using $D \to 0$ to give:

$S \to 1A \mid 0$

$A \to 1B$

$B \to 10 \mid 1B$

Reversing the right side of the productions yields:

$S \to A1 \mid 0$

$A \to B1$

$A \to 01 \mid B \mid$

which is the equivalent left linear grammar. So, given a left linear grammar, an equivalent right linear grammar can be obtained as follows:

1. Reverse the right side of every production of the given grammar.
2. Obtain a regular expression for the language generated by the grammar obtained in step 1, above.
3. Reverse the regular expression obtained in the step 2.
4. Obtain the regular, right linear grammar for the regular expression obtained in the step 3.

The resulting grammar will be an equivalent left linear grammar. For example, consider the following left linear grammar:

$S \to Sab \mid Aa$

$A \to Abb \mid bb$

Reversing the right side of the productions gives us:

$S \to baS \mid aA$

$A \to bbA \mid bb$

The regular expression that specifies the language generated by the above grammar can be obtained as follows. Replace the $\to$ symbols with "=" symbols in the productions of the above grammar to get the following set of equations:

$$S = baS \mid aA \quad \text{(I)}$$

$$A = bbA \mid bb \quad \text{(II)}$$

From equation (II), we get:

$A = (bb)^*(bb)$

Substituting this value in (I) gives us:

$S = baS \mid a(bb)^*(bb)$

Therefore,

$S = (ba)^*(a(bb)^*bb)$

and the regular expression is:

$$(ba)^*(a(bb)^*bb)$$

The reversed regular expression is:

$$(bb(bb)^*a)(ab)^*$$

The finite automata that accepts the language specified by the reversed regular expression is shown in Figure 3.18.

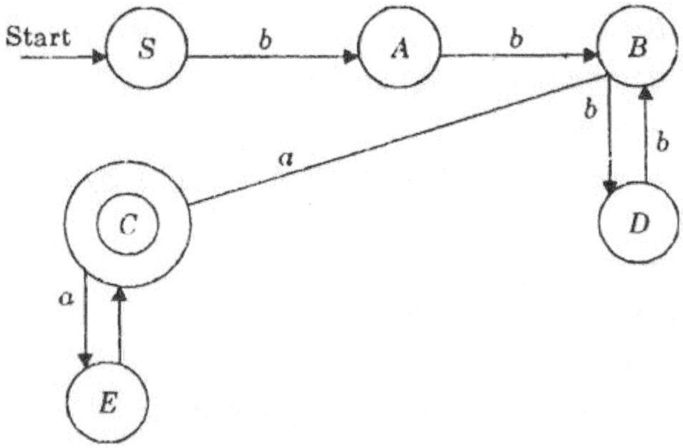

FIGURE 3.18 Transition diagram for a finite automata specified by a reversed regular expression.

Therefore, the regular grammar that generates the language accepted by the automata shown in Figure 3.18 is:

$S \rightarrow bA$

$A \rightarrow bB$

$B \rightarrow aC \mid bD \mid a$

$D \rightarrow bB$

$C \rightarrow aE$

$E \rightarrow bC \mid b$

which can be reduced to:

$S \rightarrow bbB$

$B \rightarrow aaE \mid bbB \mid a$

$E \rightarrow baE \mid b$

which is the required right linear grammar.

EXAMPLE 3.15: Consider the following grammar to obtain an equivalent left linear grammar.

$S \rightarrow gA$

$A \rightarrow aA \mid gB \mid g$

$B \rightarrow gA$

The regular expression for the above grammar is obtained as follows. Replace the $\rightarrow$ by = in the above productions to obtain the equations:

$S = gA$ (I)

$A = aA \mid gB \mid g$ (II)

$B = gA$ (III)

By substituting (III) in (II) we get:

$A = aA \mid ggA \mid g$

Therefore, $A = (a \mid gg)A \mid g$ and $A = (a \mid gg)^*g$. By substituting this value in (I) we get:

$S = a(a \mid gg)^*g$

And the regular expression is:

$a(a \mid gg)^*g$

Therefore, the reversed regular expression is:

$a(gg \mid a)^*g$

But since $(a \mid gg)^*$ is the same as $(gg \mid a)^*$, the reversed regular expression is same. Hence, the regular, right linear grammar that generates the language specified by the reversed regular expression is the given grammar itself. Therefore, an equivalent left linear grammar can be obtained by reversing the right side of the productions of the given grammar:

$S \rightarrow Ag$

$A \rightarrow Aa \mid Bg \mid g$

$B \rightarrow Ag$

EXERCISE

1. Write a CFG to specify the declarations in C. (declarations to be considered are the declarations of basic data type, array declaration)
2. Test whether the following grammar is ambiguous.

   L → L ; L | S

   S → a

3. Eliminate all $\in$-productions from the following grammar.

   S → aAB | dA

   A → bAc | $\in$

   B → dB | $\in$

4. Consider the following grammar:

   S → ABC

   A → Aa | d

   B → Bb | e

   C → Cc | f

   Eliminate left recursion from the above grammar.

5. Consider the following grammar:

   S → AB

   A → aAb | ab

   B → Bc | c

   Write the leftmost as well as rightmost derivation sequence for the string **aabbcc**.

6. If a grammar is ambiguous then we can have a single rightmost derivation but two leftmost derivations for a sentence in the language generated by the grammar. Comment on the truth/falsehood of the above statement.

7. Transform the following right-linear grammar into an equivalent left-linear grammar.

   S → abA

   A → baA | ab

8. Obtain regular grammar equivalent to the regular expressions given below:

   (*a*) a*(a|b)bb

   (*b*) (ab)*ba(ab)*

9. Obtain DFA recognizing the language generated by the following regular grammar.

   S → aA | bB | a

   A → bA | aS | b

   B → aB | bS

4 TOP-DOWN PARSING

INTRODUCTION

A syntax analyzer or parser is a program that performs syntax analysis. A parser obtains a string of tokens from the lexical analyzer and verifies whether or not the string is a valid construct of the source language-that is, whether or not it can be generated by the grammar for the source language. And for this, the parser either attempts to derive the string of tokens *w* from the start symbol *S*, or it attempts to reduce *w* to the start symbol of the grammar by tracing the derivations of *w* in reverse. An attempt to derive *w* from the grammar's start symbol *S* is equivalent to an attempt to construct the top-down parse tree; that is, it starts from the root node and proceeds toward the leaves. Similarly, an attempt to reduce *w* to the grammar's start symbol *S* is equivalent to an attempt to construct a bottom-up parse tree; that is, it starts with *w* and traces the derivations in reverse, obtaining the root *S*.

4.1 TOP-DOWN PARSING

Top-down parsing attempts to find the left-most derivations for an input string *w*, which is equivalent to constructing a parse tree for the input string *w* that starts from the root and creates the nodes of the parse tree in a predefined order. The reason that top-down parsing seeks the left-most derivations for an input string w and not the right-most derivations is that the input string w is scanned by the parser from left to right, one symbol/token at a time, and the left-most derivations generate the leaves of the parse tree in left-to-right order, which matches the input scan order.

Since top-down parsing attempts to find the left-most derivations for an input string w, a top-down parser may require backtracking (i.e., repeated scanning of the input); because in the attempt to obtain the left-most derivation of the input string w, a parser may encounter a situation in which a nonterminal A is required to be derived next, and there are multiple A-productions, such as $A \rightarrow \alpha_1 \mid \alpha_2 \mid \ldots \mid \alpha_n$. In such a situation, deciding which A-production to use for the derivation of A is a problem. Therefore, the parser will select one of the A-productions to derive A, and if this derivation finally leads to the derivation of w, then the parser announces the successful completion of parsing. Otherwise, the parser resets the input pointer to where it was when the nonterminal A was derived, and it tries another A-production. The parser will continue this until it either announces the successful completion of the parsing or reports failure after trying all of the alternatives. For example, consider the top-down parser for the following grammar:

$$S \rightarrow aAb$$
$$A \rightarrow cd \mid c$$

Let the input string be $w = acb$. The parser initially creates a tree consisting of a single node, labeled S, and the input pointer points to a, the first symbol of input string w. The parser then uses the S-production $S \rightarrow aAb$ to expand the tree as shown in Figure 4.1.

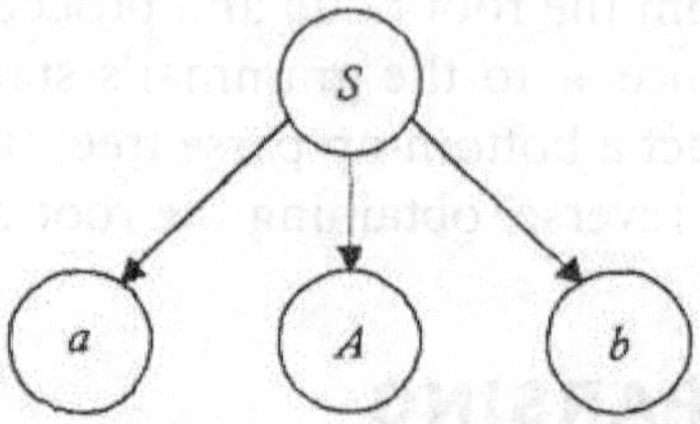

FIGURE 4.1 Parser uses the S-production to expand the parse tree.

The left-most leaf, labeled a, matches the first input symbol of w. Hence, the parser will now advance the input pointer to c, the second symbol of string w, and consider the next leaf labeled A. It will then expand A, using the first alternative for A in order to obtain the tree shown in Figure 4.2.

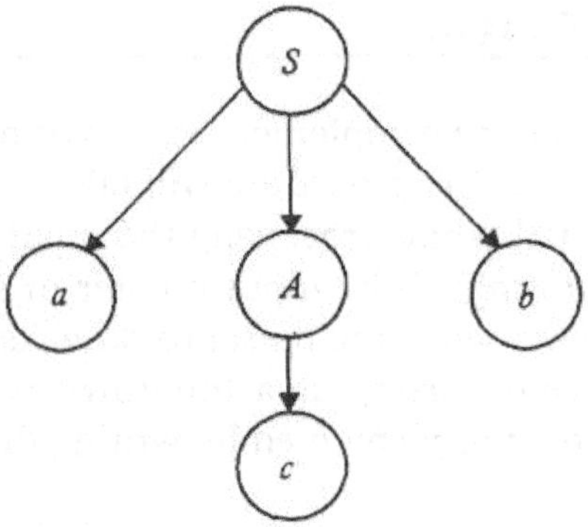

FIGURE 4.2 Parser uses the first alternative for A in order to expand the tree.

The parser now has the match for the second input symbol. So, it advances the pointer to *b*, the third symbol of *w*, and compares it to the label of the next leaf. If the label does not match *d*, it reports failure and goes back (backtracks) to *A*, as shown in Figure 4.3. The parser will also reset the input pointer to the second input symbol—the position it had when the parser encountered *A*—and it will try a second alternative for *A* in order to obtain the tree. If the leaf *c* matches the second symbol, and if the next leaf *b* matches the third symbol of *w*, then the parser will halt and announce the successful completion of parsing.

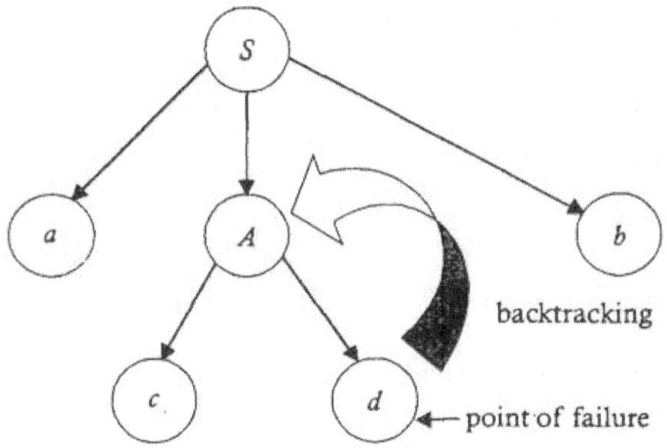

FIGURE 4.3 Parse tree obtained by applying second alternative for A.

4.2 IMPLEMENTATION

A top-down parser can be implemented by writing a set of recursive procedures to process the input. One procedure will take care of the left-most derivations for one nonterminal while processing the input. Each procedure should also provide for the storing of the input pointer in some local variable so that it can be reset properly when the parser backtracks. This implementation, called a "recursive descent parser," is a top-down parser for the above-described grammar that can be implemented by writing the following set of procedures:

```
S( )
   {
   if (input =='a' )
      {
        advance( );
        if (A( ) != error)
        if (input =='b')
          { advance(. );
          if (input == endmarker)
          return(success);
          else
          return(error);
          }
        else
        return(error);
      }
      else
      return(error);
   }

A( )
   {
   if (input =='c')
      {
      advance( );
      if (input == 'd')
      advance( );
      }
```

```
        else
        return(error);
        }

main( )
    {
    Append the endmarker to the string w to be parsed;
    Set the input pointer to the left most token of w;
    if ( S( ) != error)
    print f ("Successful completion of the parsing");
    else
    printf ("Failure");
    }
```

where advance() is a routine that, when called, advances the input's pointer to the next token of *w*.

CAUTION

In a backtracking parser, the order in which alternatives are tried affects the language accepted by the parser. For example, in the above parser, if a production $A \rightarrow c$ is tried before $A \rightarrow cd$, then the parser will fail to accept the string $w = acdb$, because it first expands S, as shown in Figure 4.4.

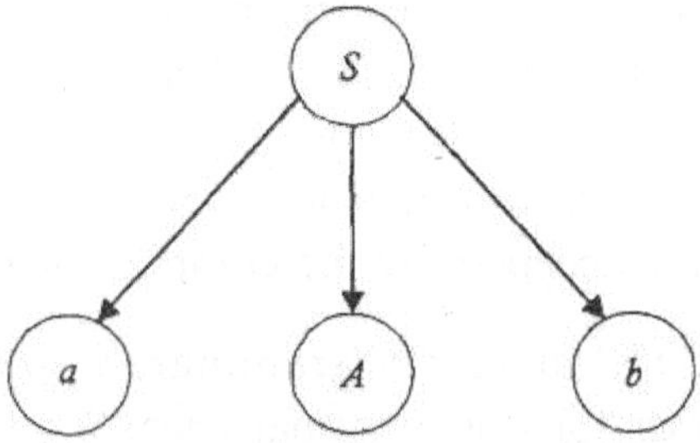

FIGURE 4.4 Result of application of S-production.

The first input symbol matches the left-most leaf; and therefore, the parser will advance the pointer to *c* and consider the nonterminal *A* for expansion in order to obtain the tree shown in Figure 4.5.

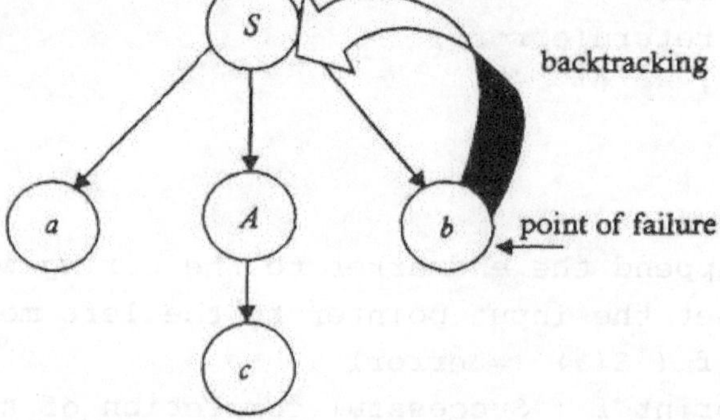

FIGURE 4.5 Result of application of A → C.

The second input symbol also matches. Therefore, the parser will advance the pointer to *d*, the third input symbol, and consider the next leaf, labeled *b* in Figure 4.5. It finds that there is no match; and therefore, it will backtrack to *S* (as shown in Figure 4.5 by the thick arrow). But since there is no alternative to *S* that can be tried, the parser will return failure. Because the point of mismatch is the descendent of a node labeled by *S*, the parser will backtrack to *S*. It cannot backtrack to *A*. Therefore, the parser will not accept the string *acdb*. Whereas, if the parser tries the alternative $A \rightarrow cd$ first and $A \rightarrow c$ second, then the parser is capable of accepting the string *acdb* as well as *acb* because, for the string $w = acb$, when the parser encounters a mismatch, it is at a node labeled by *d*, which is a descendent of a node labeled by *A*. Hence, it will backtrack to *A* and try $A \rightarrow c$, and end up in the parse tree for *acb*. Hence, we conclude that the order in which alternatives are tried in a backtracking parser affect the language accepted by the compiler or parser.

EXAMPLE 4.1: Consider a grammar $S \rightarrow aa \mid aSa$. If a top-down backtracking parser for this grammar tries $S \rightarrow aSa$ before $S \rightarrow aa$, show that the parser succeeds on two occurrences of *a* and four occurrences of *a*, but not on six occurrences of *a*.

In the case of two occurrences of *a*, the parser will first expand *S*, as shown in Figure 4.6.

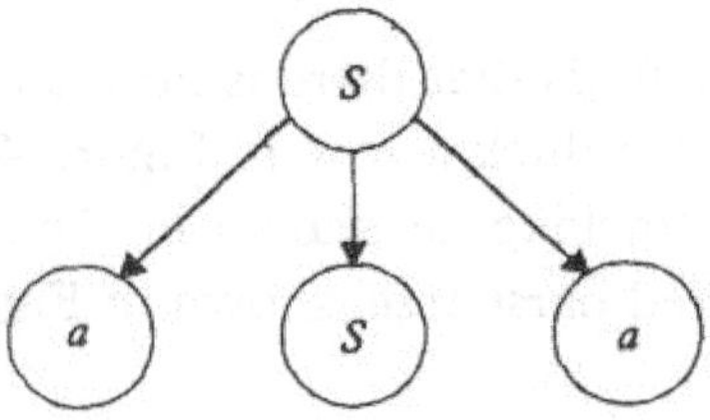

FIGURE 4.6 The parser first expands S.

The first input symbol matches the left-most leaf. Therefore, the parser will advance the pointer to a second *a* and consider the nonterminal *S* for expansion in order to obtain the tree shown in Figure 4.7.

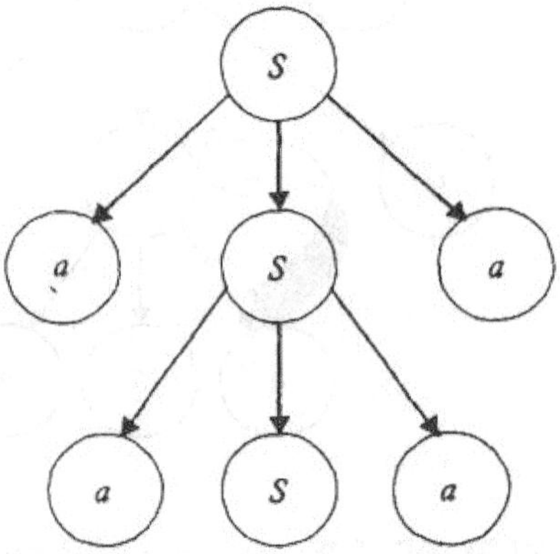

FIGURE 4.7 The parser expands the next leaf labelled S.

The second input symbol also matches. Therefore, the parser will consider the next leaf labeled *S* and expand it, as shown in Figure 4.8.

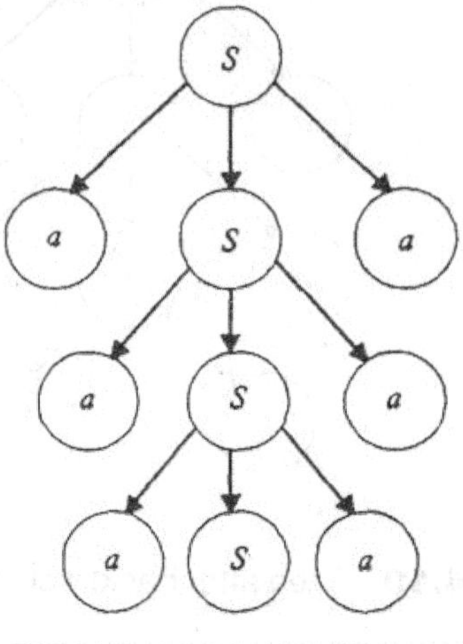

FIGURE 4.8 The parser expands the next leaf labeled S.

The parser now finds that there is no match. Therefore, it will backtrack to *S*, as shown by the thick arrow in Figure 4.9. The parser then continues matching and backtracking, as shown in Figures 4.10 through 4.15, until it arrives at the required parse tree, shown in Figure 4.16.

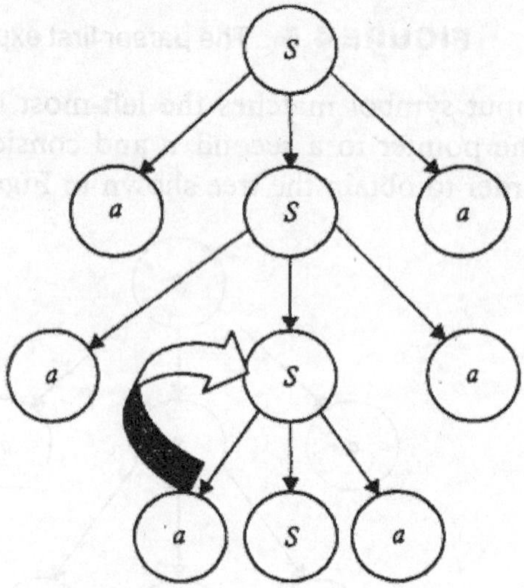

FIGURE 4.9 Tree showing point of failure.

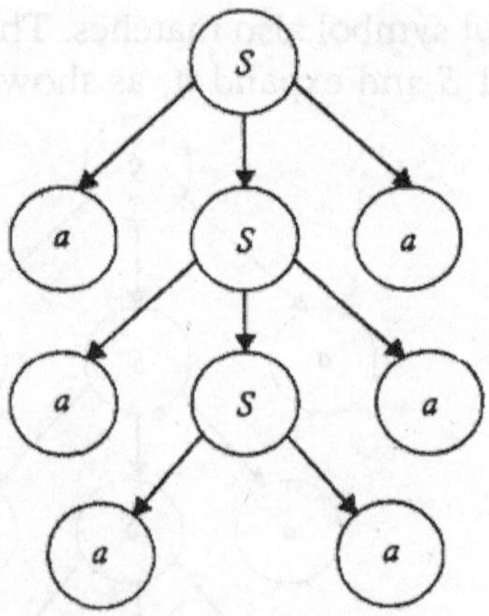

FIGURE 4.10 Tree after backtracking and applying $S \rightarrow aa$.

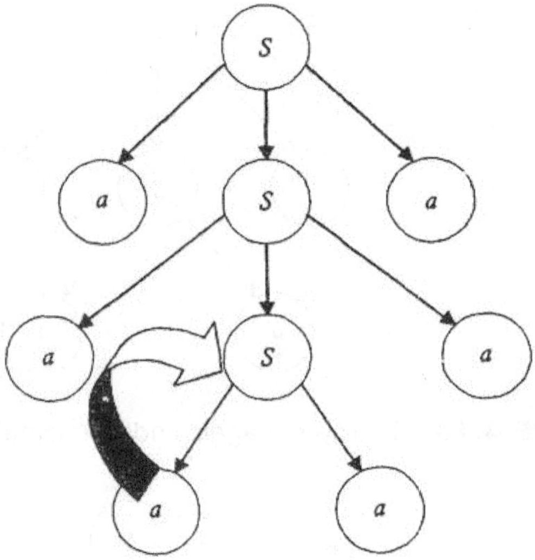

FIGURE 4.11 Tree showing point of failure.

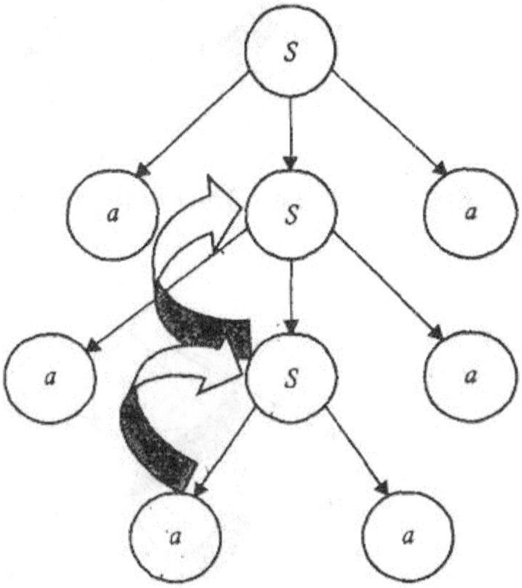

FIGURE 4.12 There is no further alternate of S that can be tried, so the parser will backtrack one more step.

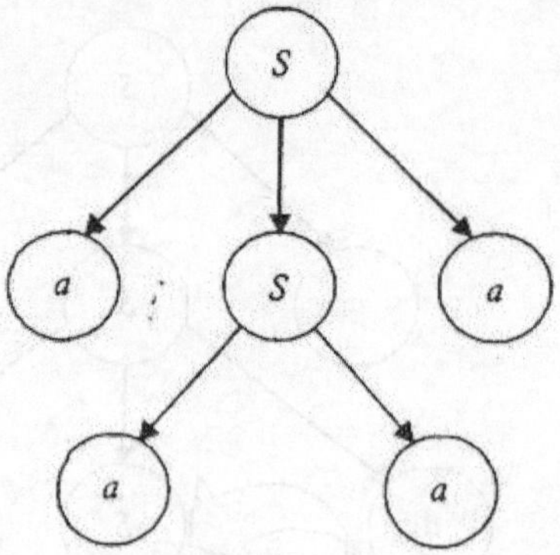

FIGURE 4.13 The parser again finds a mismatch; hence, it backtracks.

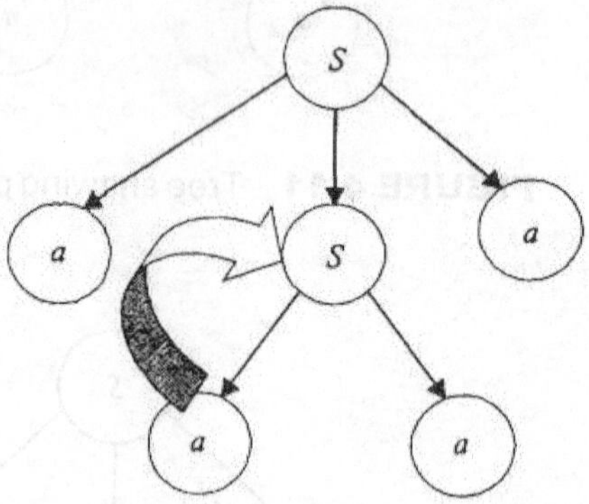

FIGURE 4.14 The parser tries an alternate aa.

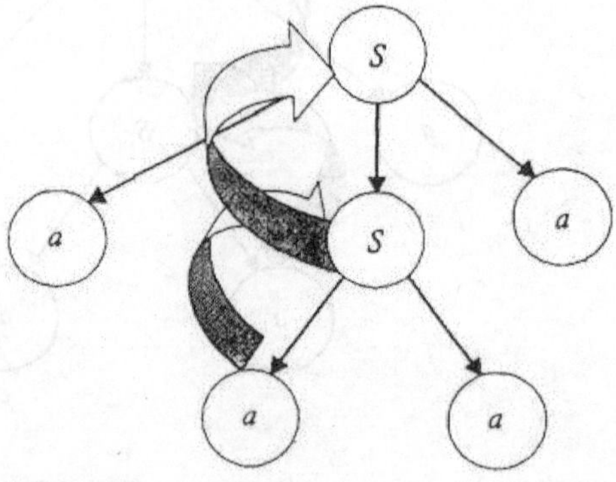

FIGURE 4.15 Since no alternate of S remains to be tried, the parser backtracks one more step.

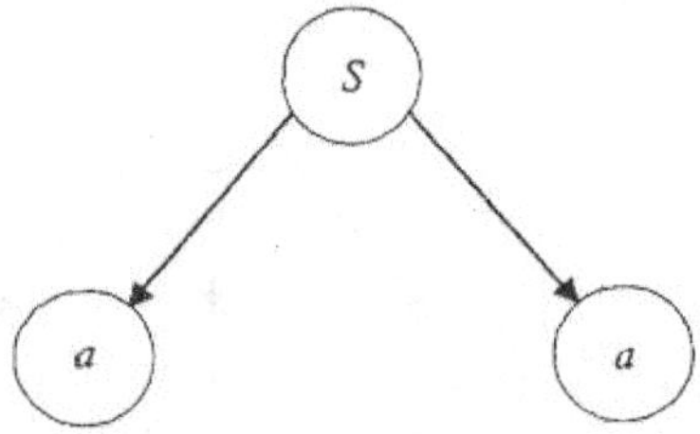

FIGURE 4.16 The parser tries an alternate aa.

Now, consider a string of four occurrences of *a*. The parser will first expand *S*, as shown in Figure 4.17.

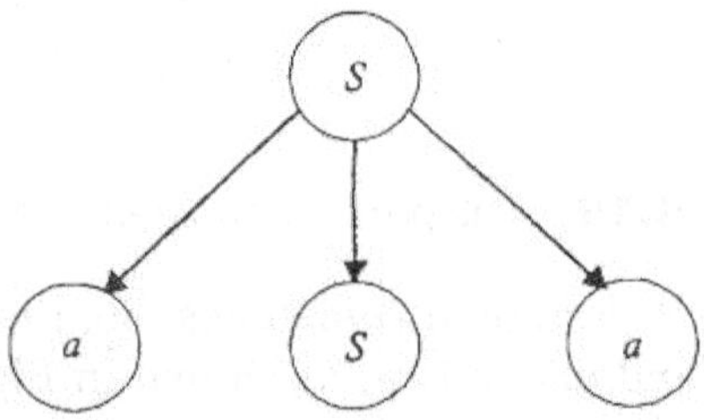

FIGURE 4.17 The parser first expands S.

The first input symbol matches the left-most leaf. Therefore, the parser will advance the pointer to a second *a* and consider the nonterminal *S* for expansion, obtaining the tree shown in Figure 4.18.

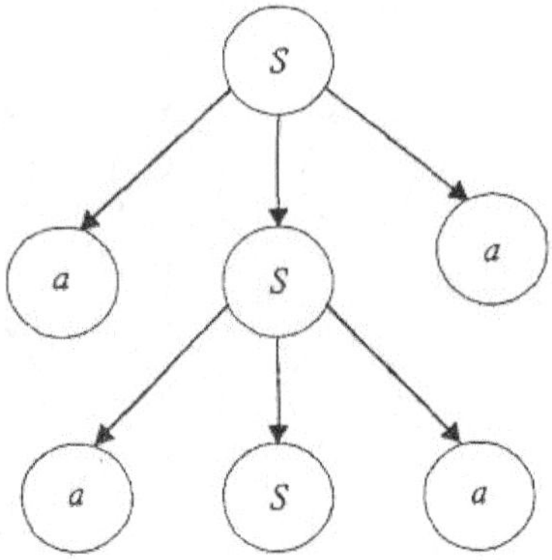

FIGURE 4.18 The parser advances the pointer to a second occurrence of a.

The second input symbol also matches. Therefore, the parser will consider the next leaf labeled by *S* and expand it, as shown in Figure 4.19.

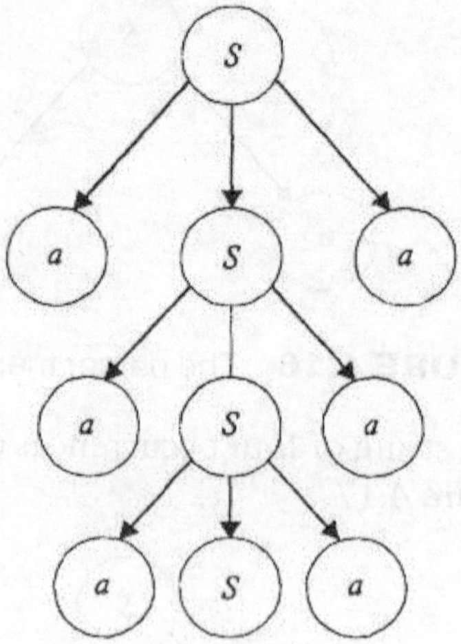

FIGURE 4.19 The parser considers the next leaf labeled by S.

The third input symbol also matches. So, the parser moves on to the next leaf labeled by *S* and expands it, as shown in Figure 4.20.

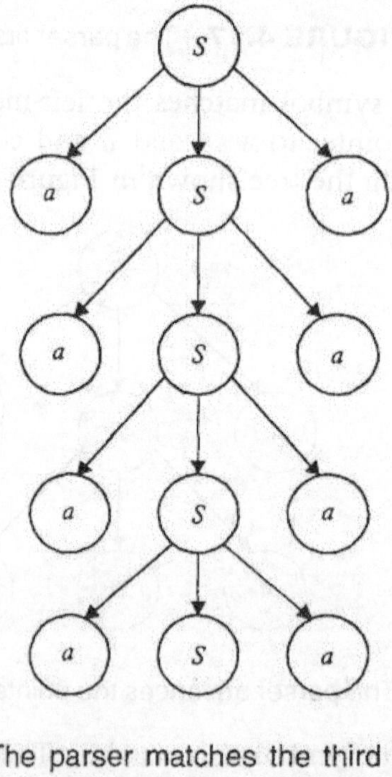

FIGURE 4.20 The parser matches the third input symbol and moves on to the next leaf labeled by S.

The fourth input symbol also matches. Therefore, the next leaf labeled by *S* is considered. The parser expands it, as shown in Figure 4.21.

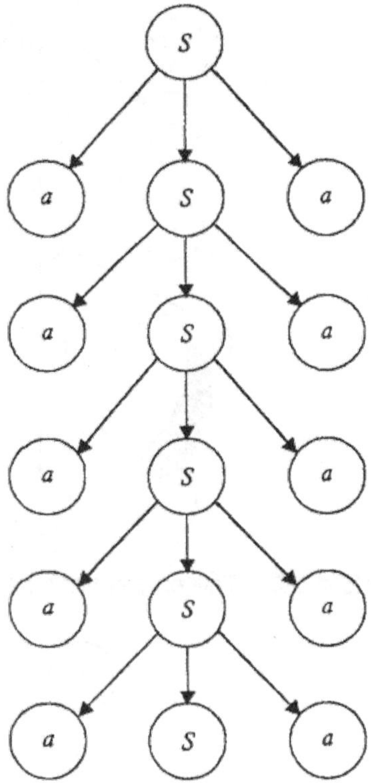

FIGURE 4.21 The parser considers the fourth occurrence of the input symbol a.

Now it finds that there is no match. Therefore, it will backtrack to *S* (Figure 4.22) and continue backtracking, as shown in Figures 4.23 through 4.30, until the parser finally arrives at the successful generation of a parse tree for *aaaa* in Figure 4.31.

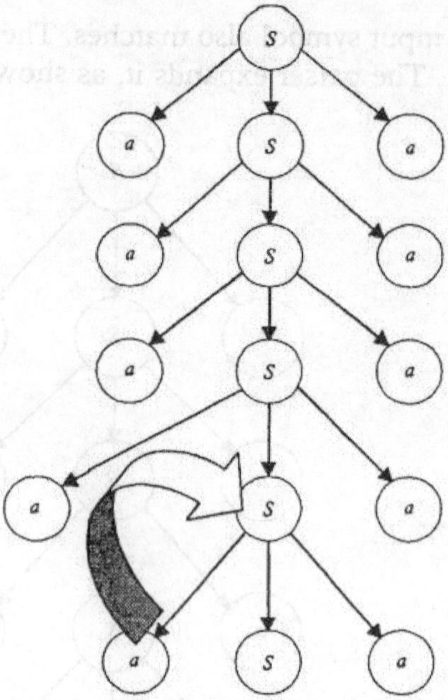

FIGURE 4.22 The parser finds no match, so it backtracks.

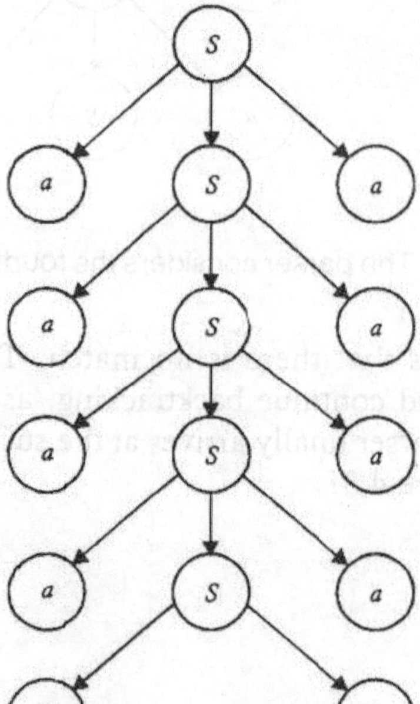

FIGURE 4.23 The parser tries an alternate aa.

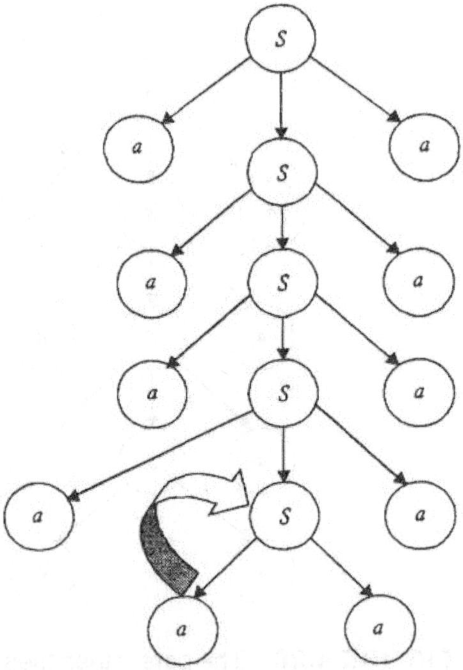

FIGURE 4.24 No alternate of S can be tried, so the parser will backtrack one more step.

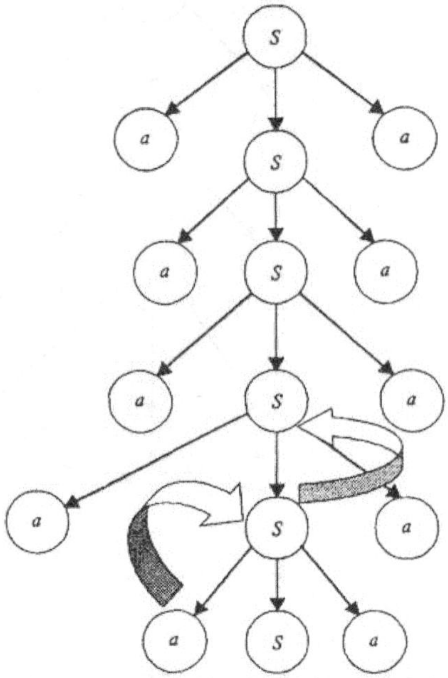

FIGURE 4.25 Again finding a mismatch, the parser backtracks.

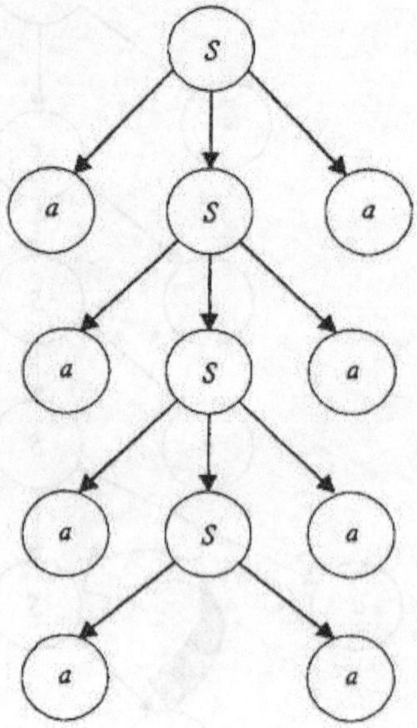

FIGURE 4.26 The parser then tries an alternate.

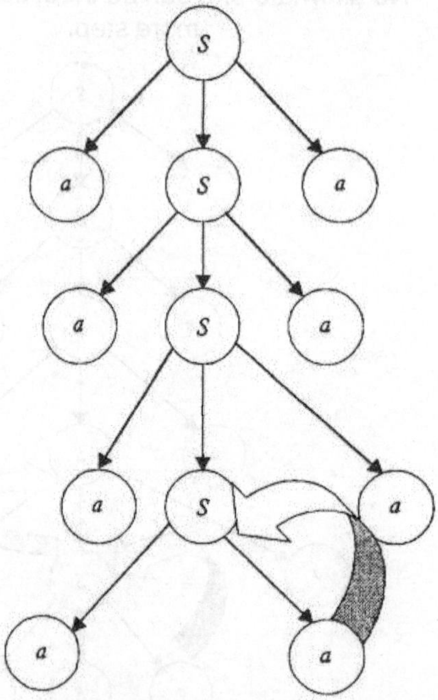

FIGURE 4.27 No alternate of S remains to be tried, so the parser will backtrack one more step.

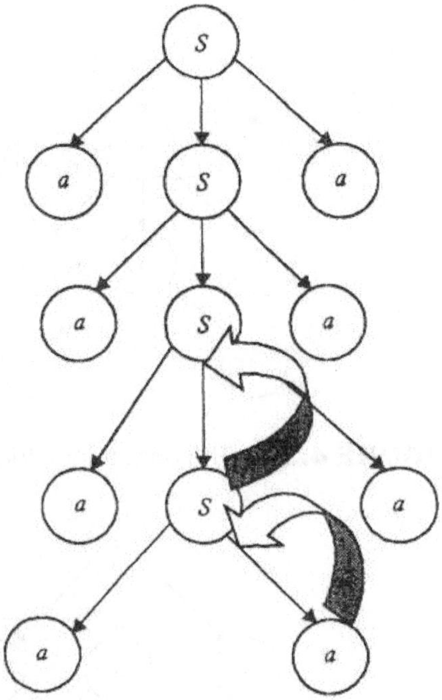

FIGURE 4.28 The parser again finds a mismatch; therefore, it backtracks.

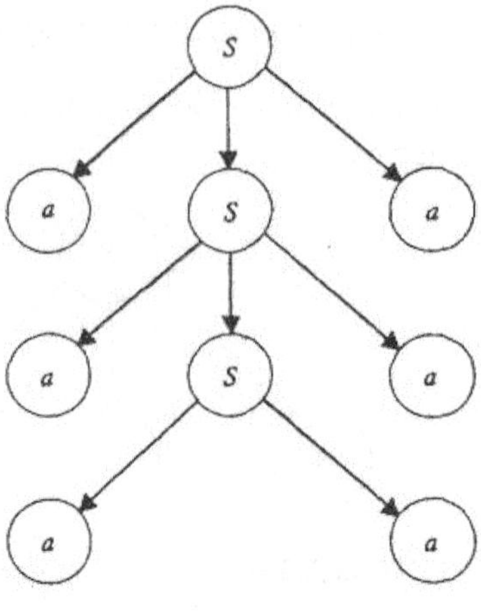

FIGURE 4.29 The parser tries an alternate aa.

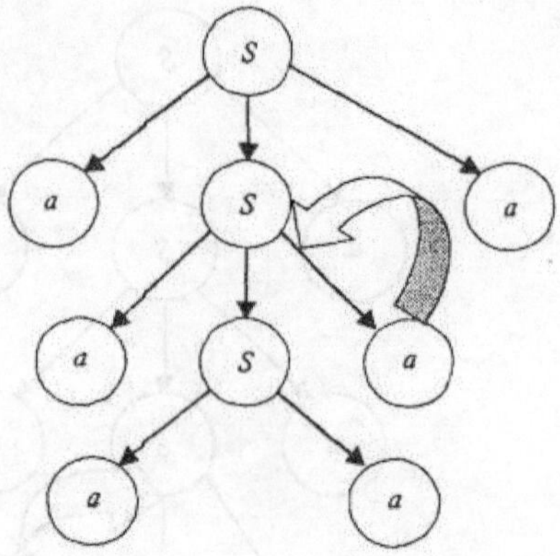

FIGURE 4.30 The parser then tries an alternate aa

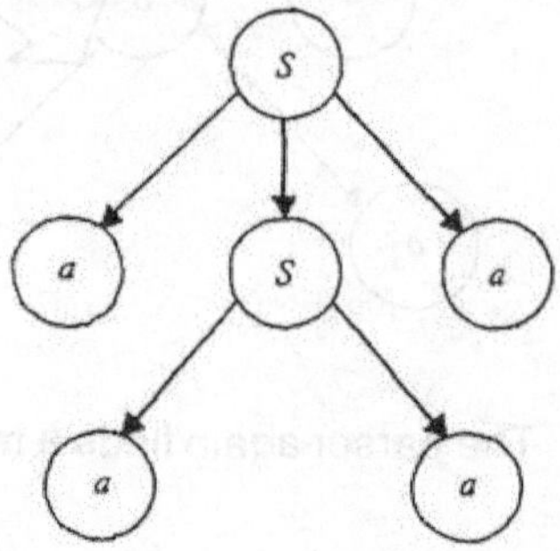

FIGURE 4.31 The parser successfully generates the parse tree for aaaa.

Now consider a string of six occurrences of *a*. The parser will first expand *S*, as shown in Figure 4.32.

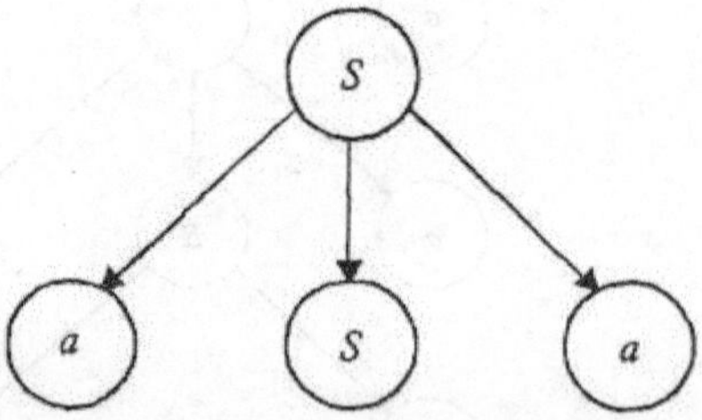

FIGURE 4.32 The parser expands S.

The first input symbol matches the left-most leaf. Therefore, the parser will advance the pointer to the second *a* and consider the nonterminal *S* for expansion. The tree shown in Figure 4.33 is obtained.

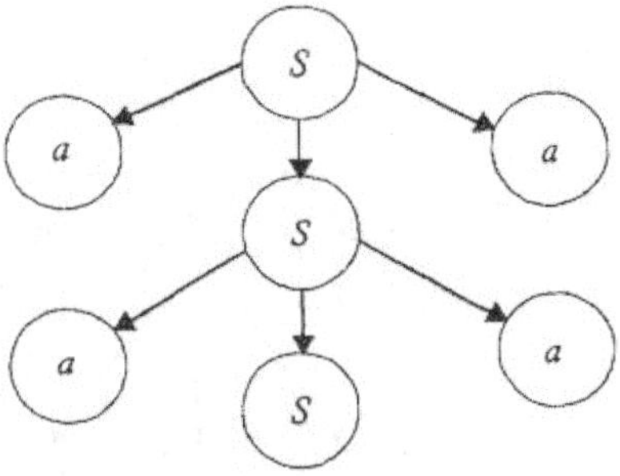

FIGURE 4.33 The parser matches the first symbol, advances to the second occurrence of a, and considers S for expansion.

The second input symbol also matches. Therefore, the parser will consider next leaf labeled *S* and expand it, as shown in Figure 4.34.

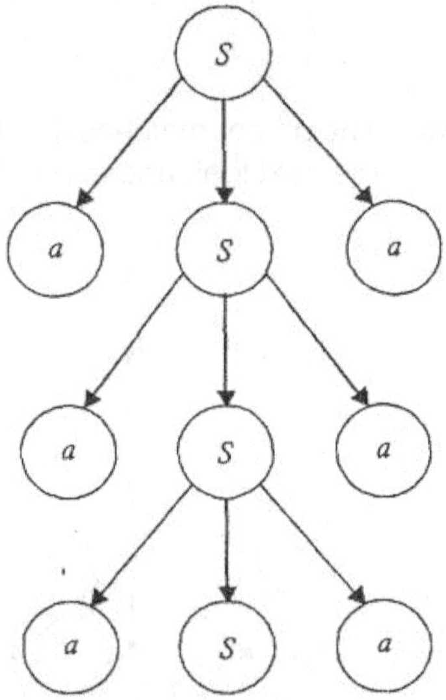

FIGURE 4.34 The parser finds a match for the second occurrence of a and expands S.

The third input symbol also matches, as do the fourth through sixth symbols. In each case, the parser will consider next leaf labeled *S* and expand it, as shown in Figures 4.35 through 4.38.

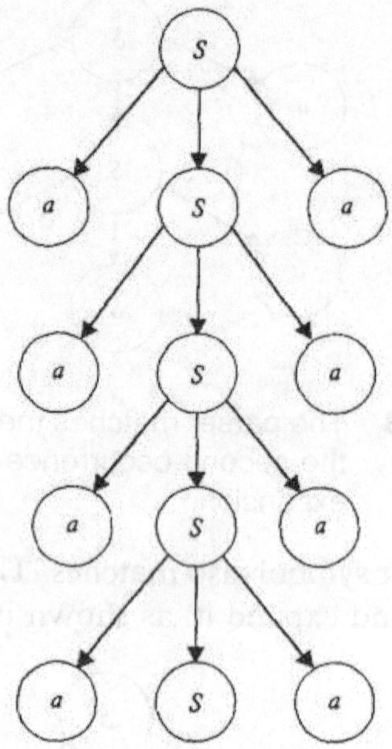

FIGURE 4.35 The parser matches the third input symbol, considers the next leaf, and expands S.

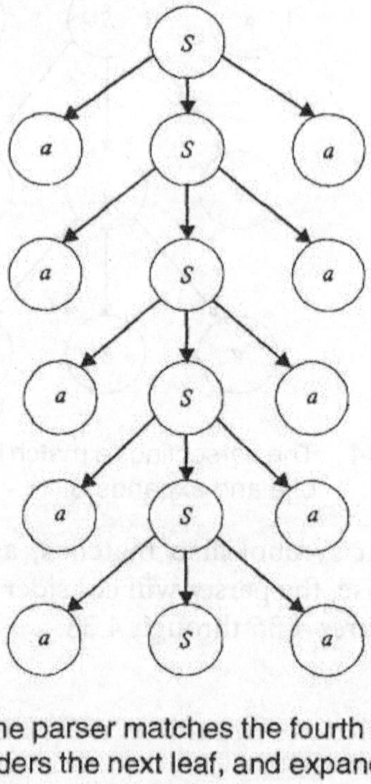

FIGURE 4.36 The parser matches the fourth input symbol, considers the next leaf, and expands S.

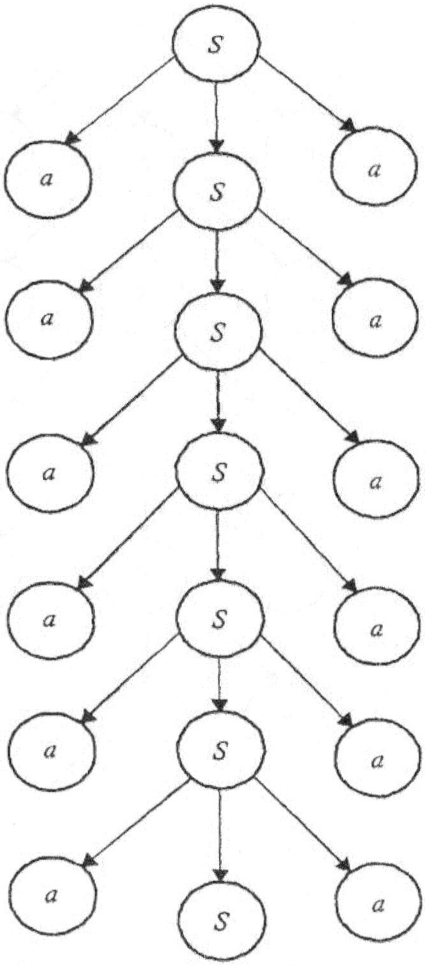

FIGURE 4.37 A match is found for the fifth input symbol, so the parser considers the next leaf, and expands S.

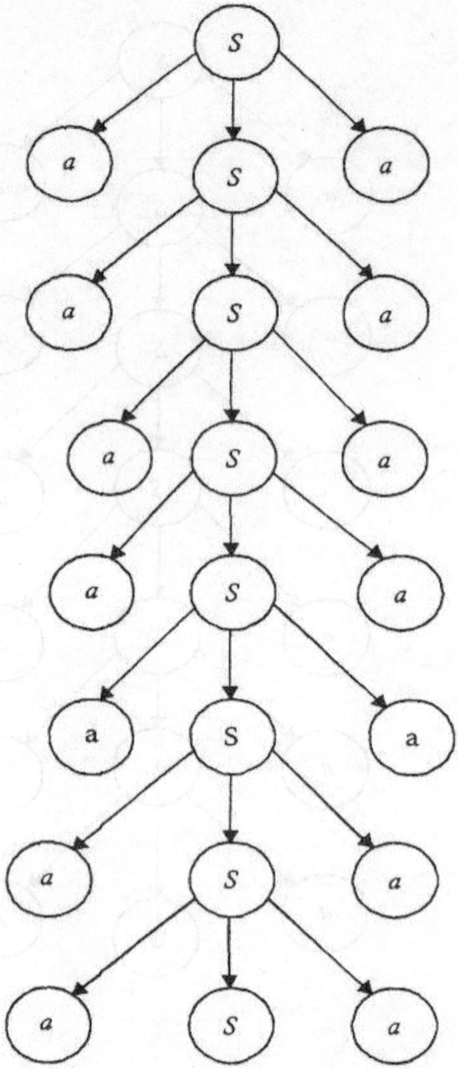

FIGURE 4.38 The sixth input symbol also matches. So the next leaf is considered, and S is expanded.

Now the parser finds that there is no match. Therefore, it will backtrack to *S*, as shown by the thick arrow in Figure 4.39.

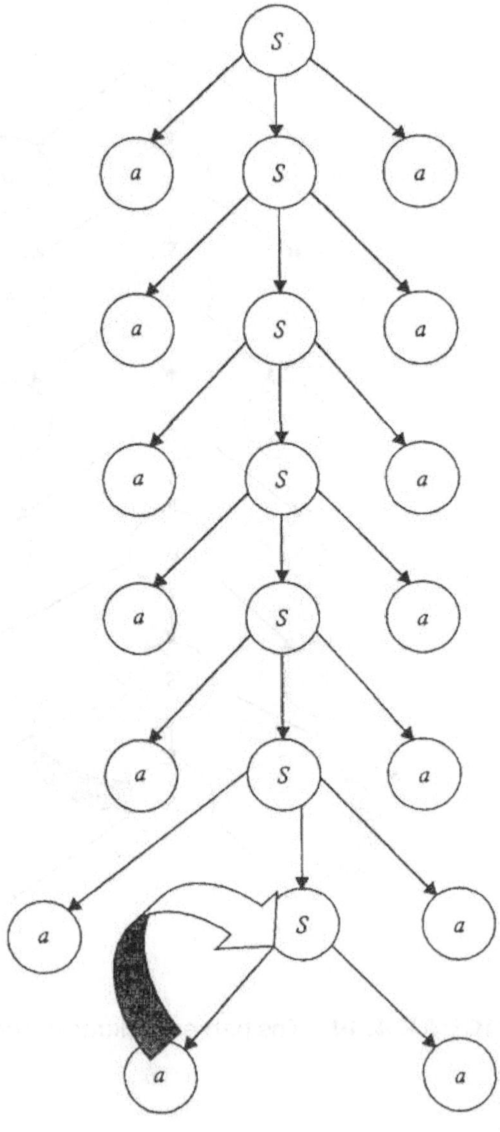

FIGURE 4.39 No match is found, so the parser backtracks to S.

Since there is no alternate of *S* that can be tried, the parser will backtrack one more step, as shown in Figure 4.40. This procedure continues (Figures 4.41 through 4.47), until the parser tries the sixth alternate *aa* (Figure 4.48) and fails to find a match.

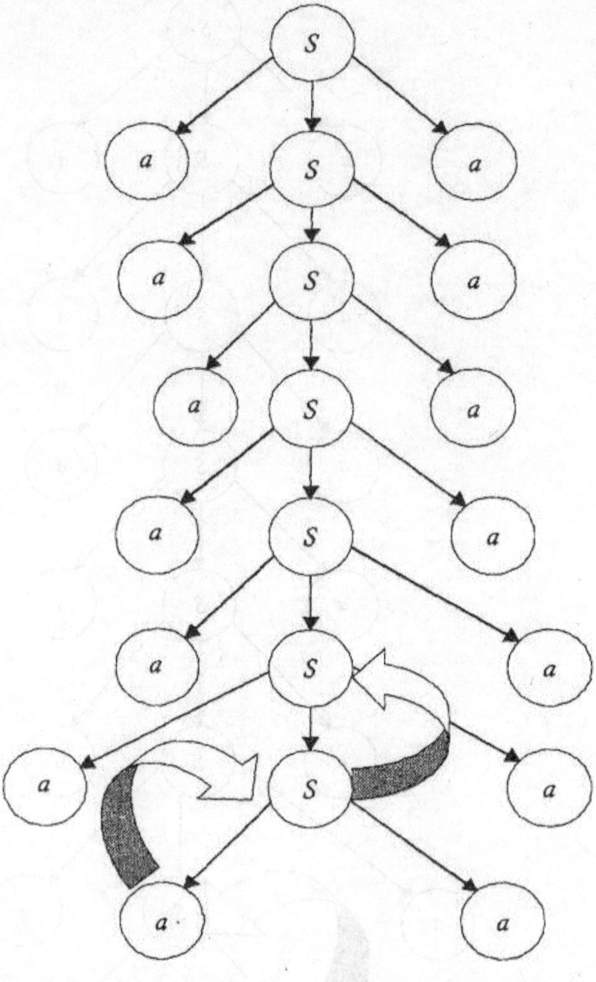

FIGURE 4.40 The parser backtracks one more step.

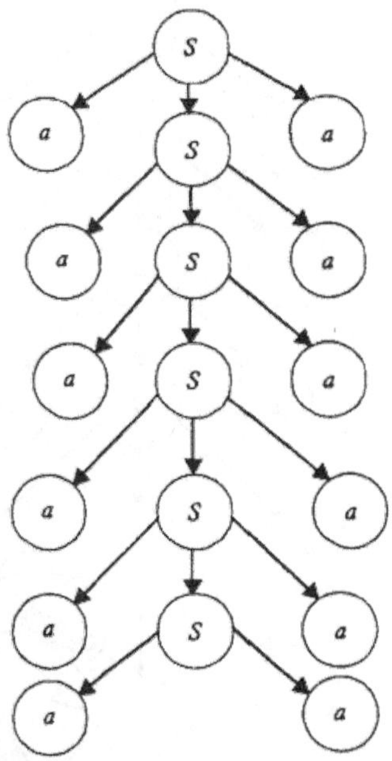

FIGURE 4.41 The parser tries the alternate aa.

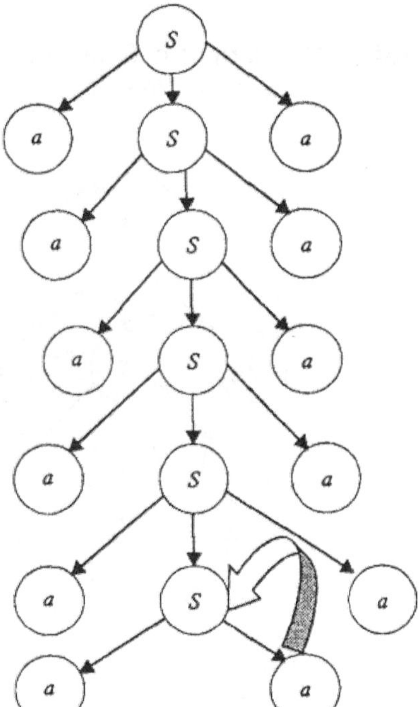

FIGURE 4.42 Again, a mismatch is found. So, the parser backtracks.

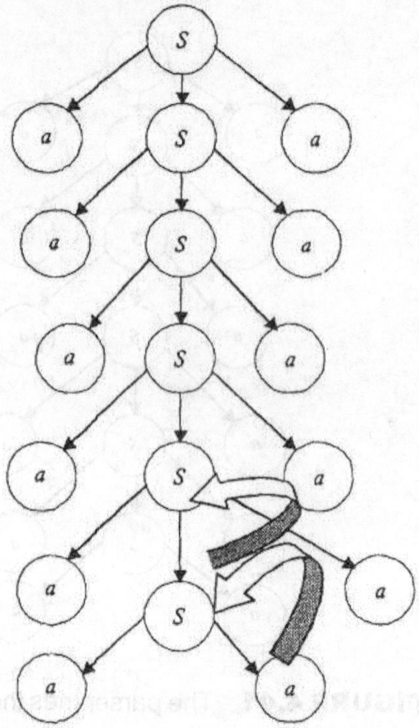

FIGURE 4.43 No alternate of S remains, so the parser will back-track one more step.

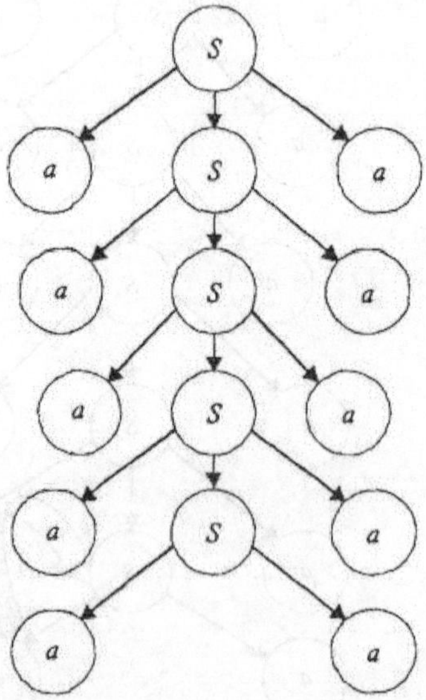

FIGURE 4.44 The parser tries an alternate aa.

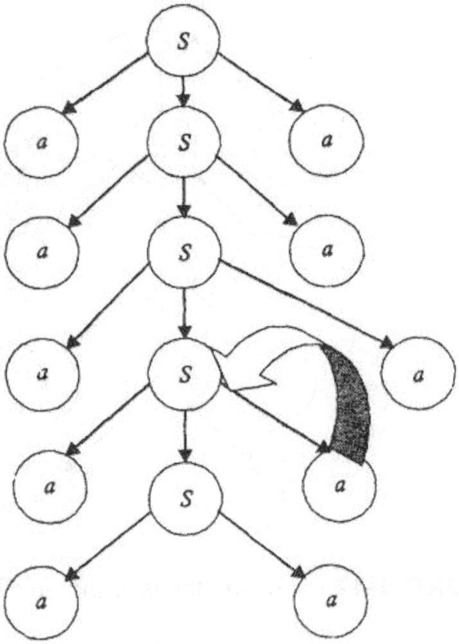

FIGURE 4.45 Again, a mismatch is found. The parser backtracks.

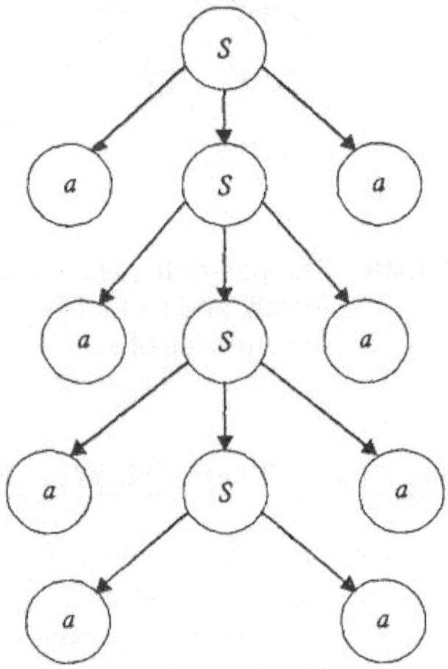

FIGURE 4.46 The parser then tries an alternate aa.

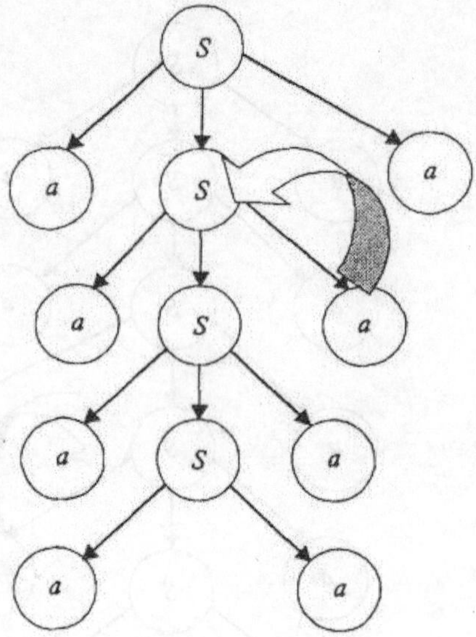

FIGURE 4.47 A mismatch is found, and the parser backtracks.

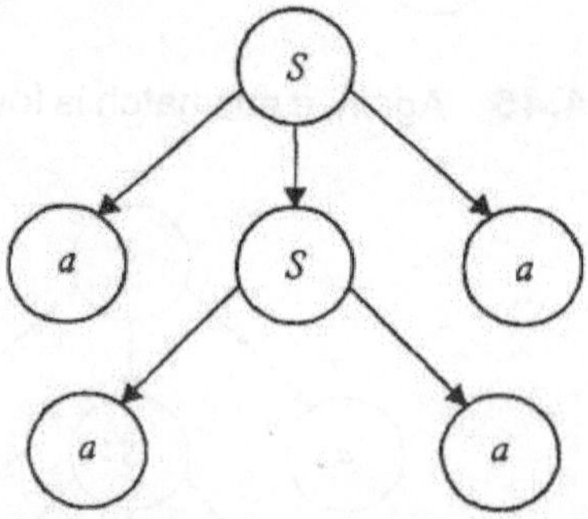

FIGURE 4.48 The parser tries for the alternate aa, fails to find a match, and cannot generate the parse tree for six occurrences of a.

4.3 THE PREDICTIVE TOP-DOWN PARSER

A backtracking parser is a non-deterministic recognizer of the language generated by the grammar. The backtracking problems in the top-down parser can be solved; that is, a top-down parser can function as a deterministic recognizer if it is capable of predicting or detecting which alternatives are right choices for the expansion of nonterminals (that derive to more than one alternative) during the parsing of input string w. By carefully writing a grammar, eliminating left recursion, and left-factoring the result, we obtain a grammar that can be parsed by a top-down parser. This grammar will be able to predict the right alternative for the expansion of a nonterminal during the parsing process; and hence, it need not backtrack.

If $A \rightarrow \alpha_1 \mid \alpha_2 \mid \dots \mid \alpha_n$ are the A-productions in the grammar, then a top-down parser can decide if a nonterminal A is to be expanded or not. And if it is to be expanded, the parser decides which A-production should be used. It looks at the next input symbol and finds out which of the α_i derives to a string that start with the terminal symbol comes next in the input. If none of the α_i derives to a string starting with a terminal symbol, the parser reports the failure; otherwise, it carries out the derivation of A using a production $A \rightarrow \alpha_i$, where α_i derives to a string whose first terminal symbol is the symbol coming next in the input. Therefore, we conclude that if the set of first-terminal symbols of the strings derivable from α_i is computed for each α_i, and this set is made available to the parser, then the parser can predict the right choice for the expansion of nonterminal A. This information can be easily computed using the productions of the grammar. We define a function FIRST(α), where α is in $(V \cup T)^*$, as follows:

FIRST(α) = Set of those terminals with which
the strings derivable from α start

If $\alpha = XYZ$, then FIRST(α) is computed as follows:

FIRST(α) = FIRST(XYZ) = $\{ X \}$ if X is terminal.

Otherwise,

FIRST(α) = FIRST(XYZ) = FIRST(X) if X does not
derive to an empty string; that is, if

FIRST(X) does not contain $\in$.

If FIRST(X) contains $\in$, then

FIRST(α) = FIRST(XYZ) = FIRST(X) $- \{ \in \} \cup$ FIRST(YZ)

FIRST(YZ) is computed in an identical manner:

FIRST(YZ) = $\{ Y \}$ if Y is terminal.

Otherwise,

FIRST(YZ) = FIRST(Y) if Y does not derive to an
empty string (i.e., if FIRST(Y) does
not contain $\in$). If FIRST(Y) contains $\in$, then

FIRST(YZ) = FIRST(Y) $- \{ \in \} \cup$ FIRST(Z)

For example, consider the grammar:

$$S \rightarrow ACB \mid CbB \mid Ba$$

$A \rightarrow da \mid BC$

$B \rightarrow g \mid \in$

$C \rightarrow h \mid \in$

$\text{FIRST}(S) = \text{FIRST}(ACB) \cup \text{FIRST}(CbB) \cup \text{FIRST}(Ba)$ (I)

$\text{FIRST}(A) = \text{FIRST}(da) \cup \text{FIRST}(BC)$

$= \{ d \} \cup \text{FIRST}(BC)$ (II)

$\text{FIRST}(B) = \text{FIRST}(g) \cup \text{FIRST}(\in)$

$= \{ g, \in \}$

$\text{FIRST}(C) = \text{FIRST}(h) \cup \text{FIRST}(\in)$

$= \{ h, \in \}$

Therefore:

$\text{FIRST}(BC) = \text{FIRST}(B) - \{ \in \} \cup \text{FIRST}(C)$

$= \{ g, \in \} - \{ \in \} \cup \{ h, \in \}$

$= \{ g, h, \in \}$

Substituting in (II) we get:

$\text{FIRST}(A) = \{ d \} \cup \{ g, h, \in \}$

$= \{ d, g, h, \in \}$

$\text{FIRST}(ACB) = \text{FIRST}(A) - \{ \in \} \cup \text{FIRST}(CB)$

$= \{ d, g, h, \in \} \cup \text{FIRST}(CB)$ (III)

$\text{FIRST}(CB) = \text{FIRST}(C) - \{ \in \} \cup \text{FIRST}(B)$

$= \{ h, \in \} - \{ \in \} \cup \{ g, \in \}$

$= \{ g, h, \in \}$

Therefore, substituting in (III) we get:

$\text{FIRST}(ACB) = \{ d, g, h, \in \} \cup \{ g, h, \in \}$

$= \{ d, g, h, \in \}$

Similarly,

$\text{FIRST}(CbB) = \text{FIRST}(C) - \{ \in \} \cup \text{FIRST}(bB)$

$= \{ h, \in \} - \{ \in \} \cup \{ b \}$

$= \{ b, h \}$

Similarly,

$\text{FIRST}(Ba) = \text{FIRST}(B) - \{ \in \} \cup \text{FIRST}(a)$

$= \{ g, \in \} - \{ \in \} \cup \{ a \}$

$= \{ a, g \}$

Therefore, substituting in (I), we get:

FIRST(S) = { $d, g, h, \in$ } ∪ { b, h} ∪ { a, g}

= { $a, b, d, g, h, \in$ }

EXAMPLE 4.2: Consider the following grammar:

$S \rightarrow aAb$

$A \rightarrow cd \mid ef$

FIRST(aAb) = { a }

FIRST(cd) = { c }, and

FIRST(ef) = { e }

Hence, while deriving S, the parser looks at the next input symbol. And if it happens to be the terminal a, then the parser derives S using $S \rightarrow aAb$. Otherwise, the parser reports an error. Similarly, when expanding A, the parser looks at the next input symbol; if it happens to be the terminal c, then the parser derives A using $A \rightarrow cd$. If the next terminal input symbol happens to be e, then the parser derives A using $A \rightarrow ef$. Otherwise, an error is reported.

Therefore, we conclude that if the first of right-hand for the production $S \rightarrow aAb$ is computed, we can decide when the parser should do the derivation using the production $S \rightarrow aAb$. Similarly, if the first of right-hand for the productions $A \rightarrow cd$ and $A \rightarrow ef$ are computed, then we can decide when derivation is to be done using $A \rightarrow cd$ and $A \rightarrow ef$, respectively. These decisions can be encoded in the form of table, as shown in Table 4.1, and can be made available to the parser for the correct selection of productions for derivations during parsing.

TABLE 4.1 Production Selections for Parsing Derivations

	a	b	c	d	e	f	$
S	$S \rightarrow aAb$						
A			$A \rightarrow cd$		$A \rightarrow ef$		

The number of rows of the table are equal to the number of nonterminals, whereas the number of columns are equal to the number of terminals, including the end marker. The parser uses of the nonterminal to be derived as the row index of the table, and the next input symbol is used as the column index when the parser decides which production is to be used. Here, the production $S \rightarrow aAb$ is added in the table at [S, a] because FIRST(aAb) contains a terminal a. Hence, S must be derived using $S \rightarrow aAb$ if and only if the terminal symbol coming next in the input is a. Similarly, the production $A \rightarrow cd$ is added at [A, c], because FIRST(cd) contain c. Hence, A must be derived using $A \rightarrow cd$ if and only if the terminal symbol coming next in the input is c. Finally, A must be derived using $A \rightarrow ef$ if and only if the terminal symbol coming next in the input is e. Hence, the production $A \rightarrow ef$ is added at $[A, e]$. Therefore, we conclude that the table can be constructed as follows:

for every production $A \rightarrow \alpha$ do
  for every a in FIRST(α) do
    TABLE$[A, a] = A \rightarrow \alpha$

Using the above method, every production of the grammar gets added into the table at the proper place when the grammar is $\in$-free. But when the grammar is not $\in$-free, $\in$-productions will not get added to the table. If there is an $\in$-production $A \rightarrow \in$ in the grammar, then deciding when A is to be derived to $\in$ is not possible using the production's right-hand FIRST. Some additional information is required to decide where the production $A \rightarrow \in$ is to be added to the table.

TIP

The derivation by $A \rightarrow \in$ is a right choice when the parser is on the verge of expanding the nonterminal A and the next input symbol happens to be a terminal, which can occur immediately following A in any string occurring on the right side of the production. This will lead to the expansion of A to $\in$, and the next leaf in the parse tree will be considered, which is labeled by the symbol immediately following A and, therefore, may match the next input symbol.

Therefore, we conclude that the production $A \rightarrow \in$ is to be added in the table at $[A, b]$ for every b that immediately follows A in any of the production's is right-hand string. To compute the set of all such terminals, we make use of the function FOLLOW(A), where A is a nonterminal, as defined below:

FOLLOW(A) = Set of terminals that immediately follow A in any string occurring on the right side of productions of the grammar

For example, if $A \rightarrow \alpha B\beta$ is a production, then FOLLOW(B) can be computed using $A \rightarrow \alpha B\beta$, as shown below:

FOLLOW(B) = FIRST(β) if FIRST(β) does not contain $\in$.
 = FIRST(β) – { $\in$ } FOLLOW(A)
 when FIRST(β) contains $\in$.

/ because when β derives to $\in$, that time the terminal symbol immediately following A, will follow B* /*

Therefore, we conclude that when the grammar is not $\in$-free, then the table can be constructed as follows:

1. Compute FIRST and FOLLOW for every nonterminal of the grammar.

2. For every production $A \rightarrow \alpha$, do:

{

for every non-$\in$ member a in FIRST(α) do

TABLE[A, a] = $A \rightarrow \alpha$

If FIRST(α) contain $\in$ then

For every b in FOLLOW(A) do

TABLE[A, b] = $A \rightarrow \alpha$

}

Therefore, we conclude that if the table is constructed using the above algorithm, a top-down parser can be constructed that will be a nonbacktracking, or 'predictive' parser.

4.3.1 Implementation of a Table-Driven Predictive Parser

A table-driven parser can be implemented using an input buffer, a stack, and a parsing table. The input buffer is used to hold the string to be parsed, The string is followed by a "\$" symbol that is used as a right-end maker to indicate the end of the input string. The stack is used to hold the sequence of grammar symbols. A "\$" indicates bottom of the stack. Initially, the stack has the start symbol of a grammar above the \$. The parsing table is a table obtained by using the algorithm presented in the previous section. It is a two-dimensional array TABLE[A, a], where A is a nonterminal and a is a terminal, or \$ symbol. The parser is controlled by a program that behaves as follows:

1. The program considers X, the symbol on the top of the stack, and the next input symbol a.
2. If $X = a = \$$, then parser announces the successful completion of the parsing and halts.
3. If $X = a \neq \$$, then the parser pops the X off the stack and advances the input pointer to the next input symbol.
4. If X is a nonterminal, then the program consults the parsing table entry TABLE[X, a]. If TABLE[X, a] = $X \rightarrow UVW$, then the parser replaces X on the top of the stack by UVW in such a manner that U will come on the top. If TABLE[X, a] = error, then the parser calls the error-recovery routine.

For example consider the following grammar:

$$S \rightarrow aABb$$
$$A \rightarrow c \mid \in$$
$$B \rightarrow d \mid \in$$

FIRST(S) = FIRST($aABb$) = { a }
FIRST(A) = FIRST(c) ∪ FIRST(∈) = { c, ∈ }
FIRST(B) = FIRST(d) ∪ FIRST(∈) = { d, ∈ }

Since the right-end marker $ is used to mark the bottom of the stack, $ will initially be immediately below S (the start symbol) on the stack; and hence, $ will be in the FOLLOW(S). Therefore:

FOLLOW(S) = { $ }

Using $S \rightarrow aABb$, we get:

FOLLOW(A) = FIRST(Bb)
= FIRST(B) − { ∈ } ∪ FIRST(b)
= { d, ∈ } − { ∈ } ∪ { b } = { d, b }
FOLLOW(B) = FIRST(b) = { b }

Therefore, the parsing table is as shown in Table 4.2.

TABLE 4.2 Parsing Table

	a	b	c	d	$
S	$S \rightarrow aABb$				
A		$A \rightarrow \epsilon$	$A \rightarrow c$	$A \rightarrow \epsilon$	
B		$B \rightarrow \epsilon$		$B \rightarrow d$	

Consider an input string $acdb$. The various steps in the parsing of this string, in terms of the contents of the stack and unspent input, are shown in Table 4.3.

TABLE 4.3 Steps Involved in Parsing the String $acdb$

Stack Contents	Unspent Input	Moves
$S	acdb$	Derivation using $S \rightarrow aABb$
$bBAa	acdb$	Popping a off the stack and advancing one position in the input
$bBA	cdb$	Derivation using $A \rightarrow c$
$bBc	cdb$	Popping c off the stack and advancing one position in the input
$bB	db$	Derivation using $B \rightarrow d$
$bd	db$	Popping d off the stack and advancing one position in the input
$b	b$	Popping b off the stack and advancing one position in the input
$	$	Announce successful completion of the parsing

Similarly, for the input string *ab*, the various steps in the parsing of the string, in terms of the contents of the stack and unspent input, are shown in Table 4.4.

TABLE 4.4 Production Selections for String *ab*

Stack Contents	Unspent Input	Moves
$S	ab$	Derivation using $S \rightarrow aABb$
$bBAa	ab$	Popping *a* off the stack and advancing one position in the input
$bBA	b$	Derivation using $A \rightarrow \in$
$bB	b$	Derivation using $B \rightarrow \in$
$b	b$	Popping *b* off the stack and advancing one position in the input
$	$	Announce successful completion of the parsing

For a string *adb*, the various steps in the parsing of the string, in terms of the contents of the stack and unspent input, are shown in Table 4.5.

TABLE 4.5 Production Selections for Parsing the String *adb*

Stack Contents	Unspent Input	Moves
$S	adb$	Derivation using $S \rightarrow aABb$
$bBAa	adb$	Popping *a* off the stack and advancing one position in the input
$bBA	ab$	Calling an error-handling routine

The heart of the table-driven parser is the parsing table-the parser looks at the parsing table to decide which alternative is a right choice for the expansion of a nonterminal during the parsing of the input string. Hence, constructing a table-driven predictive parser can be considered as equivalent to constructing the parsing table.

A parsing table for any grammar can be obtained by the application of the above algorithm; but for some grammars, some of the entries in the parsing table may end up being multiple defined entries. Whereas for certain grammars, all of the entries in the parsing table are singly defined entries. If the parsing table contains multiple entries, then the parser is still non-deterministic. The parser will be a deterministic recognizer if and only if there are no multiple entries in the parsing table. All such grammars (i.e., those grammars that, after applying the algorithm above, contain no multiple entries in the parsing table) constitute a subset of CFGs called "*LL*(1)" grammars. Therefore, a given grammar is *LL*(1) if its parsing table, constructed by algorithm above, contains no multiple entries. If the table contains multiple entries, then the grammar is not *LL*(1).

In the acronym *LL*(1), the first *L* stands for the left-to-right scan of the input, the second *L* stands for the left-most derivation, and the (1) indicates that the next input symbol is used to decide the next parsing process (i.e., length of the lookahead is "1").

In the *LL*(1) parsing system, parsing is done by scanning the input from left to right, and an attempt is made to derive the input string in a left-most order. The next input symbol is used to decide what is to be done next in the parsing process. The predictive parser discussed above, therefore, is a *LL*(1) parser, because it also scans the input from left to right and attempts to obtain the left-most derivation of it; and it also makes use of the next input symbol to decide what is to be done next. And if the parsing table used by the predictive parser does not contain multiple entries, then the parser acts as a recognizer of only the members of *L*(*G*); hence, the grammar is *LL*(1).

Therefore, *LL*(1) is the grammar *G* for which an *LL*(1) parser can be constructed, which acts as a deterministic recognizer of *L*(*G*). If a grammar is *LL*(1), then a deterministic top-down table-driven recognizer can be constructed to recognize *L*(*G*). A parsing table constructed for a given grammar *G* will have multiple entries if the grammar contains multiple productions that derive the same nonterminal-that is, the grammar contains the productions $A \rightarrow \alpha \mid \beta$, and both α and β derive to a string that starts with the same terminal symbol. Therefore, one of the basic requirements for a grammar to be considered *LL*(1) is when the grammar contains multiple productions that derive the same nonterminal, such as:

for every pair of productions $A \rightarrow \alpha \mid \beta$

FIRST(α) ∩ FIRST(β) = ϕ (i.e., FIRST(α) and FIRST(β) should be disjoint sets for every pair of productions $A \rightarrow \alpha \mid \beta$)

For a grammar to be *LL*(1), the satisfaction of the condition above is necessary as well sufficient if the grammar is ∈-free. When the grammar is not ∈-free, then the satisfaction of the above condition is necessary but not sufficient, because either FIRST(α) or FIRST(β) might contain ∈, but not both. The above condition will still be satisfied; but if FIRST(β) contains ∈, then production $A \rightarrow \beta$ will be added in the table on all terminals in

FOLLOW(A). Hence, it also required that FIRST(α) and FOLLOW(A) contain no common symbols. Therefore, an additional condition must be satisfied in order for a grammar to be $LL(1)$. When the grammar is not $\in$-free:

for every pair of productions $A \rightarrow \alpha \mid \beta$

if FIRST(β) contains $\in$, and FIRST(α) does not contain $\in$, then

FIRST(α) $\cap$ FOLLOW(A) = ϕ

Therefore, for a grammar to be $LL(1)$, the following conditions must be satisfied:

For every pair of productions

{

(1) FIRST(α) $\cap$ FIRST(β) = ϕ

and

if FIRST(β) contains $\in$, and FIRST(α) does not contain $\in$

then

(1) FIRST(α) $\cap$ FOLLOW(A) = ϕ

}

4.3.2 Examples

EXAMPLE 4.3: Test whether the grammar is $LL(1)$ or not, and construct a predictive parsing table for it.

$S \rightarrow AaAb \mid BbBa$

$A \rightarrow \in$

$B \rightarrow \in$

Since the grammar contains a pair of productions $S \rightarrow AaAb \mid BbBa$, for the grammar to be $LL(1)$, it is required that:

FIRST($AaAb$) $\cap$ FIRST($BbBa$) = ϕ

FIRST($AaAb$) = FIRST(A) – { $\in$ } $\cup$ FIRST(aAb) = { a }

FIRST($BbBa$) = FIRST(B) – { $\in$ } $\cup$ FIRST(bBa) = { b }

FIRST($AaAb$) $\cap$ FIRST($BbBa$) = { a } $\cap$ { b } = ϕ

Hence, the grammar is $LL(1)$.

To construct a parsing table, the FIRST and FOLLOW sets are computed, as shown below:

FIRST(S) = FIRST($AaAb$) $\cup$ FIRST($BbBa$)

FIRST(S) = { a } $\cup$ { b } = { a, b }

FIRST(A) = { $\in$ }

FIRST(B) = { ∈ }
FOLLOW(S) = { $ }

1. Using $S \rightarrow AaAb$, we get:
   FOLLOW(A) = FIRST(aAb) = { a }, and
   FOLLO W(A) = FIRST(b) = { b }. Therefore,
   FOLLOW(A) = { a, b }
2. Using $S \rightarrow BbBa$, we get
   FOLLOW(B) = FIRST(bBa) = { b }, and
   FOLLOW(B) = FIRST(a) = { a }. Therefore,
   FOLLOW(B) = { a, b }

TABLE 4.6 Parsing Table for Example 4.3

	a	b	$
S	$S \rightarrow AaAb$	$S \rightarrow BbBa$	
A	$A \rightarrow \in$	$A \rightarrow \in$	
B	$B \rightarrow \in$	$B \rightarrow \in$	

EXAMPLE 4.4: Consider the following grammar, and test whether the grammar is $LL(1)$ or not.

$S \rightarrow 1AB \mid \in$
$A \rightarrow 1AC \mid 0C$
$B \rightarrow 0S$
$C \rightarrow 1$

For a pair of productions $S \rightarrow 1AB \mid \in$:

FIRST($1AB$) ∩ FIRST(∈) = { 1 } ∩ { ∈ } = ϕ, and
FIRST($1AB$) ∩ FOLLOW(S) = { 1 } ∩ { $ } = ϕ

because FOLLOW(S) = { $ } (i.e., it contains only the end marker. Similarly, for a pair of productions $A \rightarrow 1AC \mid 0C$:

FIRST($1AC$) ∩ FIRST($0C$) = { 1 } ∩ { 0 } = ϕ

Hence, the grammar is $LL(1)$. Now, show that no left-recursive grammar can be $LL(1)$.

One of the basic requirements for a grammar to be *LL*(1) is: for every pair of productions $A \to \alpha \mid \beta$ in the grammar's set of productions, FIRST(α) and FIRST(β) should be disjointed.

If a grammar is left-recursive, then the set of productions will contain at least one pair of the form $A \to A\alpha \mid \beta$; and hence, FIRST($A\alpha$) and FIRST(β) will not be disjointed sets, because everything in the FIRST(β) will also be in the FIRST($A\alpha$). It thereby violates the condition for *LL*(1) grammar. Hence, a grammar containing a pair of productions $A \to A\alpha \mid \beta$ (i.e., a left-recursive grammar) cannot be *LL*(1).

Now, let X be a nullable nonterminal that derives to at least two terminal strings. Show that in *LL*(1) grammar, no production rule can have two consecutive occurrences of X on the right side of the production.

Since X is a nullable $X \overset{*}{\to} \in$, X is also deriving to at least to two terminal strings-$X \overset{*}{\to} w_1$ and $X \overset{*}{\to} w_2$-where w_1 and w_2 are the strings of terminals. Therefore, for a grammar using X to be *LL*(1), it is required that:

FIRST(w_1) $\cap$ FIRST(w_2) = ϕ

FIRST (w_1) $\cap$ FOLLOW(X) and FIRST(w_2) $\cap$ FOLLOW(X) = ϕ

If this grammar contains a production rule $A \to \alpha XX\beta$-a production whose right side has two consecutive occurrences of X-then everything in FIRST(X) will also be in the FOLLOW(X); and since FIRST(X) contains FIRST(w_1) as well as FIRST(w_2), the second condition will therefore not be satisfied. Hence, a grammar containing a production of the form $A \to \alpha XX\beta$ will never be *LL*(1), thereby proving that in *LL*(1) grammar, no production rule can have two consecutive occurrences of X on the right side of the production.

EXAMPLE 4.5: Construct a predictive parsing table for the following grammar where $S|$ is a start symbol and # is the end marker.

$$
\begin{aligned}
S| &\to S\# \\
S &\to qABC \\
A &\to a \mid bbD \\
B &\to a \mid \in \\
C &\to b \mid \in \\
D &\to c \mid \in
\end{aligned}
$$

Here, # is taken as one of the grammar symbols. And therefore, the initial configuration of the parser will be ($S|$, $w\#$), where the first member of the pair is the contents of the stack and the second member is the contents of input buffer.

$$\text{FIRST}(S|) = \text{FIRST}(S\#) \qquad \text{(I)}$$

$$\text{FIRST}(S) = \text{FIRST}(qABC) = \{ q \}$$

Therefore, by substituting in (I), we get:

$$\text{FIRST}(S|) = \{ q \}$$
$$\text{FIRST}(A) = \text{FIRST}(a) \cup \text{FIRST}(bbD) = \{ a \} \cup \{ b \}$$
$$= \{ a, b \}$$
$$\text{FIRST}(B) = \text{FIRST}(a) \cup \text{FIRST}(\in) = \{ a, \in \}$$
$$\text{FIRST}(C) = \text{FIRST}(b) \cup \text{FIRST}(\in) = \{ b, \in \}$$
$$\text{FIRST}(D) = \text{FIRST}(c) \cup \text{FIRST}(\in) = \{ c, \in \}$$
$$\text{FOLLOW}(S|) = \{ \}$$

1. Using $S| \rightarrow S\#$ we get:
   $$\text{FOLLOWS}(S) = \{ \# \}$$
2. Using $S \rightarrow qABC$ we get:
   $$\text{FOLLOW}(A) = \text{FIRST}(BC) - \{ \in \} \cup \text{FOLLOWS}(S) \quad \text{(II)}$$
   $$\text{FIRST}(BC) = \text{FIRST}(B) - \{ \in \} \cup \text{FIRST}(C)$$
   $$= \{ a, \in \} - \{ \in \} \{ b, \} = \{ a, b, \in \}$$

Substituting in (II) we get:

$$\text{FOLLOW}(A) = \{ a, b, \in \} - \{ \in \} \cup \{ \# \} = \{ a, b, \# \}$$
$$\text{FOLLOW}(B) = \text{FIRST}(C) - \{ \in \} \cup \text{FOLLOW}(S)$$
$$= \{ b, \in \} - \{ \in \} \cup \{ \# \} = \{ b, \# \}$$
$$\text{FOLLOW}(C) = \text{FOLLOW}(S) = \{ \# \}$$

3. Using $A \rightarrow bbD$ we get:
   $$\text{FOLLOW}(D) = \text{FOLLOW}(A) = \{ a, b, \# \}$$
   Therefore, the parsing table is derived as shown in Table 4.7.

TABLE 4.7 Parsing Table for Example 4.5

	q	a	b	c	#
S	$S \rightarrow S\#$				
S	$S \rightarrow qabc$				
A		$A \rightarrow a$	$A \rightarrow bbD$		
B		$B \rightarrow a$	$B \rightarrow \in$		$B \rightarrow \in$
C			$C \rightarrow b$		$C \rightarrow \in$
D		$D \rightarrow \in$	$D \rightarrow \in$	$D \rightarrow c$	$D \rightarrow \in$

EXAMPLE 4.6: Construct predictive parsing table for the following grammar:

$S \to A$
$A \to aB \mid Ad$
$B \to bBC \mid f$
$C \to g$
FIRST(S) = FIRST(A) = { a }
FIRST(B) = { b, f }
FIRST(C) = { g }

Since the grammar is $\in$-free, FOLLOW sets are not required to be computed in order to enter the productions into the parsing table. Therefore the parsing table is as shown in Table 4.8.

TABLE 4.8 Parsing Table for Example 4.6

	a	b	f	g	d
S	$S \to A$				
A	$A \to aS$			$A \to d$	
B		$B \to bBC$	$B \to f$		
C				$C \to g$	

EXAMPLE 4.7: Construct a predictive parsing table for the following grammar, where S is a start symbol.

$S \to iEtSS_1 \mid a$
$S1 \to eS \mid \in$
$E \to b$
FIRST(S) = FIRST($iEtSS1$) $\cup$ FIRST(a) = { i, a }
FIRST($S1$) = FIRST(eS) $\cup$ FIRST($\in$) = { $e, \in$ }
FIRST(E) = FIRST(b) = { b }
FOLLOW(S) = { \$ }

1. Using $S \to iEtSS_1$:
   FOLLOW(E) = { t }
   FOLLOW(S) = FIRST(S_1) - { $\in$ } $\cup$ FOLLOW(S)
   = { $e, \in$ } - { $\in$ } $\cup$ { \$ }
   = { e, \$ }
   FOLLOWS(S_1) = FOLLOW(S) = { e, \$ }

2. Using $S_1 \rightarrow eS$:
FOLLOW(S) = FOLLOW(S_1) = { e, \$ }
Therefore, the parsing table is as shown in Table 4.9.

TABLE 4.9 Parsing Table for Example 4.7

	i	a	b	e	T	\$
S	$S \rightarrow iEtSS_1$	$S \rightarrow a$				
S_1				$S1 \rightarrow eS$		$S_1 \rightarrow \in$
S_1				$S1 \rightarrow \in$		
E			$E \rightarrow b$			

EXAMPLE 4.8: Construct an $LL(1)$ parsing table for the following grammar:

$S \rightarrow aBDh$
$B \rightarrow cC$
$C \rightarrow bC \mid \in$
$D \rightarrow EF$
$E \rightarrow g \mid \in$
$F \rightarrow f \mid \in$

Computation of FIRST and FOLLOW:

FIRST(S) = FIRST($aBDh$) = { a }
FIRST(B) = FIRST(cC) = { c }
FIRST(C) = FIRST(bC) ∪ FIRST(∈) = { b } ∪ { ∈ } = { b, ∈ }
FIRST(D) = FIRST(EF) = FIRST(E) − { ∈ } ∪ FIRST(F) (I)
FIRST(E) = FIRST(g) ∪ FIRST(∈) = { g, ∈ }
FIRST(F) = FIRST(f) ∪ FIRST(∈) = { f, ∈ }

Therefore by substituting in (I) we get:

FIRST(D) = { g, ∈ } − { ∈ } ∪ { f, ∈ } = { g, f, ∈ }
FOLLOW(S) = { \$ }

1. Using the production $S \rightarrow aBDh$ we get:
FOLLOW(B) = FIRST(Dh) = FIRST(D) − { ∈ } ∪ FIRST(h)
= { g, f, ∈ } − { ∈ } ∪ { h }
= { g, f, h }
FOLLOW(D) = FIRST(h) = { h }

2. Using the production $B \to cC$, we get:
   FOLLOW(C) = FOLLOW(B) = { g, f, h }
3. Using the production $C \to bC$, we get:
   FOLLOW(C) = FOLLOW(C) = { g, f, h }
4. Using the production $D \to EF$, we get:
   FOLLOW(E) = FIRST(F) – { ∈ } ∪ FOLLOW(D)
   = { f, ∈ } – { ∈ } ∪ { h } = { f, h }
   FOLLOW(F) = FOLLOW(D) = { h }
   Therefore, the parsing table is as shown in Table 4.10.

TABLE 4.10 Production Selections for Example 4.8 Parsing Derivations

	a	b	c	g	f	h	$
S	$S \to aBDh$						
B			$B \to cC$				
C		$C \to bC$		$C \to \epsilon$	$C \to \epsilon$	$C \to \epsilon$	
D				$D \to EF$	$D \to EF$	$D \to EF$	
E				$E \to g$	$E \to \epsilon$	$E \to \epsilon$	
F					$F \to f$	$F \to \epsilon$	

EXERCISE

1. Compute the FIRST and FOLLOW sets for each nonterminal of the grammar given below:
   S → ABa | bCA
   A → cBCD | ∈
   B → CdA | ad
   C → eC | ∈
   D → bSf | a

2. Test whether the following grammar is LL(1):

   S → AB | eDa

   A → ab | c

   B → dC

   C → eC | ∈

   D → fD | ∈

3. LL(1) language is defined as the language for which there exist some LL(1) grammar generating the language. Consider the following statement:

   "There exist an algorithm to determine whether the given grammar is LL(1), but there exist no algorithm to determine whether a given language is LL(1)".

   Comment on the truth/falsehood of the above statement.

4. "There may exist a grammar that is non LL(1) but generating an LL(1) language".

   Comment on the truth/falsehood of the statement.

5. Is the following language LL(1)?

   $\{ a^n c b^n \mid n \geq 1 \}$

   (**Hint :** To show that a given language is LL(1), it is required to provide an LL(1) grammar generating the language.)

6. Design LL(1) parse table for the following grammar:

   S → aAcd | BCe

   A → b | ∈

   B → Cf | d

   C → fe

7. Consider the following grammar:

   S → aA | AB

   A → Ab | c

   B → e | f

   The grammar is not LL(1). Comment on the language generated by the grammar. That is whether the language generated by the grammar is LL(1) or not. And why?

8. Transform the following grammar so that it will be LL(1), without changing the language.

   $S \rightarrow aAC \mid bB$

   $A \rightarrow Abc \mid Abd \mid e$

   $B \rightarrow f \mid g$

   $C \rightarrow h \mid i$

9. Construct LL(1) parse table for the following grammar:

   $S \rightarrow aAC \mid bB$

   $A \rightarrow eD$

   $D \rightarrow bE \mid \epsilon$

   $E \rightarrow eD \mid dD$

   $B \rightarrow f \mid g$

   $C \rightarrow h \mid i$

10. "Every unambiguous grammar is LL(1). Comment on the truth/falsehood of the statement.

5 BOTTOM-UP PARSING

5.1 WHAT IS BOTTOM-UP PARSING?

Bottom-up parsing can be defined as an attempt to reduce the input string w to the start symbol of a grammar by tracing out the right-most derivations of w in reverse. This is equivalent to constructing a parse tree for the input string w by starting with leaves and proceeding toward the root—that is, attempting to construct the parse tree from the bottom, up. This involves searching for the substring that matches the right side of any of the productions of the grammar. This substring is replaced by the left-hand-side nonterminal of the production if this replacement leads to the generation of the sentential form that comes one step before in the right-most derivation. This process of replacing the right side of the production by the left side nonterminal is called "reduction." Hence, reduction is nothing more than performing derivations in reverse. The reason why bottom-up parsing tries to trace out the right-most derivations of an input string w in reverse and not the left-most derivations is because the parser scans the input string w from the left to right, one symbol/ token at a time. And to trace out right-most derivations of an input string w in reverse, the tokens of w must be made available in a left-to-right order. For example, if the right-most derivation sequence of some w is:

$$S \rightarrow \alpha_1 \rightarrow \alpha_2 \rightarrow \alpha_3 \rightarrow \ldots \rightarrow \alpha_{n-1} \rightarrow w$$

then the bottom-up parser starts with w and searches for the occurrence of a substring of w that matches the right side of some production $A \rightarrow \beta$ such that the replacement of β by A will lead to the generation of α_{n-1}. The parser replaces β by A, then it searches for the occurrence of a substring of α_{n-1} that matches the right side of some production $B \rightarrow \gamma$ such that replacement of γ by B will lead to the generation of α_{n-2}. This process continues until the entire w substring is reduced to S, or until the parser encounters an error.

Therefore, bottom-up parsing involves the selection of a substring that matches the right side of the production, whose reduction to the nonterminal on the left side of the production represents one step along the reverse of a right-most derivation. That is, it leads to the generation of the previous right-most derivation. This means that selecting a substring that matches the right side of production is not enough; the position of this substring in the sentential form is also important.

TIP

The substring should occur at that position in the sentential form that is currently under consideration where if it is replaced by the left-side nonterminal of the production, it leads to the generation of the previous right sentential form of the currently considered sentential form. Therefore, finding a substring that matches the right side of a production, as well as its position in the current sentential form, are both equally important. In order to take both of these factors into account, we will define a "handle" of the right sentential form.

5.2 A HANDLE OF A RIGHT SENTENTIAL FORM

A handle of a right sentential form γ is a production $A \rightarrow \beta$ and a position of β in γ. The string β will be found and replaced by A to produce the previous right sentential form in the right-most derivation of γ. That is, if $S \rightarrow \alpha A\beta \rightarrow \alpha\gamma\beta$, then $A \rightarrow \gamma$ is a handle of $\alpha\gamma\beta$, in the position following α. Consider the grammar:

$$E \rightarrow E{+}E \mid E{*}E \mid \text{id}$$

and the right-most derivation:

$$E \rightarrow E{+}E \rightarrow E{+}E{*}E \rightarrow E{+}E{+}\text{id} \rightarrow E{+}\text{id} * \text{id} \rightarrow \text{id} + \text{id} * \text{id}$$

The handles of the sentential forms occurring in the above derivation are shown in Table 5.1.

TABLE 5.1 Sentential Form Handles

Sentential Form	Handle
id + id * id	$E \rightarrow$ id at the position preceding +
E + id * id	$E \rightarrow$ id at the position following +
$E + E$ * id	$E \rightarrow$ id at the position following*
$E + E * E$	$E \rightarrow E * E$ at the position following +
$E + E$	$E \rightarrow E + E$ at the position preceding the end-marker

Therefore, the bottom-up parsing is an attempt to detect the handle of a right sentential form. And whenever a handle is detected, the reduction is performed. This is equivalent to performing right-most derivations in reverse and is called "handle pruning."

Therefore, if the right-most derivation sequence of some w is $S \rightarrow \alpha_1 \rightarrow \alpha_2 \rightarrow \alpha_3 \rightarrow \ldots \rightarrow \alpha_{n-1} \rightarrow w$, then handle pruning starts with w, the nth right sentential form, the handle $A_n \rightarrow \beta_n$ of w is located, and β_n is replaced by the left side of production $A_n \rightarrow \beta_n$ in order to obtain α_{n-1}. By continuing this process, if the parser obtains a right sentential form that consists of only a start symbol, then it halts and announces the successful completion of parsing.

EXAMPLE 5.1: Consider the following grammar, and show the handle of each right sentential form for the string $(a,(a, a))$.

$S \rightarrow (L) \mid a$

$L \rightarrow L,S \mid S$

The right-most derivation of the string $(a, (a, a))$ is:

$$S \rightarrow (L) \rightarrow (L, S) \rightarrow (L, (L)) \rightarrow (L, (L, S)) \rightarrow (L, (L, a))$$
$$\rightarrow (L, (S, a)) \rightarrow (L, (a, a)) \rightarrow (S, (a, a)) \rightarrow (a, (a, a))$$

Table 5.2 presents the handles of the sentential forms occurring in the above derivation.

TABLE 5.2 Sentential Form Handles

Sentential Form	Handle
$(a, (a, a))$	$S \rightarrow a$ at the position preceding the first comma
$(S, (a, a))$	$L \rightarrow S$ at the position preceding the first comma
$(L, (a, a))$	$S \rightarrow a$ at the position preceding the second comma
$(L, (S, a))$	$L \rightarrow S$ at the position preceding the second comma
$(L, (L, a))$	$S \rightarrow a$ at the position following the second comma
$(L, (L, S))$	$L \rightarrow L, S$, at the position following the second left bracket
$(L, (L))$	$S \rightarrow (L)$ at the position following the first comma
(L, S)	$L \rightarrow L, S$, at the position following the first left bracket
(L)	$S \rightarrow (L)$ at the position before the endmarker

5.3 IMPLEMENTATION

A convenient way to implement a bottom-up parser is to use a shift-reduce technique: a parser goes on shifting the input symbols onto the stack until a handle comes on the top of the stack. When a handle appears on the top of the stack, it performs reduction. This implementation makes use of a stack to hold grammar symbols and an input buffer to hold the string w to be parsed, which is terminated by the right endmarker \$, the same symbol used to mark the bottom of the stack. The configuration of the parser is given by a pair-the first component of which is a stack content, and second component is an unexpended input.

Initially, the parser will be in the configuration given by the pair (\$, w\$); that is, the stack is initially empty, and the buffer contains the entire string w. The parser shifts zero or more symbols from the input on to the stack until handle α appears on the top of the stack. The parser then reduces to the left side of the appropriate production. This cycle is repeated until the parser either detects an error or until the stack contains a start symbol and the input is empty, giving the configuration (\$$S$, \$). If the parser enters (\$$S$, \$), then it announces the successful completion of parsing. Thus, the primary operation of the parser is to shift and reduce.

For example consider the bottom-up parser for the grammar having the productions:

$$E \rightarrow E+T \mid T$$
$$T \rightarrow T^*F \mid F$$
$$F \rightarrow \text{id}$$

and the input string: id+id * id. The various steps in parsing this string are shown in Table 5.3 in terms of the contents of the stack and unspent input.

TABLE 5.3 Steps in Parsing the String id + id * id

Stack Contents	Input	Moves
$	id + id*id$	shift id
$id	+ id*id$	reduce by $F \rightarrow$ id
$$F$	+ id*id$	reduce by $T \rightarrow F$
$$T$	+ id*id$	reduce by $E \rightarrow T$
$$E$	+ id*id$	shift +
$$E$ +	id*id$	shift id
$$E$ + id	*id$	reduce by $F \rightarrow$ id
$$E + F$	*id$	reduce by $T \rightarrow F$
$$E + T$	*id$	shift *
$$E + T$*	id$	shift id
$$E + T$*id	$	reduce by $F \rightarrow$ id
$$E + T*F$	$	reduce by $T \rightarrow T*F$
$$E + T$	$	reduce by $E \rightarrow E + T$
$$E$	$	accept

Shift-reduce implementation does not tell us anything about the technique used for detecting the handles; hence, it is possible to make use of any suitable technique to detect handles. Depending upon the technique that is used to detect handles, we get different shift-reduce parsers. For example, an operator-precedence parser is a shift-reduce parser that uses the precedence relationship between certain pairs of terminals to guide the selection of handles. Whereas LR parsers make use of a deterministic finite automata that recognizes the set of all viable prefixes; by reading the stack from bottom to top, to determine what handle, if any, is on the top of the stack.

5.4 THE LR PARSER

The LR parser is a shift-reduce parser that makes use of a deterministic finite automata, recognizing the set of all viable prefixes by reading the stack from bottom to top. It determines what handle, if any, is available. A viable prefix of a right sentential form is that prefix that contains a handle, but no symbol to the right of the handle. Therefore, if a finite-state machine that recognizes viable prefixes of the right sentential forms is constructed, it can be used to guide the handle selection in the shift-reduce parser.

Since the LR parser makes use of a DFA that recognizes viable prefixes to guide the selection of handles, it must keep track of the states of the DFA. Hence, the LR parser stack contains two types of symbols: state symbols used to identify the states of the DFA and grammar symbols. The parser starts with the initial state of a DFA I_0 on the stack. The parser operates by looking at the next input symbol a and the state symbol I_i on the top of the stack. If there is a transition from the state I_i on a in the DFA going to state I_j, then it shifts the symbol a, followed by the state symbol I_j, onto the stack. If there is no transition from I_i on a in the DFA, and if the state I_i on the top of the stack recognizes, when entered, a viable prefix that contains the handle $A \rightarrow \alpha$, then the parser carries out the reduction by popping α and pushing A onto the stack. This is equivalent to making a backward transition from I_i on α in the DFA and then making a forward transition on A. Every shift action of the parser corresponds to a transition on a terminal symbol in the DFA. Therefore, the current state of the DFA and the next input symbol determine whether the parser shifts the next input symbol or goes for reduction.

If we construct a table mapping every state and input symbol pair as either "shift," "reduce," "accept," or "error," we get a table that can be used to guide the parsing process. Such a table is called a parsing "action" table. When carrying out the reduction by $A \rightarrow \alpha$, the parser has to pop α and push A onto the stack. This requires knowledge of where the transition goes in a DFA from the state brought onto the top of the stack after popping α on the nonterminal A; and hence, we require another table mapping every state and nonterminal pair into a state. The table of transitions on the nonterminals in the DFA is called a "goto" table. Therefore, to create an LR parser we require an action and GOTO.

If the current state of a DFA has a transition on the terminal symbol a to the state I_j, then the next move will be to shift the symbol a and enter the state I_j. But if the current state of the DFA is one in which when entered recognizes a viable prefix that contains the handle, then the next move of the parser will be to reduce.

Therefore, an LR parser is comprised of an input buffer (which holds the input string w to be parsed and assumed to be terminated by the right endmarker \$), a stack holding the viable prefixes of the right sentential forms, and a parsing table that is obtain by mapping the moves of a DFA that recognizes viable prefixes and controls the parsing actions. The configuration of a parser is given by a token pair: the first component is a stack's content, and second component is unexpended input. If, at a particular instant (and \$ is used as bottom-of-the-stack marker, also), a parser is configured as follows:

Stack Contents	**Input**
$\$I_0X_0I_1X_1 \ldots X_mI_m$	$a_ia_{i+1} \ldots a_n\$$

where I_i is a state symbol identifying the state of a DFA recognizing the viable prefixes, and X_i is the grammar symbol. The parser consults the parsing action table entry, $[I_m, a_i]$. If action$[I_m, a_i] = S_j$, then the parser shifts the next input symbol followed by the state I_j on the stack and enters into the configuration:

Stack Contents	**Input**
$\$I_0X_0I_1X_1 \ldots X_mI_ma_i\,I_j$	$a_{i+1} \ldots a_n\$$

If action$[I_m, a_i]$ = reduce by production $A \rightarrow \alpha$, then the parser carries out the reduction as follows. If $|\alpha| = r$, then the parser pops $2r$ symbols from the stack (because every shift action shifts a grammar symbol as well as state symbol), thereby bringing I_{m-r} on the top. It then consults the GOTO table entry, GOTO$[I_{m-r}, A]$. If GOTO$[I_{m-r}, A] = I_k$, then it shifts A followed by I_k onto the stack, thereby entering into the configuration:

Stack Contents	**Input**
$\$I_0X_0I_1X_1 \ldots X_{m-r}I_{m-r}AI_k$	$a_i\,a_{i+1} \ldots a_n\$$

If action$[I_m, a_i]$ = accept, then the parser halts and accepts the input string. If action$[I_m, a_i]$ = error, then the parser invokes a suitable error-recovery routine. Initially the parser will be in the configuration given by the pair ($\$I_0$, $w\$$). Therefore, we conclude that parsing table construction involves constructing a DFA that recognizes the viable prefixes of the right sentential forms, using the given grammar, and then maps its the moves into the form of the Action and GOTO table. To construct such a DFA, we make use of the items that are part of a grammar's productions. Here, an item called the "*LR*(0)" item of a production is a production with a dot placed at some position on the right side of the production. For example if $A \rightarrow XYZ$ is a production, then the following items can be generated from it:

$$A \rightarrow .XYZ$$
$$A \rightarrow X.YZ$$
$$A \rightarrow XY.Z$$
$$A \rightarrow XYZ.$$

If the length of the right side of the production is n, then there are $(n+1)$ different positions on the right side of a production where a dot can be placed. Hence, the number of items that can be generated are $(n+1)$.

The dot's position on the right side tells us how much of the right-hand side of the production is seen in the process of parsing. For example, the item $A \rightarrow X.YZ$ tells us that we have already seen a string derivable from X in the input and expect to see the string derivable from YZ next in the input.

5.4.1 Augmented Grammar

To construct a DFA that recognizes the viable prefixes, we make use of augmented grammar, which is defined as follows: if $G = (V, T, P, S)$ is a given grammar, then the augmented grammar will be $G_1 = (V \cup \{S_1\}, T, P \cup \{S_1 \rightarrow S\}, S_1)$; that is, we add a unit production $S_1 \rightarrow S$ to the grammar G and make S_1 the new start symbol. The resulting grammar will be an augmented grammar. The purpose of augmenting the grammar is to make it explicitly clear to parser when to accept the string. Parsing will stop when the parser is on the verge of carrying out the reduction using $S_1 \rightarrow S$. A NFA that recognizes the viable prefixes will be a finite automata whose states correspond to the production items of the augmented grammar. Every item represents one state in the automata, with the initial state corresponding to an item $S_1 \rightarrow S$. The transitions in the automata are defined as follows:

$\delta (A \rightarrow \alpha.X\beta, X) = A \rightarrow \alpha X.\beta$

$\delta (A \rightarrow \alpha.B\beta, \in) = B \rightarrow .\gamma$ (This transition is required, because if the current state is $A \rightarrow \alpha.B\beta$, that means we have not yet seen a string derivable from the nonterminal B; and since $B \rightarrow \gamma$ is a production of the grammar, unless we see γ, we will not get B. Therefore, we have to travel the path that recognizes γ, which requires entering into the state identified by $B \rightarrow .\gamma$ without consuming any input symbols.)

This NFA can then be transformed into a DFA using the subset construction method. For example, consider the following grammar:

$$E \rightarrow E + T \mid T$$
$$T \rightarrow T * F \mid F$$
$$F \rightarrow \text{id}$$

The augmented grammar is:

$$S \rightarrow E$$
$$E \rightarrow E + T \mid T$$
$$T \rightarrow T * F \mid F$$
$$F \rightarrow \text{id}$$

The items that can be generated using these productions are:

$$S \rightarrow .E$$
$$S \rightarrow E.$$
$$E \rightarrow .E + T$$
$$E \rightarrow E.+T$$
$$E \rightarrow E + .T$$
$$E \rightarrow E + T.$$
$$E \rightarrow .T$$
$$E \rightarrow T.$$
$$T \rightarrow .T*F$$
$$T \rightarrow T.*F$$
$$T \rightarrow T*.F$$
$$T \rightarrow T*F.$$
$$T \rightarrow .F$$
$$T \rightarrow F.$$
$$F \rightarrow .\text{id}$$
$$F \rightarrow \text{id}.$$

Therefore, the transition diagram of the NFA that recognizes viable prefixes is as shown in Figure 5.1.

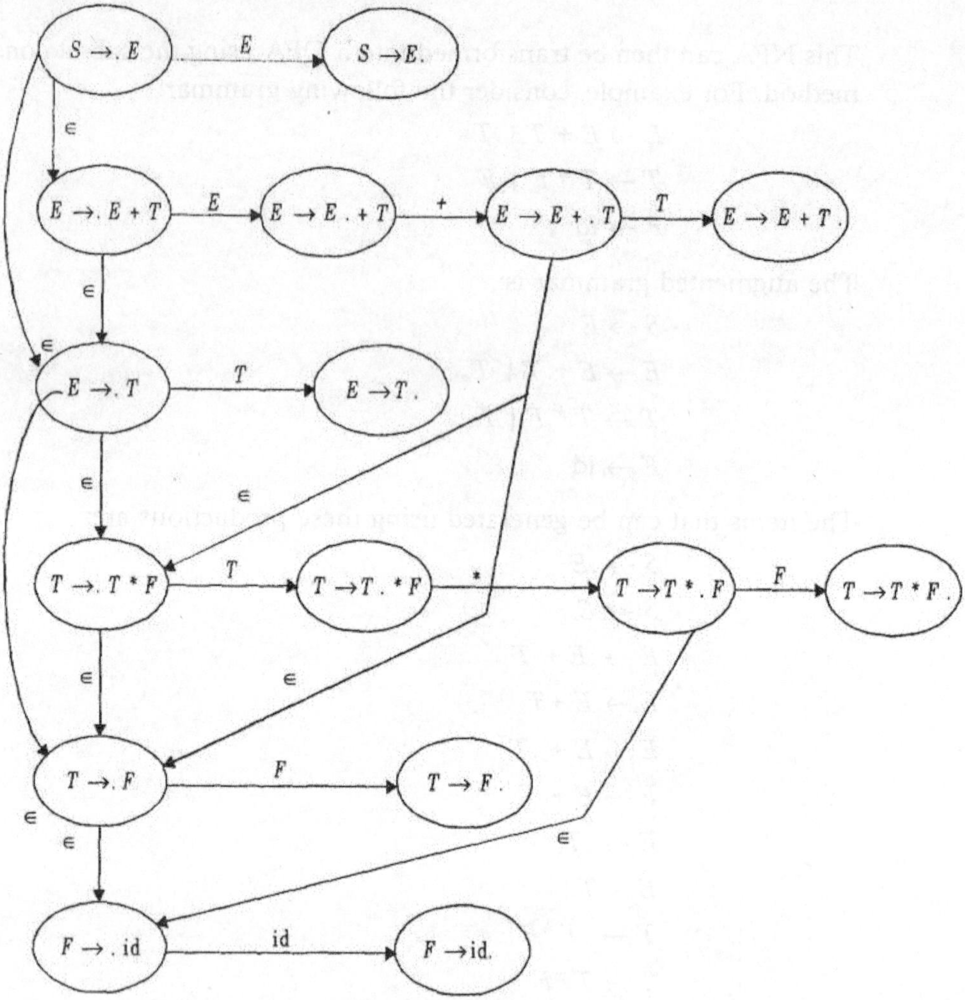

FIGURE 5.1 NFA transition diagram recognizes viable prefixes.

The DFA equivalent of the NFA shown in Figure 5.1 is, by using subset construction, illustrated in Figure 5.2.

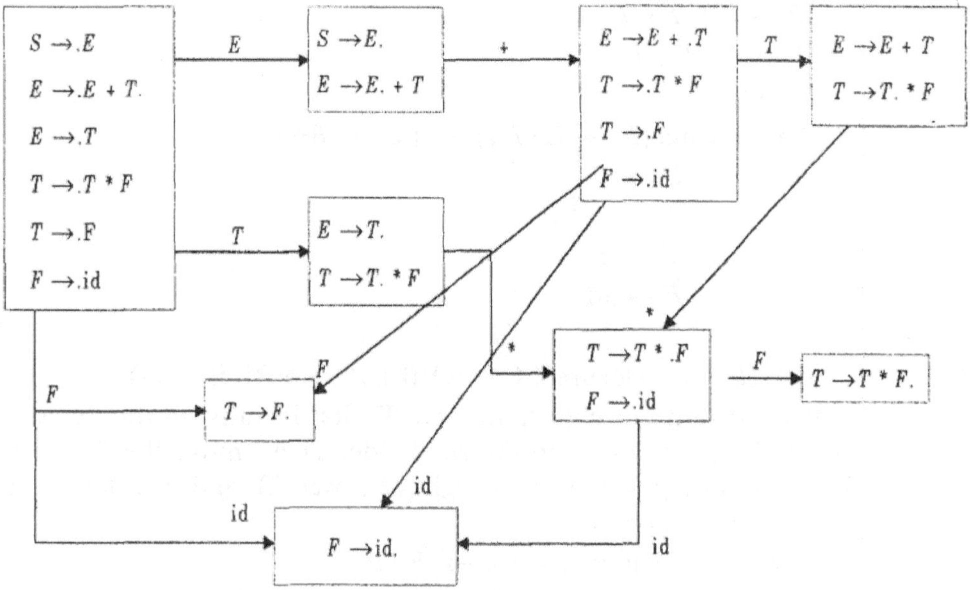

FIGURE 5.2 Using subset construction, a DFA equivalent is derived from the transition diagram in Figure 5.1.

Therefore, every state of the DFA that recognizes viable prefixes is a set of items; and hence, the set of DFA states will be a collection of sets of items—but any arbitrary collection of set of items will not correspond to the DFA set of states. A set of items that corresponds to the states of a DFA that recognizes viable prefixes is called a "canonical collection." Therefore, construction of a DFA involves finding canonical collection. An algorithm exists that directly obtains the canonical collection of LR(0) sets of items, thereby allowing us to obtain the DFA. Using this algorithm, we can directly obtain a DFA that recognizes the viable prefixes, rather than going through NFA to DFA transformation, as explained above. The algorithm for finding out the canonical collection of LR(0) sets of items makes use of the closure and goto functions. The set closure(I), where I is a set of items, is computed as follows:

1. Add every item in I to closure(I)
2. Repeat

   For every item of the form $A \to \alpha.B\beta$ in closure(I) do

       For every production $B \to \gamma$ do

       Add $B \to .\gamma$ to closure(I)

   Until no new item can be added to closure(I)

For example, consider the following grammar:

$E \rightarrow E + T \mid T$

$T \rightarrow T * F \mid F$

$F \rightarrow \text{id}$

The closure($\{E \rightarrow .E+T\}$) = $\{ E \rightarrow .E+T$

$E \rightarrow .T$

$T \rightarrow .T * F$

$T \rightarrow .F$

$F \rightarrow .\text{id}$

$\}$

goto(I, X) = closure($\{A \rightarrow \alpha X.\beta \mid A \rightarrow \alpha.X\beta$ is in $I\}$)

That is, to find out goto from I on X, first identify all the items in I in which the dot precedes X on the right side. Then, move the dot in all the selected items one position to the right(i.e., over X), and then take a closure of the set of these items.

For example, if set $I = \{ E \rightarrow .E+T$

$E \rightarrow .T$

$T \rightarrow .T*F$

$T \rightarrow .F$

$F \rightarrow .\text{id}$

$\}$

then goto(I, T) = closure ($\{E \rightarrow T.$

$T \rightarrow T.*F$

$\}$

$) = \{ E \rightarrow T.$

$T \rightarrow T.*F$

$\}$

5.4.2 An Algorithm for Finding the Canonical Collection of Sets of LR(0) Items

/* Let C be the canonical collection of sets of LR(0) items. We maintain C_{new} and C_{old} to continue the iterations*/

Input: augmented grammar

Output: canonical collection of sets of LR(0) items (i.e., set C)

1. $C_{old} = \varphi$
2. add closure ($\{S_1 \rightarrow .S\}$) to C
3. while $C_{old} \neq C_{new}$ do

   { temp = $C_{new} - C_{old}$

   $C_{old} = C_{new}$

   for every I in temp do

   for every X in $V \cup T$ (i.e., for every grammar symbol X) do

   if goto(I, X) is not empty and not in C_{new} then

   add goto(I, X) to C_{new}

   }
4. $C = C_{new}$

For example consider the following grammar:

$$E \rightarrow E + T \mid T$$
$$T \rightarrow T * F \mid F$$
$$F \rightarrow \text{id}$$

The augmented grammar is:

$$S \rightarrow E$$
$$E \rightarrow E + T \mid T$$
$$T \rightarrow T * F \mid F$$
$$F \rightarrow \text{id}$$

Initially, $C_{old} = \varphi$. First we obtain:

closure($\{S \rightarrow .E\}$) = { $S \rightarrow .E$

$E \rightarrow .E+T$

$E \rightarrow .T$

$T \rightarrow .T*F$

$T \rightarrow .F$

$F \rightarrow .\text{id}$

}

We call it I_0 and add it to C_{new}. Therefore:

$C_{new} = \{ I_0 \}$

Temp = $\{ I_0 \}$

$C_{old} = \{ I_0 \}$

In the first iteration, we obtain the goto from I_0 on every grammar symbol, as shown below:

$$\begin{aligned}
\text{goto}(I_0, E) &= \text{closure}(\{S \rightarrow E. \\
&\quad E \rightarrow E. + T\} \\
&= \{S \rightarrow E. \\
&\quad E \rightarrow E. + T \\
&\} = I_1
\end{aligned}$$

Add it to C_{new}:

$$\begin{aligned}
\text{goto}(I_0, T) &= \text{closure}(\{E \rightarrow T. \\
&\quad T \rightarrow T.{*}F\} \\
&= \{E \rightarrow T. \\
&\quad T \rightarrow T.{*}F \\
&\} = I_2
\end{aligned}$$

Add it to C_{new}:

$$\begin{aligned}
\text{goto}(I_0, F) &= \text{closure}(\{T \rightarrow F. \\
&\} \\
&= \{T \rightarrow F. \\
&\} = I_3
\end{aligned}$$

Add it to C_{new}:

$$\begin{aligned}
\text{goto}\ (I_0, \text{id}) &= \text{closure}(\{F \rightarrow \text{id}.\} \\
&= \{F \rightarrow \text{id}. \\
&\} - I_4
\end{aligned}$$

Add it to C_{new}:

goto(I_0, +) = ϕ, therefore, not added to C_{new}

goto (I_0, *) = ϕ, therefore not added to C_{new}

Therefore, at the end of first iteration:

$C_{old} = \{ I_0 \}$

$C_{new} = \{ I_0, I_1, I_2, I_3, I_4 \}$

In the second the iteration:

Temp = $\{ I_1, I_2, I_3, I_4 \}$

$C_{old} = \{ I_0, I_1, I_2, I_3, I_4 \}$

So, in the second iteration, we obtain goto from $\{I_1, I_2, I_3, I_4\}$ **on every grammar** symbol, as shown below:

goto(I_1, E) = ϕ, therefore not added to C_{new}

goto(I_1, T) = ϕ, therefore not added to C_{new}

goto(I_1, F) = ϕ, therefore not added to C_{new}

goto(I_1, id) = ϕ, therefore not added to C_{new}

goto(I_1, *) = ϕ, therefore not added to C_{new}
goto(I_1, +) = closure({$E \rightarrow E+.T$})
= { $E \rightarrow E+.T$
$T \rightarrow .T*F$
$T \rightarrow .F$
$F \rightarrow .\text{id}$
} = I_5

Add it to C_{new}:

goto(I_2, E) = ϕ, therefore not added to C_{new}
goto(I_2, T) = ϕ, therefore not added to C_{new}
goto(I_2, F) = ϕ, therefore not added to C_{new}
goto(I_2, id) = ϕ, therefore not added to C_{new}
goto(I_2, +) = ϕ, therefore not added to C_{new}
goto(I_2, *) = closure({$T \rightarrow T*.F$
}
) = { $T \rightarrow T*.F$
$F \rightarrow .\text{id}$
} = I_6

Add it to C_{new}:

goto(I_3, E) = ϕ, therefore not added to C_{new}
goto(I_3, T) = ϕ, therefore not added to C_{new}
goto(I_3, F) = ϕ, therefore not added to C_{new}
goto(I_3, id) = ϕ, therefore not added to C_{new}
goto(I_3, +) = ϕ, therefore not added to C_{new}
goto(I_3, *) = ϕ, therefore not added to C_{new}
goto(I_4, E) = ϕ, therefore not added to C_{new}
goto(I_4, T) = ϕ, therefore not added to C_{new}
goto(I_4, F) = ϕ, therefore not added to C_{new}
goto(I_4, id) = ϕ, therefore not added to C_{new}
goto(I_4, +) = ϕ, therefore not added to C_{new}
goto(I_4, *) = ϕ, therefore not added to C_{new}

Therefore, at the end of the second iteration:

C_{old} = { I_0, I_1, I_2, I_3, I_4 }
C_{new} = { $I_0, I_1, I_2, I_3, I_4, I_5, I_6$ }

In the third iteration:

$\text{Temp} = \{ I_5, I_6 \}$

$C_{\text{old}} = \{ I_0, I_1, I_2, I_3, I_4, I_5, I_6 \}$

In the third iteration, we obtain goto from $\{ I_5, I_6 \}$ on every grammar symbol, as shown below:

goto(I_5, E) = ϕ, therefore not added to C_{new}

goto(I_5, T) = closure($\{E \to E + T.$

$T \to T.*F$

$\}$

$= \{ E \to E + T.$

$T \to T.*F$

$\} = I_7$

Add it to C_{new}:

goto(I_5, F) = closure($\{ T \to F.$

$\}$

$= \{T \to F.$

$\}$ = same as I_3,

hence, not added to C_{new}

goto(I_5, id) = closure($\{F \to$ id.

$\}$

$= \{F \to$ id.

$\}$ = same as I_4,

hence, not added to C_{new}

goto(I_5, *) = ϕ, therefore not added to C_{new}

goto(I_5, +) = ϕ, therefore not added to C_{new}

goto(I_6, E) = ϕ, therefore not added to C_{new}

goto(I_6, T) = ϕ, therefore not added to C_{new}

goto(I_6, F) = closure($\{T \to T*F.$

$\}$

$= \{ T \to T*F.$

$\} = I_8$

Add it to C_{new}:

goto(I_6, id) = closure($\{F \to$ id.

$\}$

$= \{F \rightarrow \text{id}.$

$\} =$ same as I_4,

hence not added to C_{new}

goto(I_5, *) = ϕ, therefore not added to C_{new}

goto(I_5, +) = ϕ, therefore not added to C_{new}

Therefore, at the end of the third iteration:

$C_{old} = \{ I_0, I_1, I_2, I_3, I_4, I_5, I_6 \}$

$C_{new} = \{ I_0, I_1, I_2, I_3, I_4, I_5, I_6, I_7, I_8 \}$

In the fourth iteration:

Temp = $\{ I_7, I_8 \}$

$C_{old} = \{ I_0, I_1, I_2, I_3, I_4, I_5, I_6, I_7, I_8 \}$

So, in the fourth iteration, we obtain a goto from $\{ I_7, I_8 \}$ on every grammar symbol, as shown below:

goto(I_7, E) = ϕ, therefore not added to C_{new}

goto(I_7, T) = ϕ, therefore not added to C_{new}

goto(I_7, F) = ϕ, therefore not added to C_{new}

goto(I_7, id) = ϕ, therefore not added to C_{new}

goto(I_7, +) = ϕ, therefore not added to C_{new}

goto(I_7, *) = closure($\{T \rightarrow T^*.F$

$F \rightarrow .\text{id}$

$\}$

$= \{T \rightarrow T^*.F.$

$F \rightarrow .\text{id}$

$\} =$ same as I_6,

hence not added to C_{new}

goto(I_8, E) = ϕ, therefore not added to C_{new}

goto(I_8, T) = ϕ, therefore not added to C_{new}

goto(I_8, F) = ϕ, therefore not added to C_{new}

goto(I_8, id) = ϕ, therefore not added to C_{new}

goto(I_8, +) = ϕ, therefore not added to C_{new}

goto(I_8, *) = ϕ, therefore not added to C_{new}

At the end of fourth iteration:

$C_{old} = \{ I_0, I_1, I_2, I_3, I_4, I_5, I_6, I_7, I_8 \}$

$C_{new} = \{ I_0, I_1, I_2, I_3, I_4, I_5, I_6, I_7, I_8 \}$

Therefore, $C = \{ I_0, I_1, I_2, I_3, I_4, I_5, I_6, I_7, I_8 \}$

The transition diagram of the DFA is shown in Figure 5.3.

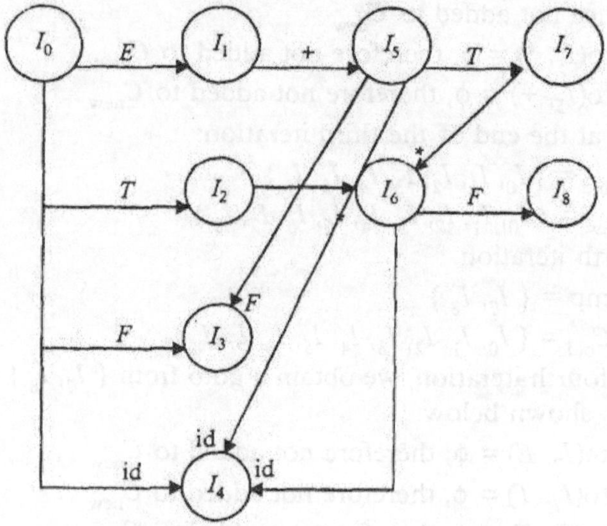

FIGURE 5.3 DFA transition diagram showing four iterations for a canonical collection of sets.

5.4.3 Construction of a Parsing Action and GOTO Table for an SLR(1) Parser

The methods for constructing the parsing Action and GOTO table are described below.

Construction of the action Table

1. For every state I_1 in C do
   for every terminal symbol a do
   if goto(I_i, a) = I_j, then
   make action[I_i, a] = S_j /*for shift and enter into the state j*/
2. For every state I_i in C whose underlying set of LR(0) items contains an item of the form A → α.do
   for every b in FOLLOW(A) do
   make action[I_i, b] = R_k /*where k is the number of the production $A \to \alpha$ standing for reduce by $A \to \alpha$ */
3. Make [I_i, \$) = accept if I_i contains an item $S_1 \to S$.

It is obvious that if a state I_i has a transition on a terminal *a* going to I_j, then the parser's next move will be to shift and enter into state *j*. Therefore, the shift entries in the action table are the mappings of the transitions in the DFA on terminals. Similarly, if state I_i corresponds to the viable prefix that contains the right side of the production $A \rightarrow \alpha$; then the parser will call a reduction by $A \rightarrow \alpha$ on all those symbols that are in the FOLLOW(A). This is because if the next input symbol happens to be a terminal symbol that can FOLLOW(A), then only the reduction by $A \rightarrow \alpha$ may lead to a previous right-most derivation. That is, if the next input symbol belongs to FOLLOW(A), then the position of α can be considered to be the one where, if it is replaced by A, we might get a previous right-most derivation. Whether or not $A \rightarrow \alpha$ is a handle is decided in this manner.

The initial state is the one whose underlying set of items' representations contain an item $S_1 \rightarrow .S$. This method is called "SLR(1)"—a Simple LR; and the (1) indicates a length of lookahead (the next symbol used by the parser to decide its next move) used. Therefore, this parsing table is an SLR parsing table. (When the parentheses are not specified, the length of the lookahead is assumed to be one.)

Construction of the Goto Table

A goto table is simply a mapping of transitions in the DFA on nonterminals. Therefore, it is constructed as follows:

For every I_i in C do

For every nonterminal A do

If goto(I_i, A) = I_j then

Make GOTO[I_i, A) = j

Therefore, the SLR parsing table for the grammar having the following productions is shown in Table 5.4.

$$S \rightarrow E$$

$$E \rightarrow E + T \mid T$$

$$T \rightarrow T * F \mid F$$

$$F \rightarrow \text{id}$$

TABLE 5.4 Action | GOTO SLR Parsing Table

	Action Table				**GOTO Table**		
	id	+	*	$	E	T	F
I_0	S_4				1	2	3
I_1		S_5		Accept			
I_2		R_2	S_6	R_2			
I_3		R_4	R_4	R_4			
I_4		R_5	R_5	R_5			
I_5	S_4					7	3
I_6	S_4						8
I_7		R_1	S_6	R_1			
I_8		R_3	R_3	R_3			

The productions are numbered as:

$$E \rightarrow E + T \qquad (1)$$

$$E \rightarrow T \qquad (2)$$

$$T \rightarrow T * F \qquad (3)$$

$$T \rightarrow F \qquad (4)$$

$$F \rightarrow \text{id} \qquad (5)$$

EXAMPLE 5.2: Consider the following grammar:

$$S \rightarrow CC$$
$$C \rightarrow cC$$
$$C \rightarrow d$$

The augmented grammar is:

$$S_1 \rightarrow S$$
$$S \rightarrow CC$$
$$C \rightarrow cC$$
$$C \rightarrow d$$

The canonical collection of sets of LR(0) items are computed as follows.

$$
\begin{aligned}
I_0 = \text{closure}(\{S_1 \to .S\}) = \{\ & S_1 \to .S \\
& S \to .CC \\
& C \to .cC \\
& C \to .d \\
& \}
\end{aligned}
$$

$\text{goto}(I_0, S) = \text{closure}(\{S_1 \to S.\}) = \{\ S_1 \to S.\ \} = I_1$

$$
\begin{aligned}
\text{goto}(I_0, C) = \text{closure}(\{S \to C.C\}) = \{\ & S \to C.C \\
& C \to .cC \\
& C \to .d\ \} = I_2
\end{aligned}
$$

$$
\begin{aligned}
\text{goto}(I_0, c) = \text{closure}(\{C \to c.C\}) = \{\ & C \to c.C \\
& C \to .cC \\
& C \to .d\} = I_3
\end{aligned}
$$

$\text{goto}(I_0, d) = \text{closure}(\{C \to d.\}) = \{\ C \to d.\ \} = I_4$

$$
\begin{aligned}
\text{goto}(I_2, C) = \text{closure}(\{S \to CC.\}) = \{\ & S \to CC. \\
& \} = I_5
\end{aligned}
$$

$$
\begin{aligned}
\text{goto}(I_2, c) = \text{closure}(\{C \to c.C\}) = \{\ & C \to c.C \\
& C \to .cC \\
& C \to .\text{d} \\
& \} = \text{same as } I_3
\end{aligned}
$$

$$
\begin{aligned}
\text{goto}(I_2, d) = \text{closure}(\{C \to d.\}) = \{\ & C \to d. \\
& \} = \text{same as } I_4
\end{aligned}
$$

$$
\begin{aligned}
\text{goto}(I_3, C) = \text{closure}(\{C \to cC.\}) = \{\ & C \to cC. \\
& \} = I_6
\end{aligned}
$$

$$
\begin{aligned}
\text{goto}(I_3, c) = \text{closure}(\{C \to c.C\}) = \{\ & C \to c.C \\
& C \to .cC \\
& C \to .d \\
& \} = \text{same as } I_3
\end{aligned}
$$

$$
\begin{aligned}
\text{goto}(I_3, d) = \text{closure}(\{C \to d.\}) = \{\ & C \to d. \\
& \} = \text{same as } I_4
\end{aligned}
$$

The transition diagram of the DFA is shown in Figure 5.4.

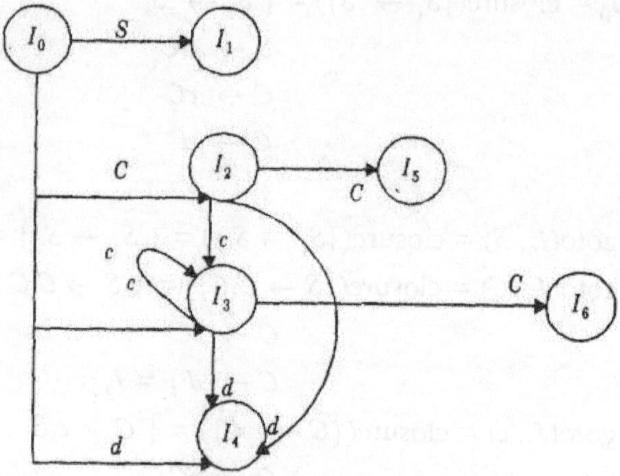

FIGURE 5.4 Transition diagram for Example 5.2 DFA.

The grammar has the following productions:

$S_1 \rightarrow S$

$S \rightarrow CC$

$C \rightarrow cC$

$C \rightarrow d$

which are numbered as:

$S \rightarrow CC$ (1)

$C \rightarrow cC$ (2)

$C \rightarrow d$ (3)

SLR parsing table as shown in Table 5.5.

TABLE 5.5 *SLR* Parsing Table

	Action Table			GOTO Table	
	c	d	$	S	C
I_0	S_3	S_4		1	2
I_1			accept		
I_2	S_3	S_4			5
I_3	S_3	S_4			6
I_4	R_3	R_3	R_3		
I_5			R_1		
I_6	R_2	R_2	R_2		

By using the method discussed above, a parsing table can be obtained for any grammar. But the action table obtained from the method above will not necessarily be without multiple entries for every grammar. Therefore, we define a SLR(1) grammar as one for which we can obtain the action table without multiple entries by using the method described. If the action table contains multiple entries, then the grammar for which the table is obtained is not SLR(1) grammar.

For example, consider the following grammar:

$$S \rightarrow AaAb$$
$$S \rightarrow BbBa$$
$$A \rightarrow \in$$
$$B \rightarrow \in$$

The augmented grammar will be:

$$S_1 \rightarrow S$$
$$S \rightarrow AaAb$$
$$S \rightarrow BbBa$$
$$A \rightarrow \in$$
$$B \rightarrow \in$$

The canonical collection sets of LR(0) items are computed as follows.

$$I_0 = \text{closure}(\{S_1 \rightarrow .S\}) = \{S_1 \rightarrow .S$$
$$S \rightarrow .AaAb$$
$$S \rightarrow .BbBa$$
$$A \rightarrow .$$
$$B \rightarrow .$$
$$\}$$

$$\text{goto}(I_0, S) = \text{closure}(\{S_1 \rightarrow S.\}) = \{ S_1 \rightarrow S. \} = I_1$$
$$\text{goto}(I_0, A) = \text{closure}(\{S \rightarrow A.aAb\}) = \{ S \rightarrow A.aAb \} = I_2$$
$$\text{goto}(I_0, B) = \text{closure}(\{S \rightarrow B.bBa\}) = \{ S \rightarrow B.bBa \} = I_3$$
$$\text{goto}(I_2, a) = \text{closure}(\{S \rightarrow Aa.Ab\}) = \{ S \rightarrow Aa.Ab$$
$$A \rightarrow .$$
$$\} = I_4$$
$$\text{goto}(I_3, b) = \text{closure}(\{S \rightarrow Bb.Ba\}) = \{ S \rightarrow Bb.Ba$$
$$B \rightarrow .$$
$$\} = I_5$$
$$\text{goto}(I_4, A) = \text{closure}(\{S \rightarrow AaA.b\}) = \{ S \rightarrow AaA.b \} = I_6$$
$$\text{goto}(I_5, B) = \text{closure}(\{S \rightarrow BbB.a\}) = \{ S \rightarrow BbB.a \} = I_7$$

goto(I_6, b) = closure({$S \to AaAb.$})= { $S \to AaAb.$ } = I_8
goto(I_7, a) = closure({$S \to BbBa.$})= { $S \to BbBa.$ } = I_9

The transition diagram for the DFA is shown in Figure 5.5.

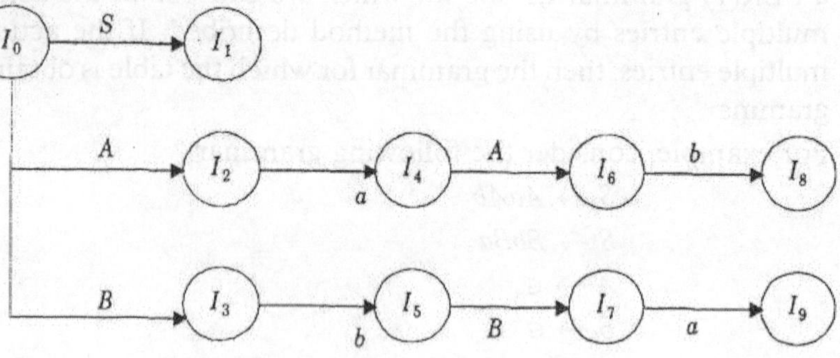

FIGURE 5.5 DFA Transition diagram.

Table 5.6 shows the SLR parsing table for the grammar having the following productions:

$S_1 \to S$
$S \to AaAb$
$S \to BbBa$
$A \to \epsilon$
$B \to \epsilon$

TABLE 5.6 Action | GOTO SLR Parsing Table

	Action Table			GOTO Table		
	a	b	\$	S	A	B
I_0	R_3/R_4	R_3/R_4		1	2	3
I_1			Accept			
I_2	S_4					
I_3		S_5				
I_4	R_3	R_3			6	
I_5	R_4	R_4				7
I_6		S_8				
I_7	S_9					
I_8			R_1			
I_9			R_2			

Where productions are numbered as follows:

$$S \rightarrow AaAb \quad (1)$$
$$S \rightarrow BbBa \quad (2)$$
$$A \rightarrow \in \quad (3)$$
$$B \rightarrow \in \quad (4)$$

Since the action table shown in Table 5.6 contains multiple entries, the above grammar is not SLR(1).

SLR(1) grammars constitute a small subset of context-free grammars, so an SLR parser can only succeed on a small number of context-free grammars. That means an SLR parser is a less-powerful LR parser. (The power of the parser is measured in terms of the number of grammars on which it can succeed.) This is because when an SLR parser sees a right-hand-side production rule $A \rightarrow \alpha$ on the top of the stack, it replaces this rule by the left-hand-side nonterminal A if the next input symbol can FOLLOW the nonterminal A. But sometimes this reduction may not lead to the generation of previous right-most derivations. For example, the parser constructed above can do the reduction by the production $A \rightarrow \in$ in the state I_0 if the next input symbol happens to be either a or b, because both a and b are in the FOLLOW(A). But since the reduction by $A \rightarrow \in$ in I_0 leads to the generation of a first instance of A in the sentential form $AaAb$, this reduction proves to be a proper one if the next input symbol is a. This is because the first instance of A in the sentential form $AaAb$ is followed by a. But if the next input symbol is b, then this is not a proper reduction, because even though b follows A, b follows a second instance of A in the sentential form $AaAb$. Similarly, if the parser carries out the reduction by $A \rightarrow \in$ in the state I_4, then it should be done if the next input symbol is b, because reduction by $A \rightarrow \in$ in I_4 leads to the generation of a second instance of A in the sentential form $AaAb$.

Therefore, we conclude that if:

1. We let terminal a follow the first instance of A and let terminal b follow the second instance of A in the sentential form $AaAb$;
2. We associate a with the item $A \rightarrow .$ in I_0 and terminal b with item $A \rightarrow .$ in I_4;
3. The parser has been asked to carry out a reduction by $A \rightarrow \in$ in I_0 on those terminals associated with the item $A \rightarrow .$ in I_0, and carry out the reduction $A \rightarrow \in$ in I_4 on those terminals associated with the item $A \rightarrow .$ in I_4;

then there would have been no conflict and the parser would have been more powerful. But this requires associating a list of terminals (lookaheads) with the items. You may recall (see Chapter 4) that lookaheads are symbols that the parser uses to 'look ahead' in the input buffer to decide whether or not reduction is to be done. That is, we have to work with items of the form $A \rightarrow \alpha.X\beta,\ a$. The item a is called as an LR(1) item, because the length of the lookahead is one; therefore, an item without a lookahead is one with lookahead of length of zero, hence LR(0) item. In the SLR method, we were working with LR(0) items. Therefore, we define an LR(k) item to be an item using lookaheads of length k. So, an LR(1) item is comprised of two parts: the LR(0) item and the lookahead associated with the item.

NOTE *We conclude that if we work with LR(1) items instead of using LR(0) items, then every state of the parser will correspond to a set of LR(1) items. When the parser looks ahead in the input buffer to decide whether reduction is to be done or not, the information about the terminals will be available in the state of the parser itself, which is not the case with the SLR parser state. Hence, with LR(1), we get a more powerful parser.*

Therefore, if we modify the closure and the goto functions to work suitably with the LR(1) items, by allowing them to compute the lookaheads, we can obtain the canonical collection of sets of LR(1). And from this we can obtain the parsing Action|GOTO table. For example, closure(I), where I is a set of LR(1) items, is computed as follows:

1. Add every item in I to closure(I).
2. Repeat

   For every item of the form $A \rightarrow \alpha.B\beta,\ a$ in closure(I) do

   For every production $B \rightarrow \gamma$ do

   Add $B \rightarrow .\gamma$, FIRST(βa) to closure(I)

/* because the reduction by $B \rightarrow \gamma$ generates B preceding β in the right side of $A \rightarrow \alpha B\beta$; and hence, the reduction by $B \rightarrow \gamma$ is proper only on those symbols that are in the FIRST(β). But if β derives to an empty string, then a will also follow B, and the lookaheads of $B \rightarrow \gamma$ will therefore be FIRST(βa).

until no new item can be added to closure(I)

For example, consider the following grammar:

$$S \rightarrow E$$
$$E \rightarrow E + T \mid T$$
$$T \rightarrow T * F \mid F$$
$$F \rightarrow \text{id}$$

The closure($\{S \rightarrow .E, \$\}$) = { $S \rightarrow .E, \$$
$E \rightarrow .E + T, \$ \mid +$
$E \rightarrow .T, \$ \mid +$
$T \rightarrow .T*F, \$ \mid + \mid *$
$T \rightarrow .F, \$ \mid + \mid *$
$F \rightarrow .\text{id}, \$ \mid + \mid *$
}

goto(I, X) = closure($\{A \rightarrow \alpha X.\beta, a \mid A \rightarrow \alpha.X\beta, a \text{ is in } I\}$)

That is, to find out goto from I on X, first identify all the items in I with a dot preceding X in the LR(0) section of the item. Then, move the dot in all the selected items one position to the right (i.e., over X), and then take this new set's closure. For example:

if set I = { $S \rightarrow .E., \$$
$E \rightarrow .E + T, \$ \mid +$
$E \rightarrow .T, \$ \mid +$
$T \rightarrow .T*F, \$ \mid + \mid *$
$T \rightarrow .F, \$ \mid + \mid *$
$F \rightarrow .\text{id}, \$ \mid + \mid *$
}

then goto(I, E) = closure ({ $S \rightarrow E., \$$
$E \rightarrow E. + T, \$ \mid +$
}
) = { $S \rightarrow E., \$$
$E \rightarrow E. +T, \$ \mid +$
}

5.4.4 An Algorithm for Finding the Canonical Collection of Sets of LR(1) Items

/* Let C be the canonical collection of sets of LR(1) items. We maintain C_{new} and C_{old} to continue the iterations */

Input : augmented grammar

Output: canonical collection of sets of LR(1) items (i.e., set C)

1. $C_{old} = \varphi$
2. add closure($\{S_1 \rightarrow .S, \$\}$) to C
3. while $C_{old} \neq C_{new}$ do

temp = $C_{new} - C_{old}$
$C_{old} = C_{new}$
for every I in temp do
for every X in $V \cup T$ (i.e., for every grammar symbol X) do
if goto(I, X) is not empty and not in C_{new}, then
add goto(I, X) to C_{new}
}

4. $C = C_{new}$

For example, consider the following grammar:

$$S \rightarrow AaAb$$
$$S \rightarrow BbBa$$
$$A \rightarrow \in$$
$$B \rightarrow \in$$

The augmented grammar will be:

$$S_1 \rightarrow S$$
$$S \rightarrow AaAb$$
$$S \rightarrow BbBa$$
$$A \rightarrow \in$$
$$B \rightarrow \in$$

The canonical collection of sets of LR(1) items are computed as follows:

I_0 = closure ({$S_1 \rightarrow .S$, \$}) = { $S_1 \rightarrow .S$, \$
$S \rightarrow .AaAb$, \$
$S \rightarrow .BbBa$, \$
$A \rightarrow .$, a
$B \rightarrow .$, b
}

goto({I_0, S}) = closure({$S_1 \rightarrow S.$, \$}) = { $S_1 \rightarrow S.$, \$ } = I_1
goto({I_0, A}) = closure({$S \rightarrow A.aAb$, \$}) = { $S \rightarrow A.aAb$, \$ } = I_2
goto({I_0, B}) = closure({$S \rightarrow B.bBa$, \$}) = { $S \rightarrow B.bBa$, \$ } = I_3
goto({I_2, a}) = closure({$S \rightarrow Aa.Ab$, \$}) = { $S \rightarrow Aa.Ab$, \$
$A \rightarrow .$, b
} = I_4
goto({I_3, b}) = closure({$S \rightarrow Bb.Ba$, \$}) = { $S \rightarrow Bb.Ba$, \$
$B \rightarrow .$, a
} = I_5

$$\text{goto}(\{I_4, A\}) = \text{closure}(\{S \rightarrow AaA.b, \$\}) = \{\ S \rightarrow AaA.b, \$\} = I_6$$
$$\text{goto}(\{I_5, B\}) = \text{closure}(\{S \rightarrow BbB.a, \$\}) = \{\ S \rightarrow BbB.a, \$\} = I_7$$
$$\text{goto}(\{I_6, b\}) = \text{closure}(\{S \rightarrow AaAb., \$\}) = \{\ S \rightarrow AaAb., \$\} = I_8$$
$$\text{goto}(\{I_7, a\}) = \text{closure}(\{S \rightarrow BbBa., \$\}) = \{\ S \rightarrow BbBa., \$\} = I_9$$

The transition diagram of the DFA is shown in Figure 5.6.

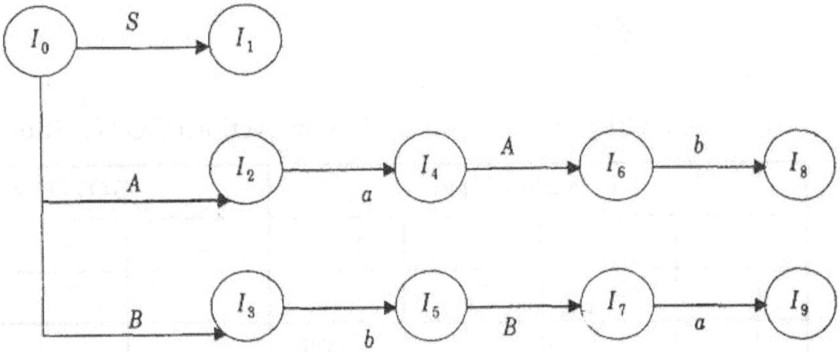

FIGURE 5.6 Transition diagram for the canonical collection of sets of LR(1) items.

5.4.5 Construction of the Action and GOTO Table for the LR(1) Parser

The following steps will construct the parsing action table for the LR(1) parser:

1. for every state I_i in C do
   for every terminal symbol a do
   if goto(I_i, a) = I_j then
   make action[I_i, a] = S_j /*for shift and enter into the state j*/
2. for every state I_i in C whose underlying set of LR(1) items contains an item of the form $A \rightarrow \alpha.$, a do
   make action[I_i, a] = R_k /*where k is the number of the production $A \rightarrow \alpha$, standing for reduce by $A \rightarrow \alpha$ */
3. make [I_i, \$] = accept if I_i contains an item $S_1 \rightarrow S.$, \$

The goto table is simply a mapping of transitions in the DFA on nonterminals. Therefore, it is constructed as follows:

for every I_i in C do
for every nonterminal A do
if goto (I_i, A) = I_j then
make goto[I_i, A] = j

This method is called as CLR(1) or LR(1), and is more powerful than SLR(1). Therefore, the CLR or LR parsing table for the grammar having the following productions is:

$$S_1 \rightarrow S$$
$$S \rightarrow AaAb$$
$$S \rightarrow BbBa$$
$$A \rightarrow \in$$
$$B \rightarrow \in$$

TABLE 5.7 CLR/LR Parsing Action | GOTO Table

	Action Table			GOTO Table		
	a	*b*	$	*S*	*A*	*B*
I_0	R_3	R_4		1	2	3
I_1			Accept			
I_2	S_4					
I_3		S_5				
I_4		R_3			6	
I_5	R_4					7
I_6		S_8				
I_7	S_9					
I_8			R_1			
I_9			R_2			

where productions are numbered as follows:

$$S \rightarrow AaAb \quad (1)$$
$$S \rightarrow BbBa \quad (2)$$
$$A \rightarrow \in \quad (3)$$
$$B \rightarrow \in \quad (4)$$

By comparing the SLR(1) parser with the CLR(1) parser, we find that the CLR(1) parser is more powerful. But the CLR(1) has a greater number of states than the SLR(1) parser; hence, its storage requirement is also greater than the SLR(1) parser. Therefore, we can devise a parser that is an intermediate between the two; that is, the parser's power will be in between that of SLR(1) and CLR(1), and its storage requirement will be the same as SLR(1)'s. Such a parser, LALR(1), will be much more useful: since each of its states corresponds to the set of LR(1) items, the information about the lookaheads is available in the state itself, making it more powerful than the SLR parser. But a state of the LALR(1) parser is obtained by combining those states of the CLR parser that have identical LR(0) (core) items, but which differ in the lookaheads in their item set representations. Therefore, even if there is no reduce-reduce conflict in the states of the CLR parser that has been combined to form an LALR parser, a conflict may get generated in the state of LALR parser. We may be able to obtain a CLR parsing table without multiple entries for a grammar, but when we construct the LALR parsing table for the same grammar, it might have multiple entries.

5.4.6 Construction of the LALR Parsing Table

The steps in constructing an LALR parsing table are as follows:

1. Obtain the canonical collection of sets of LR(1) items.
2. If more than one set of LR(1) items exists in the canonical collection obtained that have identical cores or LR(0)s, but which have different lookaheads, then combine these sets of LR(1) items to obtain a reduced collection, C_1, of sets of LR(1) items.
3. Construct the parsing table by using this reduced collection, as follows.

Construction of the Action Table

1. for every state I_i in C_1 do

    for every terminal symbol a do

    if goto(I_i, a) = I_j then

    make action[I_i, a] = S_j /*for shift and enter into the state j*/

2. for every state I_i in C_1 whose underlying set of LR(1) items contains an item of the form $A \rightarrow \alpha.$, a, do

    make action[I_i, a] = R_k /*where k is the number of the production $A \rightarrow \alpha$ standing for reduce by $A \rightarrow \alpha$ */

3. make [I_i, \$] = accept if I_i contains an item $S_1 \rightarrow S.$, \$

Construction of the Goto Table

The goto table simply maps transitions on nonterminals in the DFA. Therefore, the table is constructed as follows:

for every I_i in C_1 do
for every nonterminal A do
if goto(I_i, A) = I_j then
make goto(I_i, A) = j

For example, consider the following grammar:

$$S \rightarrow AA$$
$$A \rightarrow aA$$
$$A \rightarrow b$$

The augmented grammar is:

$$S_1 \rightarrow S$$
$$S \rightarrow AA$$
$$A \rightarrow aA$$
$$A = b$$

The canonical collection of sets of LR(1) items are computed as follows:

I_0 = closure ({$S_1 \rightarrow .S$, \$}) = {$S_1 \rightarrow .S$, \$
$S \rightarrow .AA$, \$
$A \rightarrow .aA$, a/b
$A \rightarrow .b$, a/b
}

goto(I_0, S) = closure({$S_1 \rightarrow S.$, \$}) = { $S_1 \rightarrow S.$, \$} = I_1

goto(I_0, A) = closure({$S \rightarrow A.A$, \$}) = { $S \rightarrow A.A$, \$
$A \rightarrow .aA$, \$
$A \rightarrow .b$, \$
}= I_2

goto(I_0, a) = closure({$A \rightarrow a.A$, a/b}) = { $A \rightarrow a.A$, a/b
$A \rightarrow .aA$, a/b
$A \rightarrow .b$, a/b
} = I_3

goto(I_0, b) = closure({$A \rightarrow b.$, a/b}) = { $A \rightarrow b.$, a/b
} = I_4

goto(I_2, A) = closure({$S \rightarrow AA.$, \$}) = { $S \rightarrow AA.$, \$
} = I_5

$goto(I_2, a) = closure(\{A \rightarrow a.A, \$\}) = \{ A \rightarrow a.A, \$$
$A \rightarrow .aA, \$$
$A \rightarrow .b, \$$
$\} = I_6$

$goto(I_2, b) = closure(\{A \rightarrow b., \$\}) = \{ A \rightarrow b., \$$
$\} = I_7$

$goto(I_3, A) = closure(\{A \rightarrow aA., a/b\}) = \{ A \rightarrow aA., a/b$
$\} = I_8$

$goto(I_3, a) = closure(\{A \rightarrow a.A, a/b\}) = \{ A \rightarrow a.A, a/b$
$A \rightarrow .aA, a/b$
$A \rightarrow .b, a/b$
$\} =$ same as I_3

$goto(I_3, b) = closure(\{A \rightarrow b., a/b\}) = \{ A \rightarrow b., a/b$
$\} =$ same as I_4

$goto(I_6, A) = closure(\{A \rightarrow aA., \$\}) = \{ A \rightarrow aA., \$$
$\} = I_9$

$goto(I_6, a) = closure(\{A \rightarrow a.A, \$\}) = \{ A \rightarrow a.A, \$$
$A \rightarrow .aA, \$$
$A \rightarrow .b, \$$
$\} =$ same as I_6

$goto(I_6, b) = closure(\{A \rightarrow b., \$\}) = \{ A \rightarrow b., \$$
$\} =$ same as I_7

We see that the states I_3 and I_6 have identical LR(0) set items that differ only in their lookaheads. The same goes for the pair of states I_4, I_7 and the pair of states I_8, I_9. Hence, we can combine I_3 with I_6, I_4 with I_7, and I_8 with I_9 to obtain the reduced collection shown below:

$I_0 = closure(\{S_1 \rightarrow .S, \$\}) = \{ S_1 \rightarrow .S, \$$
$S \rightarrow .AA, \$$
$A \rightarrow .aA, a/b$
$A \rightarrow .b, a/b$
$\}$

$I_1 = \{ S_1 \rightarrow S., \$ \}$

$I_2 = \{ S \rightarrow A.A, \$$
$A \rightarrow .aA, \$$
$A \rightarrow .b, \$$
$\}$

$$I_{36} = \{ A \rightarrow a.A,\ a/b/\$$$
$$A \rightarrow .aA,\ a/b/\$$$
$$A \rightarrow .b,\ a/b/\$$$
$$\}$$
$$I_{47} = \{ A \rightarrow b.,\ a/b/\$$$
$$\}$$
$$I_5 = \{ S \rightarrow AA.,\ \$$$
$$\}$$
$$I_{89} = \{ A \rightarrow aA.,\ a/b/\$$$
$$\}$$

where I_{36} stands for combination of I_3 and I_6, I_{47} stands for the combination of I_4 and I_7, and I_{89} stands for the combination of I_8 and I_9. The transition diagram of the DFA using the reduced collection is shown in Figure 5.7.

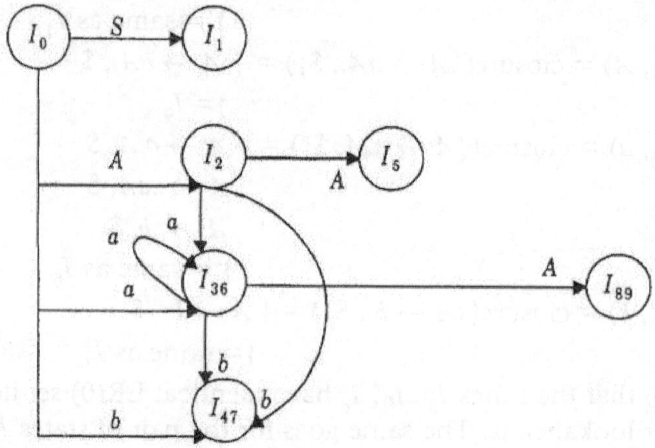

FIGURE 5.7 Transition diagram for a DFA using a reduced collection.

Therefore, Table 5.8 shows the LALR parsing table for the grammar having the following productions:

$$S_1 \rightarrow S$$
$$S \rightarrow AA$$
$$A \rightarrow aA$$
$$A \rightarrow b$$

which are numbered as:

$$A \rightarrow AA \qquad (1)$$
$$A \rightarrow aA \qquad (2)$$
$$A \rightarrow b \qquad (3)$$

TABLE 5.8 LALR Parsing Table for a DFA Using a Reduced Collection

	Action Table			GOTO Table	
	a	b	$\$$	S	A
I_0	S_{36}	S_{47}		1	2
I_1			Accept		
I_2	S_{36}	S_{47}			5
I_{36}	S_{36}	S_{47}			89
I_{47}	R_3	$R3$	R_3		
I_5			R_1		
I_{89}	R_2	R_2	R_2		

5.4.7 Parser Conflicts

An LR parser may encounter two types of conflicts: shift-reduce conflicts and reduce-reduce conflicts.

Shift-Reduce Conflict

A shift-reduce (*S*-*R*) conflict occurs in an SLR parser state if the underlying set of LR(0) item representations contains items of the form depicted in Figure 5.8, and FOLLOW(B) contains terminal a.

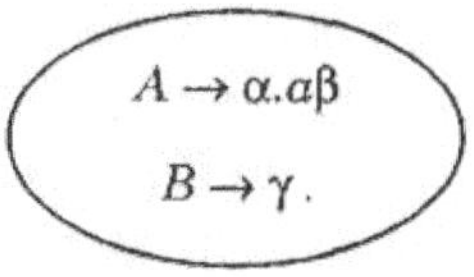

FIGURE 5.8 LR(0) underlying set representations that can cause SLR parser conflicts.

Similarly, an S-R conflict occurs in a state of the CLR or LALR parser if the underlying set of LR(1) items representation contains items of the form shown in Figure 5.9.

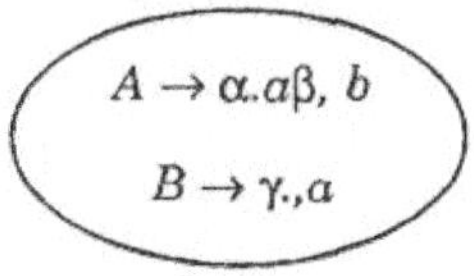

FIGURE 5.9 LR(1) underlying set representations that can cause CLR/LALR parser conflicts.

Reduce-Reduce Conflict

A reduce-reduce (*R-R*) conflict occurs if the underlying set of LR(0) items representation in a state of an SLR parser contains items of the form shown in Figure 5.10, and FOLLOW(*A*) and FOLLOW(*B*) are not disjoint sets.

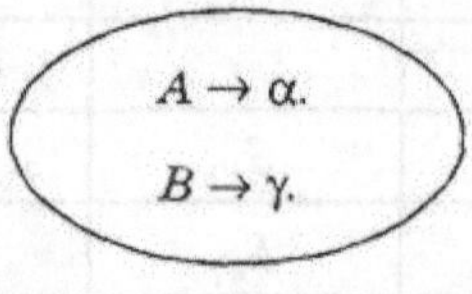

FIGURE 5.10 LR(0) underlying set representations that can cause an SLR parser *reduce-reduce conflict.*

Similarly an *R-R* conflict occurs if the underlying set of LR(1) items representation in a state of a CLR or LALR parser contains items of the form shown in Figure 5.11.

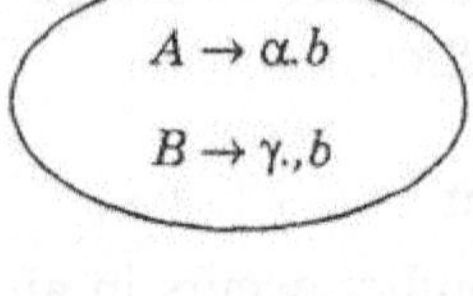

FIGURE 5.11 LR(1) underlying set representations that can cause an CLR/LALR parser.

If a set of items' representation contains only nonfinal items, then there is no conflict in the corresponding state. (An item in which the dot is in the right-most position, like $A \rightarrow XYZ.$, is called as a final item; and an item in which the dot is not in the right-most position, like $A \rightarrow X.YZ$, is a nonfinal item).

Even if there is no *R-R* conflict in the states of a CLR parser, it may be generated in the state of a LALR parser that is obtained by combining the states of the CLR parser. We combine the states of the CLR parser in order to form an LALR state. The items' lookaheads in the LALR parser state are obtained by combining the lookaheads of the corresponding items in the states of the CLR parser. And since reduction depends on the lookaheads, even if there is no *R-R* conflict in the states of the CLR parser, a conflict may become generated in the state of the LALR parser as a result of this state combination. For example, consider the sets of LR(1) items that represent the two different states of the CLR(1) parser, as shown in Figure 5.12.

FIGURE 5.12 Sets of LR(1) items represent two different CLR(1) parser states.

There is no *R-R* conflict in these states. But when we combine these states to form an LALR, the state's set of items representation will be as shown in Figure 5.13.

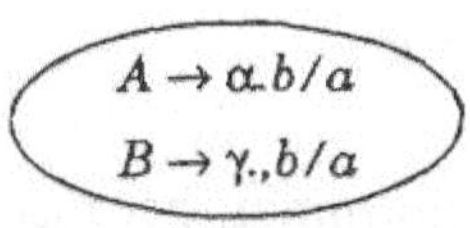

FIGURE 5.13 States are combined to form an LALR.

We see that there is an *R-R* conflict in this state, because the parser will call a reduction by $A \to \alpha$ as well as by $B \to \gamma$ on both *a* and *b*. If there is no *S-R* conflict in the CLR(1) states, it will never be reflected in the LALR(1) state obtained by combining the CLR(1) states. For example consider the sets of LR(1) items representing the two different states of the CLR(1) parser as shown in Figure 5.14.

FIGURE 5.14 LR(1) items represent two different states of the CLR(1) parser.

There is no *S-R* conflict in these states. When we combine these states, the resulting LALR state set will be as shown in Figure 5.15. There is no *S-R* conflict in this state, as well.

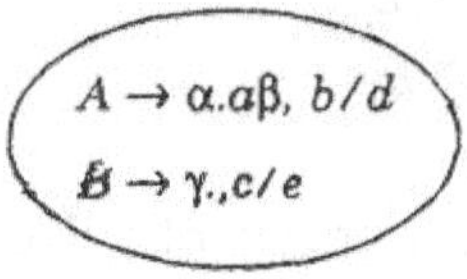

FIGURE 5.15 LALR state set resulting from the combination of CLR(1) state sets.

5.4.8 Handling Ambiguous Grammars

Since every ambiguous grammar fails to be LR, they will not belong to either the SLR, CLR, or LALR grammar classes. But some ambiguous grammars are quite useful for specifying languages. Hence, the question is how to deal with these grammars in the framework of LR parsing. For example, the natural grammar that specifies nonparenthesized expressions with + and * operators is:

$$E \rightarrow E + E$$
$$E \rightarrow E * E$$
$$E \rightarrow \text{id}$$

But this is ambiguous grammar, because the precedence and associations of the operators has not been specified. Even so, we prefer this grammar, because we can easily change the precedence and associations as required, thereby allowing us more flexibility. Similarly, if we use unambiguous grammar instead of the above grammar to specify the same language, it will have the following productions:

$$E \rightarrow E + T \mid T$$
$$T \rightarrow T * F \mid F$$
$$F \rightarrow \text{id}$$

This parser will spend a substantial portion its time in carrying out reductions by the unit productions $E \rightarrow T$ and $T \rightarrow F$. These production are in the grammar to enforce associations and precedence, thereby making the parsing time excessive. With an ambiguous grammar, every LR parser construction method will have conflicts. But these conflicts can be resolved by using the precedence and association information of + and * as per the language's usage. For example, consider the SLR parser construction for the above grammar. The augmented grammar is:

$$S \rightarrow E$$
$$E \rightarrow E + E$$
$$E \rightarrow E * E$$
$$E \rightarrow \text{id}$$

The canonical collection of sets of LR(0) items is shown below:

$$I_0 = \text{closure}(\{S \rightarrow .E\}) = \{\ S \rightarrow .E$$
$$E \rightarrow .E + E$$
$$E \rightarrow .E * E$$
$$E \rightarrow .\text{id}$$
$$\}$$

$$
\begin{aligned}
\text{goto}(I_0, E) = \text{closure}(\{&S \to .E \\
&E \to E. + E \\
&E \to E. * E \\
&\} \\
) = \{\ &S \to .E \\
&E \to E. + E \\
&E \to E. * E \\
&\} = I_1
\end{aligned}
$$

$$
\begin{aligned}
\text{goto}(I_0, \text{id}) = \text{closure}(\{&E \to \text{id}. \\
&\} \\
) = \{\ &E \to \text{id}. \\
&\} = I_2
\end{aligned}
$$

$$
\begin{aligned}
\text{goto}(I_1, +) = \text{closure}(\{&E \to \text{E} +.E \\
&\} \\
) = \{&E \to E + .E \\
&E \to .E + E \\
&E \to .E * E \\
&E \to .\text{id} \\
&\} = I_3
\end{aligned}
$$

$$
\begin{aligned}
\text{goto}(I_1, *) = \text{closure}(\{\ &E \to E *.E \\
&\} \\
) = \{\ &E \to E *. E \\
&E \to .E + E \\
&E \to .E * E \\
&E \to .\text{id} \\
&\} = I_4
\end{aligned}
$$

$$
\begin{aligned}
\text{goto}(I_1, \text{id}) = \text{closure}(\{&E \to \text{id}. \\
&\} \\
) = \{\ &E \to \text{id}. \\
&\} = \text{same as } I_2
\end{aligned}
$$

$$
\begin{aligned}
\text{goto}(I_3, E\,) = \text{closure}(\{\ &E \to E + E. \\
&E \to E. + E \\
&E \to E. * E \\
&\}
\end{aligned}
$$

$$
\begin{aligned}
&) = \{\ E \rightarrow E + E. \\
&\qquad E \rightarrow E. + E \\
&\qquad E \rightarrow E. * E \\
&\qquad \} = I_5 \\
\text{goto}(I_1, \text{id}) &= \text{closure}(\{E \rightarrow \text{id}. \\
&\qquad \} \\
&) = \{E \rightarrow \text{id}. \\
&\qquad \} = \text{same as } I_2 \\
\text{goto}(I_4, E) &= \text{closure}(\{\ E \rightarrow E * E. \\
&\qquad E \rightarrow E. + E \\
&\qquad E \rightarrow E. * E \\
&\qquad \} \\
&) = \{E \rightarrow E * E. \\
&\qquad E \rightarrow E. + E \\
&\qquad E \rightarrow E. * E \\
&\qquad \} = I_6 \\
\text{goto}(I_4, \text{id}) &= \text{closure}(\{E \rightarrow \text{id}. \\
&\qquad \} \\
&) = \{\ E \rightarrow \text{id}. \\
&\qquad \} = \text{same as } I_2 \\
\text{goto}(I_5, +) &= \text{closure}(\ \{\ E \rightarrow E + .E \\
&\qquad \} \\
&) = \{\ E \rightarrow E + .E \\
&\qquad E \rightarrow .E + E \\
&\qquad E \rightarrow .E * E \\
&\qquad E \rightarrow .\text{id} \\
&\qquad \} = \text{same as } I_3 \\
\text{goto}(I_5, *) &= \text{closure}(\{\ E \rightarrow E * .E \\
&\qquad \} \\
&) = \{\ E \rightarrow E * .E \\
&\qquad E \rightarrow .E + E \\
&\qquad E \rightarrow .E * E \\
&\qquad E \rightarrow .\text{id} \\
&\qquad \} = \text{same as } I_4
\end{aligned}
$$

$$
\begin{aligned}
\text{goto}(I_6, +) = \text{closure}(\{ & E \rightarrow E +. E \\
& \} \\
) = \{ & E \rightarrow E + .E \\
& E \rightarrow .E + E \\
& E \rightarrow .E * E \\
& E \rightarrow .\text{id} \\
\} & = \text{same as } I_3 \\
\text{goto}(I_6, *) = \text{closure}(\{ & E \rightarrow E *.E \\
& \} \\
) = \{ & E \rightarrow E * .E \\
& E \rightarrow .E + E \\
& E \rightarrow .E * E \\
& E \rightarrow .\text{id} \\
\} & = \text{same as } I_4
\end{aligned}
$$

The transition diagram of the DFA for the augmented grammar is shown in Figure 5.16. The SLR parsing table is shown in Table 5.9.

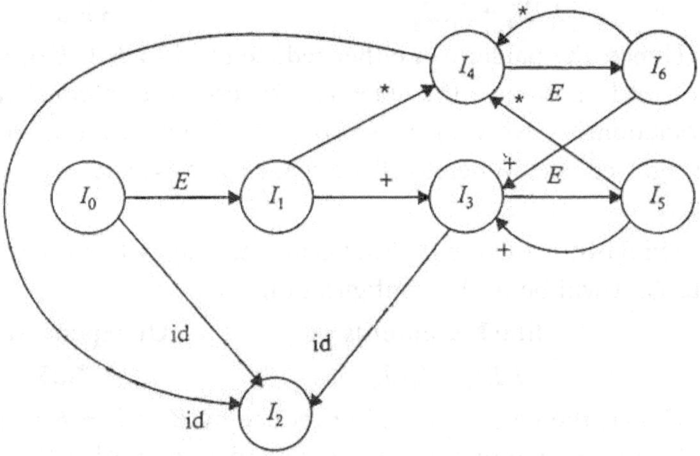

FIGURE 5.16 Transition diagram for augmented grammar DFA.

TABLE 5.9 SLR Parsing Table for Augmented Grammar

Action Table					GOTO Table
	+	*	id	\$	E
I_0			S_2		1
I_1	S_3	S_4		accept	
I_2	R_3	R_3		R_3	
I_3			S_2		5
I_4			S_2		6
I_5	S_3/R_1	S_4/R_1		R_1	
I_6	S_3/R_2	S_4/R_2		R_2	

We see that there are shift-reduce conflicts in I_5 and I_6 on + as well as *. Therefore, for an input string id + id + id\$, when the parser enters into the state I_5, the parser will be in the configuration:

Stack Contents	Unexpended Input
$I_0EI_1 + I_3EI_5$	+id\$

Hence, the parser can either reduce by $E \rightarrow E + E$ or shift the + onto the stack and enter into the state I_3. To resolve this conflict, we make use of associations. If we want left-associativity, then a reduction by $E \rightarrow E + E$ is the right choice. Whereas if we want right-associativity, then shift is a right choice.

Similarly, if the input string is id + id * id\$ when the parser enters into the state I_5, it will be in the configuration:

Stack Contents	Unexpended Input
$I_0EI_1 + I_3EI_5$	*id\$

Hence, the parser can either reduce by $E \rightarrow E + E$ or shift the * onto the stack and enter into the state I_4 in order to resolve this conflict. We must make use of precedence if we want a higher precedence for + then the reduction by $E \rightarrow E + E$. If we want a higher precedence for *, then shift is a right choice.

Similarly if the input string is id * id + id\$ when the parser enters into the state I_6, it will be in the configuration:

Stack Contents	Unexpended Input
$I_0EI_1 * I_4EI_6$	+id\$

Hence, the parser can either reduce by $E \rightarrow E * E$ or shift the + onto the stack and enter into the state I_3 in order to resolve this conflict. We have to make use of precedence if we want a higher precedence for *; then reduction by $E \rightarrow E * E$ is a right choice. Whereas if we want a higher precedence for +, then shift is right choice.

Similarly, if the input string is id * id * id$ when the parser enters into the state $I6$, the parser will be in the configuration:

Stack Contents	**Unexpended Input**
$I_0EI_1 * I_4EI_6$	*id$

The parser can either reduce by $E \rightarrow E * E$ or shift the * onto the stack and enter into the state I_4. To resolve this conflict, we have to make use of associations. If we want left-associativity, then a reduction by $E \rightarrow E * E$ is a right choice. If we want right-associativity, then shift is a right choice.

Therefore, for a higher precedence to *, and for left-associ^tivity for both + and *, we get the SLR parsing table shown in Table 5.10.

TABLE 5.10 SLR Parsing Table Reflects Higher Precedence and Left-Associativity

	Action Table				**GOTO Table**
	+	*	id	$	E
I_0			S_2		1
I_1	S_3	S_4		Accept	
I_2	R_3	R_3		R_3	
I_3			S_2		5
I_4			S_2		6
I_5	R_1	S_4		R_1	
I_6	R_2	R_2		R_2	

Therefore, we have a way to deal with ambiguous grammars. We can make use of disambiguiting rules to resolve parsing action conflicts.

5.5 DATA STRUCTURES FOR REPRESENTING PARSING TABLES

Since there are only a few entries in the goto table, separate data structures must be used for the action table and the goto table. These data structures are described below.

Representing the Action Table

One of the simplest ways to represent the action table is to use a two-dimensional array. But since many rows of the action table are identical, we can save considerable space (and expend a negligible cost in processing time) by creating an array of pointers for each state. Then, pointers for states with the same actions will point to the same location, as shown in Figure 5.17.

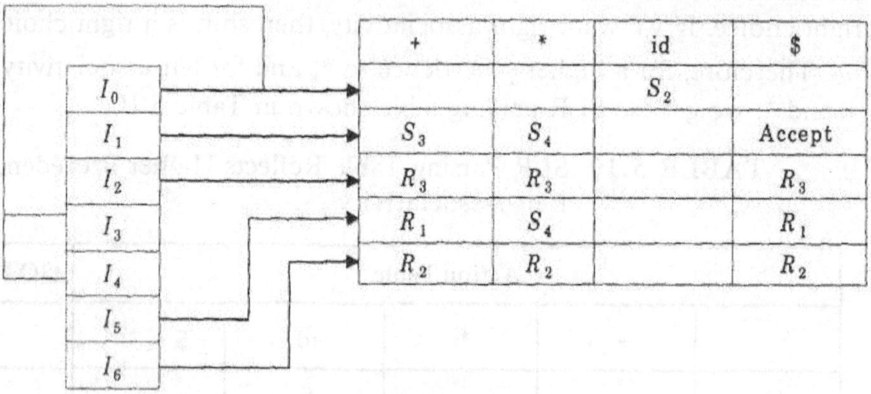

FIGURE 5.17 States with actions in common point to the same location via an array.

To access information, we assign each terminal a number from zero to one less than the number of terminals. We use this integer as an offset from the pointer value for each state. Further reduction in the space is possible at the expense of speed by creating a list of actions for each state. Each node on a list will be comprised of a terminal symbol and the action for that terminal symbol. It is here that the most frequent actions, like error actions, can be appended at the end of the list. For example, for the state I_0 in Table 5.10, the list will be as shown in Figure 5.18.

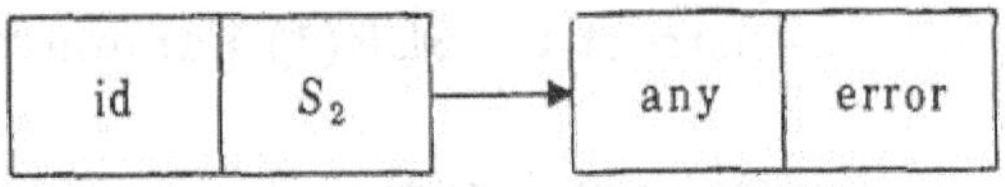

FIGURE 5.18 List that incorporates the ability to append actions.

Representing the GOTO Table

An efficient way to represent the goto table is to make a list of pairs for each nonterminal A. Each pair is of the form:

(current-state, goto(current-state, A))

Since the error entries in the goto table are never consulted, we can replace each error entry by the most common nonerror entry **in its column is represented by any in place of current-state.**

5.6 WHY LR PARSING IS ATTRACTIVE

There are several reasons why LR parsers are attractive:

1. An LR parser can be constructed to recognize virtually all programming language constructs for which a CFG can be written.
2. The LR parsing method is the most general, nonbacktracking shift-reduce method known. Yet it can be implemented as efficiently as any other method.
3. The class of grammars that can be parsed by using the LR method is a proper superset of the class of grammars that can be parsed with a predictive parser.
4. The LR parser can quickly detect a syntactic error while left-to-right scanning of input.

The main drawback of the LR method is that it is too much work to construct an LR parser by hand for a typical programming language grammar. But fortunately, many LR parser generators are available that automatically generate the required LR parser.

5.7 EXAMPLES

The examples that follow further illustrate the concepts covered within this chapter.

EXAMPLE 5.3: Construct an SLR(1) parsing table for the following grammar:

$$S \rightarrow xAy \mid xBy \mid xAz$$
$$A \rightarrow aS \mid q$$
$$B \rightarrow q$$

First, augment the given grammar by adding a production $S1 \rightarrow S$ to the grammar. Therefore, the augmented grammar is:

$$S_1 \rightarrow S$$
$$S \rightarrow xAy \mid xBy \mid xAz$$
$$A \rightarrow aS \mid q$$
$$B \rightarrow q$$

Next, we obtain the canonical collection of sets of LR(0) items, as follows:

$$\text{closure}(\{S_1 \rightarrow .S\}) = \{\ S_1 \rightarrow .S,\ S \rightarrow .xAy,\ S \rightarrow .xBy,\ S \rightarrow .xAz\ \} = I_0$$

$$\text{goto}(I_0, S) = \text{closure}(\{S_1 \rightarrow S.\}) = \{\ S_1 \rightarrow S.\ \} = I_1$$

$$\text{goto}(I_0, x) = \text{closure}(\{S \rightarrow x.Ay,\ S \rightarrow x.By,\ S \rightarrow x.Az\}) = \{S \rightarrow x.Ay,\ S \rightarrow x.By,\ S \rightarrow x.Az,\ A \rightarrow .qS,\ A \rightarrow .q,\ B \rightarrow .q\ \} = I_2$$

$$\text{goto}(I_2, A) = \text{closure}(\{\ S \rightarrow xA.y,\ S \rightarrow xA.z\ \}) = \{\ S \rightarrow xA.y,\ S \rightarrow xA.z\ \} = I_3$$

$$\text{goto}(I_2, B) = \text{closure}(\{S \rightarrow xB.y\ \}) = \{\ S \rightarrow xB.y\ \} = I_4$$

$$\text{goto}(I_2, q) = \text{closure}(\{A \rightarrow q.S,\ A \rightarrow q.$$

$$
\begin{aligned}
B \to q.\}) = \{\ & A \to q.S \\
& A \to q. \\
& B \to q. \\
& S \to .xAy \\
& S \to .xBy \\
& S \to .xAz \\
\}\ & = I_5
\end{aligned}
$$

$$
\begin{aligned}
&\text{goto}(I_3, y) = \text{closure}(\{S \to xAy.\}) = \{\ S \to xAy.\ \} = I_6 \\
&\text{goto}(I_3, z) = \text{closure}(\{S \to xAz.\ \}) = \{\ S \to xAz.\ \} = I_7 \\
&\text{goto}(I_4, y) = \text{closure}(\{S \to xBy.\}) = \{\ S \to xBy.\ \} = I_8 \\
&\text{goto}(I_5, S) = \text{closure}(\{A \to qS.\}) = \{\ A \to qS.\ \} = I_9 \\
&\text{goto}(I_5, x) = \text{closure}(\{\ S \to x.Ay \\
&\qquad\qquad\qquad\qquad\qquad S \to x.By \\
&\qquad\qquad\qquad\qquad\qquad S \to x.Az \\
&\qquad\qquad\qquad\qquad\qquad \}) = I_2
\end{aligned}
$$

The transition diagram of this DFA is shown in Figure 5.19.

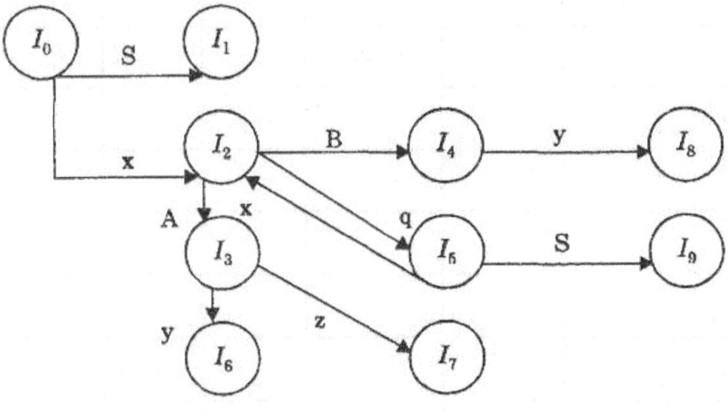

FIGURE 5.19 Transition diagram for the canonical collection of sets of LR(0) items in Example 5.3.

The FOLLOW sets of the various nonterminals are FOLLOW(S_1) = {\$}. Therefore:

1. Using $S_1 \to S$, we get FOLLOW(S) = FOLLOW(S_1) = {\$}
2. Using $S \to xAy$, we get FOLLOW(A) = $\{y\}$
3. Using $S \to xBy$, we get FOLLOW(B) = $\{y\}$
4. Using $S \to xAz$, we get FOLLOW(A) = $\{z\}$

Therefore, FOLLOW(A) = {y, z}. Using $A \rightarrow qS$, we get FOLLOW(S) = FOLLOW(A) = {y, z}. Therefore, FOLLOW(S) = {y, z, \$}. Let the productions of the grammar be numbered as follows:

$$S \rightarrow xAy \quad (1)$$
$$S \rightarrow xBy \quad (2)$$
$$S \rightarrow xAz \quad (3)$$
$$A \rightarrow qS \quad (4)$$
$$A \rightarrow q \quad (5)$$
$$B \rightarrow q \quad (6)$$

The SLR parsing table for the productions above is shown in Table 5.11.

TABLE 5.11 SLR(1) Parsing Table

	Action Table					GOTO Table		
	x	y	z	q	\$	S	A	B
I_0	S_2					1		
I_1			Accept					
I_2				S_5			3	4
I_3		S_6	S_7					
I_4		S_8						
I_5	S_2	R_5/R_6	R_5			9		
I_6		R_1	R_1		R_1			
I_7		R_3	R_3		R_3			
I_8		R_2	R_2		R_2			
I_9		R_4	R_4					

EXAMPLE 5.4: Construct an SLR(1) parsing table for the following grammar:

$$S \rightarrow 0S0 \mid 1S1 \mid 10$$

First, augment the given grammar by adding the production $S_1 \rightarrow S$ to the grammar. The augmented grammar is:

$$S_1 \rightarrow S$$
$$S \rightarrow 0S0 \mid 1S1 \mid 10$$

Next, we obtain the canonical collection of sets of LR(0) items, as follows:

$$\text{closure}(\{S_1 \rightarrow .S\}) = \{\ S1 \rightarrow .S \\ S \rightarrow .0S0 \\ S \rightarrow .1S1 \\ S \rightarrow .10 \\ \} = I_0$$

$$\text{goto}(I_0, S) = \text{closure}(\{S_1 \rightarrow S.\}) = \{S_1 \rightarrow S.\} = I_1$$

$$\text{goto}(I_0, 0) = \text{closure}(\{S \rightarrow 0.S0\}) = \{\ S \rightarrow 0.S0 \\ S \rightarrow .0S0 \\ S \rightarrow .1S1 \\ S \rightarrow .10 \\ \} = I_2$$

$$\text{goto}(I_0, 1) = \text{closure}(\{\ S \rightarrow 1.S1 \\ S \rightarrow 1.0 \\ \}) = \{S \rightarrow 1.S1 \\ S \rightarrow 1.0 \\ S \rightarrow .0S0 \\ S \rightarrow .1S1 \\ S \rightarrow .10\} = I_3$$

$$\text{goto}(I_2, S) = \text{closure}(\{S \rightarrow 0S.0\}) = \{\ S \rightarrow 0S.0\ \} = I_4$$

$$\text{goto}(I_2, 0) = \text{closure}(\{S \rightarrow 0.S0 \\ \}) = I_2$$

$$\text{goto}(I_2, 1) = \text{closure}(\{S \rightarrow 1.S1 \\ S \rightarrow 1.0 \\ \}) = I_3$$

$$\text{goto}(I_3, S) = \text{closure}(\{S \rightarrow 1S.1 \\ \}) = I_5$$

$$\text{goto}(I_3, 0) = \text{closure}(\{S \rightarrow 10. \\ S \rightarrow 0.S0$$

$$
\begin{aligned}
&\}) = \{S \rightarrow 10.\\
&\quad S \rightarrow 0.S0\\
&\quad S \rightarrow .0S0\\
&\quad S \rightarrow .1S1\\
&\quad S \rightarrow .10\\
&\} = I_6
\end{aligned}
$$

$$
\begin{aligned}
\text{goto}(I_3, 1) &= \text{closure}(\{\ S \rightarrow 1S.1\\
&\qquad S \rightarrow 1.0\\
&\quad \}) = I_3\\
\text{goto}(I_4, 0) &= \text{closure}(\{S \rightarrow 0S0.\\
&\quad \}) = I_7\\
\text{goto}(I_5, 1) &= \text{closure}(\{S \rightarrow 1S1.\\
&\quad \}) = I_8\\
\text{goto}(I_6, S) &= \text{closure}(\{S \rightarrow 0S.0\\
&\quad \}) = I_4\\
\text{goto}(I_6, 0) &= \text{closure}(\{S \rightarrow 0.S0\\
&\quad \}) = I_2\\
\text{goto}(I_6, 1) &= \text{closure}(\{S \rightarrow 1.S1\\
&\qquad S \rightarrow 1.0\\
&\quad \}) = I_3
\end{aligned}
$$

The transition diagram of the DFA is shown in Figure 5.20.

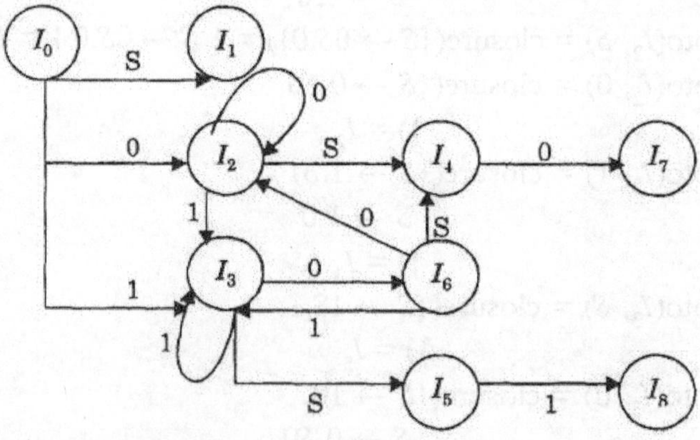

FIGURE 5.20 DFA transition diagram for Example 5.4.

The FOLLOW sets of the various nonterminals are FOLLOW(S_1) = {\$}. Therefore:

1. Using $S_1 \rightarrow S$, we get FOLLOW(S) = FOLLOW(S_1) = {\$}
2. Using $S \rightarrow 0S0$, we get FOLLOW(S) = { 0 }
3. Using $S \rightarrow 1S1$, we get FOLLOW(S) = {1}

So, FOLLOW(S) = {0, 1, \$}. Let the productions be numbered as follows:

$$S \rightarrow 0S0 \qquad \text{(I)}$$
$$S \rightarrow 1S1 \qquad \text{(II)}$$
$$S \rightarrow 10 \qquad \text{(III)}$$

The SLR parsing table for the production set above is shown in Table 5.12.

TABLE 5.12 SLR Parsing Table for Example 5.4

	Action Table		GOTO Table	
	0	1	\$	S
I_0	S_2	S_3		1
I_1				accept
I_2	S_2	S_3		4
I_3	S_6	S_3		5
I_4	S_7			
I_5		S_8		
I_6	$S2/R_3$	S_3/R_3	R_3	4
I_7	R_1	R_1		R_1
I_8	R_2	R_2		R_2

EXAMPLE 5.5: Consider the following grammar, and construct the LR(1) parsing table.

$$S \rightarrow aSbS \mid bSaS \mid \epsilon$$

The augmented grammar is:

$$S| \rightarrow S$$
$$S \rightarrow aSbS \mid bSaS \mid \epsilon$$

The canonical collection of sets of LR(1) items is:

I_0 = {
S| → .S, \$
S →. aSbS, \$
S → .bSaS, \$
S → ., \$
}

goto(I_0, S) = {S| → S. , \$ } = I_1

goto(I_0, a) = {S → a.SbS, \$
S → .aSbS, b
S →.bSaS, b
S →., b
} = I_2

goto(I_0, b) = {S → b.SaS, \$
S → .aSbS, a
S → .bSaS, a
S → ., a
} = I_3

goto(I_2, S) = {S→ aS.bS, \$ } = I_4

goto(I2, a) = {S→ a.SbS, b
S → .aSbS, b
S → .bSaS, b
S → ., b
} = I_5

goto(I_2, b) = {S→ b.SaS, b
S →. aSbS, a
S → .bSaS, a
S → ., a
} = I_6

goto(I_3, S) = {S→ bS.aS, \$ } = I_7

goto(I_3, a) = {S→ a.SbS, a
S →. aSbS, b
S → .bSaS, b
S → ., b
} = I_8

goto(I_3, b) = {$S \rightarrow b.SaS, a$
$S \rightarrow .aSbS, a$
$S \rightarrow .bSaS, a$
$S \rightarrow ., a$
} = I_9

goto(I_4, b) = {
$S \rightarrow aSb.S, \$$
$S \rightarrow .aSbS, \$$
$S \rightarrow .bSaS, \$$
$S \rightarrow ., \$$
} = I_{10}

goto(I_5, S) = {$S \rightarrow aS.bS, b$ } = I_{11}
goto(I_5, a) = I_5
goto(I_5, b) = I_6
goto(I_6, S) = { $S \rightarrow bS.aS, b$ } = I_{12}
goto(I_6, a) = I_8
goto(I_6, b) = I_9
goto(I_7, a) = {
$S \rightarrow bSa.S, \$$
$S \rightarrow . aSbS, \$$
$S \rightarrow .bSaS, \$$
$S \rightarrow ., \$$
} = I_{13}

goto(I_8, S) = {$S \rightarrow aS.bS, a$} = I_{14}
goto(I_8, a) = I_5
goto(I_8, b) = I_6
goto(I_9, S) = { $S \rightarrow bS.aS, a$ } = I_{15}
goto(I_9, a) = I_8
goto(I_9, b) = I_9
goto(I_{10}, S) = { $S \rightarrow aSbS., \$$ } = I_{16}
goto(I_{10}, a) = I_2
goto(I_{10}, b) = I_3
goto(I_{11}, b) = {
$S \rightarrow aSb.S, b$
$S \rightarrow . aSbS, b$

$S \rightarrow .bSaS, b$
$S \rightarrow ., b$
$\} = I_{17}$
goto(I_{12}, a) = {
$S \rightarrow bSa.S, b$
$S \rightarrow .aSbS, b$
$S \rightarrow .bSaS, b$
$S \rightarrow ., b$
$\} = I_{18}$
goto(I_{13}, S) = { $S \rightarrow bSaS., \$$ } = I_{19}
goto(I_{13}, a) = I_2
goto(I_{13}, b) = I_3
goto(I_{14}, b) = {
$S \rightarrow aSb.S, a$
$S \rightarrow .aSbS, a$
$S \rightarrow .bSaS, a$
$S \rightarrow ., a$
$\} = I_{20}$
goto(I_{15}, a) = {
$S \rightarrow bSa.S, a$
$S \rightarrow .aSbS, a$
$S \rightarrow .bSaS, a$
$S \rightarrow ., a$
$\} = I_{21}$
goto(I_{17}, S) = { $S \rightarrow aSbS., b$ } = I_{22}
goto(I_{17}, a) = I_5
goto(I_{17}, b) = I_6
goto(I_{18}, S) = { $S \rightarrow bSaS., b$ } = I_{23}
goto(I_{18}, a) = I_5
goto(I_{18}, b) = I_6
goto(I_{20}, S) = { $S \rightarrow aSbS., a$ } = I_{24}
goto(I_{20}, a) = I_8
goto(I_{20}, b) = I_9
goto(I_{21}, S) = { $S \rightarrow bSaS., a$ } = I_{25}
goto(I_{21}, a) = I_8
goto(I_{21}, b) = I_9

The parsing table for the production above is shown in Table 5.13.

TABLE 5.13 Parsing Table for Example 5.5

	Action Table		GOTO Table	
	a	b	$\$$	S
I_0	S_2	S_3	R_3	1
I_1			Accept	
I_2	S_5	S_6/R_3		4
I_3	S_8/R_3	S_9		7
I_4		S_{10}		
I_5	S_5	S_6/R_3		11
I_6	S_8/R_3	S_9		12
I_7	S_{13}			
I_8	S_5	S_6/R_3		14
I_9	S_8/R_3	S_9		15
I_{10}	S_2	S_3	R_3	16
I_{11}		S_{17}		
I_{12}	S_{18}			
I_{13}	S_2	S_3	R_3	19
I_{14}		S_{20}		
I_{15}		S_{21}		
I_{16}			R_1	
I_{17}	S_5	S_6/R_3		22
I_{18}	S_5	S_6/R_3		23
I_{19}			R_2	
I_{20}	S_8/R_3	S_9		24
I_{21}	S_8/R_3	S_9		25
I_{22}		R_1		
I_{23}		R_2		
I_{24}	R_1			
I_{25}	R_2			

The productions for the grammar are numbered as shown below:

$$S \rightarrow aSbS \quad (1)$$
$$S \rightarrow .bSaS \quad (2)$$
$$S \rightarrow \epsilon \quad (3)$$

EXAMPLE 5.6: Construct an LALR(1) parsing table for the following grammar:

$$S \rightarrow Aa \mid bAc \mid dc \mid bda$$
$$A \rightarrow d$$

The augmented grammar is:

$$S| \rightarrow S$$
$$S \rightarrow Aa$$
$$S \rightarrow bAc$$
$$S \rightarrow dc$$
$$S \rightarrow bda$$
$$A \rightarrow d$$

The canonical collection of sets of LR(1) items is:

$I_0 = \{S| \rightarrow .S, \$$
$S \rightarrow .Aa, \$$
$S \rightarrow .bAc, \$$
$S \rightarrow .dc, \$$
$S \rightarrow .bda, \$$
$A \rightarrow .d, a$
$\}$

goto(I_0, S) = $\{S| \rightarrow S., \$ \} = I_1$
goto(I_0, A) = $\{S \rightarrow A.a, \$ \} = I_2$
goto(I_0, b) = $\{S \rightarrow b.Ac, \$$
$S \rightarrow b.da, \$$
$A \rightarrow .d, c$
$\} = I_3$
goto(I_0, d) = $\{S \rightarrow d.c, \$$
$A \rightarrow d., a$
$\} = I_4$
goto(I_2, a) = $\{S \rightarrow Aa., \$ \} = I_5$
goto(I_3, A) = $\{S \rightarrow bA.c, \$ \} = I_6$

$$\text{goto}(I_3, d) = \{\ S \to bd.a,\ \$ \\ A \to d.,\ c \\ \} = I_7$$

$$\text{goto}(I_4, c) = \{\ S \to dc.,\ \$\ \} = I_8$$

$$\text{goto}(I_6, c) = \{\ S \to bAc.,\ \$\ \} = I_9$$

$$\text{goto}(I_7, a) = \{\ S \to bda.,\ \$\ \} = I_{10}$$

There no sets of LR(1) items in the canonical collection that have identical LR(0)-part items and that differ only in their lookaheads. So, the LALR(1) parsing table for the above grammar is as shown in Table 5.14.

TABLE 5.14 LALR(1) Parsing Table for Example 5.5

	Action Table					GOTO Table	
	a	b	c	d	$\$$	S	A
I_0		S_3		S_4		1	2
I_1					Accept		
I_2	S_5						
I_3				S_7		1	
I_4	R_5		S_8				
I_5					R_1		
I_6	S_{10}		S_9				
I_7			R_5				
I_8					R_3		
I_9					R_2		
I_{10}					R_4		

The productions of the grammar are numbered as shown below:

1. $S \to Aa$
2. $S \to bAc$
3. $S \to dc$
4. $S \to bda$
5. $A \to d$

EXAMPLE 5.7: Construct an LALR(1) parsing table for the following grammar:

$$S \rightarrow Aa \mid aAc \mid Bc \mid bBa$$
$$A \rightarrow d$$
$$B \rightarrow d$$

The augmented grammar is:

$$S| \rightarrow S$$
$$S \rightarrow Aa \mid aAc \mid Bc \mid bBa$$
$$A \rightarrow d$$
$$B \rightarrow d$$

The canonical collection of sets of LR(1) items is:

I_0 = {

$S| \rightarrow .S, \$$

$S \rightarrow .Aa, \$$

$S \rightarrow .aAc, \$$

$S \rightarrow .Bc, \$$

$S \rightarrow .bBa\ , \$$

$A \rightarrow .d, a$

$B \rightarrow .d, c$

}

goto(I_0, S) = { $S| \rightarrow S., \$$ } = I_1

goto(I_0, A) = { $S \rightarrow A.a, \$$ } = I_2

goto(I_0, B) = { $S \rightarrow B.c, \$$ } = I_3

goto(I_0, a) = {$S \rightarrow a.Ac, \$$

$A \rightarrow .d, c$

} = I_4

goto(I_0, b) = {

$S \rightarrow b.Ba, \$$

$B \rightarrow .d, a$

} = I_5

goto(I_0, d) = {

$A \rightarrow d., a$

$B \rightarrow d., c$

} = I_6

goto(I_2, a) = {$S \to Aa.$, \$ } = I_7
goto(I_3, c) = {$S \to Bc.$, \$ } = I_8
goto(I_4, A) = {$S \to aA.c$, \$ } = I_9
goto(I_4, d) = {$A \to d.$, c} = I_{10}
goto(I_5, B) = {$S \to bB.a$, \$ } = I_{11}
goto(I_5, d) = {$B \to d.$, a} = I_{12}
goto(I_9, c) = {$S \to aAc.$, \$} = I_{13}
goto(I_{11}, a) = {$S \to bBa.$, \$ } = I_{14}

Since no sets of LR(1) items in the canonical collection have identical LR(0)-part items and differ only in their lookaheads, the LALR(1) parsing table for the above grammar is as shown in Table 5.15.

TABLE 5.15 LALR(1) Parsing Table for Example 5.6

	Action Table					GOTO Table		
	a	b	c	d	\$	S	A	B
I_0	S_4	S_5		S_6		1	2	3
I_1					Accept			
I_2	S_7							
I_3			S_8					
I_4				S_{10}			9	
I_5				S_{12}				11
I_6	R_5		R_6					
I_7					R_1			
I_8					R_3			
I_9			S_{13}					
I_{10}			R_5					
I_{11}	S_{14}							
I_{12}	R_6							
I_{13}					R_2			
I_{14}					R_4			

The productions of the grammar are numbered as shown below:

1. $S \rightarrow Aa$
2. $S \rightarrow aAc$
3. $S \rightarrow Bc$
4. $S \rightarrow bBa$
5. $A \rightarrow d$
6. $B \rightarrow d$

EXAMPLE 5.8: Construct the nonempty sets of LR(1) items for the following grammar:

$$S \rightarrow A$$
$$A \rightarrow AB \mid \in$$
$$B \rightarrow aB \mid b$$

The collection of nonempty sets of LR(1) items is shown in Figure 5.21.

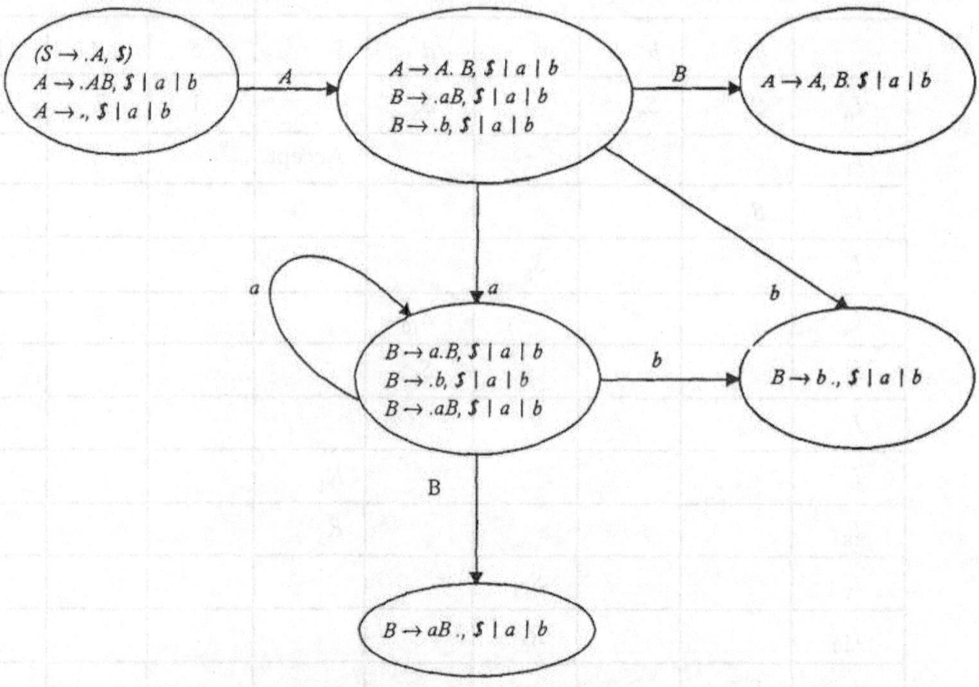

FIGURE 5.21 Collection of nonempty sets of LR(1) items for Example 5.7.

EXERCISE

1. Explain the meaning of the following terms by giving suitable examples:
   (*a*) Handle
   (*b*) Viable prefix
2. Give an example of a grammar that is LL(1), but not SLR(1).
3. A grammar is said to be LR(0), if it can be parsed by LR parser using zero symbols look-ahead. Consider the statement: "Every LR(0) grammar is SLR(1), but vice versa need not necessarily be true". Comment on the truth/falsehood of the statement.
4. A grammar containing left recursion cannot be LL(1), therefore a grammar containing right recursion cannot be LR(1). Comment.
5. What is the advantage of left recursive grammar over right recursive grammar in LR parsing. Explain with suitable example.
6. Consider the following grammar:
   $S \rightarrow aAb$
   $A \rightarrow Aa \mid \epsilon$
   Construct CLR(1)/LR(1) parsing table for the above grammar.
7. Design SLR(1) parser for the grammar of problem 6. if LALR(1) parser is designed for this grammar. How many states the LALR(1) parser will have?
8. "If the grammar is ambiguous then there exist exactly one handle for each right sentential form". Comment.
9. Design LALR(1) parser for the following grammar:
   $S \rightarrow aAd \mid bBd \mid aBc \mid bAc$
   $A \rightarrow e$
   $B \rightarrow e$
10. Design SLR(1) parser for the following grammar.
    $S \rightarrow aAb \mid bB$
    $A \rightarrow Aa \mid \epsilon$
    $B \rightarrow Bb \mid \epsilon$

6 SYNTAX-DIRECTED DEFINITIONS AND TRANSLATIONS

6.1 SPECIFICATION OF TRANSLATIONS

The specification of a construct's translation in a programming language involves specifying what the construct is, as well as specifying the translating rules for the construct. Whenever a compiler encounters that construct in a program, it will translate the construct according to the rules of translation. Here, the term "translation" is used in a much broader sense. Translation does not necessarily mean generating either intermediate code or object code. Translation also involves adding information into the symbol table as well as performing construct-specific computations. For example, if a construct is a declarative statement, then its translation adds information about the construct's type attribute into the symbol table. Whereas, if the construct is an expression, then its translation generates the code for evaluating the expression.

When we specify what the construct is, we specify the syntactic structure of the construct; hence, syntactic specification is the part of the specification of the construct's translation. Therefore, if we suitably extend the notation that we use for syntactic specification so that it will allow for both the syntactic structure and the rules of translation that go along with it, then we can use this notation as a framework for the specification of the construct translation.

Translation of a construct involves manipulating the values of various quantities. For example, when translating the declarative statement ***int a b c*** the compiler needs to extract the type int and add it to the symbol table records of *a, b,* and *c*. This requires that the compiler keep track of the type int, as well as the pointers to the symbol records containing *a, b,* and *c*.

Since we use a context-free grammar to specify the syntactic structure of a programming language, we extend that context-free grammar by associating sets of attributes with the grammar symbols and the set of semantic rules with the productions. These sets hold the values of the quantities, which a compiler is required to track, as well as the associated set of semantic rules specify how the attributed values of the grammar symbols of the production are manipulated. These extensions allow us to specify the translations. Syntax-directed definitions and translation schemes are examples of these extensions of context-free grammars, allowing us to specify the translations.

Syntax-directed definitions use CFG to specify the syntactic structure of the construct. It associates a set of attributes with each grammar symbol; and with each production, it associates a set of semantic rules for computing the values of the attributes of the grammar symbols appearing in that production. Therefore, the grammar and the set of semantic rules constitute syntax-directed definitions.

6.2 IMPLEMENTATION OF THE TRANSLATIONS SPECIFIED BY SYNTAX-DIRECTED DEFINITIONS

Attributes are associated with the grammar symbols that are the labels of the parse tree nodes. They are thus associated with the construct's parse tree. Therefore, when a semantic rule is evaluated, the parser computes the value of an attribute at a parse tree node. For example, a semantic rule could specify the computation of the value of an attribute val that is associated with the grammar symbol *X* (a labeled parse tree node). To refer to the attribute val associated with the grammar symbol *X*, we use the notation *X*.val. Therefore, to evaluate the semantic rules and carry out translations, we must traverse the parse tree and get the values of the attributes at the nodes computed. The order in which we traverse the parse tree nodes depends on the dependencies of the attributes at the parse tree nodes. That is, if an attribute val at a parse tree node *X* depends on the attribute val at the parse tree node *Y*, as shown in Figure 6.1, then the val attribute at node *X* cannot be computed unless the val attribute at *Y* is computed.

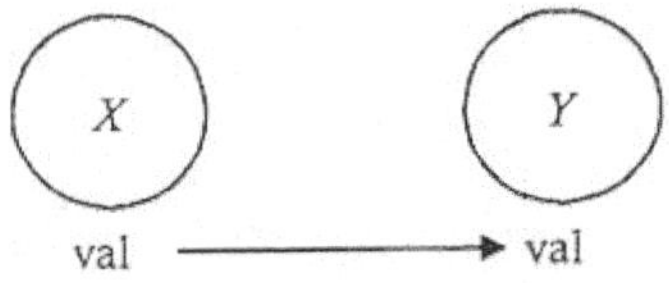

FIGURE 6.1 The attribute value of node X is dependent on the attribute value of node Y.

Hence, carrying out the translation specified by the syntax-directed definitions involves:

1. Generating the parse tree for the input string *w*,
2. Finding out the traversal order of the parse tree nodes by generating a dependency graph and doing a topological sort of that graph, and
3. Traversing the parse tree in the proper order and getting the semantic rules evaluated.

If the parse tree attribute's dependencies are such that an attribute of node *X* depends on the attributes of nodes generated before it in the parse tree-construction process, then it is possible to get *X* s attribute value computed during the parsing itself; the parser is not required to generate an explicit parse tree, and the translations can be carried out along with the parsing. The attributes associated with a grammar symbol are classified into two categories: the synthesized and the inherited attributes of the grammar symbol.

Synthesized Attributes

An attribute is said to be synthesized if its value at a parse tree node is determined by the attribute values at the child nodes. A synthesized attribute has a desirable property; it can be evaluated during a single bottom-up traversal of the parse tree. Synthesized attributes are, in practice, extensively used. Syntax-directed definitions that use synthesized attributes only are shown below:

$E \rightarrow E_1 + T$	E.val : = $E1$.val + T.val
$E \rightarrow T$	E.val : = T.val
$T \rightarrow T_1 * F$	T.val : = $T1$.val * F.val
$T \rightarrow F$	T.val : = F.val
$F \rightarrow id$	F.val : = num.lexval

These definitions specify the translations that must be carried by the expression evaluator. A parse tree, along with the values of the attributes at the nodes (called an "annotated parse tree"), for an expression 2+3*5 is shown in Figure 6.2.

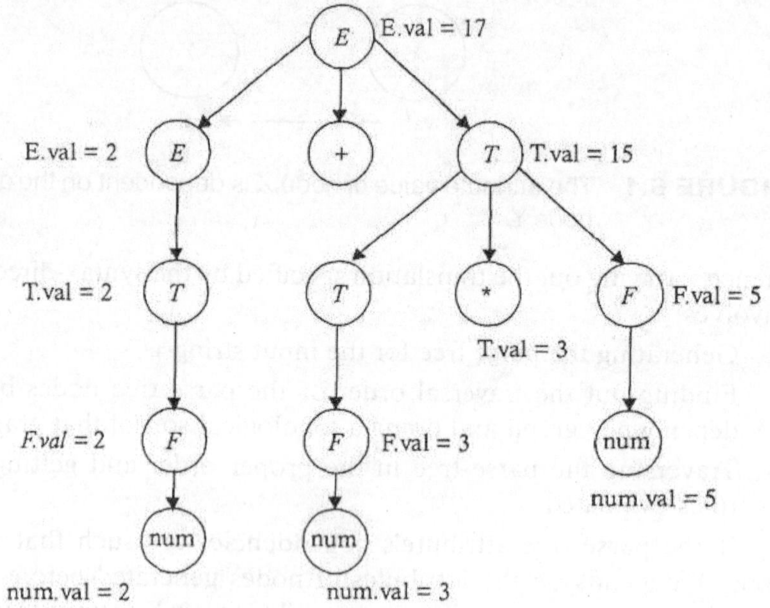

FIGURE 6.2 An annotated parse tree.

Syntax-directed definitions that use synthesized attributes only are known as "*S*-attributed" definitions. If translations are specified using *S*-attributed definitions, then the semantic rules can be conveniently evaluated by the parser itself during the parsing, thereby making translation more efficient. Therefore, *S*-attributed definitions constitute a subclass of the syntax-directed definitions that can be implemented along with parsing.

Inherited Attributes

Inherited attributes are those whose initial value at a node in the parse tree is defined in terms of the attributes of the parent and/or siblings of that node. For example, syntax-directed definitions that use inherited attributes are given below:

$D \rightarrow TL$	*L*.type = *T*.type
$T \rightarrow$ int	*T*.type = int
$T \rightarrow$ real	*T*.type = real
$L \rightarrow L1$.id	*L*1.type = *L*.type enter(id.prt, *L*.type)
$L \rightarrow$ id	enter(id.prt, *L*.type)

A parse tree, along with the attributes' values at the parse tree nodes, for an input string ***int id1,id2,id3*** is shown in Figure 6.3.

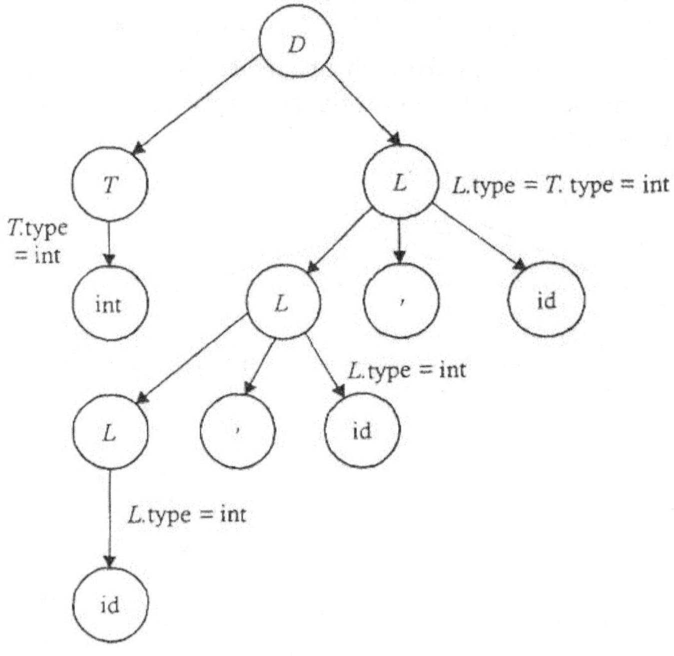

FIGURE 6.3 Parse tree with node attributes for the string int id1,id2,id3.

Inherited attributes are convenient for expressing the dependency of a programming language construct on the context in which it appears. When inherited attributes are used, then the interdependencies among the attributes at the nodes of the parse tree must be taken into account when evaluating their semantic rules, and these interdependencies among attributes are depicted by a directed graph called a "dependency graph." For example, if a semantic rule is of the form A.val = f(X.val, Y.val, Z.val)—that is, if A.val is function of X.val, Y.val, and Z.val)-and is associated with a production $A \rightarrow XYZ$, then we conclude that A.val depends on X.val, Y.val, and Z.val. Therefore, every semantic rule must adopt the above form (if it hasn't already) by introducing a dummy, synthesized attribute.

Dummy Synthesized Attributes

If the semantic rule is in the form of a procedure call fun(a1,a2,a3,..., ak), then we can transform it into the form b = fun(a1,a2,a3,..., ak), where b is a dummy synthesized attribute. The dependency graph has a node for each attribute and an edge from node *b* to node *a* if attribute *a* depends on attribute *b*. For example, if a production $A \rightarrow XYZ$ is used in the parse tree, then there will be four nodes in the dependency graph—*A*.val, *X*.val, *Y*.val, and *Z*.val—with edges from *X*.val, *Y*.val, and *Z*.val to *A*.val.

The dependency graph for such a parse tree is shown in Figure 6.4. The ellipses denote the nodes of the dependency graph, and the circles denote the nodes of the parse tree.

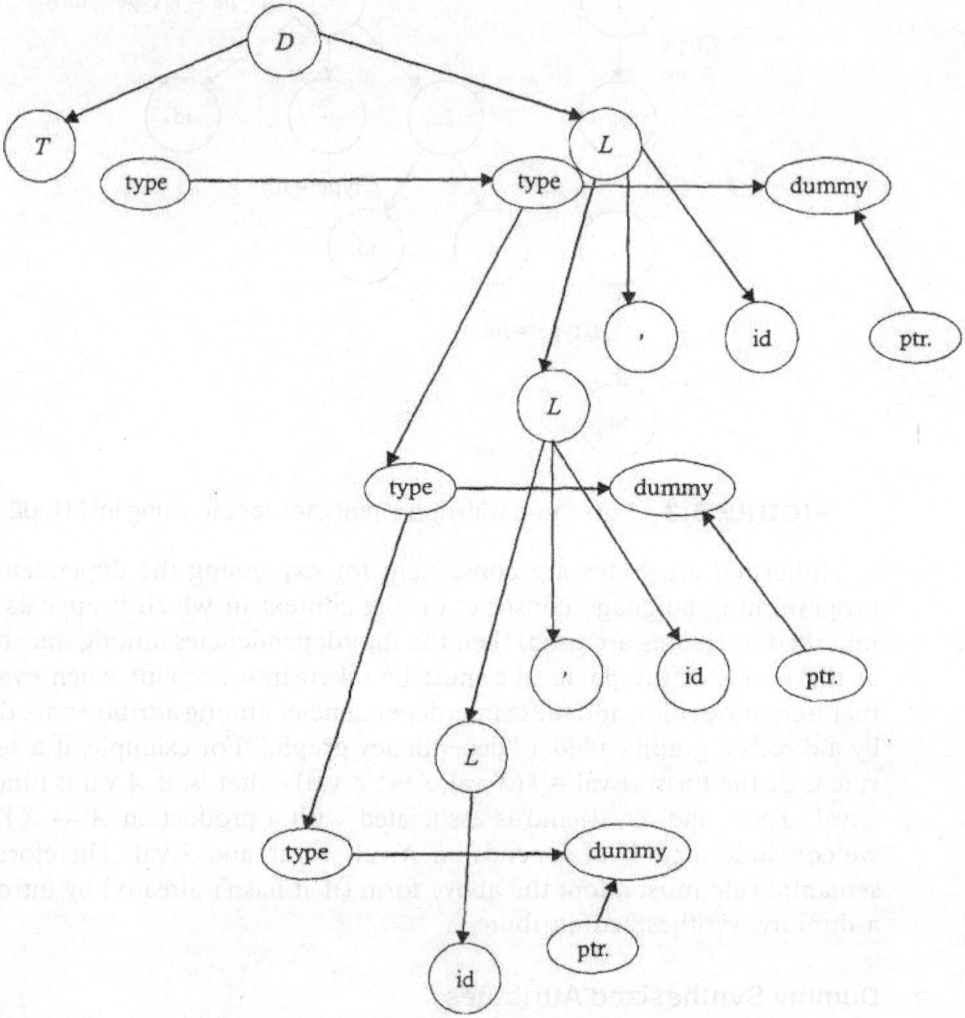

FIGURE 6.4 Dependency graph with four nodes.

This topological sort of a dependency graph results in an order in which the semantic rules can be evaluated. But for reasons of efficiency, it is better to get the semantic rules evaluated (i.e., carry out the translation) during the parsing itself. If the translations are to be carried out during the parsing, then the evaluation order of the semantic rules gets linked to the order in which the parse tree nodes are created, even though the actual parse tree is not required to be generated by the parser. Many top-down as well as bottom-up parsers generate nodes in a depth-first left-to-right order; so the semantic rules must be evaluated in this same order if the translations are to be carried out during the parsing itself. A class of syntax-directed definitions, called "*L*-attributed" definitions, has attributes that can always be evaluated in depth-first, left-to-right order. Hence, if the translations are specified using *L*-attributed definitions, then it is possible to carry out translations during the parsing.

6.3 L-ATTRIBUTED DEFINITIONS

A syntax-directed definition is *L*-attributed if for every production $A \rightarrow X_1 X_2 \rightarrow X_n$, and each inherited attribute of X_j for i lies between 1 and n,

1. The attributes (both inherited as well as synthesized) of the symbols $X_1, X_2, \ldots, X_{j-1}$ (i.e., the symbols to the left of X_j in the production, and
2. The inherited attributes of A.

The syntax-directed definition above is an example of the *L*-attributed definition, because the inherited attribute *L*.type depends on *T*.type, and *T* is to the left of *L* in the production $D \rightarrow TL$. Similarly, the inherited attribute L_1.type depends on the inherited attribute *L*.type, and *L* is parent of L_1 in the production $L \rightarrow L_1$,id.

When translations carried out during parsing, the order in which the semantic rules are evaluated by the parser must be explicitly specified. Hence, instead of using the syntax-directed definitions, we use syntax-directed translation schemes to specify the translations. Syntax-directed definitions are more abstract specifications for translations; therefore, they hide many implementation details, freeing the user from having to explicitly specify the order in which translation takes place. Whereas the syntax-directed translation schemes indicate the order in which semantic rules are evaluated, allowing some implementation details to be specified.

6.4 SYNTAX-DIRECTED TRANSLATION SCHEMES

A syntax-directed translation scheme is a context-free grammar in which attributes are associated with the grammar symbols, and semantic actions, enclosed within braces ({ }), are inserted in the right sides of the productions. These semantic actions are basically the subroutines that are called at the appropriate times by the parser, enabling the translation. The position of the semantic action on the right side of the production indicates the time when it will be called for execution by the parser. When we design a translation scheme, we must ensure that an attribute value is available when the action refers to it. This requires that:

1. An inherited attribute of a symbol on the right side of a production must be computed in an action immediately preceding (to the left of) that symbol, because it may be referred to by an action computing the inherited attribute of the symbol to the right of (following) it.
2. An action that computes the synthesized attribute of a nonterminal on the left side of the production should be placed at the end of the right side of the production, because it might refer to the attributes of any of the right-side grammar symbols. Therefore, unless they are computed, the synthesized attribute of a nonterminal on the left cannot be computed.

These restrictions are motivated by the *L*-attributed definitions. Below is an example of a syntax-directed translation scheme that satisfies these requirements, which are implemented during predictive parsing:

$D \rightarrow T$ { L.type : = T.type }L;
$T \rightarrow$ int{ T.type : = int }
$T \rightarrow$ real{ T.type : = real }
$L \rightarrow$ { $L1$.type = L.type }$L1$, id{enter(id.prt, L.type);}
$L \rightarrow$ id{enter(id.prt, L.type);}

The advantage of a top-down parser is that semantic actions can be called in the middle of the productions. Thus, in the above translation scheme, while using the production $D \rightarrow TL$ to expand D, we call a routine after recognizing T (i.e., after T has been fully expanded), thereby making it easier to handle the inherited attributes. Whereas a bottom-up parser reduces the right side of the production $D \rightarrow TL$ by popping T and L from the top of the parser stack and replacing them by D, the value of the synthesized attribute T.type is already on the parser stack at a known position. It can be inherited by L. Since L.type is defined by a copy rule, L.type = T.type, the value of T.type can be used in place of L.type. Thus, if the parser stack is implemented as two parallel arrays—state and value—and state [I] holds a grammar symbol X, then value [I] holds a synthesized attribute of X. Therefore, the translation scheme implemented during bottom-up parsing is as follows, where [top] is value of stack top before the reduction and [newtop] is the value of the stack top after the reduction:

$D \rightarrow Tl;$

$T \rightarrow$ int{value[newtop] = int}

$T \rightarrow$ real{value[newtop] = real}

$L \rightarrow L1$, id{enter(value[top], value[top-3]);}

$L \rightarrow$ id{enter(value[top], value[top-1]);}

6.5 INTERMEDIATE CODE GENERATION

While translating a source program into a functionally equivalent object code representation, a parser may first generate an intermediate representation. This makes retargeting of the code possible and allows some optimizations to be carried out that would otherwise not be possible. The following are commonly used intermediate representations:

1. Postfix notation
2. Syntax tree
3. Three-address code

Postfix Notation

In postfix notation, the operator follows the operand. For example, in the expression $(a - b) * (c + d) + (a - b)$, the postfix representation is:

$$ab - cd + ab - +$$

Syntax Tree

The syntax tree is nothing more than a condensed form of the parse tree. The operator and keyword nodes of the parse tree (Figure 6.5) are moved to their parent, and a chain of single productions is replaced by single link (Figure 6.6).

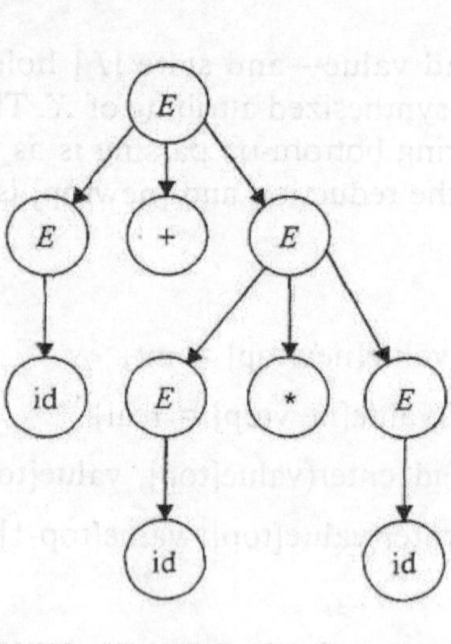

FIGURE 6.5 Parse tree for the string id+id*id.

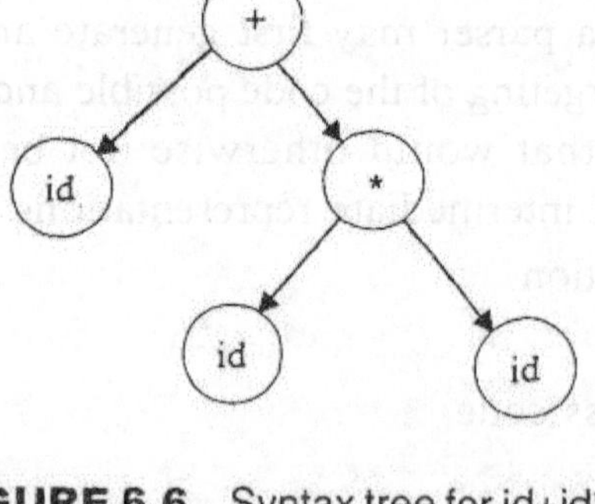

FIGURE 6.6 Syntax tree for id+id*id.

Three-Address Code

Three address code is a sequence of statements of the form $x = y \ op \ z$. Since a statement involves no more than three references, it is called a "three-address statement," and a sequence of such statements is referred to as three-address code. For example, the three-address code for the expression $a + b * c + d$ is:

$$T_1 = b * c$$
$$T_2 = a + T_2$$
$$T_3 = T_3 + d.$$

Sometimes a statement might contain less than three references; but it is still called a three-address statement. The following are the three-address statements used to represent various programming language constructs:

- Used for representing arithmetic expressions:

  $X = Y\ op\ Z$

  $X = op\ Y$

  X = Y
- Used for representing Boolean expressions:

  if $A > B$ goto L

  goto L
- Used for representing array references and dereferencing operations:

  $x = y[i]$

  $x[i] = y$

  $x = *y$

  $*x = y$
- Used for representing a procedure call:

  param T

  call p, n

6.6 REPRESENTING THREE-ADDRESS STATEMENTS

Records with fields for the operators and operands can be used to represent three-address statements. It is possible to use a record structure with four fields: the first holds the operator, the next two hold the operand1 and operand2, respectively, and the last one holds the result. This representation of a three-address statement is called a "quadruple representation."

Quadruple Representation

Using quadruple representation, the three-address statement $x = y\ op\ z$ is represented by placing *op* in the operator field, y in the operand1 field, z in the operand2 field, and x in the result field. The statement $x = op\ y$, where *op* is a unary operator, is represented by placing *op* in the operator field, y in the operand1 field, and x in the result field; the operand2 field is not used. A statement like param $t1$ is represented by placing param in the operator field and $t1$ in the operand1 field; neither operand2 nor the result field are used. Unconditional and conditional jump statements are represented by placing the target labels in the result field. For example, a quadruple representation of the three-address code for the statement $x = (a + b) * -c/d$ is shown in Table 6.1. The numbers in parentheses represent the pointers to the quadruple structure.

TABLE 6.1 Quadruple Representation of $x = (a + b) * - c/d$

	Operator	Operand1	Operand2	Result
(1)	+	a	b	$t1$
(2)	–	c		$t2$
(3)	*	$t1$	$t2$	$t3$
(4)	/	$t3$	d	$t4$
(5)	=	$t4$		x

Triple Representation

The contents of the operand1, operand2, and result fields are therefore normally the pointers to the symbol records for the names represented by these fields. Hence, it becomes necessary to enter temporary names into the symbol table as they are created. This can be avoided by using the position of the statement to refer to a temporary value. If this is done, then a record structure with three fields is enough to represent the three-address statements: the first holds the operator value, and the next two holding values for the operand1 and operand2, respectively. Such a representation is called a "triple representation." The contents of the operand1 and operand2 fields are either pointers to the symbol table records, or they are pointers to records (for temporary names) within the triple representation itself. For example, a triple representation of the three-address code for the statement $x = (a+b)*-c/d$ is shown in Table 6.2.

TABLE 6.2 Triple Representation of $x = (a + b) * - c/d$

	Operator	Operand1	Operand2
(1)	+	a	b
(2)	–	c	
(3)	*	(1)	(2)
(4)	/	(3)	d
(5)	=	x	(4)

Indirect Triple Representation

Another representation uses an additional array to list the pointers to the triples in the desired order. This is called an indirect triple representation. For example, a triple representation of the three-address code for the statement $x = (a+b)*-c/d$ is shown in Table 6.3.

TABLE 6.3 Indirect Triple Representation of $x = (a + b) * - c/d$

(1)
(2)
(3)
(4)
(5)

	Operator	Operand1	Operand2
(1)	+	a	b
(2)	-	c	
(3)	*	(1)	(2)
(4)	/	(3)	d
(5)	=	x	(4)

Comparison

By using quadruples, we can move a statement that computes A without requiring any changes in the statements using A, because the result field is explicit. However, in a triple representation, if we want to move a statement that defines a temporary value, then we must change all of the pointers in the operand1 and operand2 fields of the records in which this temporary value is used. Thus, quadruple representation is easier to work with when using an optimizing compiler, which entails a lot of code movement. Indirect triple representation presents no such problems, because a separate list of pointers to the triple structure is maintained. When statements are moved, this list is reordered, and no change in the triple structure is necessary; hence, the utility of indirect triples is almost the same as that of quadruples.

6.7 SYNTAX-DIRECTED TRANSLATION SCHEMES TO SPECIFY THE TRANSLATION OF VARIOUS PROGRAMMING LANGUAGE CONSTRUCTS

Specifying the translation of the construct involves specifying the construct's syntactic structure, using CFG, and associating suitable semantic actions with the productions of the CFG. For example, if we want to specify the translation of the arithmetic expressions into postfix notation so they can be carried along with the parsing, and if the parsing method is LR, then first we write a grammar that specifies the syntactic structure of the arithmetic expressions. We then associate suitable semantic actions with the productions of the grammar. These associations are covered below.

6.7.1 Arithmetic Expressions

The grammar that specifies the syntactic structure of the expressions in a typical programming language will have the following productions:

$E \rightarrow E + T$

$E \rightarrow T$

$T \rightarrow T * F$

$T \rightarrow F$

$F \rightarrow id$

Translating arithmetic expressions involves generating code to evaluate the given expression. Hence, for an expression $a + b * c$, the postfix representation that is required to be generated is:

abc * +

Syntax-directed translation schemes to specify the translation of an expression into postfix notation are as follows:

$E \rightarrow E_1 + T$	{*E*.code = concate(E_1.code, *T*.code,"+");}
$E \rightarrow T$	{*E*.code = *T*.code;}
$T \rightarrow T_1 * F$	{*T*.code = concate(T_1.code, *F*.code,"*");}
$T \rightarrow F$	{*T*.code = *F*.code;}
$F \rightarrow id$	{*F*.code = getname(id.place);}

where code is a string value attribute used to hold the postfix expression, and place is pointer value attribute used to link the pointer to the symbol record that contains the name of the identifier. The label getname returns the name of the identifier from the symbol table record that is pointed to by ptr, and concate(s_1, s_2, s_3) returns the concatenation of the strings s_1, s_2, and s_3, respectively. For the string *a*+*b***c*, the values of the attributes at the parse tree node are shown in Figure 6.7.

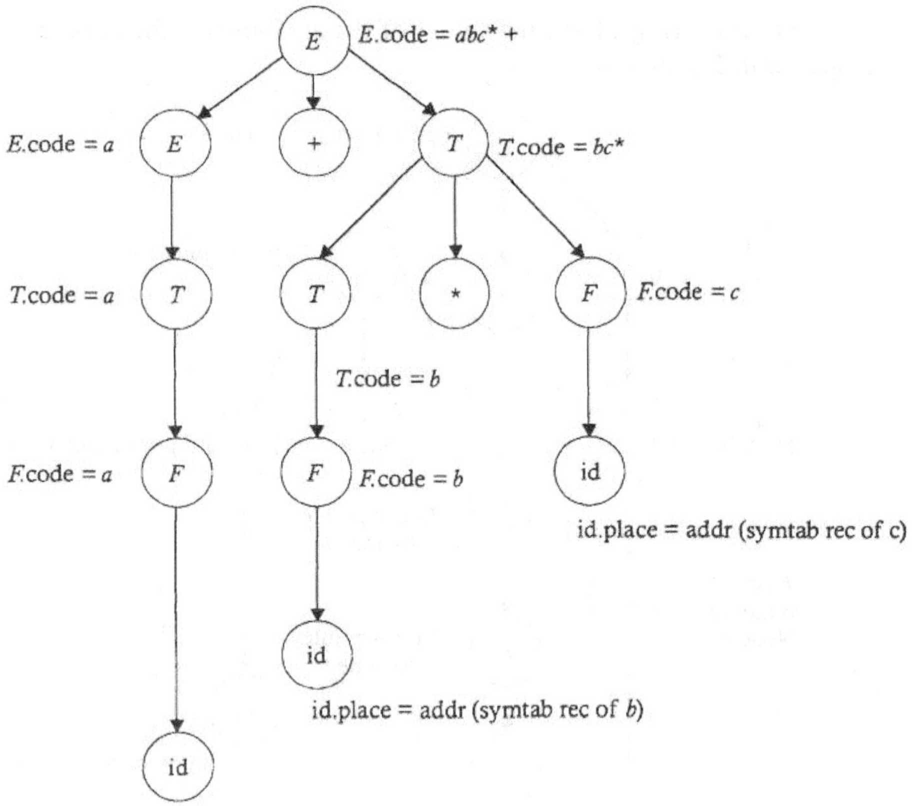

FIGURE 6.7 Values of attributes at the parse tree node for the string a + b * c.

id.place = addr(symtab rec of *a*)

Syntax-directed translation schemes to specify the translation of an expression into the syntax tree are as follows:

$E \rightarrow E_1 + T$	$\{E.\text{ptr} = \text{mknode}(\text{'+'}, E_1.\text{ptr}, T.\text{ptr})\}$
$E \rightarrow T$	$\{E.\text{ptr} = T.\text{ptr}\}$
$T \rightarrow T_1 * F$	$\{T.\text{ptr} = \text{mknode}(\text{'*'}, T_1.\text{ptr}, F.\text{ptr})$
$T \rightarrow F$	$\{T.\text{ptr} = F.\text{ptr}\}$
$F \rightarrow \text{id}$	$\{F.\text{ptr} = \text{mkleaf}(\text{id.place})\}$

where ptr is pointer value attribute used to link the pointer to a node in the syntax tree, and place is pointer value attribute used to link the pointer to the symbol record that contains the name of the identifier. The mkleaf generates leaf nodes, and mknode generates intermediate nodes.

For the string *a*+*b***c*, the values of the attributes at the parse tree nodes are shown in Figure 6.8.

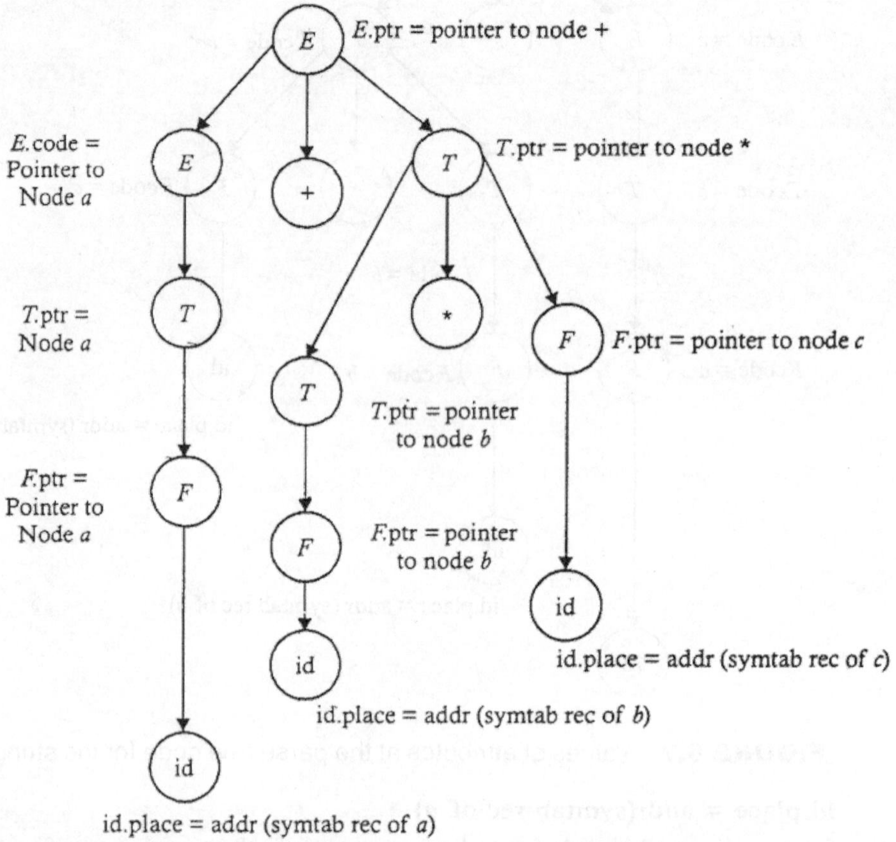

FIGURE 6.8 Values of the attributes at the parse tree nodes for a + b * c, id.place = addr(symtab rec of a).

id.place = addr(sumtab rec of *a*)

Syntax-directed translation schemes specifying the translation of an expression into three-address code are as follows:

$E \rightarrow E_1 + T$ {$\$_2$ =gentemp ( );
gencode ('+', E_1.place, T.place);
E.place = $\$_2$}

$E \rightarrow T$ {E.place = T.place}

$T \rightarrow T_1 * F$ {$\$_1$ = gentemp ( );

$$\text{gencode}\ (\text{'*'}, T_1.\text{place}, F.\text{place});$$
$$T.\text{place} = \$_1\}$$
$$T \rightarrow F \qquad \{T.\text{ptr} = F.\text{ptr}\}$$
$$F \rightarrow \text{id} \qquad \{F.\text{ptr} = \text{id.place}\}$$

where ptr is a pointer value attribute used to link the pointer to the symbol record that contains the name of the identifier, mkleaf generates leafnodes, and mknode generates intermediate nodes. For the string $a+b*c$, the values of the attributes at the parse tree nodes are shown in Figure 6.9.

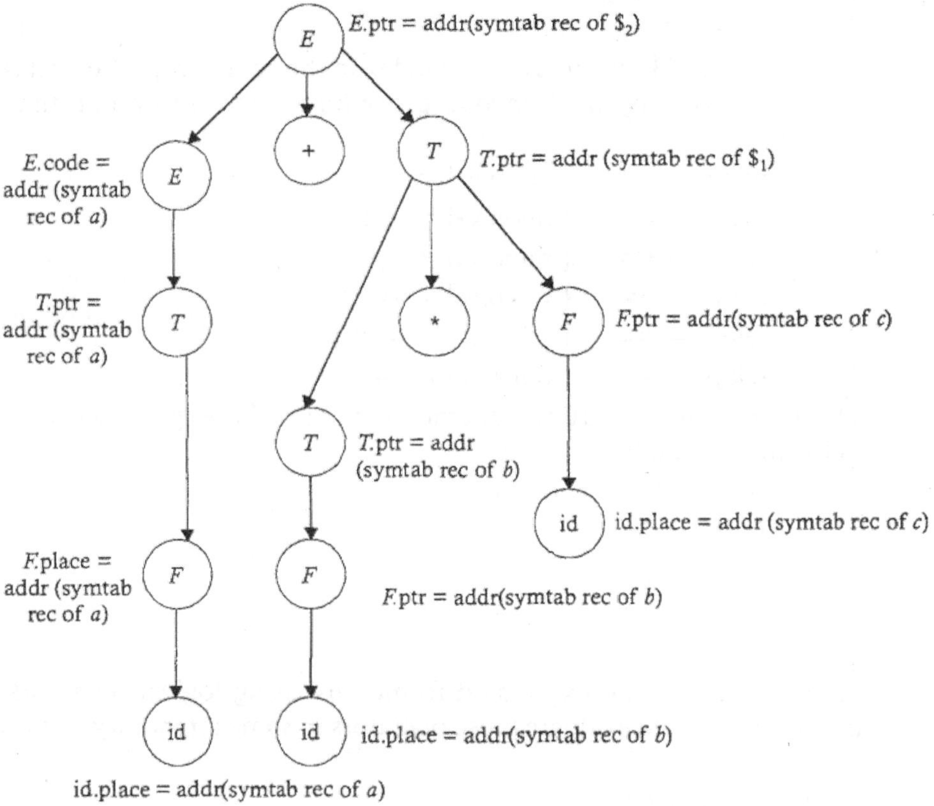

FIGURE 6.9 Values of the attributes at the parse tree nodes for a + b * c, id.place = addr(sumtab rec of a).

6.7.2 Boolean Expressions

One way of translating a Boolean expression is to encode the expression's true and false values as the integers one and zero, respectively. The code to evaluate the value of the expression in some temporary is generated as shown below:

```
E → E1 relop E2
    {
        t1 = gentemp();
        gencode(if E1.place relop.val E2.place
        goto(nextquad + 3));
        gencode(t1 = 0);
        gencode(goto(nextquad+2))
        gencode(t1 = 1)}
        E.place = t1;
    }
```

where nextquad keeps track of the index in the code array. The next statement will be inserted by the gencode procedure, and will update the value of nextquad.

```
relop → <     { relop.val = '<' }
relop → >     { relop.val ='>' }
relop → <=    { relop.val = '<=' }
relop → >=    { relop.val ='>=' }
relop → ==    { relop.val = '==' }
relop → !=    { relop.val = '!=' }
```

The following translation scheme translates the expression $a < b$ to the following three-address code:

```
i)      if a<b goto i + 3
i+1)    t1 = 0
i+2)    goto i+4
i+3)    t1 = 1
i+4)
```

Similarly, a Boolean expression formed by using logical operators involves generating code to evaluate those operators in some temporary form, as shown below:

```
E → E1 lop E2
    {
        t1 = gentemp();
        gencode (t1 = E1.place lop.val E2.place);
        E.place = t1;
    }
E → not E1
```

```
{
   t1 = gentemp();
   gencode (t1 = not E1.place)
   E.place = t1
}
lop → and { lop.val = and}
lop → or  { lop.val = or}
```

The translation scheme above translates the expressions $a < b$ and $c > d$ to the following three-address code:

```
i)     if a<b goto i+3
i+1)   t1 = 0
i+2)   goto i+4
i+3)   t1 = 1
i+4)   if c>d goto i+7
i+5)   t2 = 0
i+6)   goto i+8
i+7)   t2 = 1
i+8)   t3 = t1 and t2
```

Another way to translate a Boolean expression is to represent its value by a position in the three-address code sequence. For example, if we point to the statement labeled $L1$, then the value of the expression is true (1); whereas if we point to the statement labeled $L2$, then the value of the expression is false (0). In this case, the use of a temporary to hold either a one or zero, depending upon the true of false value of the expression, becomes redundant. This also makes it possible to decide the value of the expression without evaluating it completely. This is called a "short circuit" or "jumping the code." To discover the true/false value of the expression $a<b$ or $c>d$, it is not necessary to completely evaluate the expression; if $a<b$ is true, then the entire expression will be true. Similarly to discover the true/false value of the expression $a<b$ and $c>d$, it is not necessary to completely evaluate the expression, because if $a<b$ is false, then the entire expression will be false.

TIP *Therefore a Boolean expression can be translated into two to three address statements, a conditional jump, and an unconditional jump. But the targets of these jumps are not known at the time of translating a Boolean expression; hence, these jumps are generated without their targets, which are filled in later on.*

Therefore, we must remember the indices of these jumps in the code array by using suitable attributes of *E*. For this, we use two pointer value attributes: *E*.true and *E*.false. The attribute *E*.true will hold the pointer to the list that contains the index of the conditional jump in the code array, whereas the attribute *E*.false will hold the pointer to the list that contains the index of the unconditional jump. The translation scheme for the Boolean expression that uses relational operators is as follows:

$E \rightarrow E_1$ relop E_2
{
  E.true = mklist(nextquad);
  E.false = mklist(nextquad + 1);
  gencode (if E_1.place relop.val E_2.place goto);
  gencode (goto_);
}

where mklist(ind) is a procedure that creates a list containing ind and returns a pointer to the created list.

relop → < { relop.val = '<' }
relop → > { relop.val = '>' }
relop → <= { relop.val = '<=' }
relop → >= { relop.val = '>=' }
relop → == { relop.val = '==' }
relop → != { relop.val = '!=' }

The above translation scheme translates the expression $a < b$ to the following three address code:

E.true ⟶ *I*) if $a < b$ goto_
E.false ⟶ *I*+2) goto_

6.7.3. Short-Circuit Code for Logical Expressions

AND OPERATOR

Logical expressions that use the 'and' operator are expressions defined by the production *E* → *E*1 and *E*2. Generating the short-circuit code for these logical expressions involves setting the true value of the first expression, *E*1, to the start of the second expression, *E*2, in the code array. We make the true value of *E* the same as the true value of expression *E*2; and we make the false value of *E* the same as the false values of both *E*1 and *E*2. This requires remembering where *E*2 starts in the code array index, which means we must provide for the memory of the nextquad value just before $E2$ is processed. This can accomplished by introducing a nullable nonterminal M before $E2$ in the above production, providing for a reduction by $M \rightarrow \in$ just before the processing of $E2$. Hence, we can get a semantic action associated with this production and executed at this point. We therefore have a method for remembering the value of nextquad just before the $E2$ code is generated.

$E \rightarrow E_1$ and $M\ E_2$ { backpatch($E1$.true, M.quad);
E.true = $E2$.true;
E.false = merge($E1$.false, $E2$.false);
}

$M \rightarrow \in$ {M.quad = nextquad; }

where backpatch(ptr,L) is a procedure that takes a pointer ptr to a list containing indices of the code array and fills the target of the statements at these indices in the code array by L.

OR OPERATOR

For an expression using the 'or' operator-that is, an expression defined by the production $E \rightarrow E1$ or $E2$—generating the short-circuit code involves setting the false value of the first expression, $E1$, to the start of code of $E2$ in the code array, and making the false value of E the same as the false value of $E2$. The true value of E is assigned the same true value both $E1$ and $E2$. This requires remembering where $E2$ starts in the code array index, which requires making a provision for remembering the value of nextquad just before the expression $E2$ is processed. This can be achieved by introducing a nullable nonterminal M before $E2$ in the above production, providing for a reduction by $M \rightarrow \in$ just before the processing of $E2$. Hence, we obtain a semantic action that is associated with this production and executed at this point; therefore, we have provisioned the recall of the value of nextquad just before the $E2$ code is generated.

$E \rightarrow E1$ or $M\ E2$ { backpatch($E1$.false, M.quad);
E.false = $E2$.false;
E.true = merge($E1$.true, $E2$.true);
}

$M \rightarrow \in$ {M.quad = nextquad; }

NOT OPERATOR

For the logical expression using the 'not' operator, that is, one defined by the production $E \rightarrow$ not $E1$, generating the short-circuit code involves making the false value of the expression E as the true value of $E1$. And the true value of E is assigned the false value of $E1$.

```
E → not E1    {
                 E.true = E1.false
                 E.false = E1.true
              }
```

The above translation scheme translates the expression $a < b$ and $c > d$ to the following three-address code:

```
I)     if a<b goto I+2
I+1)   goto_
+2)    if c>d goto_
I+3)   goto_
```

E.true → [I + 2]   E.false → [I + 1] — [I + 3]

For example, consider the following Boolean expression:

not ($P<Q$ and $R<S$ or not ($T<U$ and $R<Q$))

When the above translation scheme is used to translate this construct, the three-address code generated for it is as shown below.

```
i)      if p < q goto(i+2)
i+1)    goto(i+4)
i+2)    if r < s goto_
i+3)    goto(i+4)
i+4)    if t < u goto(i+6)
i+5)    goto_
i+6)    if r < q goto_
i+7)    goto_
```

E.true → [I+6]

E.false → [I+2] → [I+5] → [I+7]

FIGURE 6.10 Translation scheme for a Boolean expression containing and, not, and or.

IF-THEN-ELSE

Since an if-then-else statement is composed of three components—a boolean expression E, a statement $S1$ that is to be executed when E is true, and a statement $S2$ that is to be executed when E is false—the translation of if-then-else involves making a provision for transferring control to the start of $S1$ if E is true, for transferring control to the start of $S2$ if E is false, and for transferring control to the next statement after the execution of $S1$ and $S2$ is over. This requires remembering where code of $S1$ starts in the code array as well as remembering where code of $S2$ starts in the code array.

This is achieved by introducing a nullable nonterminal $M1$ before the $S1$ and a nullable nonterminal $M2$ before the $S2$ in the above production, providing for the reduction by $M1 \rightarrow \in$ just before processing $S1$. Hence, we get a semantic action associated with this production and executed at this point, which enables the recall of the value of nextquad just before generating $S1$ code. Similarly, it provides for the reduction by $M2 \rightarrow \in$ just before processing $S2$, and we get a semantic action associated with production executed at this point, enabling the recall of the value of nextquad just before generating $S2$ code.

In addition, an unconditional jump is required at the end of $S1$ in order to transfer control to the statement that follows the if-then-else statement. To generate this unconditional jump, we add a nullable nonterminal N after $S1$ to the production and associate a semantic action with the production $N \rightarrow \in$, which takes care of generating this unconditional jump, as shown in Figure 6.11.

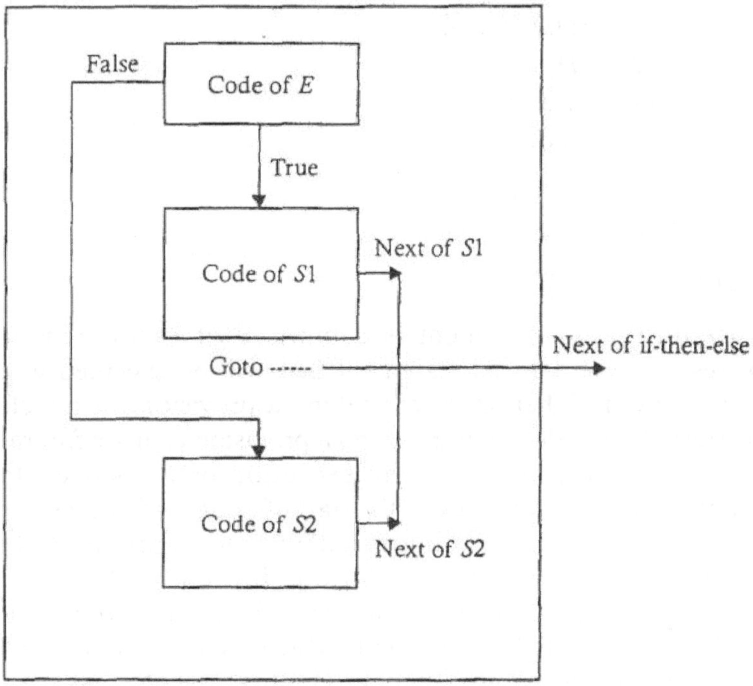

FIGURE 6.11 The addition of the nullable nonterminal N facilitates an unconditional jump.

$S \rightarrow$ if E then $M1$ $S1$ N
    else $M2$ $S2$ {
        backpatch (E.true, $M1$.quad)
        backpatch (E.false, $M2$.quad)
        S.next:
            = merge ($S1$.next, $S2$.next, N.next)
        }
$M1 \rightarrow \in$ { $M1$.quad = nextquad;}
$M2 \rightarrow \in$ { $M2$.quad = nextquad}
$N \rightarrow \in$ {
        N.next = mklist (nextquad);
        gencode (goto...);
    }

Hence, for the statement if $a<b$ then $x = y + z$ else $p = q + r$, the three-address code that is required to be generated is:

i)	if $a < b$ goto(i + 2)
i+1)	goto(i + 5)
i+2)	$t1 = y + z$
i+3)	$x = t1$
i+4)	goto...
i+5)	$t2 = q + r$
i+6)	$p = t2$

IF-THEN

Since an if-then statement is comprised of two components, a Boolean expression E and an $S1$ statement that will be executed when E is true, the translation of if-then involves making a provision for transferring control to the start of $S1$ code if E is true, and a provision is made for transferring control to the next statement after the execution of $S1$ is over if E is false. This requires recalling the index of the start of code of $S1$ in the code array, and can be achieved by introducing a nullable nonterminal M before $S1$ in the production. This will provide for a reduction by $M \rightarrow \in$, just before the processing of S1. Hence, we can get a semantic action associated with this production executed at this point, which makes a provision for remembering the value of nextquad just before generating code of S1, as shown in Figure 6.12 below:

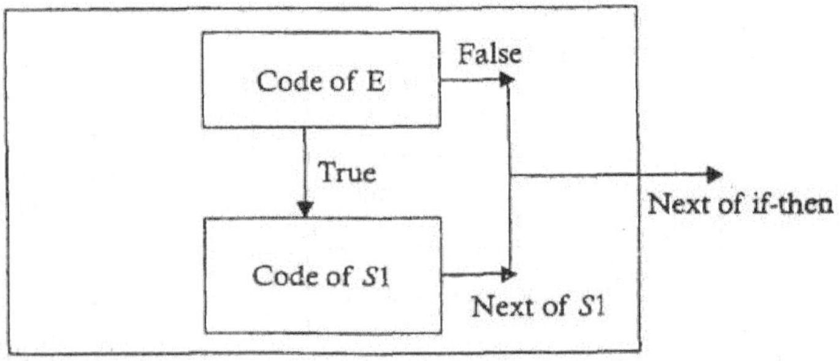

FIGURE 6.12 A nullable nonterminal M provisions the translation of if-then.

S → if E then M S1 {
backpatch (E.true, M.quad);
S.next = merge(*E*.false, *S*1.next)
}

M → ∈ { *M*.quad = nextquad; }

Hence, for the statement if $a<b$ then $x = y + z$, the three-address code that is required to be generated is:

i)	if $a<b$ goto(i+2)	
i+1)	goto...	
i+2)	$t1 = y + z$	
i+3)	$x = t1$	*S*.Next → $i + 1$

WHILE

Since a while statement has two components, a Boolean expression *E* and a statement *S*1, which is the statement to be executed repeatedly as long as *E* is true, the translation of while involves provisioning the transfer of control to the start of *S*1 code if *E* is true. The expression must be tested again after *S*1 execution is over, control must be transferred to the next statement if *E* is false. This requires remembering the index in the code array where *S*1 code starts as well as where the *E* code starts. This can be achieved by introducing a nullable nonterminal *M*2 before *S*1 in the production. This will provide for the reduction by *M*2 → ∈ just before the processing of *S*1. Hence, a semantic action is associated with this production and is executed at this point, enabling the recall of the value of nextquad just before generating *S* code. Similarly, introducing a nullable nonterminal *M*1 before *E* will provide for the reduction by *M*1 → ∈ just before the processing of *E*. Hence, a semantic action is now associated with this production and is executed at this point, provisioning the recall of the value of nextquad just before *E* code is generated, as shown in Figure 6.13.

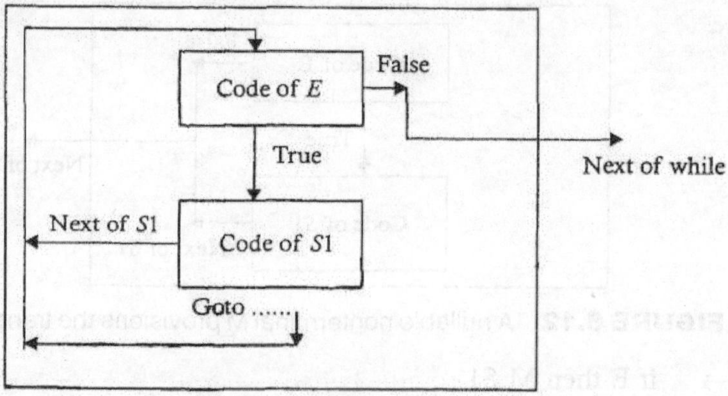

FIGURE 6.13 The translation of the Boolean while statement is facilitated by a nullable nonterminal M.

$S \rightarrow$ while $M1$ E
do $M2$ $S1$ {
backpatch (E.true, $M2$.quad)
backpatch ($S1$.next, $M1$.quad)
S.next = E.false
gencode (goto($M1$.quad))
}
$M1 \rightarrow \in$ { $M1$.quad = nextquad; }
$M2 \rightarrow \in$ { $M2$.quad = nextquad; }

Hence, for the statement while $a<b$ do $x = y + z$, the three-address code that is required to be generated is:

i)	if $a < b$ goto(i+2)
i+1)	goto...
i+2)	$t1 = y + z$
i+3)	$x = t1$
i+4)	goto(i)
	S.Next $\rightarrow$ $i + 1$

DO-WHILE

Since a do-while statement is comprised of two components, a Boolean expression E and statement $S1$ that is executed repeatedly as long as E is true, translation involves provisioning the transfer of control to test the expression after the execution of $S1$ is over. Control must also be transferred to the start of $S1$ code if E is true, and conversely to the next statement if E is false.

This requires recalling the $S1$ start index in the code array as well as the E start index. We introduce a nullable nonterminal $M1$ before $S1$ in the production, providing for the reduction by $M1 \rightarrow \in$ just before the processing of $S1$. Hence, a semantic action is now associated with this production and is executed at this point, provisioning the recall of the value of nextquad just before $S1$ code generates. Similarly, introducing a nullable nonterminal $M2$ before E will provide for the reduction by $M2 \rightarrow \in$ just before the processing of E. We then have a semantic action associated with this production and executed at this point, and which provisions the recall of the value of nextquad just before E code generates, as shown in Figure 6.14.

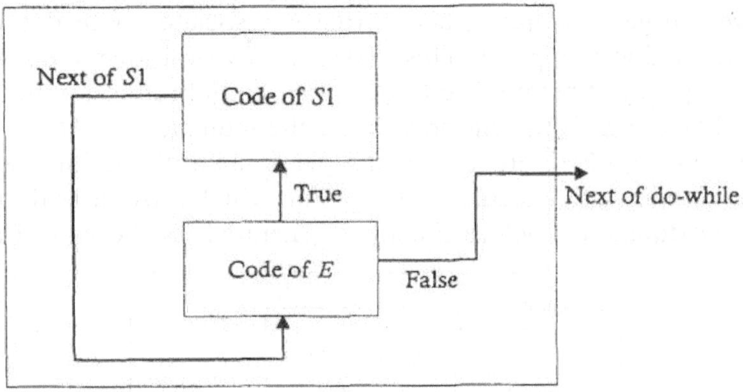

FIGURE 6.14 Translation of the Boolean do-while.

$S \rightarrow$ do $M1$ $S1$ while $M2$ E {

backpatch (E.true, $M1$.quad)
backpatch ($S1$.next, $M2$.quad)
S.next = F.false

}

$M1 \rightarrow \in$ { $M1$.quad = nextquad; }
$M2 \rightarrow \in$ { $M2$.quad = nextquad; }

Hence, for a statement do $x = y + z$ while $a<b$, the three-address code that is required to be generated is:

i)	$t1 = y + z$
i+1)	$x = t1$
i+2)	if $a < b$ goto(i)
i+3)	goto…

S.Next $\rightarrow$ $\boxed{i + 3}$

REPEAT-UNTIL

Since a repeat-until statement has two components, a Boolean expression *E* and a *S*1 statement *S*1 that is executed repeatedly until *E* becomes true, the translation of repeat-until involves provisioning transfer of control to a test of the expression after the execution of *S*1 is over. We must also engineer a transfer a control to the start code of *S*1 if *E* is false and to the next statement if *E* is true.

This requires recalling the index in the code array where *S*1 code starts as well as the index in the code array where *E* code starts. We achieve this by introducing a nullable nonterminal *M*1 before *S*1 in the production. This will provide for the reduction by $M_1 \rightarrow \in$, just before the processing of *S*1. Hence, we can get a semantic action that is associated with this production and is executed at this point. This makes a provision for remembering the value of nextquad just before *S* code generates, and introduces a nullable non-terminal *M*2 before *E*. This will provide for the reduction by $M_2 \rightarrow \in$, just before the processing of *E*. Hence we can get a semantic action associated with this production and executed at this point, which provisions the recall of the value of nextquad just before *E* code is generated, as shown in Figure 6.15.

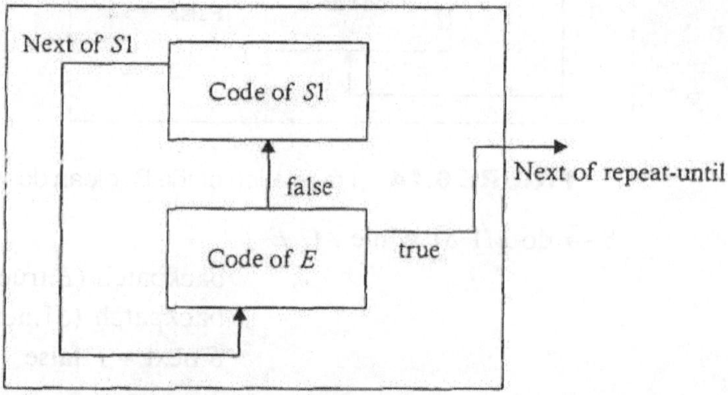

FIGURE 6.15 Translation of Boolean repeat-until.

```
S → repeat M1 S1
      until M2 E      {
                          backpatch (E.false, M1.quad)
                          backpatch (S1.next, M2.quad)
                          S.next = E.true
                      }
M1 →∈ { M1.quad = nextquad; }
M2 →∈ { M2.quad = nextquad; }
```

Hence, for the Boolean statement repeat $x = y + z$ until $a<b$, the three-address code that is required to be generated is:

i)	$t1 = y + z$
i+1)	$x = t1$
i+2)	if $a < b$ goto...
i+3)	goto(i)
	S.Next $\rightarrow$ $\boxed{i + 2}$

FOR

A for statement is composed of four components: an expression $E1$, which is used to initialize the iteration variable; an expression $E2$, which is a Boolean expression used to test whether or not the value of the iteration variable exceeds the final value; an expression $E3$, which is used to specify the step by which the value of the iteration variable is to be incremented or decremented; and statement, $S1$ which is the statement to be executed as long as the value of the iteration variable is not or equal to the final value. Hence, the translation of a for statement involves provisioning the transfer a control to the start of $S1$ code if $E2$ is true, transferring control to the start of $E3$ code after the execution of $S1$ is over, transferring control to the start of $E2$ code after $E3$ code is executed, and transferring control to the next statement if $E2$ is false, as shown in Figure 6.16.

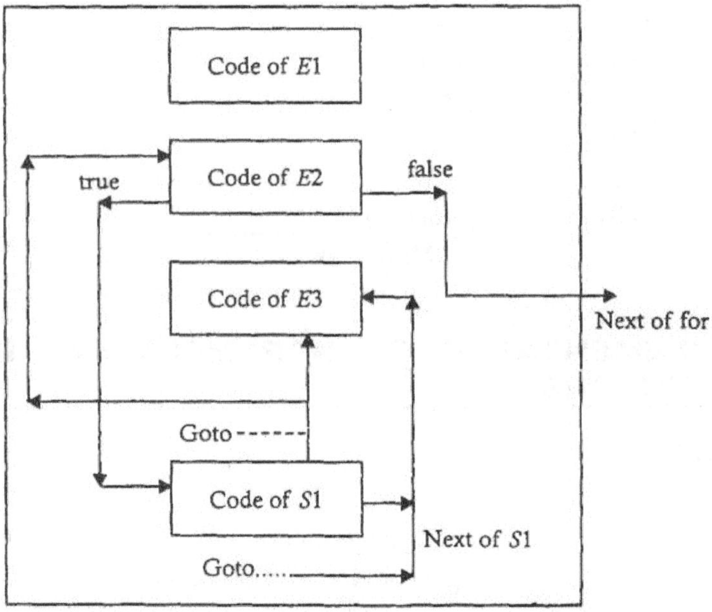

FIGURE 6.16 Handling the translation of the Boolean for.

```
S → for (E1; M1 E2; M2 E3) M3 S1
                {
                        backpatch (E2.true, M3.quad)
                        backpatch (M3.next, M1.quad)
                        backpatch (S1.next, M2.quad)
                        gencode (goto(M2.quad))
                        S.next = E2.false
                }
M1 → ∈ { M1.quad = nextquad; }
M2 → ∈ { M2.quad = nextquad; }
M3 → ∈          {
                M3.next: = mklist (nextquad)
                gencode (goto...)
                M3.quad = nextquad;
                }
```

Hence, for a statement for(i = 1; i<= 20; i++) $x = y + z$, the three-address code that is required to be generated is:

```
j )        i = 1
j+1)       if i <= 20 goto(j + 6)
j+2)       goto...
j+3)       t1 = i+1
j+4)       i = t1
j+5)       goto(j+1)
j+6)       t2 = y + z
j+7)       x = t2
j+8)       goto(j+3)
              S.Next  →  [J + 2]
```

6.8 IMPLEMENTATION OF INCREMENT AND DECREMENT OPERATORS

```
L → id++      {
                    t1 = gentemp();
                    t2 = gentemp();
                    gencode(t1 = id.place);
                    gencode(t2 = id.place +1);
```

```
                    gencode (id.place = t2);
                    L.place = t1;
           }
L → ++id   {
                    t1 = gentemp();
                    gencode(t1 = id.place +1);
                    gencode(id.place = t1);
                    L.place = t1;
           }
L → id--   {
                    t1 = gentemp();
                    t2 = gentemp();
                    gencode(t1 = id.place);
                    gencode(t2 = id.place -1);
                    gencode(id.place = t2);
                    L.place = t1;
           }
L → --id   {
                    t1 = gentemp();
                    gencode (t1 = id.place -1);
                    gencode (id.place = t1);
                    L.place = t1;
           }
```

6.9 THE ARRAY REFERENCE

An array reference is an expression with an *l*-value. Therefore, to capture its syntactic structure, we add the following productions to the grammar:.

$L \rightarrow$ id[elist]

elist $\rightarrow$ elist*l*, E | E

An array reference in a source program is replaced by the *l*-value of an expression that specifies reference to an element of the array. Computing the *l*-value involves finding the offset of the referred element of the array and then adding it to the base. But since deriving an offset depends on the subscripts used in an array reference, and the values of these subscripts are not known during the compilation, unless the subscripts are constant expressions, a compiler has to generate the code for evaluating the *l*-value of an expression that specifies the reference to an element of an array. This *l*-value computation is achieved as follows:

$$l\text{-value}(a[i1, i2, i3, \ldots, ik]) = \text{addr}(a) + \text{offset}$$

$$\text{Offset} = [(i1 - lb1)(ub2 - lb2+1)(ub3 - lb3+1) \ldots (ubk - lbk+1) + (i2 - lb2)(ub3 - lb3+1)(ub4 - lb4+1) \ldots (ubk - lbk+1) + \ldots + (ik - lbk)] * \text{size of element}$$

where *lbi* and *ubi* are the lower and upper bounds of the *i*th dimension.

If the lower bound of each dimension is one, and the upper bound of the *i*th dimension is *di*, then the offset computing formula becomes:

$$\text{Offset} = [(i1 - 1)*d2*d3* \ldots *dk+(i2 - 1)*d3*d4* \ldots *dk+ \ldots +(ik - 1))*bpw$$

$$\text{Offset} = [i1*d2*d3* \ldots *dk+ i2*d3*d4* \ldots *dk+ \ldots + ik)*bpw$$

$$[d2*d3* \ldots *dk+ d3*d4* \ldots *dk + \ldots + dk]*bpw$$

The $[i1*d2*d3*\ldots*dk + i2*d3*d4*\ldots*dk + \ldots + ik]*bpw$ is a variable part of the offset computation, whereas $[d2* d3*\ldots*dk + d3*d4*\ldots*dk + \ldots +dk]*bpw$ is a constant part of the offset computation and is not required to be computed for every reference to an array *a*. It can be computed once while processing the declaration of the array *a*. We call this value "constant *C*." Therefore:

$$\text{Offset} = V - C$$

where *V* is the variable part, and

$$l\text{-value}(a[i1, i2, i3, \ldots, ik]) = \text{addr}(a) + V - C$$

Since addr(*a*) is fixed, we can combine *C* with addr(*a*) and store this value in an attribute, *L*.place, and we can store *V* in another attribute, *L*.off, so that:

$$l\text{-value}(a[i1, i2, i3, \ldots, ik]) = L.\text{place}[L.\text{off}]$$

Hence, the translation of an array reference involves generating code for computing *V*, and *V* is made a value of attribute *L*.off. We compute addr(*a*) – *C* and make it the value of the attribute *L*.place. Computing *V* involves evaluating the expression:

$$[i1*d2*d3* \ldots *dk+ i2*d3*d4* \ldots *dk+ \ldots + ik]*bpw$$

This expression can be rewritten as:

$((((i1)d2 + i2)d3+i3)d4 +\ldots+1)*bpw$

Therefore, the three-address code that is required to be generated for computing V is:

```
t1 = i1
t1 = t1*d2
t1 = t1+i2
t1 = t1*d3
t1 = t1+i3

t1 = t1 * dk
t1 = t1 + ik
V = t1 * bpw
```

Therefore, the translation scheme is:

```
elist →E             (Initialize queue by adding E.place)
elist → elist1, E    (Append E.place to queue)
L → id[elist]        { T1: = gentemp ( )
                             elist.Ndim = 1
                     gencode(T1 = retrieve();
                     while (queue not empty ) do
                     {
                             gencode (T1= T1 * limit (id.place, elist.Ndim))
                             gencode (T1 : = T1 + retrieve())
                             elist.Ndim = elist.Ndim + 1
               }
               V = gentemp();
               U = gentemp();
               gencode (V : = T1 * bpw)
               gencode (U : = id.place – C)
               L.off = V
               L.place: = U
               }
```

where retrieve() is a function that retrieves a value from the queue, and limit() returns the upper bound of the dimension of the array.

In this translation scheme, the attribute id.place cannot be accessed in the semantic action associated with the production elist → *E* or in the semantic action associated with the production elist → elist *l*, *E*. So it is not possible to make use of the value of the subscript that is available in *E*.place to get the required three-address statements generated. Hence, a queue is necessary in order to maintain the subscripts' storage. These subscripts are used later on for generating the code for computing the offset.

Another way to approach this is to modify the grammar to make it suitable for translation. This requires rewriting the productions in such a manner that both id and *E* exist in the same production so that the pointer to the symbol table record of the array name is available in id.place. This can be used to retrieve the upper-bound dimension information of the array. And the value of the subscript is available *E*.place; so by using both of these, the required three-address statements can be generated, and the value of the subscript does not need to be stored. Therefore, the modified grammar, along with the semantic actions, is:

```
L →elist   {   U = newtemp(); V = newtemp()
               V = elist.place * bpw
               U = gencode (elist.array – C)
               L.place = U
               L.off = V
           }
elist →id      E {elist.place = E.place
               elist.array = id.place
               elist.Ndim = 1; }
elist → elist, E          {    T1 = newtemp ();
                               gencode (T1 = elist.place *
                               limit (elist.array, elist.Ndim +1))
                               gencode (T1 = T1 + E.place)
                               elist.array = elist1.array
                               elist.place = T1,
                               elist.Ndim = elist.Ndim +1
                          }
```

For example, consider the following assignment statement:

$$c[a[ij]] = b[i, j] + c[a[i, j]] + d[i + j]$$

where *a* and *b* are arrays of size 30 × 40, and *c* and *d* are arrays of size 20.

There are four bytes per word, and the arrays are allocated statically. When the above translation scheme is used to translate this construct, the three-address code generated is:

$t1 = i * 40$
$t1 = t1 + j$
$t1 = t1 * 4$
$t1 = \text{addr}(a) - 164$
$t3 = t2[t1]$
$t3 = t3 * 4$
$t4 = \text{addr}(c) - 4$
$t5 = i * 40$
$t5 = t5 + j$
$t5 = t5 * 4$
$t6 = \text{addr}(b) - 164$
$t7 = t6[t5]$
$t8 = i * 40$
$t8 = t8 + j$
$t8 = t8 * 4$
$t9 = \text{addr}(a) - 164$
$t10 = t9[t8]$
$t10 = t10 * 4$
$t11 = \text{addr}(c) - 4$
$t12 = t11[t10]$
$t13 = i + j$
$t14 = \text{addr}(d) - 4$
$t15 = t14[t13]$
$t16 = t7 + t12$
$t16 = t16 + t15$
$t4[t3] = t16$

6.10 SWITCH/CASE

To capture the syntactic structure of the switch statement, we add the following productions to the grammar. Here, break is assumed to be a part of statement that is derivable from a nonterminal S.

$S \rightarrow$ switch E { caselist}

caselist $\rightarrow$ caselist case V : S

caselist $\rightarrow$ case V: S

caselist $\rightarrow$ default: S

caselist $\rightarrow$ caselist default: S

A switch statement is comprised of two components: an expression E, which is used to select a particular case from the list of cases; and a caselist, which is a list of n number of cases, each of which corresponds to one of the possible values of the expression E, perhaps including a default case.

NOTE *A case statement can be implemented in a variety of different ways. If the number of cases is not too great, then a case statement can be implemented by generating a sequence of conditional jumps, each of which tests for an individual value and transfers to the code for the corresponding statement. If the number of cases is large, then it is more efficient to construct a hash table for the case values with the labels of the various statements as entries.*

A syntax-directed translation scheme that translates a case statement into a sequence of conditional jumps, each of which tests for an individual value and transfers to the code for the corresponding statement, is considered below. We begin with a typical switch statement:

```
switch (E)
  {
     case V1: S1
     case V2: S2



     case Vn:Sn
  }
```

The generated three-address that is required for the statement is shown in Figure 6.17. Here, next is the label of the code for the statement that comes next of the switch statement in execution order.

```
Code for evaluating E

goto L

L1 : Code for S1

goto Next

L2 : Code for S2

goto Next
.
.
goto Next.

Ln : Code for Sn

goto Next

Ln : Code for default

        goto Next
L: if v1 = t1 goto L1
   if v2 = t1 goto L2
        .
        .
   if Vn = t1 goto Ln
   goto Ld
```

FIGURE 6.17 A switch/case three-address translation.

Therefore, switch statement translation involves generating an unconditional jump after the code of every *S*1, *S*2,..., *Sn* statement in order to transfer control to the next element of the switch statement, as well as to remember the code start of *S*1, *S*2,..., *Sn*, and to generate the conditional jumps. Each of these jumps tests for an individual value and transfers to the code for the corresponding statement. This requires introducing nullable nonterminals before *S*1, as shown in Figure 6.18.

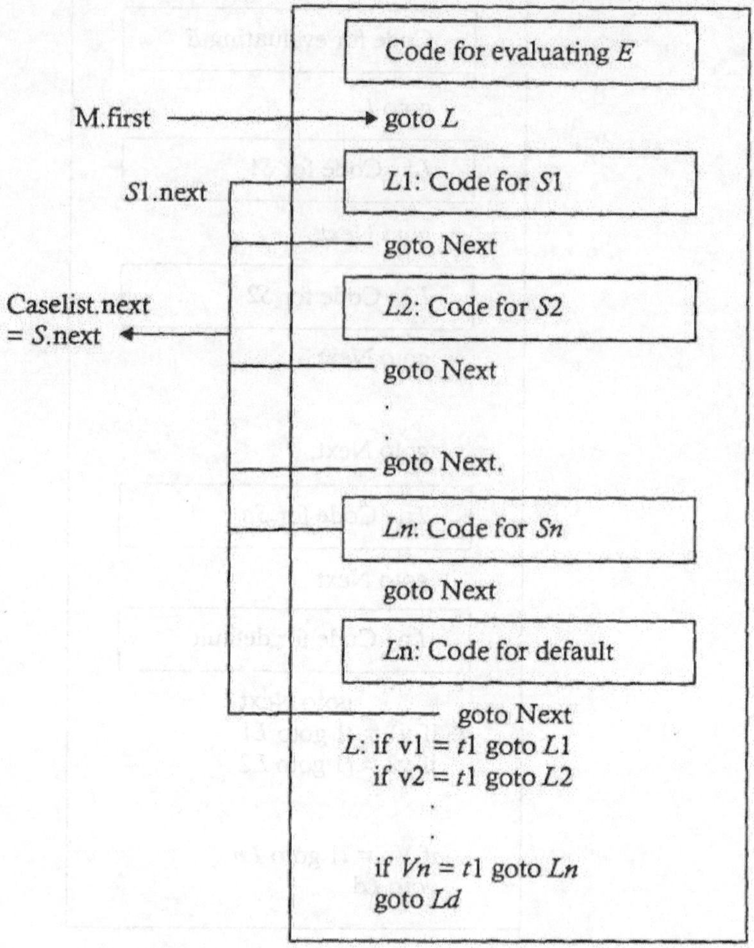

FIGURE 6.18 Nullable nonterminals are introduced into a switch statement translation.

EXAMPLE 6.1: Consider the following switch statement:

```
switch (i + j)
{
    case 1: x = y + z
    default: p = q + r
    case 2: u = v + w
}
```

The above translation scheme translates into the following three-address code, which is also shown in Figure 6.19:

```
i)      t1 = i + j
i + 1)  goto(i + 11)
i + 2)  t1 =y + z
i + 3)  x = t1
i + 4)  goto_
i + 5)  t2 = q+r
i + 6)  p = t2
i + 7)  goto_
i + 8)  t3 = u+w
i + 9)  u = t3
i + 10) goto_
i + 11) if t1 = 1 goto(i+2)
i + 12) if t1 = 2 goto(i+8)
i + 13) goto(i + 5)
```

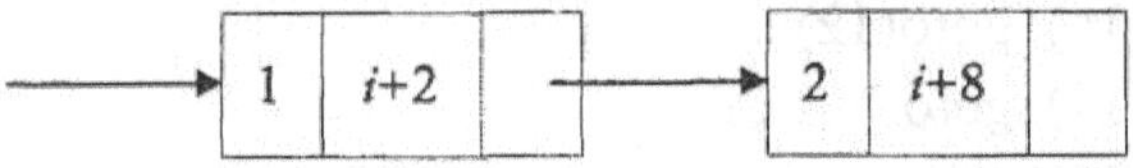

FIGURE 6.19 Contents of queue during the translation.

EXAMPLE 6.2: Using the above translation scheme translates the following switch statement:

```
switch (a+b)
  {
          case 2: { x = y; break; }
          case 5: {switch x
                  {
                          case 0: { a = b + 1; break; }
                          case 1: { a = b + 3; break; }
                          default: { a = 2; break; }
                  }
                  break;
          case 9: { x = y – 1; break; }
          default: { a = 2; break; }
  }
```

The three address code is:

(1) $t1 = a + b$
(2) goto(23)
(3) $x = y$
(4) goto NEXT
(5) goto(14)
(6) $t3 = b + 1$
(7) $a = t3$
(8) goto NEXT
(9) $t4 = b + 3$
(10) $a = t4$
(11) goto NEXT
(12) $a = 2$
(13) goto NEXT
(14) if $x = 0$ goto(6)
(15) if $x = 1$ goto(9)
(16) goto(12)
(17) goto NEXT
(18) $t5 = y - 1$
(19) $x = t5$
(20) goto NEXT
(21) $a = 2$
(22) goto NEXT
(23) if $t1 = 2$ goto(3)
(24) if $t1 = 5$ goto(5)
(25) if $t1 = 9$ goto(18)
(26) goto(21)

6.11 THE PROCEDURE CALL

$S \rightarrow$ call id (arglist)

{ for every value T in queue generate
Param T gencode
(call id.place, arglist.count)

arglist → arglist, E{ append (queue, E.place)
arglist.count:= arglist. count + 1}

arglist → E { initialize queue by E.place
arglist.count: = 1}

6.12 EXAMPLES

Following are additional examples of syntax-directed definitions and translations.

EXAMPLE 6.3: Generate the three-address code for the following C program:

```
main()
{   int i = 1;
    int a[10];
    while(i <= 10)
      a[i] = ;
}
```

The three-address code for the above C program is:

(1) $i = 1$

(2) if i <= 10 goto(4)

(3) goto(8)

(4) $t1 = i$ * width

(5) $t2$ = addr(a) – width

(6) $t2[t1] = 0$

(7) goto(2)

where width is the number of bytes required for each element.

EXAMPLE 6.4: Generate the three-address code for the following program fragment:

```
while (A < C and B > D) do
   if A = 1 then C = C+1
     else
        while A <= D do
                  A = A + 3
```

The three-address code is:

```
(1) if a < c goto(3)
(2) goto(16)
(3) if b >d goto(5)
(4) goto(16)
(5) if a = 1 goto(7)
(6) goto(10)
(7) t1 = c+1
(8) c = t1
(9) goto(1)
(10) if a <= d goto
(11) goto(1)
(12) t2 = a+3
(13) a = t2
(14) goto(10)
(15) goto(1)
```

EXAMPLE 6.5: Generate the three-address code for the following program fragment, where *a* and *b* are arrays of size 20 × 20, and there are four bytes per word.

```
begin
   add = 0;
   i = 1;
   j = 1;
   do
     begin
        add = add + a[i,j] * b[j,i]
        i = i + 1;
        j = j + 1;
     end
   while i <= 20 and j <= 20;
end
```

The three-address code is:

```
(1) add = 0
(2) i = 1
```

```
(3) j = 1
(4) t1 = i * 20
(5) t1 = t1 + j
(6) t1 = t1 * 4
(7) t2 = addr(a) - 84
(8) t3 = t2[t1]
(9) t4 = j * 20
(10) t4 = t4 + i
(11) t4 = t4 * 4
(12) t5 = addr(b) - 84
(13) t6 = t5[t4]
(14) t7 = t3 * t6
(15) t7 = add + t7
(16) t8 = i + 1
(17) i = t8
(18) t9 = j + 1
(19) j = t9
(20) if i <= 20 goto(22)
(21) goto NEXT
(22) if j <= 20 goto(4)
(23) goto NEXT
```

EXAMPLE 6.6: Consider the program fragment:

```
sum = 0
for(i = 1; i<= 20; i++)
    sum = sum + a[i] + b[i];
```

and generate the three-address code for it. There are four bytes per word. The three address code is:

```
(1) sum = 0
(2) i = 1
(3) if i <= 20 goto(8)
(4) goto NEXT
(5) t1 = i+1
(6) i = t1
```

(7) goto(3)
(8) $t2 = i * 4$
(9) $t3 = \text{addr}(a) - 4$
(10) $t4 = t3[t2]$
(11) $t5 = i * 4$
(12) $t6 = \text{addr}(b) - 4$
(13) $t7 = t6[t5]$
(14) $t8 = \text{sum} + t4$
(15) $t8 = t8 + t7$
(16) $\text{sum} = t8$
(17) goto(5)

EXERCISE

1. Explain why every S-attributed definition is L-attributed?
2. Write a grammar for expressions, and write syntax directed translations to count the number of operators in the given expression, to go along with your grammar.
3. Write a grammar for expressions, and write syntax directed translations to count the number of reductions made by the parser, to go along with your grammar.
4. Discuss the advantages and disadvantages of short circuit evaluation of Boolean expressions with suitable examples.
5. Write a grammar for the following control structure:

   do N times S

   Write syntax directed translations to go along with this grammar to translate it into three address code.
6. What is the advantage of using lower bound for each dimension of an array to be 0?, (As is the case with C language).
7. Write a grammar for comma expression in C, and write syntax directed translations to translate into three address code, to go along with this grammar.
8. Consider the following assignment statement:

   A[i][j] = a[i][j] + b[c[k],l]

   Where a and b are arrays of 10 by 20, and C is an array of 10 elements (assume lower bound to be 0 for each dimension).

Translate the above statement into three address code by assuming 4 bytes word size.

9. Consider the following grammar defining binary numbers:

   binarynumber → *binarynumber binarydigit* | *binarydigit*

   binarydigit → *0* | *1*

   Add semantic rules or semantic actions to the above grammar using suitable attributes to compute the integer value of the binary number.

10. A **switch** statement can be implemented by generating sequence of test for each case as well as using **jump table**, which is a table of unconditional jumps, and the value of case is used as offset into this table. When this **jump table** implementation is advantageous.

7 SYMBOL TABLE MANAGEMENT

7.1 THE SYMBOL TABLE

A symbol table is a data structure used by a compiler to keep track of scope/binding information about names. These names are used in the source program to identify the various program elements, like variables, constants, procedures, and the labels of statements. The symbol table is searched every time a name is encountered in the source text. When a new name or new information about an existing name is discovered, the content of the symbol table changes. Therefore, a symbol table must have an efficient mechanism for accessing the information held in the table as well as for adding new entries to the symbol table.

For efficiency, our choice of the implementation data structure for the symbol table and the organization of its contents should stress on minimal cost when adding new entries or accessing the information of existing entries. Also, if the symbol table can grow dynamically as necessary, then it is more useful for a compiler.

7.2 IMPLEMENTATION

Each entry in a symbol table can be implemented as a record that consists of several fields. These fields are dependent on the information to be saved about the name. But since the information about a name depends on the usage of the name (i.e., on the program element identified by the name), the entries in the symbol table records will not be uniform. Hence, to keep the symbol table records uniform, some of the information about the name is kept outside of the symbol table record, and a pointer to this information is stored in the symbol table record, as shown in Figure 7.1. Here, the information about the lower and upper bounds of the dimension of the array named *a* is kept outside of the symbol table record, and the pointer to this information is stored within the symbol table record.

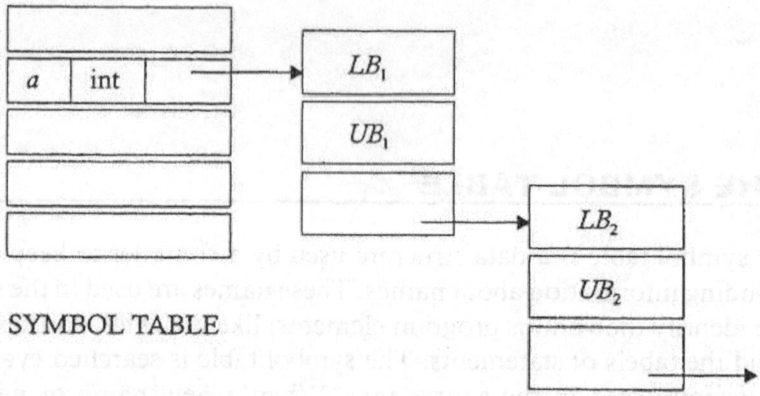

FIGURE 7.1 A pointer steers the symbol table to remotely stored information for the array a.

7.3 ENTERING INFORMATION INTO THE SYMBOL TABLE

Information is entered into the symbol table in various ways. In some cases, the symbol table record is created by the lexical analyzer as soon as the name is encountered in the input, and the attributes of the name are entered when the declarations are processed. But very often, the same name is used to denote different objects, perhaps even in the same block. For example, in C programming, the same name can be used as a variable name and as a member name of a structure, both in the same block. In such cases, the lexical analyzer only returns the name to the parser, rather than a pointer to the symbol table record. That is, a symbol table record is not created by the lexical analyzer; the string itself is returned to the parser, and the symbol table record is created when the name's syntactic role is discovered.

7.4 WHERE SHOULD NAMES BE HELD?

If there is a modest upper bound on the length of the name, then the name can be stored in the symbol table record itself. But if there is no such limit, or if the limit is rarely reached, then an indirect scheme of storing name is used. A separate array of characters, called a "string table," is used to store the name, and a pointer to the name is kept in the symbol table record, as shown in Figure 7.2.

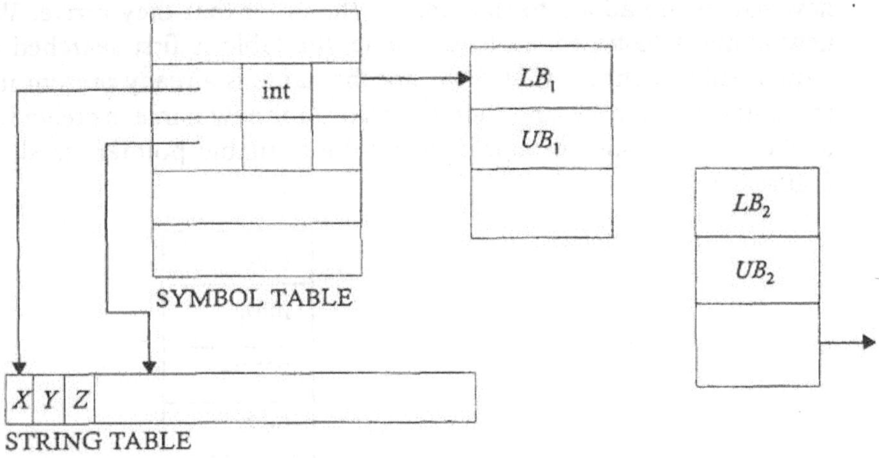

FIGURE 7.2 Symbol table names are held either in the symbol table record or in a separate string table.

7.5 INFORMATION ABOUT THE RUNTIME STORAGE LOCATION

The information about the runtime, name storage location is kept in the symbol table. If the compiler is going to be generating assembly code, then the assembler takes care of the storage locations of the various names. After generating the assembly code, the compiler scans the symbol table and generates the assembly language data definitions. These are appended to the assembly language code for each name. But if machine code is being generated, then the compiler must ascertain the position of each data object relative to a fixed origin.

7.6 VARIOUS APPROACHES TO SYMBOL TABLE ORGANIZATION

There are several methods of organizing the symbol table. These methods are discussed below.

7.6.1 The Linear List

A linear list of records is the easiest way to implement a symbol table. The new names are added to the table in the order that they arrive. Whenever a new name is to be added to the table, the table is first searched linearly or sequentially to check whether or not the name is already present in the table. If the name is not present, then the record for new name is created and added to the list at a position specified by the available pointer, as shown in the Figure 7.3.

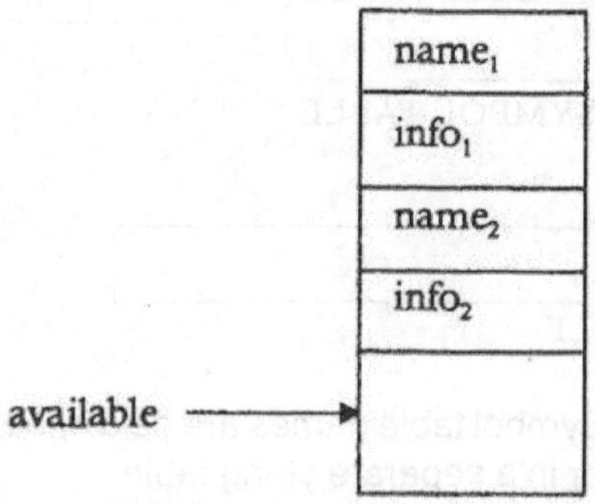

FIGURE 7.3 A new record is added to the linear list of records.

To retrieve the information about the name, the table is searched sequentially, starting from the first record in the table. The average number of comparisons, p, required for search are $p = (n + 1)/2$ for successful search and $p = n$ for an unsuccessful search, where n is the number of records in symbol table. The advantage of this organization is that it takes less space, and additions to the table are simple. This method's disadvantage is that it has a higher accessing time.

7.6.2 Search Trees

A search tree is a more efficient approach to symbol table organization. We add two links, left and right, in each record, and these links point to the record in the search tree. Whenever a name is to be added, first the name is searched in the tree. If it does not exist, then a record for the new name is created and added at the proper position in the search tree. This organization has the property of alphabetical accessibility; that is, all the names accessible from $name_i$ by following a left link, precede $name_1$ in alphabetical order. Similarly, all the name accessible from $name_i$ by following right link follow $name_i$ in alphabetical order (see Figure 7.4). The expected time needed to enter n names and to make m queries is proportional to $(m + n) \log_2 n$; so for greater numbers of records (higher n) this method has advantages over linear list organization.

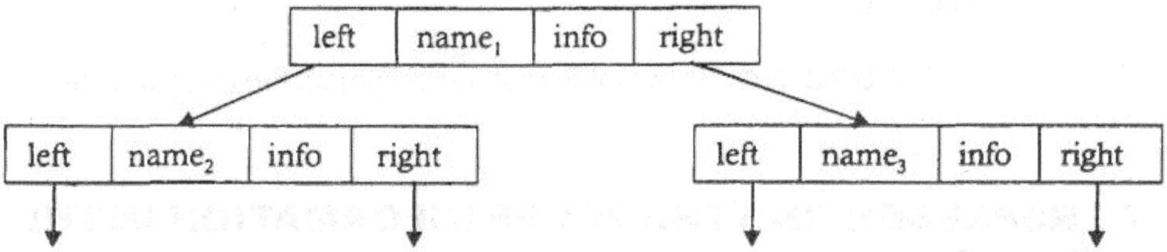

FIGURE 7.4 The search tree organization approach to a symbol table.

7.6.3 Hash Tables

A hash table is a table of k pointers numbered from zero to k–1 that point to the symbol table and a record within the symbol table. To enter a name into symbol table, we find out the hash value of the name by applying a suitable hash function. The hash function maps the name into an integer between zero and k–1, and using this value as an index in the hash table, we search the list of the symbol table records that are built on that hash index. If the name is not present in that list, we create a record for name and insert it at the head of the list. When retrieving the information associated with the name the hash value of the name is first obtained, and then the list that was built on this hash value is searched for information about the name (Figure 7.5).

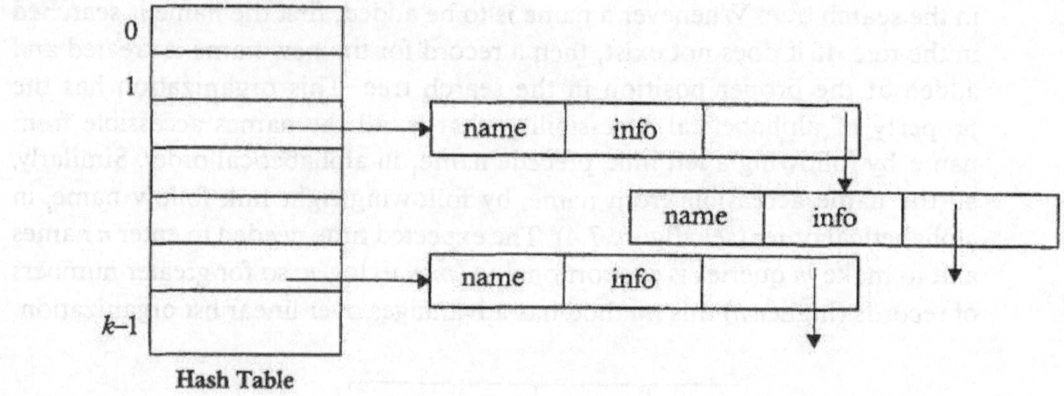

FIGURE 7.5 Hash table method of symbol table organization.

7.7 REPRESENTING THE SCOPE INFORMATION IN THE SYMBOL TABLE

Every name possesses a region of validity within the source program, called the "scope" of that name. The rules governing the scope of names in a block-structured language are as follows:

1. A name declared within a block *B* is valid only within *B*.
2. If block *B*1 is nested within *B*2, then any name that is valid for *B*2 is also valid for *B*1, unless the identifier for that name is re-declared in *B*1.

These scope rules require a more complicated symbol table organization than simply a list of associations between names and attributes. One technique that can be used is to keep multiple symbol tables, one for each active block, such as the block that the compiler is currently in. Each table is list of names and their associated attributes, and the tables are organized into a stack. Whenever a new block is entered, a new empty table is pushed onto the stack for holding the names that are declared as local to this block. And when a declaration is compiled, the table on the stack is searched for a name. If the name is not found, then the new name is inserted. When a reference to a name is translated, each table is searched, starting from the top table on the stack, ensuring compliance with static scope rules. For example, consider following program structure. The symbol table organization will be as shown in Figure 7.6.

Program main

Var x,y : integer :

```
Procedure P :
Var x,a : boolean;
Procedure q
Var x,y,z : real;
Begin
.
.
end
begin
:
end
begin
:
end
```

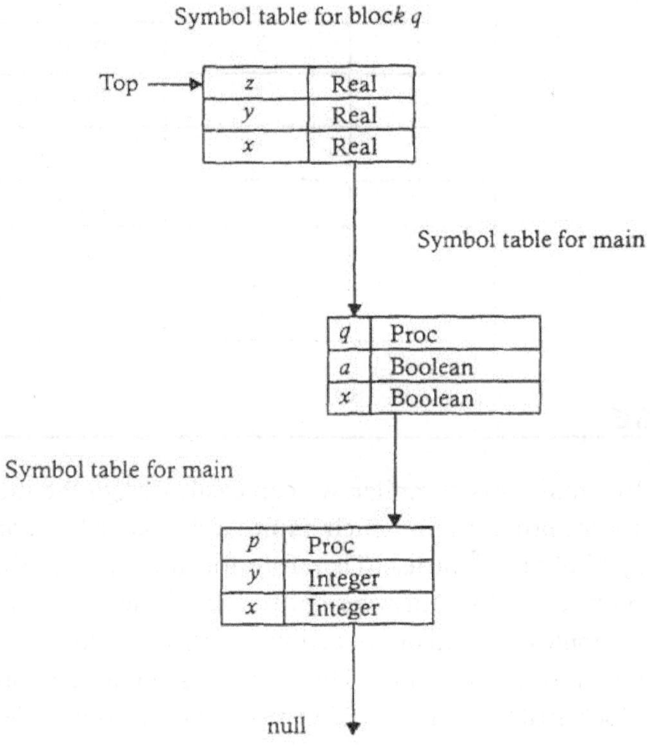

FIGURE 7.6 Symbol table organization that complies with static scope information rules.

Another technique can be used to represent scope information in the symbol table. We store the nesting depth of each procedure block in the symbol table and use the [procedure name, nesting depth] pair as the key to accessing the information from the table. A nesting depth of a procedure is a number that is obtained by starting with a value of one for the main and adding one to it every time we go from an enclosing to an enclosed procedure. This number is basically a count of how many procedures are there in the referencing environment of the procedure.

For example, refer to the program code structure above. The symbol table's contents are shown in Table 7.1.

TABLE 7.1 Symbol Table Contents Using a Nesting Depth Approach

X	1	real
Y	1	real
Z	1	real
q	3	proc
a	3	Boolean
X	3	Boolean
P	2	proc
Y	2	integer
X	2	integer

EXERCISE

1. In a multipass compiler, we can easily design the intermediate form of the source program, in which names are replaced by some form of pointers to symbol table entries. Therefore for latter passes the symbol table that is required is the only the collection of independent entries that contains attributes, instead of collection of entries containing name, attributes, block structure information. Therefore it is possible to strip off the names and block structure information from the symbol table entries. Comment

2. Consider the following C code fragment:

```
void fun()
        {
            int a,b,c;
                ←———————— (A)
            .
            .
            {
                int b,c;
                    ←———————— (B)
                .
                .
                {
                    char a,d;
                        ←———————— (C)
                    .
                    {
                        int x;
                        ←———————— (D)
                        .
                        .
                    }
                }
            }
        }
```

Show the contents of the symbol table at points (A),(B),(C), and (D), assuming that only one symbol table is maintained. (i.e., No new table is created on entry to a block).

3. Repeat the exercise of problem 2, assuming that new symbol table is built for each block on stack.

4. Consider the following code:

```
program test;
    var i,j : integer;
    procedure a;
        var i : integer;
```

```
procedure b;
    var i : real;
        j : real;
        i := i + 10;
        a.i := i * 10;...........................(A)
    end; { of procedure b}
    .
    .
  end; { procedure a}
begin { of main}
  .
a; { call to procedure a}
end.
```

In the above program procedure **b** is defined inside procedure **a**, and therefore variable **i** which is local to procedure **a** is accessible to procedure **b**. But there is a local declaration of variable **i** in procedure **b** which therefore hides variable **i** local to procedure **a**, inside the body of procedure **b**, which again becomes available after exiting procedure **b.** If we modify the language scope rules in such a way that **i** in procedure **a** can be accessed inside the body of procedure **b** using the notation: **block-name.variable-name** as shown at point (A). How it will affect the symbol table organization. Discuss.

8 STORAGE MANAGEMENT

8.1 STORAGE ALLOCATION

One of the important tasks that a compiler must perform is to allocate the resources of the target machine to represent the data objects that are being manipulated by the source program. That is, a compiler must decide the run-time representation of the data objects in the source program. Source program run-time representations of the data objects, such as integers and real variables, usually take the form of equivalent data objects at the machine level; whereas data structures, such as arrays and strings, are represented by several words of machine memory.

The strategies that can be used to allocate storage to the data objects are determined by the rules defining the scope and duration of the names in the programming language. The simplest strategy is static allocation, which is used in languages like FORTRAN. With static allocation, it is possible to determine the run-time size and relative position of each data object during compilation. A more-complex strategy for dynamic memory allocation that involves stacks is required for languages that support recursion: an entry to a new block or procedure causes the allocation of space on a stack, which is freed on exit from the block or procedure. An even more-complex strategy is required for languages, which allows the allocation and freeing of memory for some data in a non-nested fashion. This storage space can be allocated and freed arbitrarily from an area called a "heap." Therefore, implementation of languages like PASCAL and C allow data to be allocated under program control. The run-time organization of the memory will be as shown in Figure 8.1.

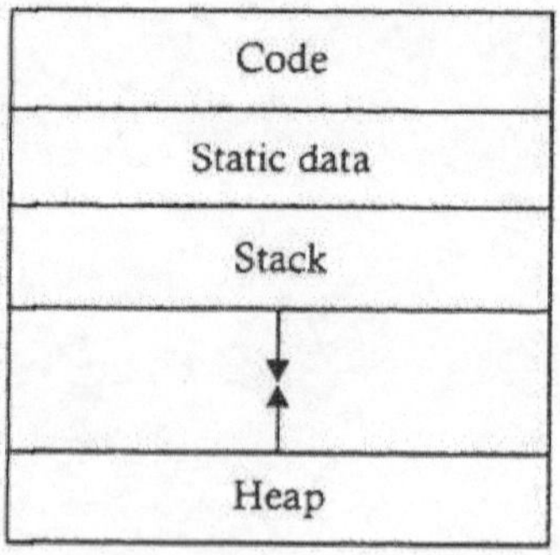

FIGURE 8.1 Heap memory storage allows program-controlled data allocation.

The run-time storage has been subdivided to hold the generated target code and the data objects, which are allocated statically for the stack and heap. The sizes of the stack and heap can change as the program executes.

8.2 ACTIVATION OF THE PROCEDURE AND THE ACTIVATION RECORD

Each execution of a procedure is referred to as an activation of the procedure. This is different from the procedure definition, which in its simplest form is the association of an identifier with a statement; the identifier is the name of the procedure, and the statement is the body of the procedure.

If a procedure is non-recursive, then there exists only one activation of procedure at any one time. Whereas if a procedure is recursive, several activations of that procedure may be active at the same time. The information needed by a single execution or a single activation of a procedure is managed using a contiguous block of storage called an "activation record" or "activation frame" consisting of the collection of fields. (Very often, registers take the place of one or more of the fields in the activation record.) The activation record contains the following information:

1. Temporary values, such as those arising during the evaluation of the expression.
2. Local data of a procedure.

3. The information about the machine state (i.e., the machine status) just before a procedure is called, including PC values and the values of the registers that must be restored when control is relinquished after the procedure.
4. Access links (optional) referring to non-local data that is held in other activation records. This is not required for a language like FORTRAN, because non-local data is kept in fixed place. But it is required for Pascal.
5. Actual parameters (i.e., the parameters supplied to the called procedure). These parameters may also be passed in machine registers for greater efficiency.
6. The return value, used by called procedure to return a value to calling procedure. Again, for greater efficiency, a machine register may be used for returning value.

The size of almost all of the fields of the activation record can be determined at compile time. An exception is if a called procedure has a local array whose size is determined by the values of the actual parameters.

The information in the activation record is organized in a manner that enables easy access at execution time. A pointer to the activation record is required. This pointer is called the current environment pointer (CEP), and it points to one of the fixed fields in the activation record. Using the proper offset from this pointer, and depending upon the format of the activation record, the contents of the activation record can be accessed. Figure 8.2 shows the organization of information in a typical activation record.

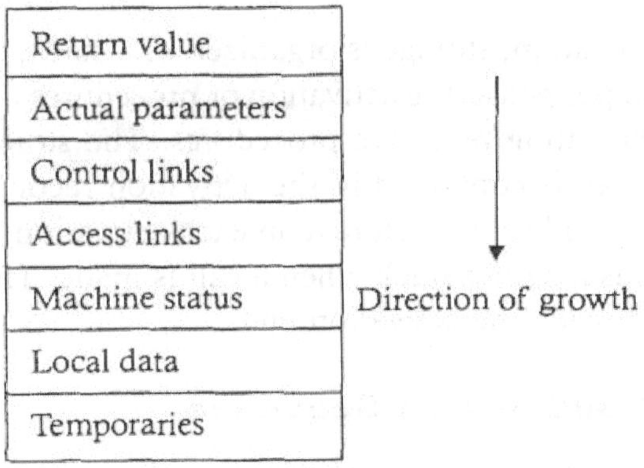

FIGURE 8.2 Typical format of an activation record.

8.3 STATIC ALLOCATION

In static allocation, the names are bound to specific storage locations as the program is compiled. These storage locations cannot be changed during the program's execution. Since the binding does not change at run time, every time a procedure is called, its names are bound to the same storage locations. Hence, if the local names are allocated statically, then their values will be retained throughout the activation of a procedure. The compiler uses the name type to determine the amount of storage to set aside for that name. The address of this storage consists of an offset from an end-of-activation record for the procedure. The compiler must decide where the activation records go relative to the target code and relative to other activation records. Once this decision is made, the storage position for each name in the record is fixed. Therefore, at compile time, it is possible to fill in both the address at which the target code can find the data and the address at which information is saved. However, there are some limitations to using static allocation:

1. The size of the data object and any constraints on its position in memory must be known at compile time.
2. Recursive procedures cannot be permitted, because all activations of a procedure use the same binding for local names.
3. Data structures cannot be created dynamically, since there is no mechanism for storage allocation at run time.

8.4 STACK ALLOCATION

In stack allocation, storage is organized as a stack, and activation records are pushed and popped as the activation of procedures begin and end, respectively, thereby permitting recursive procedures. The storage for the locals in each procedure call is contained in the activation record for that call. Hence, the locals are bound to fresh storage in each activation, because a new activation record is pushed onto stack when a call is made. The storage values of locals are deleted when the activation ends.

8.4.1 The Call and Return Sequence

Procedure calls are implemented by generating what is called a "call sequence and return sequence" in the target code. The job of a call sequence is to set up an activation record. Setting up an activation record means entering the information into the fields of the activation record if the storage for the activation record is allocated statically. When the storage for the activation record is allocated dynamically, storage is allocated for it on the stack, and the information is entered in its fields.

On the other hand, the job of a return sequence is to restore the state of machine so that the machine's calling procedure can continue executing. This also involves destroying the activation record if it was allocated dynamically on the stack.

The code in a call sequence is often divided between the caller and the callee. But there is no exact division of run-time tasks between the caller and callee. It depends on the source language, the target machine, and the operating system. Hence, even when using a common language, the call sequence may differ from implementation to implementation. But it is desirable to put as much of the calling sequence into the callee as possible, because there may be several calls for a procedure. And even though that portion of the calling sequence is generated for each call by the various callers, the portion of the calling sequence is shared within the callee, so it is generated only once. Figure 8.3 shows the format of a typical activation record. Here, the contents of the activation record are accessed using the CEP pointer.

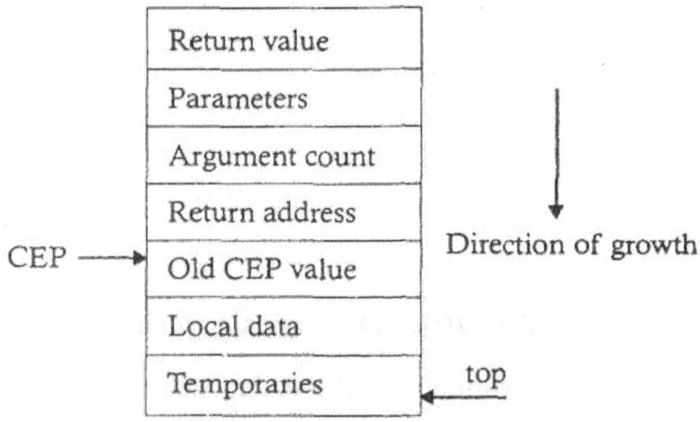

FIGURE 8.3 The CEP pointer is used to access the contents of the activation record.

The stack is assumed to be growing from higher to lower addresses. A positive offset will be used to access the contents of the activation record when we want to go in a direction opposite to that of the growth of the stack (in Figure 8.3, the field pointed to by the CEP). A negative offset will be used to access the contents of the activation record when we want to go in the same direction as the growth of stack. A typical call sequence for caller code to evaluate parameters is as follows:

push ( ) /* for return value
push (T_1) /* T_1 is holding the first argument
push (T_2) /* T_2 is holding the second argument
.
.
.
push (T_n) /* T_n is holding the *n*th argument
push (*n*) /* *n* is the count of arguments
push (*return address*)
push (*CEP*)
goto *start of code segment of callee*

A typical callee code segment is shown in Figure 8.4.

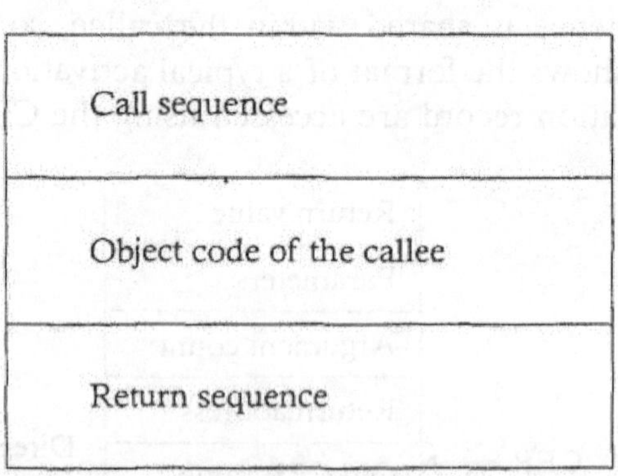

FIGURE 8.4 Typical callee code segment.

A typical call sequence in the callee will be:

CEP = top /*
Code for pushing the local data of
  the callee

And a typical return sequence is:

top = *CEP* + 1
l = *top /* for retrieving return address
top = top + 1

CEP = **CEP* / for resetting the CEP to point to the activation record of the caller

top = top+ *top +2 /*for resetting top to point to the top of the activation record of caller goto1

goto *l* → add two statements

8.4.2 Access to Nonlocal Names

The way that the nonlocals are accessed depends on the scope rules of the language (see Chapter 7). There are two different types of scope rules: static scope rules and dynamic scope rules.

Static scope rules determine which declaration a name's reference will be associated with, depending upon the program's language, thereby determining from where the name's value will be obtained at run time. When static scope rules are used during compilation, the compiler knows how the declarations are bound to the name references, and hence, from where their values will be obtained at run time. What the compiler has to do is to provision the retrieval of the nonlocal name value when it is accessed at run time.

Whereas when dynamic scope rules are used, the values of nonlocal names are retrieved at run time by scanning down the stack, starting at the top-most activation record. The rule for associating a nonlocal reference to a declaration is simple when procedure nesting is not permitted. In the absence of nested procedures, the storage for all names declared outside any procedure can be allocated statically. The position of this storage is known at compile time, so if a name is nonlocal in some procedure's body, its statically determined address is used; whereas if a name is local, it is assessed via a CEP pointer using the suitable offset.

An important benefit of static allocation for nonlocals is that declared procedures can be freely passed as parameters and returned as results. For example, a function inCis passed by address; that is, a pointer is passed to it. When the procedures are nested, declarations are bound to name references according to the following rule: if a name x is not declared in a procedure P, then an occurrence of x in P is in the scope of a declaration of x in an enclosing procedure P_1 such that:

1. The enclosing procedure P_1 has a declaration of x, and
2. P_1 is more closely nested around P than any other procedure with a decla ration of x.

Therefore, a reference to a nonlocal name x is resolved by associating it with the declaration of x in P_1, and the compiler is required to provision for getting the value of x at run time from the most-recent activation record of P_1 by generating a suitable call sequence.

One of the ways to implement this is to add a pointer, called an "access link," to each activation record. And if a procedure P is nested immediately within Q in the source text, then make the access link in the activation record P, pointing to the most-recent activation record of Q. This requires an activation record with a format like that shown in Figure 8.5.

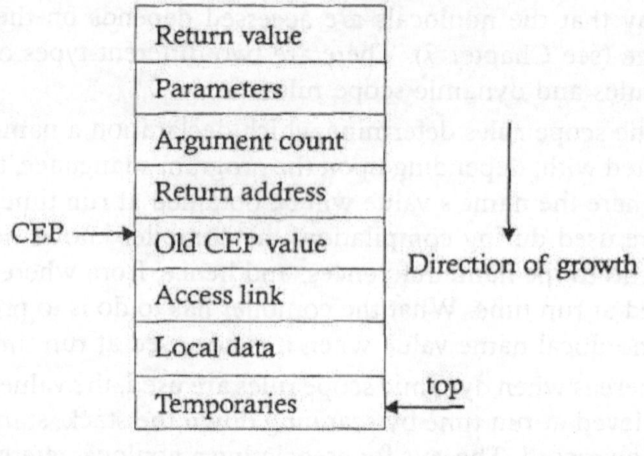

FIGURE 8.5 An activation record that deals with nonlocal name references.

The modified call and return sequence, required for setting up the activation record shown in Figure 8.5, is:

push ( ) /* for return value

push (T_1) /* T_1 is holding the first argument

push (T_2) /* T_2 is holding the second argument

.

.

.

push (T_n) /* T_n is holding the nth argument

push(n) /* n is the count of arguments

push (*return address*)

push (*CEP*)

code to set up access link

goto *start of code segment of callee*

A typical callee segment is shown in Figure 8.6.

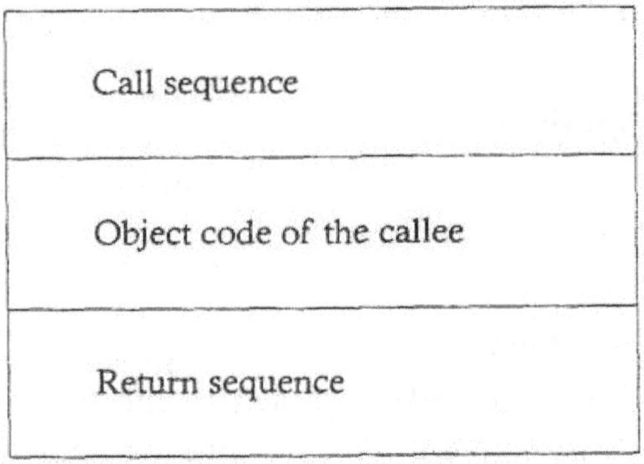

FIGURE 8.6 A typical callee segment.

A typical call sequence in the callee is:

CEP = top+1/* code for pushing the local data of the callee

A typical return sequence is:

top = *CEP*+1

1 = *top /* for retrieving return address

top = top+1

CEP = **CEP* / for resetting the CEP to point to
the activation record of caller

top = top + *top +2/* for resetting top to point to the top of
the activation record of caller goto 1

8.4.3 Setting Up the Access Link

To generate the code for setting up the access link, a compiler makes use of the following information: the nesting depth of the caller procedure and the nesting depth of the callee procedure. A procedure's nesting depth is number that is obtained by starting with value of one for the main and adding one to it every time we go from an enclosing to an enclosed procedure. This number is basically a count of how many procedures are there in the referencing environment of the procedure.

Suppose that procedure *p* at a nesting depth *Np* calls a procedure *q* at nesting depth *Nq*. Then the access link in the activation record of procedure *q* is set up as follows:

if ($Nq > Np$) then

The access link in the activation record of procedure q is set to point to the activation record of procedure p.

else

if ($Nq = Np$) then

Copy the access link in the activation record of procedure p into the activation record of procedure q.

else

if ($Nq < Np$) then

Follow ($Np - Nq$) links to reach to the activation record, and copy the access link of this activation record into the activation record of procedure q.

The Block Structure

A block is a statement that contains its own local data declarations. Blocks can either be independent—like *B*1 begin and *B*1 end, then *B*2 begin and *B*2 end—or they can be nested—like *B*1 begin and *B*2 begin, then *B*2 end and *B*1 end. This nesting property is sometimes called a "block structure." The scope of a declaration in a block-structured language is given by the most closely nested rule:

1. The scope of a declaration in a block *B* includes *B*.
2. If a name *X* is not declared in a block *B*, then an occurrence of *X* in *B* is in the scope of a declaration of *X* in an enclosing block *B*, such that:

(*a*) *B* has a declaration of *X*, and

(*b*) *B* is more closely nested around *B* than any other block with a declaration of *X*.

Block structure can be implemented using stack allocation. Space is allocated for declared names. The block is entered by pushing an activation record, and it is de-allocated when control leaves the block and the activation record is destroyed. That is, a block is treated like a parameter-less procedure, called only at the entry to the block and returned upon exit from the block. An alternative is to allocate storage for a complete procedure body at one time. If there are blocks within the procedure, then an allowance is made for the storage needed by the declarations within the block, as shown in Figure 8.7. For example, consider the following program structure:

```
main ()
{
   int a;
   {
   int b;
         {
         int c;
         printf ("% d% d\n", b,c);
         }
         {
         intd;
         printf("% d% d\n", b, d);
         }
   }
   printf("% d\n",a);
}
```

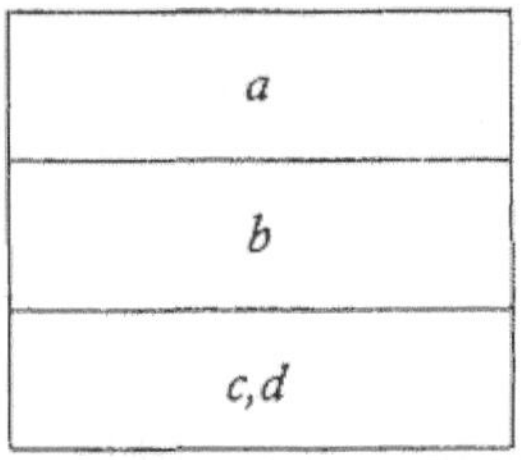

FIGURE 8.7 Storage for declared names.

EXERCISE

1. If we want to support local arrays of variable size, then suggest the storage allocation that is suitable to meet the requirement.
2. Consider the following function:

```
void fun(int x , float y , char z)
   {
      int *a;
      float b[10];
```

```
        .
        .
        .
    }
```

Assuming that storage requirements of various data objects are as follow:

int – 2 bytes

char – 1 byte

float – 4 bytes

pointer – 4 bytes

Determine offset from CEP of x,y,z,a,b[20], and b[5], using the activation record structure discussed in the chapter.

3. Consider the following C code:

```
int a = 1;
void fun(int x)
   {
        static int b;
                  <------------ (B)
        b = x + 1;
   }
void main()
   {
        int n = 5;
                  <------------ (A)
        fun(n);
   }
```

Give the possible organization of run-time environment at the points marked (A) and (B) in the code.

4. Compare display implementation with static chain pointer implementation.
5. A variation of call by name is call by need (also called as lazy evaluation) which prevents reevaluation of arguments. That means the argument is evaluated only first time it is used, and uses the value computed by this evaluation at every subsequent use of that argument. Give an example showing that it gives different results from call by name.
6. Compare call by value result and call by reference parameter passing mechanisms. Can they produce different results? When?
7. Where the static internal variables in C program are allocated? Why?

9 ERROR HANDLING

9.1 ERROR RECOVERY

One of the important tasks that a compiler must perform is the detection of and recovery from errors. Recovery from errors is important, because the compiler will be scanning and compiling the entire program, perhaps in the presence of errors; so as many errors as possible need to be detected.

Every phase of a compilation expects the input to be in a particular format, and whenever that input is not in the required format, an error is returned. When detecting an error, a compiler scans some of the tokens that are ahead of the error's point of occurrence. The fewer the number of tokens that must be scanned ahead of the point of error occurrence, the better the compiler's error-detection capability. For example, consider the following statement:

if $a = b$ then $x\!: = y + z$;

The error in the above statement will be detected in the syntactic analysis phase, but not before the syntax analyzer sees the token "then"; but the first token, itself, is in error.

After detecting an error, the first thing that a compiler is supposed to do is to report the error by producing a suitable diagnostic. A good error diagnostic should possess the following properties.

1. The message should be produced in terms of the original source program rather than in terms of some internal representation of the source program. For example, the message should be produced along with the line numbers of the source program.

2. The error message should be easy to understand by the user.
3. The error message should be specific and should localize the problem. For example, an error message should read, "x is not declared in function fun," and not just, "missing declaration."
4. The message should not be redundant; that is, the same message should not be produced again and again.

Therefore, a compiler should report errors by generating messages with the above properties. The errors captured by the compiler can be classified as either syntactic errors or semantic errors. Syntactic errors are those errors that are detected in the lexical or syntactic analysis phase by the compiler. Semantic errors are the other errors detected by the compiler.

9.2 RECOVERY FROM LEXICAL PHASE ERRORS

The lexical analyzer detects an error when it discovers that an input's prefix does not fit the specification of any token class. After detecting an error, the lexical analyzer can invoke an error recovery routine. This can entail a variety of remedial actions.

The simplest possible error recovery is to skip the erroneous characters until the lexical analyzer finds another token. But this is likely to cause the parser to read a deletion error, which can cause severe difficulties in the syntax-analysis and remaining phases. One way the parser can help the lexical analyzer can improve its ability to recover from errors is to make its list of legitimate tokens (in the current context) available to the error recovery routine. The error-recovery routine can then decide whether a remaining input's prefix matches one of these tokens closely enough to be treated as that token.

9.3 RECOVERY FROM SYNTACTIC PHASE ERRORS

A parser detects an error when it has no legal move from its current configuration. The $LL(1)$ and $LR(1)$ parsers use the valid prefix property; therefore, they are capable of announcing an error as soon as they read an input that is not a valid continuation of the previous input's prefix. This is earliest time that a left-to-right parser can announce an error. But there are a variety of other types of parsers that do not necessarily have this property.

The advantages of using a parser with a valid-prefix-property capability is that it reports an error as soon as possible, and it minimizes the amount of erroneous output passed to subsequent phases of the compiler.

Panic Mode Recovery

Panic mode recovery is an error recovery method that can be used in any kind of parsing, because error recovery depends somewhat on the type of parsing technique used. In panic mode recovery, a parser discards input symbols until a statement delimiter, such as a semicolon or an end, is encountered. The parser then deletes stack entries until it finds an entry that will allow it to continue parsing, given the synchronizing token on the input. This method is simple to implement, and it never gets into an infinite loop.

9.4 ERROR RECOVERY IN LR PARSING

A systematic method for error recovery in *LR* parsing is to scan down the stack until a state *S* with a goto on a particular nonterminal *A* is found, and then discard zero or more input symbols until a symbol *a* is found that can legitimately follow *A*. The parser then shifts the state goto [*S*, *A*] on the stack and resumes normal parsing.

There might be more than one choice for the nonterminal *A*. Normally, these would be nonterminals representing major program pieces, such as statements.

Another method of error recovery that can be implemented is called "phrase level recovery." Each error entry in the *LR* parsing table is examined, and, based on language usage, an appropriate error-recovery procedure is constructed. For example, to recover from an construct error that starts with an operator, the error-recovery routine will push an imaginary id onto the stack and cover it with the appropriate state. While doing this, the error entries in a particular state that call for a particular reduction on some input symbols are replaced by that reduction. This has the effect of postponing the error detection until one or more reductions are made; but the error will still be caught before a shift.

A phrase level error-recovery implementation for an *LR* parser is shown below. The parsing table's grammar is:

$$E \rightarrow E + E \mid E * E \mid \text{id}$$

The *SLR* parsing table for the above grammar is shown in Table 9.1.

TABLE 9.1 Parsing Table for $E \to E + E \mid E * E \mid \text{id}$

	id	+	*	$	E
I_0	S_2				1
I_1		S_3	S_4	Accept	
I_2		R_3	R_3	R_3	
I_3	S_2				5
I_4	S_2				6
I_5		S_3/R_1	S_4/R_1	R_1	
I_6		S_3/R_2	S_4/R_2	R_2	

The conflict is resolved by giving higher precedence to * and using left-associativity, as shown in Table 9.2.

TABLE 9.2 Parsing Table without Parsing Action Conflicts

	id	+	*	$	E
I_0	S_2				1
I_1		S_3	S_4	Accept	
I_2		R_3	R_3	R_3	
I_3	S_2				5
I_4	S_2				6
I_5		R_1	S_4	R_1	
I_6		R_2	R_2	R_2	

The parsing table with error routines is shown in Table 9.3,

TABLE 9.3 Parsing Table with Error Routines

	id	+	*	$	E
I_0	S_2	e_1	e_1	e_1	1
I_1	e_2	S_3	S_4	Accept	
I_2	R_3	R_3	R_3	R_3	
I_3	S_2	e_1	e_1	e_1	5
I_4	S_2	e_1	e_1	e_1	6
I_5	R_1	R_1	S_4	R_1	
I_6	R_2	R_2	R_2	R_2	

where routine e_1 is called from states I_0, I_3, and I_4, which pushes an imaginary id onto the stack and covers it with state I_2. The routine e_2 is called from state I_1, which pushes + onto stack and covers it with state I_3.

For example, if we trace the behavior of the parser described above for the input id + *id $:

Stack Contents	**Unspent Input**	**Moves**
$\$I_0$	id+*id$	shift and enter into state 2
$\$I_0\text{id}I_2$	+*id$	reduce by production number 3
$\$I_0EI_1$	+*id$	shift and enter into state 3
$\$I_0EI_1+I_3$	*id$	call error routine *e*1
$\$I_0EI_1+I_3$**id I**$_2$ (**id** I_2 **pushed by** ***e*1**)	*id$	reduce by production number 3
$\$I_0EI_1+I_3EI_5$	*id$	shift and enter into state 4
$\$I_0EI_1+I_3EI_5*I_4$	id$	shift and enter into state 2
$\$I_0EI_1+I_3EI_5*I_4\text{id}I_2$	$	reduce by production number 3
$\$I_0EI_1+I_3EI_5*I_4EI_6$	$	reduce by production number 2
$\$I_0EI_1+I_3EI_5$	$	reduce by production number 1
$\$I_0EI_1$	$	accept

Similarly, if we trace the behavior of the parser for the input id id*id $:

Stack Contents	Unspent Input	Moves
$\$I_0$	id id*id$	shift and enter into state 2
$\$I_0\text{id}I_2$	id*id$	reduce by production number 3
$\$I_0EI_1$	id*id$	call error routine e_2
$\$I_0EI_1+I_3$	id*id$	shift and enter into state 2
(I_3 pushed by *e*2)		
$\$I_0EI_1+I_3\text{id}\,I_2$	*id$	reduce by production number 3
$\$I_0EI_1+I_3EI_5$	*id$	shift and enter into state 4
$\$I_0EI_1+I_3EI_5{*}I_4$	id$	shift and enter into state 2
$\$I_0EI_1+I_3EI_5{*}I_4\text{id}I_2$	$	reduce by production number 3
$\$I_0EI_1+I_3EI_5{*}I_4EI_6$	$	reduce by production number 2
$\$I_0EI_1+I_3EI_5$	$	reduce by production number 1
$\$I_0EI_1$	$	accept

9.5 AUTOMATIC ERROR RECOVERY IN YACC

The tool YACC can generate a parser with the ability to automatically recover from the errors. Major nonterminals, such as those for program blocks or statements, are identified; and then error productions of the form $A \rightarrow$ error α are added to the grammar, where α is usually $\in$.

When YACC-generated parser encounters an error, it finds the top-most state on its stack, whose underlying set of items includes an item of the form $A \rightarrow$ .error. Therefore, the parser shifts the token error, and a reduction to A is immediately possible. The parser then invokes a semantic action associated with production $A \rightarrow$ error, and this semantic action takes care of recovering from the error.

9.6 PREDICTIVE PARSING ERROR RECOVERY

An error is detected during predictive parsing when the terminal on the top of the stack does not match the next input symbol, or when nonterminal A is on top of the stack and a is the next input symbol. $M[A,a]$ is the error entry.

Panic mode recovery can be used to recover from an error detected by the *LL* parser. The effectiveness of panic mode recovery depends on the choice of the synchronizing token. Several heuristics can be used when selecting the synchronizing token in order to ensure quick recovery from common errors:

1. All the symbols in the FOLLOW(A) must be kept in the set of synchronizing tokens, because if we skip until an a symbol in FOLLOW(A) is read, and we pop A from the stack, it is likely that the parsing can continue.
2. Since the syntactic structure of a language is very often hierarchical, we add the symbols that begin higher constructs to the synchronizing set of lower constructs. For example, we add keywords to the synchronizing sets of nonterminals that generate expressions.
3. We also add the symbols in FIRST(A) to the synchronizing set of nonterminal A. This provides for a resumption of parsing according to A if a symbol in FIRST(A) appears in the input.
4. A derivation by an $\in$-production can be used as a default. Error detection will be postponed, but the error will still be captured. This method reduces the number of nonterminals that must be considered during error recovery.

Another method of error recovery that can be implemented is called "phrase level recovery." In phrase level recovery, each error entry in the LL parsing table is examined, and based on language usage, an appropriate error-recovery procedure is constructed. For example, to recover from a construct error that starts with an operator, the error-recovery routine will insert an imaginary id into the input. Then, if some state terminal symbols are derived using an $\in$-production, the error entries in that state are replaced by the derivation using the imaginary-id $\in$-production. This has the effect of postponing error detection.

A phrase level error-recovery implementation for an *LR* parser is shown in Tables 9.4 and 9.5. The parsing table is constructed for the following grammar:

$$E \rightarrow TE_1$$
$$E_1 \rightarrow +TE_1 \mid \in$$
$$T \rightarrow FT_1$$
$$T_1 \rightarrow * FT_1 \mid \in$$
$$F \rightarrow \text{id}$$

TABLE 9.4 *LR* Parsing Table

	id	+	*	$
E	$E \rightarrow TE_1$			
T	$T \rightarrow FT_1$			
F	$F \rightarrow$ id			
E_1		$E_1 \rightarrow +TE_1$		$E_1 \rightarrow \epsilon$
T_1		$T_1 \rightarrow \epsilon$	$T_1 \rightarrow *FT_1$	$T_1 \rightarrow \epsilon$
id	pop			
+		pop		
*			pop	
$				accept

The modified table is shown in Table 9.5. Routine e_1, when called, pushes an imaginary id into the input; and routine e_2, when called, removes all the remaining symbols from the input.

TABLE 9.5 Phrase Level Error-Recovery Implementation

	id	+	*	$
E	$E \rightarrow TE_1$	e_1	e_1	e_1
T	$T \rightarrow FT_1$	e_1	e_1	e_1
	$F \rightarrow$ id	e_1	e_1	e_1
E_1	$E_1 \rightarrow \epsilon$	$E_1 \rightarrow +TE_1$	$E_1 \rightarrow \epsilon$	$E_1 \rightarrow \epsilon$
T_1	$T_1 \rightarrow \epsilon$	$T_1 \rightarrow \epsilon$	$T_1 \rightarrow *FT_1$	$T_1 \rightarrow \epsilon$
id	pop			
+		pop		
*			pop	
$	e_2	e_2	e_2	accept

For example, if we trace the behavior of the parser shown in Table 9.5 for the input id + *id $:

Stack Contents	Unspent Input	Moves
$\$E$	id+*id$	derive using $E \rightarrow TE_1$
$\$E_1T$	id+*id$	derive using $T \rightarrow FT_1$
$\$E_1T_1F$	id+*id$	derive using $F \rightarrow$ id
$\$E_1T_1$id	id+*id$	pop
$\$E_1T_1$	+*id$	derive using $T_1 \rightarrow \in$
$\$E_1$	+*id$	derive using $E_1 \rightarrow +TE_1$
$\$E_1T+$	+*id$	pop
$\$E_1T$	*id$	call error routine $e1$
$\$E_1T$	**id*id$**	derive using $T \rightarrow FT_1$
	(imaginary id is pushed by e_1)	
$\$E_1T_1$F	id*id$	derive using $F \rightarrow$ id
$\$E_1T_1$id	id*id$	pop E_1T_1F Id pop
$\$E_1T_1$	*id$	derive using $T_1 \rightarrow *FT_1$
$\$E_1T_1$F	id$	derive using $F \rightarrow$ id
$\$E_1T_1$F	id$	pop
$\$E_1T_1$id	id$	pop
$\$E_1T_1$	$	derive using $T_1 \rightarrow \in$
$\$E_1$	$	derive using $E_1 \rightarrow \in$
$	$	accept

Similarly, if we trace the behavior for the input id id*id $:

Stack Contents	Unspent Input	Moves
$\$E$	id id*id$	derive using $E \rightarrow TE_1$
$\$E_1T$	id+*id$	derive using $T \rightarrow FT_1$
$\$E_1T_1F$	id+*id$	derive using $F \rightarrow$ id
$\$E_1T_1$id	id+*id$	pop
$\$E_1T_1$	id*id$	derive using $T_1 \rightarrow \in$
$\$E_1$	id*id$	derive using $E_1 \rightarrow \in$
$	**id*id$**	call error routine e_2
	(id*id$ is removed by e_2)	
$	$	accept

9.7 RECOVERY FROM SEMANTIC ERRORS

The primary sources of semantic errors are undeclared names and type incompatibilities. Recovery from an undeclared name is rather straightforward. The first time the undeclared name is encountered, an entry can be made in the symbol table for that name with an attribute that is appropriate to the current context. For example, if missing declaration error of *x* is encountered, then the error-recovery routine enters the appropriate attribute for *x* in *x's* symbol table, depending on the current context of *x*. A flag is then set in the *x* symbol table record to indicate that an attribute has been added, and to recover from an error or not in response to the declaration of *x*.

EXERCISE

1. In which phase of compilation process type errors are detected.
2. In which phase of compilation process the type of literal becomes known to the compiler.
3. Give an example of an error detected during code optimization phase.
4. Detect errors if any in the following constructs. Also find out, on what token appearing next, those errors are detected:
   (*a*) whilea = bx=y+z;
   (*b*) a + b * + c;
   (*c*) (a + b) = c;
5. Trace out the moves of the parser whose parsing table is given in Table 9.3, for the input: id + id * * id

10 CODE OPTIMIZATION

10.1 INTRODUCTION TO CODE OPTIMIZATION

The translation of a source program to an object program is basically one to many mappings; that is, there are many object programs for the same source program, which implement the same computations. Some of these object-programs may be better than other object programs when it comes to storage requirements and execution speeds. Code optimization refers to techniques a compiler can employ in order to produce an improved object code for a given source program.

How beneficial the optimization is depends upon the situation. For a program that is only expected to be run a few times, and which will then be discarded, no optimization is necessary. Whereas if a program is expected to run indefinitely, or if it is expected to run many times, then optimization is useful, because the effort spent on improving the program's execution time will be paid back, even if execution time is only reduced by a small percentage.

What follows are some optimization techniques that are useful when designing optimizing compilers.

10.2 WHAT IS CODE OPTIMIZATION?

Code optimization refers to the techniques used by the compiler to improve the execution efficiency of the generated object code. It involves a complex analysis of the intermediate code and the performance of various transformations; but every optimizing transformation must also preserve the semantics of the program. That is, a compiler should not attempt any optimization that would lead to a change in the program's semantics.

Optimization can be machine-independent or machine-dependent. Machine-independent optimizations can be performed independently of the target machine for which the compiler is generating code; that is, the optimizations are not tied to the target machine's specific platform or language. Examples of machine-independent optimizations are: elimination of loop invariant computation, induction variable elimination, and elimination of common subexpressions.

On the other hand, machine-dependent optimization requires knowledge of the target machine. An attempt to generate object code that will utilize the target machine's registers more efficiently is an example of machine-dependent code optimization. Actually, code optimization is a misnomer; even after performing various optimizing transformations, there is no guarantee that the generated object code will be optimal. Hence, we are actually performing code improvement. When attempting any optimizing transformation, the following criteria should be applied:

1. The optimization should capture most of the potential improvements without an unreasonable amount of effort.
2. The optimization should be such that the meaning of the source program is preserved.
3. The optimization should, on average, reduce the time and space expended by the object code.

10.3 LOOP OPTIMIZATION

Loop optimization is the most valuable machine-independent optimization because a program's inner loops are good candidates for improvement. The important loop optimizations are elimination of loop invariant computations and elimination of induction variables. A loop invariant computation is one that computes the same value every time a loop is executed. Therefore, moving such a computation outside the loop leads to a reduction in the execution time. Induction variables are those variables used in a loop; their values are in lock-step, and hence, it may be possible to eliminate all except one.

10.3.1 Eliminating Loop Invariant Computations

To eliminate loop invariant computations, we first identify the invariant computations and then move them outside loop if the move does not lead to a change in the program's meaning. Identification of loop invariant computation requires the detection of loops in the program. Whether a loop exists in the program or not depends on the program's control flow, therefore, requiring a control flow analysis. For loop detection, a graphical representation, called a "program flow graph," shows how the control is flowing in the program and how the control is being used. To obtain such a graph, we must partition the intermediate code into basic blocks. This requires identifying leader statements, which are defined as follows:

1. The first statement is a leader statement.
2. The target of a conditional or unconditional goto is a leader.
3. A statement that immediately follows a conditional goto is a leader.

A basic block is a sequence of three-address statements that can be entered only at the beginning, and control ends after the execution of the last statement, without a halt or any possibility of branching, except at the end.

10.3.2 Algorithm to Partition Three-Address Code into Basic Blocks

To partition three-address code into basic blocks, we must identify the leader statements in the three-address code and then include all the statements, starting from a leader, and up to, but not including, the next leader. The basic blocks into which the three-address code is partitioned constitute the nodes or vertices of the program flow graph. The edges in the flow graph are decided as follows. If *B*1 and *B*2 are the two blocks, then add an edge from *B*1 to *B*2 in the program flow graph, if the block *B*2 follows *B*1 in an execution sequence. The block *B*2 follows *B*1 in an execution sequence if and only if:

1. The first statement of block *B*2 immediately follows the last statement of block *B*1 in the three-address code, and the last statement of block *B*1 is not an unconditional goto statement.
2. The last statement of block *B*1 is either a conditional or unconditional goto statement, and the first statement of block *B*2 is the target of the last statement of block *B*1.

For example, consider the following program fragment:

```
Fact(x)
{
    int f = 1;
    for(i = 2; i<=x; i++)
    f = f*i;
    return(f);
}
```

The three-address-code representation for the program fragment above is:

(1) $f = 1;$

(2) $i = 2$

(3) if $i <= x$ goto(8)

(4) $f = f * i$

(5) $t1 = i + 1$

(6) $i = t1$

(7) goto(3)

(8) goto calling program

The leader statements are:

- Statement number 1, because it is the first statement.
- Statement number 3, because it is the target of a goto.
- Statement number 4, because it immediately follows a conditional goto statement.
- Statement number 8, because it is a target of a conditional goto statement.

Therefore, the basic blocks into which the above code can be partitioned are as follows, and the program flow graph is shown in Figure 10.1.

- Block *B*1:

$f = 1;$ $i = 2$

- Block *B*2:

if $i <= x$ goto(8)

- Block *B*3:

$f = f * i$ $t1 = i + 1$ $i = t1$ goto(3)

- Block *B*4:

goto calling program

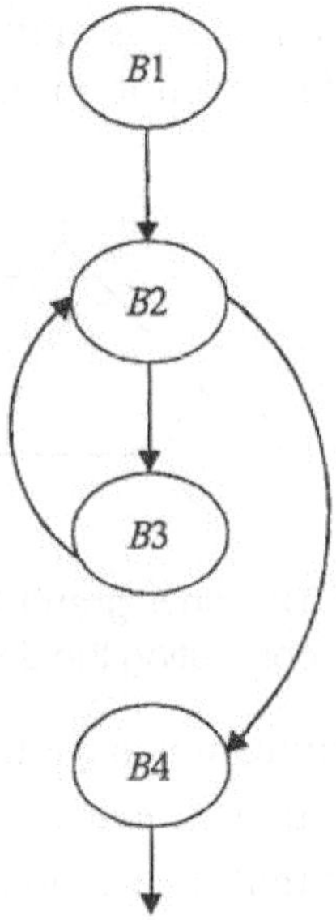

FIGURE 10.1 Program flow graph.

10.3.3 Loop Detection

A loop is a cycle in the flow graph that satisfies two properties:

1. It should have a single entry node or header, so that it will be possible to move all of the loop invariant computations to a unique place, called a "preheader," which is a block/node placed outside the loop, just in front of the header.
2. It should be strongly connected; that is, it should be possible to go from any node of the loop to any other node while staying within the loop. This is required until at least some of the loops get executed repeatedly.

If the flow graph contains one or more back edges, then only one or more loops/cycles exist in the program. Therefore, we must identify any back edges in the flow graph.

10.3.4 Identification of the Back Edges

To identify the back edges in the flow graph, we compute the dominators of every node of the program flow graph. A node *a* is a dominator of node *b* if all the paths starting at the initial node of the graph that reach to node *b* go through *a*. For example, consider the flow graph in Figure 10.2. In this flow graph, the dominator of node 3 is only node 1, because all the paths reaching up to node 3 from node 1 do not go through node 2.

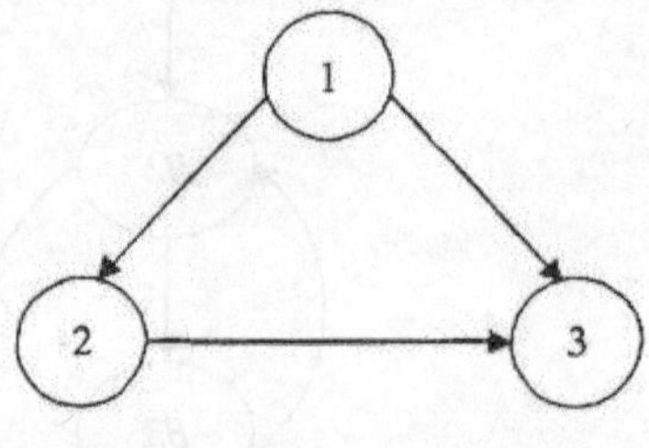

FIGURE 10.2 The flow graph back edges are identified by computing the dominators.

Dominator (dom) relationships have the following properties:

1. They are reflexive; that is, every node dominates itself.
2. That are transitive; that is, if *a* dom *b* and *b* dom *c*, this implies *a* dom *c*.

10.3.5 Reducibie Flow Graphs

Several code-optimization transformations are easy to perform on reducible flow graphs. A flow graph *G* is reducible if and only if we can partition the edges into two disjointed groups, forward edges and back edges, with the following two properties:

1. The forward edges form an acyclic graph in which every node can be reached from the initial node *G*.
2. The back edges consist only of edges whose heads dominate their tails.

For example, consider the flow graph shown in Figure 10.3. This flow graph has no back edges, because no edge's head dominates the tail of that edge. Hence, it could have been a reducible graph if the entire graph had been acyclic. But that is not the case. Therefore, it is not a reducible flow graph.

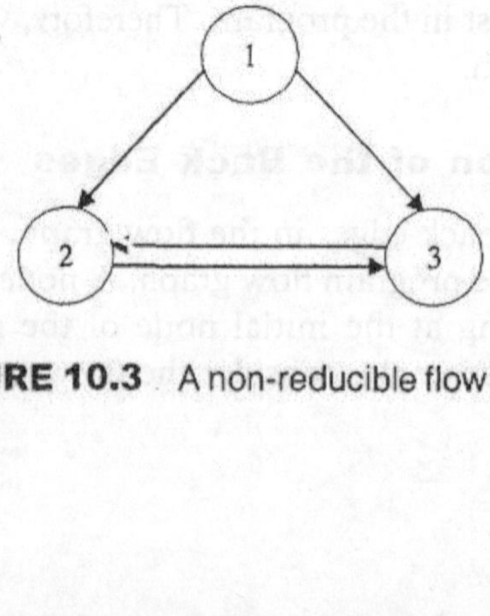

FIGURE 10.3 A non-reducible flow graph.

After identifying the back edges, if any, the natural loop of every back edge must be identified. The natural loop of a back edge $a \rightarrow b$ is the set of all those nodes that can reach a without going through b, including node b itself. Therefore, to find a natural loop of the back edge $n \rightarrow d$, we start with node n and add all the predecessors of node n to the loop. Then we add the predecessors of the nodes that were just added to the loop; and we continue this process until we reach node d. These nodes plus node d constitute the set of all those nodes that can reach node n without going through node d. This is the natural loop of the edge $n \rightarrow d$. Therefore, the algorithm for detecting the natural loop of a back edge is:

Input : back edge $n \rightarrow d$.

Output: set loop, which is a set of nodes forming the natural loop of the back edge $n \rightarrow d$.

```
main()
{
        loop = { d } / * Initialize by adding node d to the set loop*/
        insert(n); /* call a procedure insert with the node n */
}
procedure insert(m)
{
        if m is not in the loop then
          {
          loop = loop ∪ { m }
          for every predecessor p of m do
             insert(p);
          }
}
```

For example in the flow graph shown in Figure 10.1, the back edges are edge $B3 \rightarrow B2$, and the loop is comprised of the blocks $B2$ and $B3$.

After the natural loops of the back edges are identified, the next task is to identify the loop invariant computations. The three-address statement $x = y$ op z, which exists in the basic block B (a part of the loop), is a loop invariant statement if all possible definitions of b and c that reach upto this statement are outside the loop, or if *b* and *c* are constants, because then the calculation *b op c* will be the same each time the statement is encountered in the loop. Hence, to decide whether the statement $x = b\ op\ c$ is loop invariant or not, we must compute the *u–d* chaining information. The *u–d* chaining information is computed by doing a global data flow analysis of the flow graph. All of the definitions that are capable of reaching to a point immediately before the start of the basic block are computed, and we call the set of all such definitions for a block *B* the IN(*B*). The set of all the definitions capable of reaching to a point immediately after the last statement of block *B* will be called OUT(*B*). We compute both IN(*B*) and OUT(*B*) for every block *B*, GEN(*B*) and KILL(*B*), which are defined as:

- GEN(*B*): The set of all the definitions generated in block *B*.
- KILL(*B*): The set of all the definitions outside block *B* that define the same variables as are defined in block *B*.

Consider the flow graph in Figure 10.4.

The GEN and KILL sets for the basic blocks are as shown in Table 10.1.

TABLE 10.1 GEN and KILL sets for Figure 10.4 Flow Graph

Block	GEN	KILL
*B*1	{1,2}	{6,10,11}
*B*2	{3,4}	{5,8}
*B*3	{5}	{4,8}
*B*4	{6,7}	{2,9,11}
*B*5	{8,9}	{4,5,7}
*B*6	{10,11}	{1,2,6}

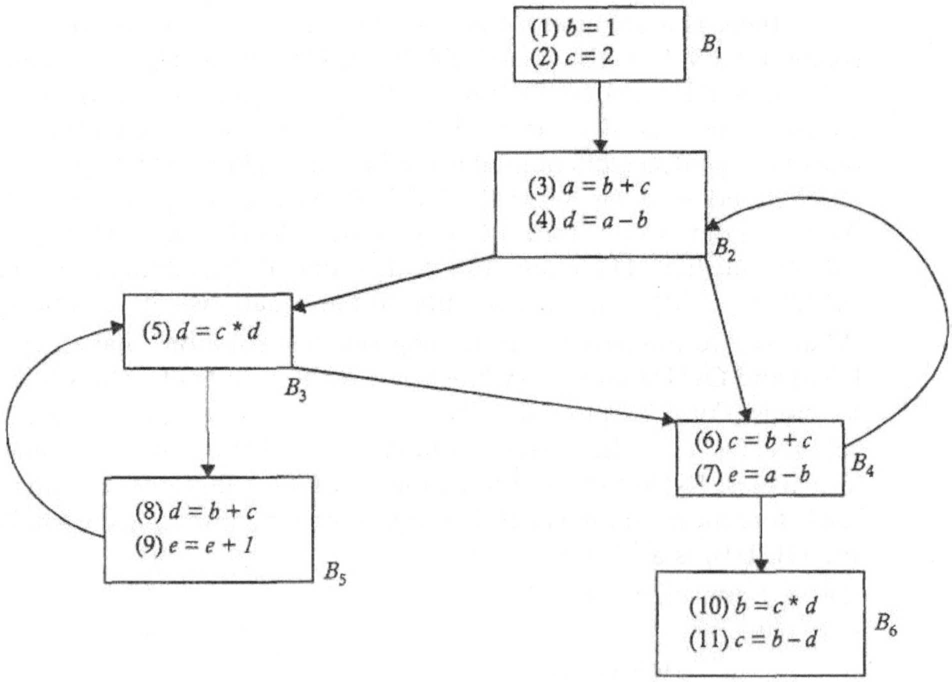

FIGURE 10.4 Flow graph with GEN and KILL block sets.

IN(B) and OUT(B) are defined by the following set of equations, which are called "data flow equations":

$$\text{IN}(B) = \cup\ \text{OUT}(P)$$

$$\text{OUT}(B) = \text{IN}(B) - \text{KILL}(B) \cup \text{GEN}(B)$$

The next step, therefore, is to solve these equations. If there are n nodes, there will be $2n$ equations in $2n$ unknowns. The solution to these equations is not generally unique. This is because we may have a situation like that shown in Figure 10.5, where a block B is a predecessor of itself.

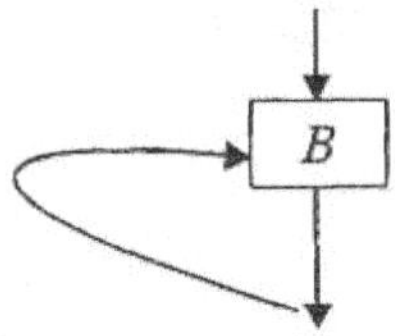

FIGURE 10.5 Nonunique solution to a data flow equation, where B is a predecessor of itself.

If there is a solution to the data flow equations for block B, and if the solution is $IN(B) = IN_0$ and $OUT(B) = OUT_0$, then $IN_0 \cup \{d\}$ and $OUT_0 \cup \{d\}$, where d is any definition not in IN_0. OUT_0 and KILL(B) also satisfy the equations, because if we take $OUT_0 \cup \{d\}$ as the value of OUT(B), since B is one of the predecessors of itself according to $IN(B) = \cup\, OUT(P)$, d gets added to IN(B), because d is not in the KILL(B). Hence, we get $IN(B) = IN_0 \cup \{d\}$. And according to OUT(B) = IN(B) – KILL(B) GEN(B), $OUT(B) = OUT_0 \cup \{d\}$ gets satisfied. Therefore, IN_0, OUT_0 is one of the solutions, whereas $IN_0 \cup \{d\}, OUT_0 \cup \{d\}$ is another solution to the equations—no unique solution. What we are interested is in finding smallest solution, that is, the smallest IN(B) and OUT(B) for every block B, which consists of values that are in all solutions. For example, since IN_0 is in $IN_0 \cup \{d\}$, and OUT_0 is in $OUT_0 \cup \{d\}$, IN_0, OUT_0 is the smallest solution. And this is what we want, because the smallest IN(B) turns out to be the set of all definitions reaching the point just before the beginning of B. The algorithm for computing the smallest IN(B) and OUT(B) is as follows:

```
(1)    For each block B do
       {
               IN(B)= φ
               OUT(B)= GEN(B)
       }
(2)    flag = true
(3)    while (flag) do
       {
               flag = false
               for each block B do
               {
               IN_new(B) = Φ
               for each predecessor P of B
               IN_new(B) = IN_new(B) ∪ OUT(P)
               if IN_new(B) ≠ IN(B) then
                   {
                       flag = true
                       IN(B) = IN_new(B)
                       OUT(B) = IN(B) – KILL(B) ∪ GEN(B)
                   }
               }
       }
```

Initially, we take IN(B) for every block that is to be an empty set, and we take OUT(B) to be GEN(B), and we compute $IN_{new}(B)$. If it is different from IN(B), we compute a new OUT(B) and go for the next iteration. This is continued until IN(B) comes out to be the same for every B in a previous and current iteration.

For example, for the flow graph shown in Figure 10.5, the IN and OUT iterations for the blocks are computed using above algorithm, as shown in Tables 10.2–10.6.

TABLE 10.2 IN and OUT Computation for Figure 10.5

Block	IN	OUT
*B*1	Φ	{1,2}
*B*2	Φ	{3,4}
*B*3	Φ	{5}
*B*4	Φ	{6,7}
*B*5	Φ	{8,9}
*B*6	Φ	{10,11}

TABLE 10.3 First Iteration for the IN and OUT Values

Block	IN	OUT
*B*1	Φ	{1,2}
*B*2	{1,2,6,7}	{1,2,3,4,6,7}
*B*3	{3,4,8,9}	{3,5,9}
*B*4	{3,4,5}	{3,4,5,6,7}
*B*5	{5}	{8,9}
*B*6	{6,7}	{7,10,11}

TABLE 10.4 Second Iteration for the IN and OUT Values

Block	IN	OUT
*B*1	Φ	{1,2}
*B*2	{1,2,3,4,5,6,7}	{1,2,3,4,6,7}
*B*3	{1,2,3,4,6,7,8,9}	{1,2,3,5,6,7,9}
*B*4	{1,2,3,4,5,6,7,9}	{1,3,4,5,6,7}
*B*5	{3,5,9}	{3,8,9}
*B*6	{3,4,5,6,7}	{3,4,5,7,10,11}

TABLE 10.5 Third Iteration for the IN and OUT Values

Block	IN	OUT
*B*1	Φ	{1,2}
*B*2	{1,2,3,4,5,6,7}	{1,2,3,4,6,7}
*B*3	{1,2,3,4,6,7,8,9}	{1,2,3,5,6,7,9}
*B*4	{1,2,3,4,5,6,7,9}	{1,3,4,5,6,7}
*B*5	{1,2,3,5,6,7,9}	{1,2,3,6,8,9}
*B*6	{1,3,4,5,6,7}	{1,3,4,5,7,10,11}

TABLE 10.6 Fourth Iteration for the IN and OUT Values

Block	IN	OUT
*B*1	Φ	{1,2}
*B*2	{1,2,3,4,5,6,7}	{1,2,3,4,6,7}
*B*3	{1,2,3,4,6,7,8,9}	{1,2,3,5,6,7,9}
*B*4	{1,2,3,4,5,6,7,9}	{1,3,4,5,6,7}
*B*5	{1,2,3,5,6,7,9}	{1,2,3,6,8,9}
*B*6	{1,3,4,5,6,7}	{1,3,4,5,7,10,11}

The next step is to compute the *u–d* chains from the reaching definitions information, as follows.

If the use of *A* in block *B* is preceded by its definition, then the *u–d* chain of *A* contains only the last definition prior to this use of *A*. If the use of *A* in block *B* is not preceded by any definition of *A*, then the *u–d* chain for this use consists of all definitions of *A* in IN(*B*).

For example, in the flow graph for which IN and OUT were computed in Tables 10.2–10.6, the use of *a* in definition 4, block *B*2 is preceded by definition 3, which is the definition of *a*. Hence, the *u–d* chain for this use of *a* only contains definition 3. But the use of *b* in *B*2 is not preceded by any definition of *b* in *B*2. Therefore, the *u–d* chain for this use of *B* will be {1}, because this is the only definition of *b* in IN(*B*2).

The *u–d* chain information is used to identify the loop invariant computations. The next step is to perform the code motion, which moves a loop invariant statement to a newly created node, called "preheader," whose only successor is a header of the loop. All the predecessors of the header that lie outside the loop will become predecessors of the preheader.

But sometimes the movement of a loop invariant statement to the preheader is not possible because such a move would alter the semantics of the program. For example, if a loop invariant statement exists in a basic block that is not a dominator of all the exits of the loop (where an exit of the loop is the node whose successor is outside the loop), then moving the loop invariant statement in the preheader may change the semantics of the program. Therefore, before moving a loop invariant statement to the preheader, we must check whether the code motion is legal or not. Consider the flow graph shown in Figure 10.6.

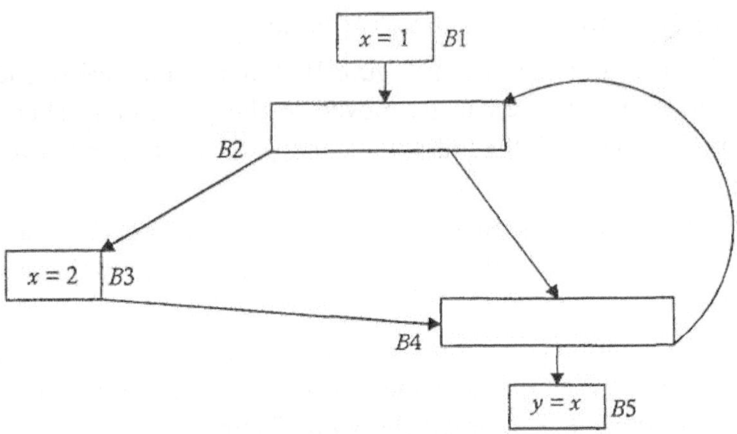

FIGURE 10.6 A flow graph containing a loop invariant statement.

In the flow graph shown in Figure 10.6, $x = 2$ is the loop invariant. But since it occurs in *B*3, which is not the dominator of the exit of loop, if we move it to the preheader, as shown in Figure 10.7, a value of 2 will always get assigned to *y* in *B*5; whereas in the original program, *y* in *B*5 may get value 1 as well as 2.

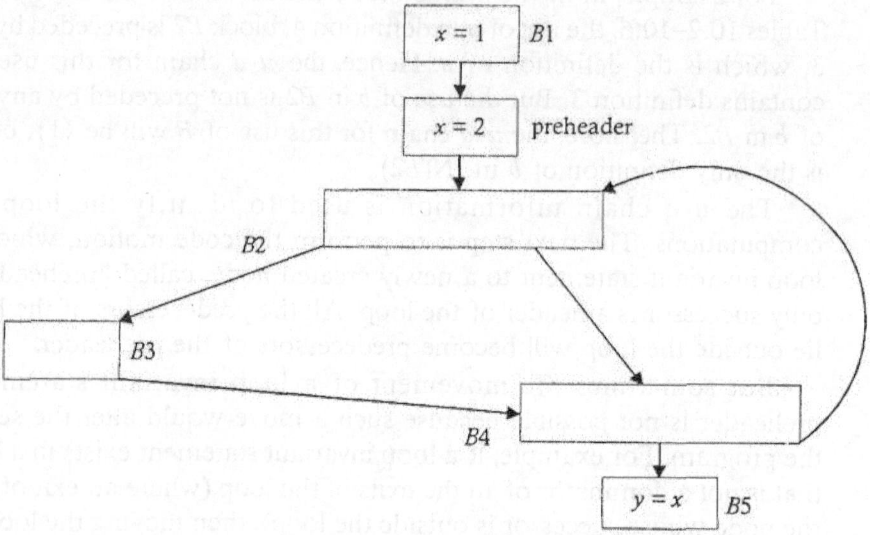

FIGURE 10.7 Moving a loop invariant statement changes the semantics of the program.

After Moving $x = 2$ to the Preheader

In the flow graph shown in Figure 10.7, if *x* is not used outside the loop, then the statement $x = 2$ can be moved to the preheader. Therefore, for a code motion to be legal, the following conditions must be met, even if no errors are encountered:

1. The block in which a loop invariant statement occurs should be a dominator of all exits of the loop, or the name assigned to the block should not be used outside the loop.
2. We cannot move a loop invariant statement assigned to *A* into preheader if there is another statement in the loop that assigns to *A*. For example, consider the flow graph shown in Figure 10.8.

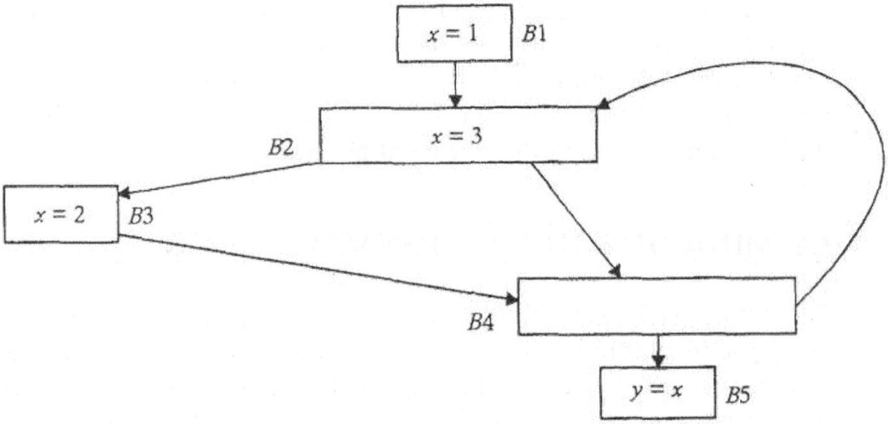

FIGURE 10.8 Moving the preheader changes the meaning of the program.

Even though the statement $x = 3$ in $B2$ satisfies condition (1), moving it to the preheader will change the meaning of the program. Because if $x = 3$ is moved to the preheader, then the value that will be assigned to y in $B5$ will be two if the execution path is $B1$–$B2$–$B3$–$B4$–$B2$–$B4$–$B5$. Whereas for the same execution path, the original program assigns a 3 to y in $B5$.

3. The move is illegal if A is used in the loop, and A is reached by any definition of A other than the statement to be moved. For example, consider the flow graph shown in Figure 10.9.

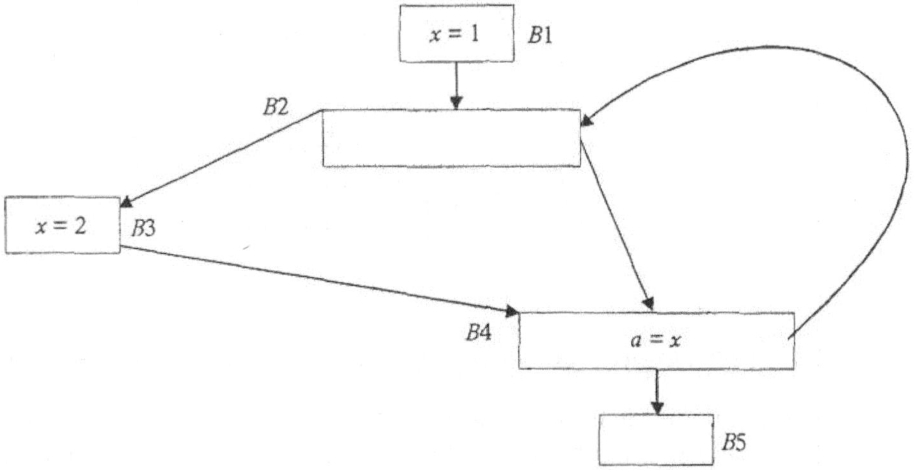

FIGURE 10.9 Moving a value to the preheader changes the original meaning of the program.

Even though x is not used outside the loop, the statement $x = 2$ in the block $B2$ cannot be moved to the preheader, because the use of x in $B4$ is also reached by the definition $x = 1$ in $B1$. Therefore, if we move $x = 2$ to the preheader, then the value that will get assigned to a in $B4$ will always be a 1, which is not the case in the original program.

10.4 ELIMINATING INDUCTION VARIABLES

We define basic induction variables of a loop as those names whose only assignments within the loop are of the form $I = I \pm C$, where C is a constant or a name whose value does not change within the loop. A basic induction variable may or may not form an arithmetic progression at the loop header.

For example, consider the flow graph shown in Figure 10.10. In the loop formed by $B2$, I is a basic induction variable.

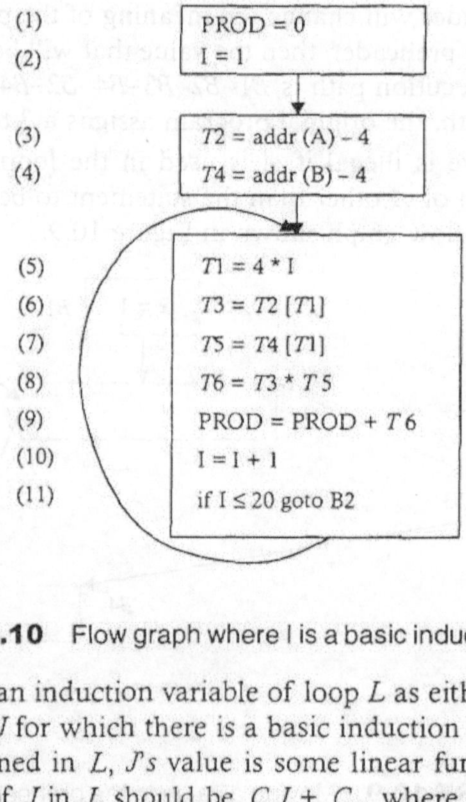

FIGURE 10.10 Flow graph where I is a basic induction variable.

We then define an induction variable of loop L as either a basic induction variable or a name J for which there is a basic induction variable I, such that each time J is assigned in L, J's value is some linear function or value of I. That is, the value of J in L should be $C_1I + C_2$, where C_1 and C_2 could be functions of both constants and loop invariant names. For example, in loop L, I is a basic induction variable; and $T1$ is also an induction variable, because the only assignment of $T1$ in the loop assigns a value to $T1$ that is a linear function of I, computed as $4 * I$.

Algorithm for Detecting and Eliminating Induction Variables

An algorithm exists that will detect and eliminate induction variables. Its method is as follows:

1. Find all of the basic induction variables by scanning the statements of loop L.
2. Find any additional induction variables, and for each such additional induction variable A, find the family of some basic induction B to which A belongs. (If the value of A at the point of assignment is expressed as $C_1B + C_2$, then A is said to belong to the family of basic induction variable B). Specifically, we search for names A with single assignments to A within loop L, and which have one of the following forms:

   $$A = B * C$$
   $$A = C * B$$
   $$A = B/C$$
   $$A = B \pm C$$
   $$A = C \pm B$$

   where C is a loop constant, and B is an induction variable, basic or otherwise. If B is basic, then A is in the family of B. If B is not basic, let B be in the family of D, then the additional requirements to be satisfied are:

   (*a*) There must be no assignment to D between the lone point of assignment to B in L and the assignment to A.

   (*b*) There must be no definition of B outside of L reaches A.
3. Consider each basic induction variable B in turn. For every induction variable A in the family of B:

   (*a*) Create a new name, temp.

   (*b*) Replace the assignment to A in the loop with A = temp.

   (*c*) Set temp to $C_1B + C_2$ at the end of the preheader by adding the statements:

   temp = $C_1 * B$
   temp = temp + C_2 /* omit if $C_2 = 0$*/

(*d*) Immediately after each assignment $B = B + D$, where D is a loop invariant, append:

temp = temp + $C_1 * D$

If D is a loop invariant name, and if $C_1 \neq 1$, create a new loop invariant name for $C_1 * D$, and add the statements:

temp1 = $C_1 * D$

temp = temp + temp1

(*e*) For each basic induction variable B whose only uses are to compute other induction variables in its family and in conditional branches, take some A in B's family, preferably one whose function expresses its value simply, and replace each test of the form B reloop X goto Y by:

temp2 = $C_1 * X$

temp2 = temp2 + C_2 /* omit if $C_2 = 0$ */

if temp reloop temp2 goto Y

Delete all assignments to B from the loop, as they will now be useless.

(*f*) If there is no assignment to temp between the introduced statement A = temp (step 1) and the only use of A, then replace all uses of A by temp and delete the statement A = temp.

In the flow graph shown in Figure 10.10, we see that I is a basic induction variable, and $T1$ is the additional induction variable in the family of I, because the value of $T1$ at the point of assignment in the loop is expressed as $T1 = 4 * I$. Therefore, according to step 3b, we replace $T1 = 4 * I$ by $T1$ = temp. And according to step 3c, we add temp = $4 * I$ to the preheader. We then append the statement temp = temp + 4 after statement (10), as shown in Figure 10.10 as per step 3d. And according to step 3e, we replace the statement if $I \leq 20$ goto $B2$ by:

temp1 = 80

if (temp ≤ temp1) goto $B2$, and delete $I = I + 1$

The results of these modifications are shown in Figure 10.11.

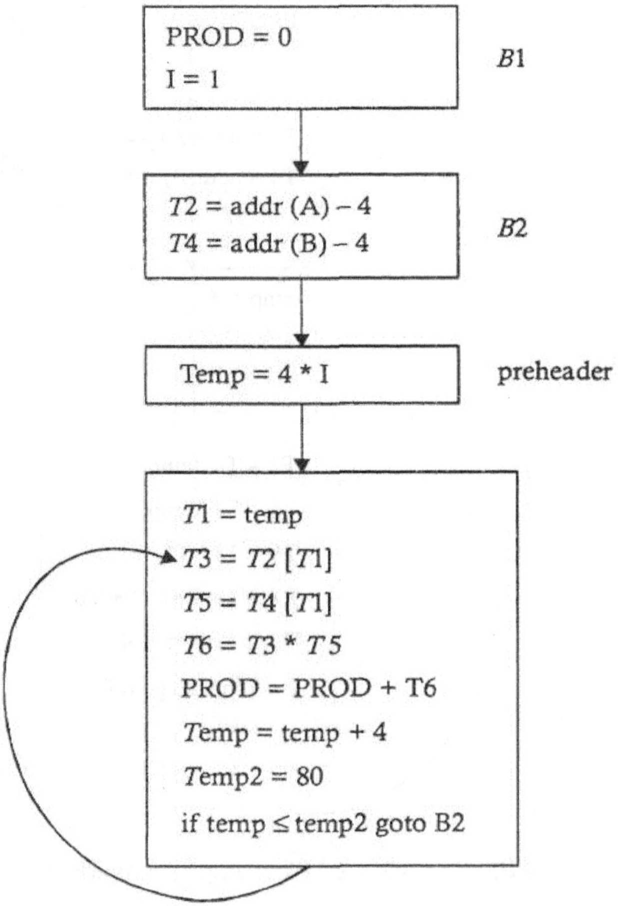

FIGURE 10.11 Modified flow graph.

By step 3f, replace *T1* by temp. And by copy propagation, temp = 4 * *I*, in the preheader, can be replaced by temp = 4, and the statement *I* = 1 can be eliminated. In *B*1, the statement if temp ≤ temp2 goto *B2* can be replaced by if temp ≤ 80 goto *B2*, and we can eliminate temp2 = 80, as shown in Figure 10.12.

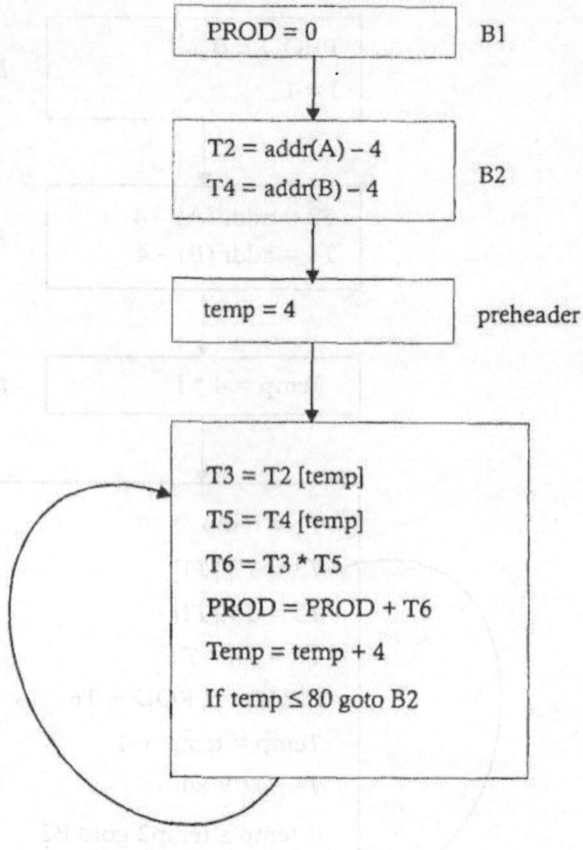

FIGURE 10.12 Flow graph preheader modifications.

10.5 ELIMINATING LOCAL COMMON SUBEXPRESSIONS

The first step in eliminating local common subexpressions is to detect the common subexpression in a basic block. The common subexpressions in a basic block can be automatically detected if we construct a directed acyclic graph (DAG).

DAG Construction

For constructing a basic block DAG, we make use of the function node(id), which returns the most recently created node associated with id. For every three-address statement $x = y\ op\ z$, $x = op\ y$, or $x = y$ in the block we:

do

{

1. If node(y) is undefined, create a leaf labeled y, and let node(y) be this node. If node(z) is undefined, create a leaf labeled z, and let that leaf be node(z). If the statement is of the form $x = op\ y$ or $x = y$, then if node(y) is undefined, create a leaf labeled y, and let node(y) be this node.
2. If a node exists that is labeled op whose left child is node(y) and whose right child is node(z) (to catch the common subexpressions), then return this node. Otherwise, create such a node, and return it. If the statement is of the form $x = op\ y$, then check if a node exists that is labeled op whose only child is node(y). Return this node. Otherwise, create such a node and return. Let the returned node be n.
3. Append x to the list of identifiers for the node n returned in step 2. Delete x from the list of attached identifiers for node(x), and set node(x) to be node n.

}

Therefore, we first go for a DAG representation of the basic block. And if the interior nodes in the DAG have more than one label, then those nodes of the DAG represent the common subexpressions in the basic block. After detecting these common subexpressions, we eliminate them from the basic block. The following example shows the elimination of local common subexpressions, and the DAG is shown in Figure 10.13.

(1) $S1 := 4 * I$

(2) $S2$: addr(A) – 4

(3) $S3 : S2\ [S1]$

(4) $S4 : 4 * I$

(5) $S5$: = addr(B) – 4

(6) $S6 := S5\ [S4]$

(7) $S7 := S3 * S6$

(8) $S8$: PROD + $S7$

(9) PROD : = $S8$

(10) $S9 := I + 1$

(11) $I = S9$

(12) if $I \leq 20$ goto (1).

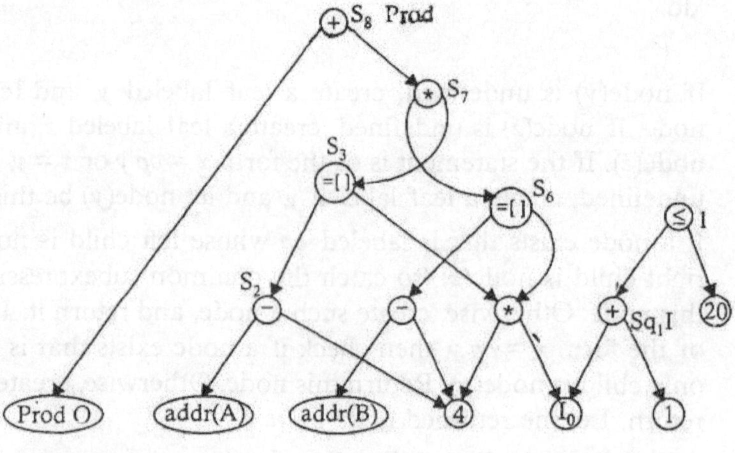

FIGURE 10.13 DAG representation of a basic block.

In Figure 10.13, PROD 0 indicates the initial value of PROD, and *I*0 indicates the initial value of *I*. We see that the same value is assigned to *S*8 and PROD. Similarly, the value assigned to *S*9 is the same as *I*. And the value computed for *S*1 and *S*4 are the same; hence, we can eliminate these common subexpressions by selecting one of the attached identifiers (one that is needed outside the block). We assume that none of the temporaries is needed outside the block. The rewritten block will be:

(1) $S1 := 4 * I$
(2) $S2 :=$ addr(A) – 4
(3) $S3 := S2\ [S1]$
(4) $S5 :=$ addr(B) – 4.
(5) $S6 := S5\ [S1]$
(6) $S7 := S3 * S6$
(7) PROD : = PROD + $S7$
(8) $I := I + 1$
(9) if $I \leq 20$ goto (1)

10.6 ELIMINATING GLOBAL COMMON SUBEXPRESSIONS

Global common subexpressions are expressions that compute the same value but in different basic blocks. To detect such expressions, we need to compute available expressions.

10.6.1 Available Expressions

An expression *x op y* is available at a point *p* if every path from the initial node of the flow graph reaching to *p* evaluates *x op y*, and if after the last such evaluation and prior to reaching *p* there are no subsequent assignments to *x* or *y*. To eliminate global common subexpressions, we need to compute the set of all the expressions available at the point just before the start of every block. This requires computing the set all the expressions available at a point just after the end of every block. We call these sets IN(*b*) and OUT(*b*), respectively. The computation of IN(*b*) and OUT(*b*) requires computing the set of all expressions generated by the basic block and the set of all expressions killed by the basic block, respectively:

- A block kills an expression *x op y* if it assigns to *x* or *y* and if does not subsequently recompute *x op y*.
- A block generates an expression *x op y* if it evaluates *x op y* and subsequently does not redefine *x* or *y*.

To compute the available expressions, we solve the following equations:

$$\text{OUT}(b) = \text{IN}(b) - \text{KILL}(b) \cup \text{GEN}(b)$$
$$\text{IN}(b) = \cap\ \text{OUT}(p)$$

Here, also, we obtain the smallest solution.

The algorithm for computing the smallest IN(*b*) and OUT(*b*) is given below, where *b*1 is the initial block, and *U* is a "universal" set of all expressions appearing on the right of one or more statements of the program.

```
1. IN(b1) = φ
   OUT(b1) = GEN(b1);
2. for (i=2; i <= n; i++)
   {
       IN(b) = U
       OUT(b) = U - GEN(b)
   }
3. flag = true
4. while (flag) do
       {
       flag = false
       for (i=2; i <= n; i++)
           {
```

```
        IN_new(bi) = Φ
        for each predecessor p of bi
        IN_new(bi) = IN_new(bi) ∩ OUT(p)
        if IN_new(bi) ≠ IN(bi) then
            {
            flag = true
            IN(bi) = IN_new(bi)
            OUT(bi) = IN(bi) − KILL(bi) ∪ GEN(bi)
            }
        }
    }
```

After computing IN(b) and OUT(b), eliminating the global common subexpressions is done as follows. For every statement s of the form $x = y\ op\ z$ such that $y\ op\ z$ is available at the beginning of the block containing s, and neither y nor z is defined prior to the statement $x = y\ op\ z$ in that block, do:

1. Find all definitions reaching up to the s statement block that have $y\ op\ z$ on the right.
2. Create a new temp.
3. Replace each statement $U = y\ op\ z$ found in step 1 by:
   temp = $y\ op\ z$
   U = temp
4. Replace the statement $x = y\ op\ z$ in block by x = temp.

10.7 LOOP UNROLLING

Loop unrolling involves replicating the body of the loop to reduce the required number of tests if the number of iterations are constant. For example consider the following loop:

```
I = 1
while (I <= 100)
{
    x[I] = 0;
    I++;
}
```

In this case, the test $I <= 100$ will be performed 100 times. But if the body of the loop is replicated, then the number of times this test will need to be performed will be 50. After replication of the body, the loop will be:

```
I = 1
while(I<= 100)
{
    x[I] = 0;
    I++;
    X[I] = 0;
    I++;
}
```

It is possible to choose any divisor for the number of times the loop is executed, and the body will be replicated that many times. Unrolling once—that is, replicating the body to form two copies of the body—saves 50% of the maximum possible executions.

10.8 LOOP JAMMING

Loop jamming is a technique that merges the bodies of two loops if the two loops have the same number of iterations and they use the same indices. This eliminates the test of one loop. For example, consider the following loop:

```
{
for (I = 0; I < 10; I++)
    for (J = 0; J < 10; J++)
        X[I,J] = 0;
    for (I = 0; I < 10; I++)
        X[I,I] = 1;
}
```

Here, the bodies of the loops on I can be concatenated. The result of loop jamming will be:

```
{
for (I = 0; I < 10; I++)
    {
        for (J = 0; J < 10; J++)
```

```
            X[I,J] = 0;
        X[I,J] = 1;
        }
    }
```

The following conditions are sufficient for making loop jamming legal:

1. No quantity is computed by the second loop at the iteration I if it is computed by the first loop at iteration $J \geq I$.
2. If a value is computed by the first loop at iteration $J \geq I$, then this value should not be used by second loop at iteration I.

EXERCISE

1. Consider the following C code:

```
count = 0;
result = 0;
while ( count++ < 20)
    {
        increment = 2 * count;
        result += increment;
    }
```

   Optimize this code.
2. "Removing a statement from a loop because it computes same value in each iteration of loop may lead to increase in execution cost". Comment.
3. What is meant by reducible flow graph? Explain with suitable example.
4. Define the term basic block, and suggest data structure for it. Also give C type declarations required for implementing this data structure.

5. Consider the flow graph given below:

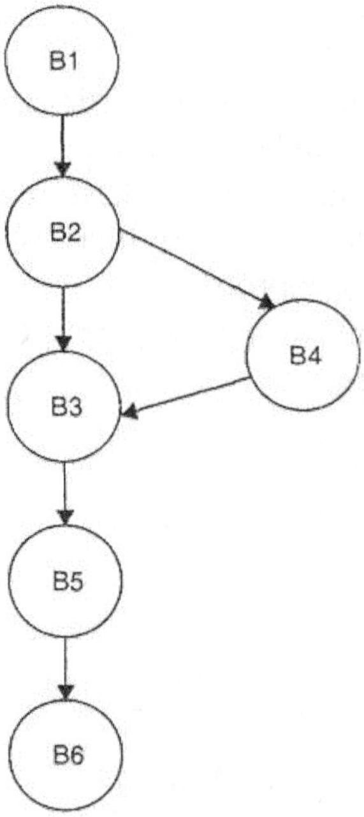

Find the dominators of each basic block of the above flow graph.

6. Construct DAG for the basic block whose code is given below:

t1 = b +c

t2 = d * e

t3 = t2 * t1

t3 = t3 * f

x = t1 – t3

7. Consider the following basic block:

t1 = b +c

t2 = d * e

t3 = b + c

t4 = t2 * t3

t5 = t4 * f

x = t1 – t5

Which of the following optimizations are possible to be carried out with the above basic block:

(1) common sub-expression elimination
(2) copy propagation
(3) dead code elimination

8. Define the meaning of terms basic induction variable and other induction variable with suitable examples.
9. Define the meaning of terms Live variable and available expression. with suitable examples. Which of them is a forward flow problem, and which is a backward flow problem.
10. Consider the following flow graph, Compute the reaching definitions for each basic block.

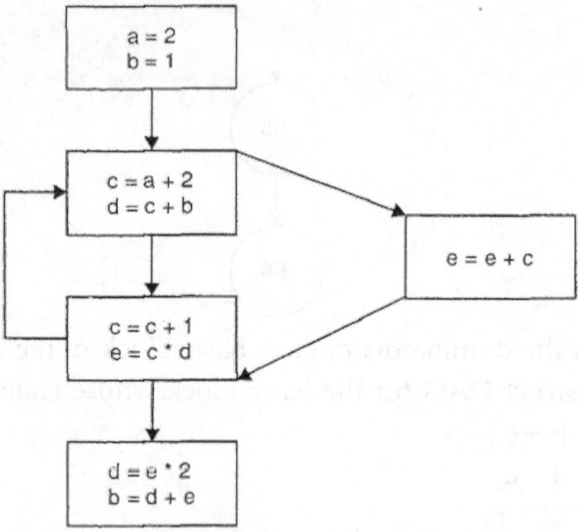

11 CODE GENERATION

11.1 AN INTRODUCTION TO CODE GENERATION

Code generation is the last phase in the compilation process. Being a machine-dependent phase, it is not possible to generate good code without considering the details of the particular machine for which the compiler is expected to generate code. Even so, a carefully selected code-generation algorithm can produce code that is twice as fast as code generated by an ill-considered code-generation algorithm.

In this chapter, we first discuss straightforward code generation from a sequence of three-address statements. This is followed by a discussion of the code-generation algorithm that takes into account the flow of control structures in the program when assigning registers to names. Then we will look at a code-generation algorithm that is capable of generating reasonably good code from a basic block. Finally, various machine-dependent optimizations that are capable of improving the efficiency of object code are discussed. Throughout our discussion, we assume that the input to the code-generation algorithm is a sequence of three-address statements partitioned into basic blocks.

11.2 PROBLEMS THAT HINDER GOOD CODE GENERATION

There are three main difficulties that we face when attempting to generate efficient object code, namely:

1. Selection of the most-efficient instructions to represent the computation specified by the three-address statement;
2. Deciding on a computation order that leads to the generation of the more-efficient object code; and
3. Deciding which registers to use.

Selecting the Most-Efficient Instructions to Represent the Computation Specified by the Three-Address Statement

Many machines allow certain computations to be done in more than one way. For example, if a machine permits an instruction AOS for incrementing the contents of a storage location directly, then for a three-address statement $a = a + 1$, it is possible to generate the instruction AOS a, rather than a sequence of instructions like the following:

```
MOVE a, R
    ADD #1, R
    MOVE R, a
```

Now, deciding which instruction sequence is better is the problem. This decision requires an extensive knowledge about the context in which these three-address statements will appear.

Deciding on the Computation Order that Will Lead to the Generation of More-Efficient Object Code

Some computation orders require fewer registers to hold intermediate results than others. Now, deciding the best order is very difficult. For example, consider the basic block:

$$t1 = a + b$$

$$t2 = c + d$$

$$t3 = e - t2$$

$$t4 = t1 - t3$$

If the order of computation used is the one given in the basic block *t*1-*t*2-*t*3-*t*4, then the number of registers required for holding the intermediate result is more than when the order *t*2-*t*3-*t*1-*t*4 is used.

Deciding on Registers

Deciding which register should handle the computation is another problem that stands in the way of good code generation. The problem is further complicated when a machine requires register-pairs for some operands and results.

11.3 THE MACHINE MODEL

Being a machine-dependent phase, we will need to describe some of the features of a typical computer in order to discuss the various issues involved in code generation. For this purpose, we describe a hypothetical machine model, as follows.

We assume that the machine is byte-addressable with two bytes per word, having 2^{16} bytes, and eight general-purpose registers, $R0$ to $R7$, that are capable of holding a 16-bit quantity. The format of the instruction is an ***op* source destination** with four-bit opcode, and the source and destination are each six-bit fields. Since a six-bit field is not capable of holding a memory address (a memory address is a 16-bit), when sources and destinations are memory addresses, then these six-bit fields hold certain bit patterns specifying that the words following an instruction contain memory addresses used as source and destination operands, respectively. The following addressing modes are assumed to be supported by the machine model:

1. r (register addressing)
2. $*r$ (indirect register)
3. X (absolute address)
4. #data (immediate)
5. $X(r)$ (indexed address)
6. $*X(r)$ (indirect indexed address)

We assume that opcodes like the one listed below are available:

- MOV (for moving source to destination),
- ADD (for adding source to destination), and
- SUB (for subtracting source from destination), and so on.

The cost of the instruction is considered to be its length, because generating a shorter instruction not only reduces the storage requirement of the object code, but it also reduces the time taken to perform the operation. This is because most machines spend more time fetching words from memory than they spend in executing the instruction. Hence, by minimizing the instruction length, we minimize the time taken to perform the instruction, as well.

For example, length of the instruction MOV R0, R1 is one memory word, because, three-bit code is enough for uniquely identifying each of the registers. Therefore, the six-bit fields, each for source and destination operand, can easily hold the three-bit codes for the registers shown in Table 11.1.

TABLE 11.1 Instruction MOV R0, R1

MOV	*R0*	R1

Similarly, the length of the instruction MOV R0, M is two memory words, because since the destination operand is a memory address, it will occupy the word following an instruction, as shown in Table 11.2.

TABLE 11.2 For the Instruction MOV R0, M

MOV	*R0*	bit pattern
	M	

Similarly, the length of the instruction MOV M1, M2 is three memory words, because the source and the destination operands, being memory addresses, will occupy the words following the instruction, as shown in Table 11.3.

TABLE 11.3 Instruction MOV M1, M2

MOV	bit pattern	bit pattern
	M1	
	M2	

For example, consider a three-address statement, $a = b + c$. We can generate the following different instruction sequences for this statement, depending upon where the values of operand *b* and *c* can be found.

If the values of *b* and *c* can be found in the memory locations of the same name, then the following instruction sequences can be generated:

1. MOV *b*, *R0*
ADD c, *R0*
MOV *R0*, *a* length = six words
2. MOV *b*, *a*
ADD *c*, *a* length = six words

If *a*, *b*, and *c* are assumed to be in registers $R0$, $R1$, and $R2$, respectively then the following instruction sequence can be generated:

3. MOV *$R1$, *$R0$
   ADD *$R2$, *$R0$ length = two words

If the values of *b* and *c* are assumed to be in registers $R0$ and $R1$, respectively, then the following instruction sequence can be generated:

4. ADD $R2$, $R1$
   MOV $R1$, *a* length = three words

Therefore, we conclude that for generating good code, we must utilize the addressing capabilities of the machine efficiently. And this will be possible if we keep the *r*-value of the name in the register if it is going to be used in the future.

11.4 STRAIGHTFORWARD CODE GENERATION

Given a sequence of three-address statements partitioned into basic blocks, straightforward code generation involves generating code for each three-address statement in turn by taking the advantage of any of the operands of the three-address statements that are in the register, and leaving the computed result in the register as long as possible. We store it only if the register is needed for another computation or just before a procedure call, jump, or labeled statement, such as at the end of a basic block is encountered. The reason for this is that after leaving a basic block, we may go to several different blocks, or we may go to one particular block that can be reached from several others. In either case, we cannot assume that a datum used by a block appears in the same register, no matter how the program's control reached that block. Hence, to avoid possible error, our code-generation strategy stores everything across the basic block boundaries.

TIP

When generating code by using the above strategy, we need to keep track of what is currently in each register. For this, we maintain what is called a "register descriptor," which is simply a pointer to a list that contains information about what is currently in each of the registers. Initially, all of the registers are empty.

We also need to keep track of the locations for each name—where the current value of the name can be found at run time. For this, we maintain what is called an "address descriptor" for each name in the block. This information can be stored in the symbol table.

We also need a location to perform the computation specified by each of the three-address statements. For this, we make use of the function getreg(). When called, getreg() returns a location for the computation performed by a three-address statement. For example, if $x = y\ op\ z$ is to be performed, getreg() returns a location L where the computation $y\ op\ z$ should be performed; and if possible, it returns a register.

Algorithm for code generation

What follows is an algorithm for code generation.

{

For every three-address statement of the form $x = y\ op\ z$ in the basic block do

{

1. Call getreg() to obtain the location L in which the computation $y\ op\ z$ should be performed. /* This requires passing the three-address statement $x = y\ op\ z$ as a parameter to getreg(), which can be done by passing the index of this statement in the quadruple array.
2. Obtain the current location of the operand y by consulting its address descriptor, and if the value of y is currently both in the memory location as well as in the register, then prefer the register. If the value of y is currently not available in L, then generate an instruction MOV y, L (where y as assumed to represent the current location of y).
3. Generate the instruction OP z, L, and update the address descriptor of x to indicate that x is now available in L, and if L is in a register, then update its descriptor to indicate that it will contain the run-time value of x.
4. If the current values of y and /or z are in the register, and we have no further uses for them, and they are not live at the end of the block, then alter the register descriptor to indicate that after the execution of the statement $x = y\ op\ z$, those registers will no longer contain y and /or z.

}

Store all the results.

}

The function getreg(), when called upon to return a location where the computation specified by the three-address statement $x = y\ op\ z$ should be performed, returns a location L as follows:

1. First, it searches for a register already containing the name y. If such a register exists, and if y has no further use after the execution of $x = y \ op \ z$, and if it is not live at the end of the block and holds the value of no other name, then return the register for L.
2. Otherwise, getreg() searches for an empty register; and if an empty register is available, then it returns it for L.
3. If no empty register exists, and if x has further use in the block, or *op* is an operator such as indexing that requires a register, then getreg() finds a suitable, occupied register. The register is emptied by storing its value in the proper memory location M, the address descriptor is updated, the register is returned for L. (The least-recently used strategy can be used to find a suitable, occupied register to be emptied.)
4. If x is not used in the block or no suitable, occupied register can be found, getreg() selects a memory location and returns it for L.

EXAMPLE 11.1: Consider the expression:

$$x = (a + b) - ((c + d) - e)$$

The three-address code for this is:

$$t1 = a + b$$
$$t2 = c + d$$
$$t3 = t2 - e$$
$$x = t1 - t3$$

Applying the algorithm above results in Table 11.4.

TABLE 11.4 Computation for the Expression $x = (a + b) - ((c + d) - e)$

Statement	L	Instructions Generated	Register Descriptor	Address Descriptor
			All registers empty	
$t1 = a + b$	$R0$	MOV a, $R0$ ADD b, $R0$	$R0$ will hold $t1$	$t1$ is in $R0$
$t2 = c + d$	$R1$	MOV c, $R1$ ADD d, $R1$	$R1$ will hold $t2$	$t2$ is in $R1$
$t3 = t2 - e$	$R1$	SUB e, $R1$	$R1$ will hold $t3$	$t3$ is in $R1$

$x = t1 - t3$	$R0$	SUB $R1, R0$	$R0$ will hold x	x is in $R0$
		MOV $R0, x$		x is in $R0$ and memory

The algorithm makes use of the next-use information of each name in order to make more-informed decisions regarding register allocation. Therefore, it is required to compute the next-use information. If:

- A statement at the index i in a block assigns a value to name x,
- And if a statement at the index j in the same block uses x as an operand,
- And if the path from the statement at index i to the statement at index j is a path without any intervening assignment to name x, then

we say that the value of x computed by the statement at index i is used in the statement at index j. Hence, the next use of the name x in the statement i is statement j. For each three-address statement i, we need to compute information about those three-address statements in the block that are the next uses of the names coming in statement i. This requires the backward scanning of the basic block, which will allow us to attach to every statement i under consideration the information about those statements that are the next uses of each name in the statement i. The algorithm is as follows:

```
For each statement i of the form x = y op z do
{
    attach information about the next uses of x, y, and z
    to statement i
    set the information for x to no next-use /* This information
    can be kept into the symbol table */
    set the information for y and z to be the next use
    in statement i
}
```

Consider the basic block:

$t1 = a + b$

$t2 = c + d$

$t3 = e - t2$

$t4 = t1 - t3$

When straightforward code generation is done using the above algorithm, and if only two registers, $R0$ and $R1$, are available, then the generated code is as shown in Table 11.5.

TABLE 11.5 Generated Code with Only Two Available Registers, R0 and R1

Statement	L	Instructions Generated	Cost	Register Descriptor	Address Descriptor
				*R*0 and *R*1 empty	
*t*1 = *a* + *b*	*R*0	MOV *a*, *R*0 ADD *b*, *R*0	2 words 2 words	*R*0 will hold *t*1	*t*1 is in *R*0
*t*2 = *c* + *d*	*R*1	MOV *c*, *R*1 ADD *d*, *R*1	2 words 2 words	*R*1 will hold *t*2	*t*2 is in *R*1
*t*3 = *e* – *t*2		MOV *R*0, *t*1 (generated by getreg())	2 words		*t*1 is in
					*t*3 is in *R*0
	*R*0	MOV *e*, *R*0 SUB *R*1, *R*0	2 words 1 word	*R*0 will hold *t*3 *R*1 will be empty because *t*2 has no next use	
x = *t*1 - *t*3	*R*1	MOV *t*1, *R*1 SUB *R*0, *R*1	2 words 1 word	*R*1 will hold *x* *R*0 will be empty because *t*3 has no next use	*x* is in *R*1
		MOV *R*1, *x*	2 words		*x* is in *R*1 and memory

We see that the total length of the instruction sequence generated is 18 memory words. If we rearrange the final computations as:

$t2 = c + d$
$t3 = e - t2$
$t1 = a + b$
$t4 = t1 - t3$

and then generate the code, we get Table 11.6.

TABLE 11.6 Generated Code with Rearranged Computations

Statement	L	Instructions Generated	Cost	Register Descriptor	Address Descriptor
				$R0$ and $R1$ empty	
$t2 = c + d$	R0	MOV c, $R0$ ADD d, $R0$	2 words 2 words	$R0$ will hold $t2$	$t2$ is in $R0$
$t3 = e - t2$	$R1$	MOV e, $R1$ SUB $R0$, $R1$	2 words 1 word	$R1$ will hold $t3$ $R0$ will be empty because $t2$ has no next use	$t3$ is in $R1$
$t1 = a + b$	R0	MOV a, $R0$ ADD b, $R0$	2 words 2 words	$R0$ will hold $t1$	$t1$ is in $R0$
$x = t1 - t3$	$R1$	SUB $R1$, $R0$	1 word	$R0$ will hold x $R1$ will be empty because $t3$ has no next use	x is in $R0$
		MOV $R0$, x	2 words		x is in $R0$ and memory

Here, the length of the instruction sequence generated is 14 memory words. This indicates that the order of the computation is a deciding factor in the cost of the code generated. In the above example, the cost is reduced when the order *t*2-*t*3-*t*1-*t*4 is used, because *t*1 gets computed immediately before the statement that computes *t*4, which uses *t*1 as its left operand. Hence, no intermediate store-and-load is required, as is the case when the order *t*1-*t*2-*t*3-*t*4 is used. Good code generation requires rearranging the final computation order, and this can be done conveniently with a DAG representation of a basic block rather than with a linear sequence of three-address statements.

11.5 USING DAG FOR CODE GENERATION

To rearrange the final computation order for more-efficient code-generation, we first obtain a DAG representation of the basic block, and then we order the nodes of the DAG using heuristics. Heuristics attempts to order the nodes of a DAG so that, if possible, a node immediately follows the evaluation of its left-most operand.

11.5.1 Heuristic for Ordering Nodes of DAG

The algorithm for heuristic ordering is given below. It lists the nodes of a DAG such that the node's reverse listing results in the computation order.

```
{
 While there exists an unlisted interior node do
    {
    select an unlisted node n whose parents have been listed
         list n
         while there exists a left-most child m of n that has no
    unlisted parents and m is not a leaf do
         {
         list m
                m = n
         }
    }
order = reverse of the order of listing of nodes
}
```

EXAMPLE 11.2: Consider the DAG shown in Figure 11.1.

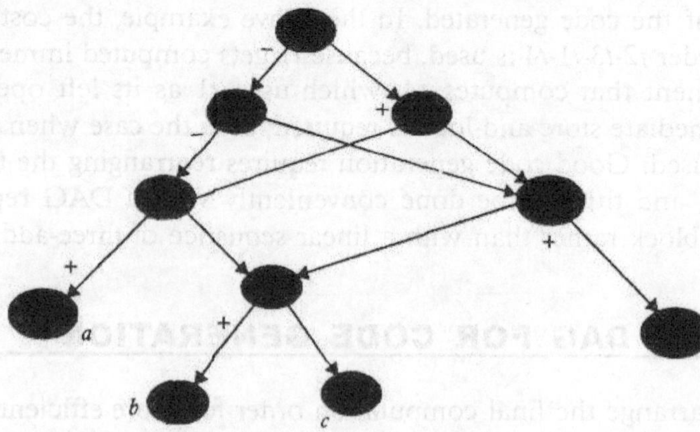

FIGURE 11.1 DAG Representation.

The order in which the nodes are listed by the heuristic ordering is shown in Figure 11.2.

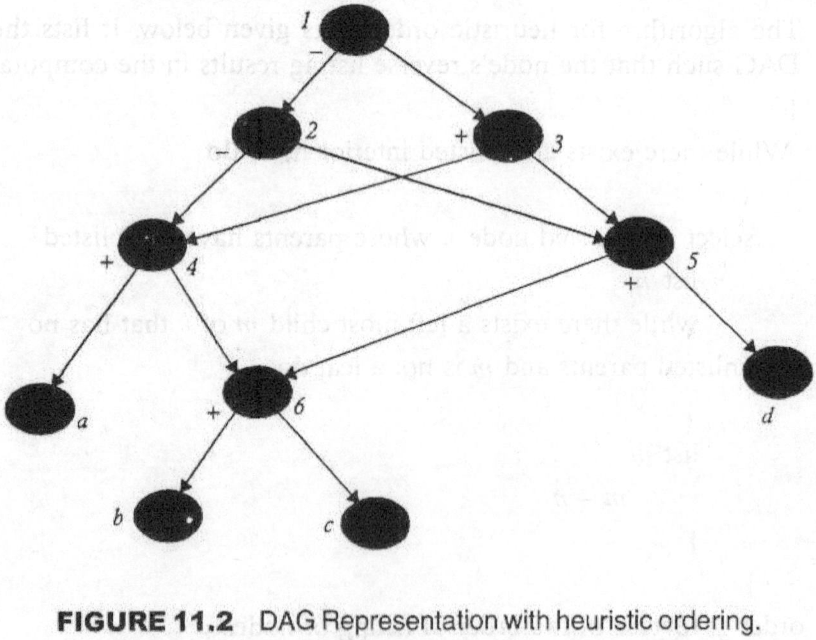

FIGURE 11.2 DAG Representation with heuristic ordering.

Therefore, the computation order is:

$t6 = b + c$

$t5 = t6 + d$

$t4 = a + t6$

$t3 = t4 + t5$

$t2 = t4 - t5$

$t1 = t2 - t3$

If the DAG representation turns out to be a tree, then for the machine model described above, we can obtain the optimal order using the algorithm described in Section 11.5.2, below. Here, an optimal order means the order that yields the shortest instruction sequence.

11.5.2 The Labelling Algorithm

This algorithm works on the tree representation of a sequence of three-address statements. It could also be made to work if the intermediate code form was a parse tree. This algorithm has two parts: the first part labels each node of the tree from the bottom up, with an integer that denotes the minimum number of registers required to evaluate the tree and with no storing of intermediate results. The second part of the algorithm is a tree traversal that travels the tree in an order governed by the computed labels in the first part, and which generates the code during the tree traversal.

The labelling algorithm.

```
{
if n is a leaf node then
    if n is the left-most child of its parent then
        label(n) = 1
    else
        label(n) = 0
    else
        label(n) = max[label(n_i) + (i - 1)]
              for i = 1 to k
/* where n_1, n_2,..., n_k are the children of n, ordered by their labels; that is,
label(n_1) ≥ label(n_2) ≥ ... ≥ label(n_k) */
}
```

For $k = 2$, the formula label(n) = max[label(n_i) + (i – 1)] becomes:

label(n) = max[11, 12 + 1]

where 11 is label(n_1), and 12 is label(n_2). Since either 11 or 12 will be same, or since there will be a difference of at least one between 11 and 12 (i.e., 11 – 12), which is greater than or equal to one, we get:

$$\text{label}(n) = l_1 + 1 \text{ if } l_1 = l_2$$
$$= \max(l_1, l_2) \text{ if } l_1 \neq l_2$$

EXAMPLE 11.3: Consider the following three-address code and its DAG representation, shown in Figure 11.3:

$t1 = a + b$

$t2 = c + d$

$t3 = e - t2$

$t4 = t1 - t3$

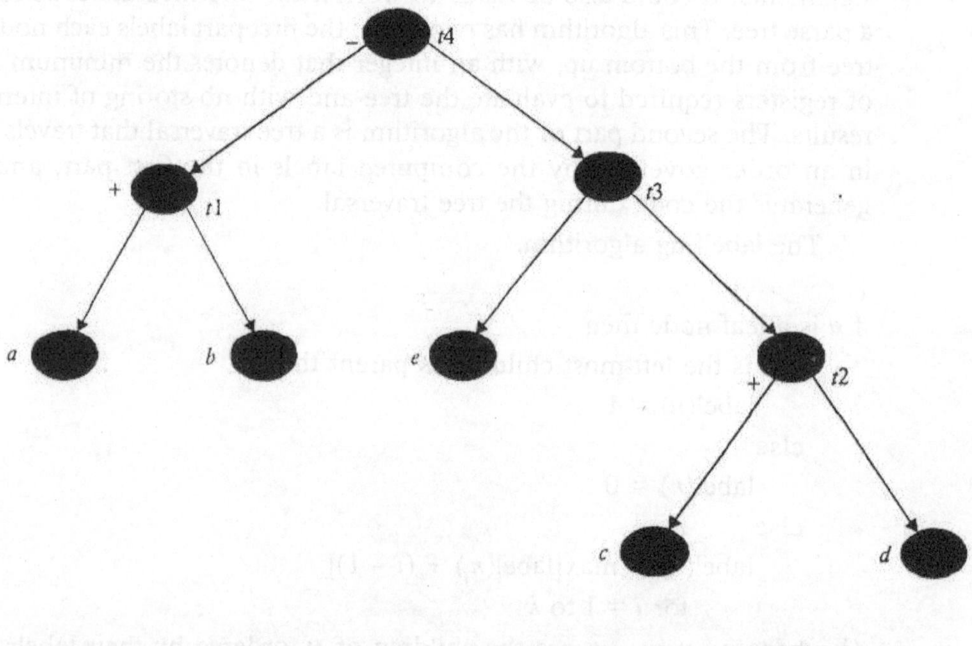

FIGURE 11.3 DAG representation of three-address code for Example 11.3.

The tree, after labeling, is shown in Figure 11.4.

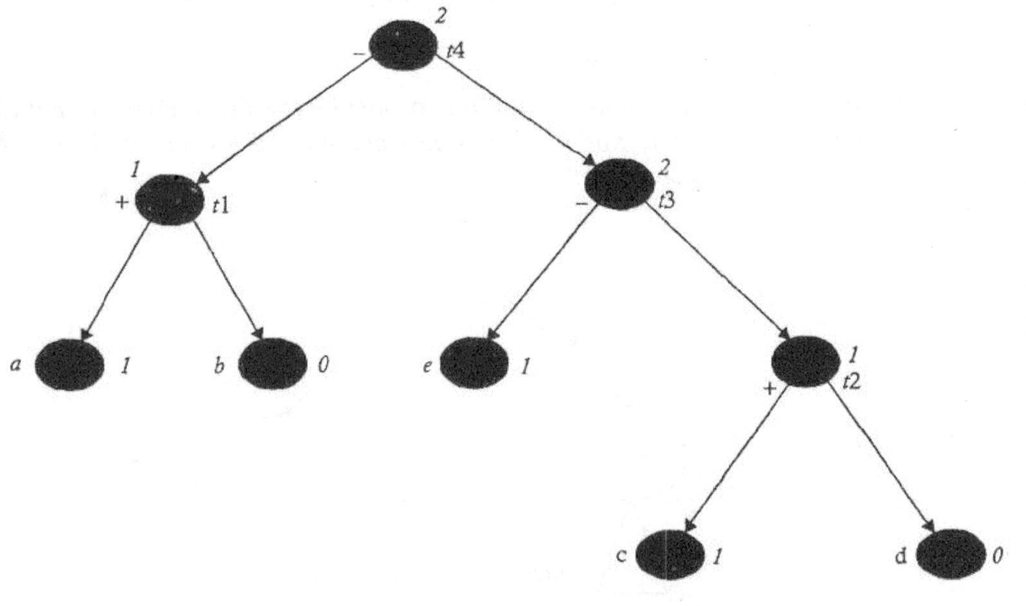

FIGURE 11.4 DAG representation tree after labeling.

11.5.3 Code Generation by Traversing the Labeled Tree

We will now examine an algorithm that traverses the labeled tree and generates machine code to evaluate the tree in the register $R0$. The content of $R0$ can then be stored in the appropriate memory location. We assume that only binary operators are used in the tree. The algorithm uses a recursive procedure, gencode(n), to generate the code for evaluating into a register a subtree that has its root in node n. This procedure makes use of RSTACK to allocate registers.

Initially, RSTACK contains all available registers. We assume the order of the registers to be $R0$, $R1$,..., from top to bottom. A call to gencode() may find a subset of registers, perhaps in a different order in RSTACK, but when gencode() returns, it leaves the registers in RSTACK in the same order in which they were found. The resulting code computes the value of the tree in the top register of RSTACK. It also makes use of TSTACK to allocate temporary memory locations. Depending upon the type of node n with which gencode() is called, gencode() performs the following:

1. If n is a leaf node and is the left-most child of its parent, then gencode() generates a load instruction for loading the top register of RSTACK by the label of node n:

   MOV name, RSTACK[top]

2. If n is an interior node, it will be an operator node labeled by *op* with the children n_1 and n_2, and n_2 is a simple operand and not a root of the subtree, as shown in Figure 11.5.

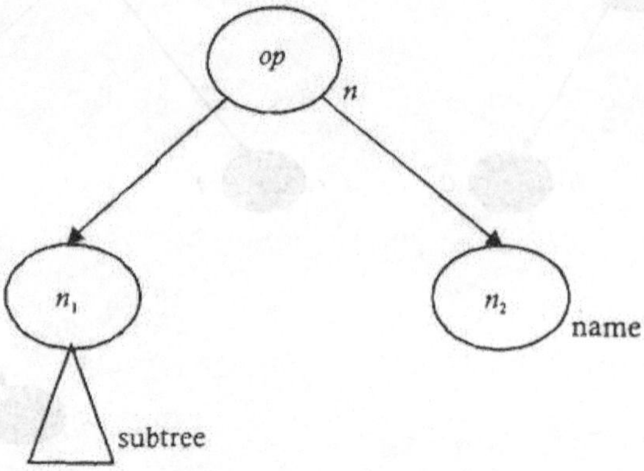

FIGURE 11.5 The node n is an operand and not a subtree root.

In this case, gencode() will first generate the code to evaluate the subtree rooted at n_1 in the RSTACK[top]. It will then generate the instruction, OP name, RSTACK[top].

3. If n is an interior node, it will be an operator node labeled by *op* with the children n_1 and n_2, and both n_1 and n_2 are roots of subtrees, as shown in Figure 11.6.

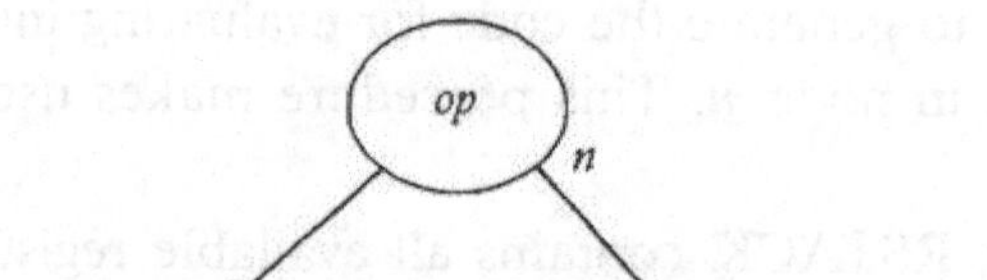

FIGURE 11.6 The node n is an operator, and n_1 and n_2 are subtree roots.

In this case, gencode() examines the labels of n_1 and n_2. If label(n_2) > label(n_1), then n_2 requires a greater number of registers to evaluate without storing the intermediate results than n_1 does. Therefore, gencode() checks whether the total number of registers available to r is greater than the label(n_1). If it is, then the subtree rooted at n_1 can be evaluated without storing the intermediate results. It first swaps the top two registers of RSTACK, then generates the code for evaluating the subtree rooted at n_2, which is harder to evaluate in RSTACK[top]. It removes the top-most register from RSTACK and stores it in R, then generates code for evaluating the subtree rooted at n_1 in RSTACK[top]. An instruction, OP R, RSTACK[top], is generated, pushing R onto RSTACK. The top two registers are swapped so that the register holding the value of n will be in the top register of RSTACK.

4. If label(n_2) <= label(n_1), then n_1 requires a greater number of register to evaluate without storing the intermediate results than n_2 does. Therefore, gencode() checks whether the total number of registers available r is greater than label(n_2). If it is, then the subtree rooted at n_2 can be evaluated without storing the intermediate results. Hence, it first generates the code for evaluating subtree rooted at n_1, which is harder to evaluate in RSTACK[top], removes the top-most register from RSTACK, and stores it in R. It then generates code for evaluating the subtree rooted at n_2 in RSTACK[top]. An instruction, OP RSTACK[top], R, is generated then pushes register R onto RSTACK. In this case, the top register, after pushing R onto RSTACK, holds the value of n. Therefore, swapping and reswapping is needed.
5. If label(n_1) as well as label(n_2) are greater than or equal to r (i.e., both subtrees require r or more registers to evaluate without intermediate storage), a temporary memory location is required. In this case, gencode() first generates the code for evaluating n_2 in a temporary memory location, then generates code to evaluate n_1, followed by an instruction to evaluate root n in the top register of RSTACK.

Algorithm for Implementing Gencode()

The procedure for gencode() is outlined as follows:

```
Procedure gencode(n)
{
    if n is a leaf node and the left-most child of its parent then
        generate MOV name, RSTACK[top]
    if n is an interior node with children n1 and n2, with
        label(n2) = 0 then
```

```
        {
        gencode(n1)
        generate op name RSTACK[top] /* name is the operand
        represented by n2 and op is the operator
        represented by n*/
        }
    if n is an interior node with children n1 and n2,
        label(n2) > label(n1), and label(n1) < r then
            {
            swap top two registers of RSTACK
        gencode(n2)
        R = pop(RSTACK)
        gencode(n1)
        generate op R, RSTACK[top] /* op is the operator
        represented by n */
        PUSH(R,RSTACK)
        swap top two registers of RSTACK
        }
    if n is an interior node with children n1 and n2,
            label(n2) <= label(n1), and label(n2) < r then
        {
        gencode(n1)
        R = pop(RSTACK)
        gencode(n2)
        generate op RSTACK[top], R /* op is the operator
        represented by n */
        PUSH(R, RSTACK)
        }
    if n is an interior node with children n1 and n2,
        label(n2) <= label(n1), and label(n1) > r as well as
        label(n2) > r then
            {
            gencode(n2)
            T = pop(TSTACK)
```

```
            generate MOV RSTACK[top], T
            gencode(n1)
                 generate op T, RSTACK[top] /* op is the operator
            represented by n */
            PUSH(T, TSTACK)
       }
  }
```

The algorithm above can be used when the DAG represented is a tree; but when there are common subexpressions in the basic block, the DAG representation will no longer be a tree, because the common subexpressions will correspond to nodes with more than one parent. These are called "shared nodes." In this case, we can apply the labeling and the gencode() algorithm by partitioning the DAG into a set of trees. We find, for each shared node as well as root n, the maximal subtree with n as a root that includes no other shared nodes, except as leaves. For example, consider the DAG shown in Figure 11.7. It is not a tree, but it can be partitioned into the set of trees shown in Figure 11.8. The procedure gencode() can be used to generate code for each of this tree,

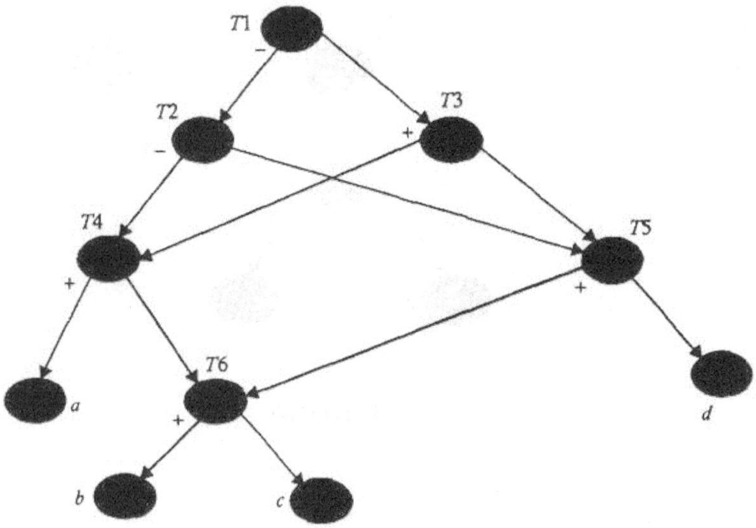

FIGURE 11.7 A nontree DAG.

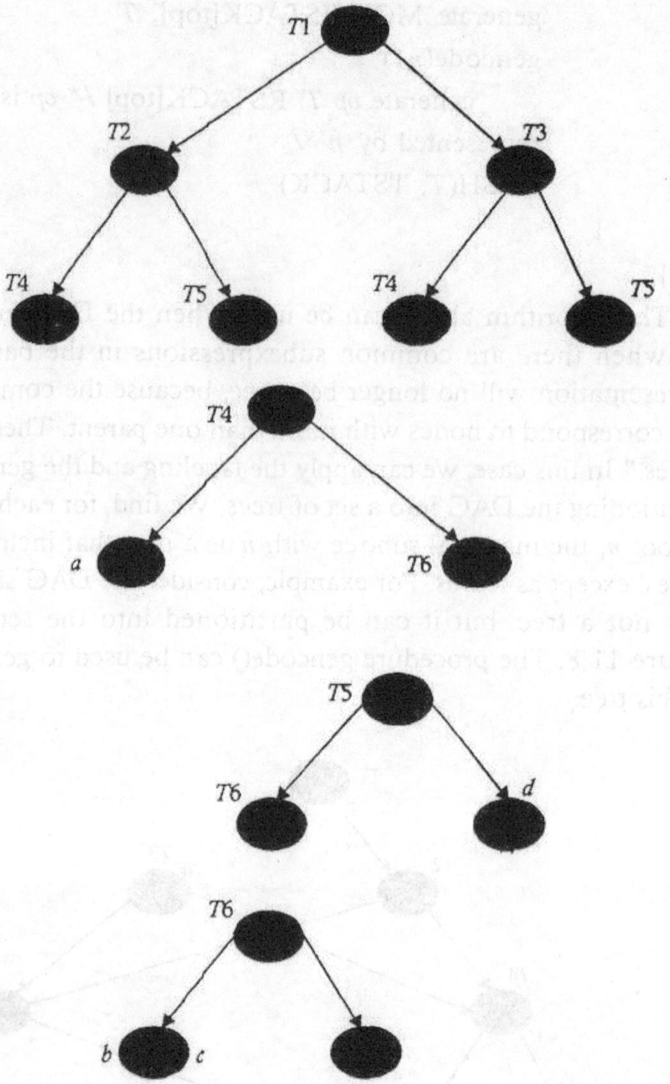

FIGURE 11.8

EXAMPLE 11.4: Consider the labeled tree shown in Figure 11.9.

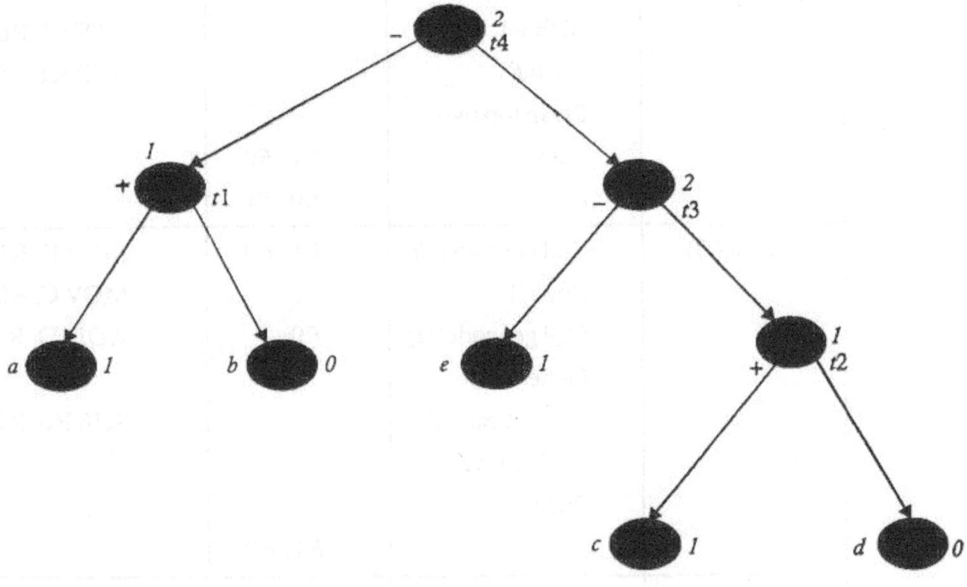

FIGURE 11.9 A DAG that has been partitioned into a set of trees.

The code generated by gencode() when this tree of Figure 11.4 is given as input along with the recursive calls of gencode is shown in Table 11.7. It starts with call to gencode() of *t*4. Initially, the top two registers will be *R*0 and *R*1.

TABLE 11.7 Recursive Gencode Calls

Call to Gencode()	Action Taken	RSTACK Contents Top Two Registers	Code Generated
		*R*0, *R*1	
gencode(*t*4)	Swap top two registers	*R*1, *R*0	MOV E, R1
	Call gencode(*t*3)		MOV C, R0
	Pop *R*1		ADD D, R0
	Call gencode(*t*1)	*R*0	SUB R0, R1
	Generate an		

	instruction
	SUB R1,R0
	Push $R1$
	Swap top two
	registers
		$R1$, $R0$
		$R0$, $R1$
			MOV A, R0
			ADD B, R0
			SUB R1, R0

gencode($t3$)	Call gencode(E)
	Pop $R1$
	Call gencode($t2$)
	Generate an
	instruction
	SUB R0,R1
	Push $R1$
		$R1$, $R0$
		
		$R0$
		
		$R1$, $R0$
			MOV E, R1
			MOV C, R0
			ADD D, R0
			
			SUB R0, R1

gencode(E)	Generate an instruction MOV E, R1	$R1$, $R0$	MOV E, R1

gencode($t2$)	gencode(c)
	Generate an
	instruction
	ADD D, R0
		$R0$	MOV C, R0
			
			ADD D, R0

gencode(c)	Generate an instruction MOV C, R0	$R0$	

gencode($t1$)	gencode(A)
	Generate an
	instruction
	ADD B, R0
		$R0$	MOV A, R0
			
			ADD B, R0

gencode(A)	Generate an instruction MOV A, R0	$R0$	MOV A, R0

11.6 USING ALGEBRAIC PROPERTIES TO REDUCE THE REGISTER REQUIREMENT

It is possible to make use of algebraic properties like operator commutativity and associativity to reduce the register requirements of the tree. For example, consider the tree shown in Figure 11.10.

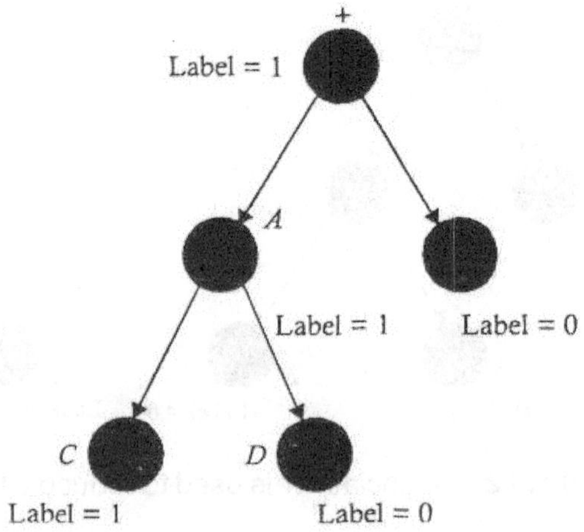

FIGURE 11.10 Tree with a label of two.

The label of the tree in Figure 11.10 is two, but since + is a commutative operator, we can interchange the left and the right subtrees, as shown in Figure 11.11. This brings the register requirement of the tree down to one.

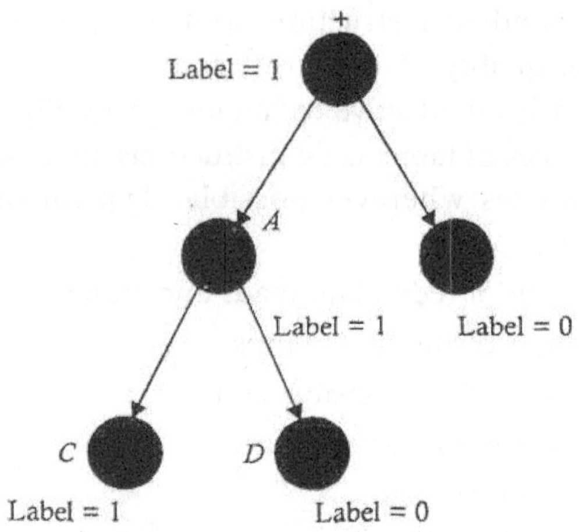

FIGURE 11.11 The left and right subtrees have been interchanged, reducing the register requirement to one.

Similarly, associativity can be used to reduce the register requirement. Consider the tree shown in Figure 11.12.

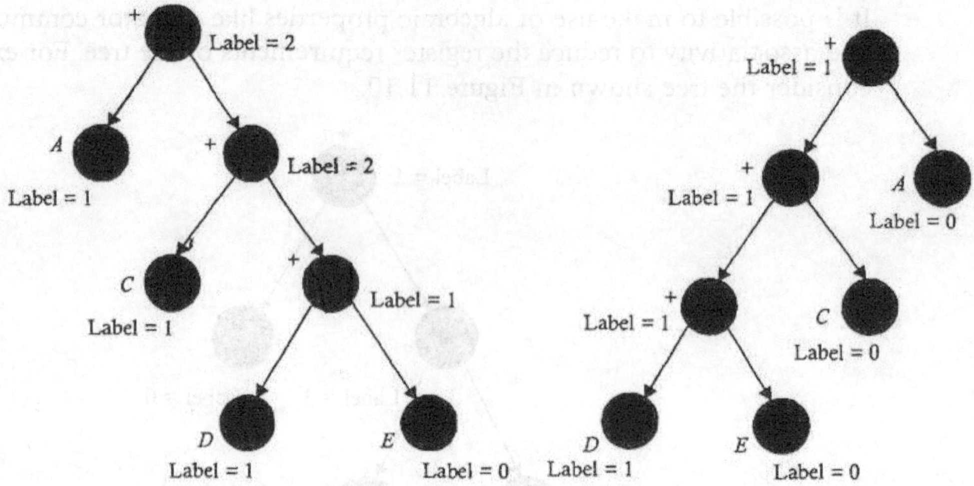

FIGURE 11.12 Associativity is used to reduce a tree's register requirement.

11.7 PEEPHOLE OPTIMIZATION

Code generated by using the statement-by-statement code-generation strategy contains redundant instructions and suboptimal constructs. Therefore, to improve the quality of the target code, optimization is required. Peephole optimization is an effective technique for locally improving the target code. Short sequences of target code instructions are examined and replacement by faster sequences wherever possible. Typical optimizations that can be performed are:

- Elimination of redundant loads and stores
- Elimination of multiple jumps
- Elimination of unreachable code
- Algebraic simplifications
- Reducing for strength
- Use of machine idioms

Eliminating Redundant Loads and Stores

If the target code contains the instruction sequence:

1. MOV R, a
2. MOV a, R

we can delete the second instruction if it an unlabeled instruction. This is because the first instruction ensures that the value of *a* is already in the register *R*. If it is labeled, there is no guarantee that step 1 will always be executed before step 2.

Eliminating Multiple Jumps

If we have jumps to other jumps, then the unnecessary jumps can be eliminated in either intermediate code or the target code. If we have a jump sequence:

```
        goto L1
        ...
L1:     goto L2
```

then this can be replaced by:

```
        goto L2
        ...
L1:     goto L2
```

If there are now no jumps to *L*1, then it may be possible to eliminate the statement, provided it is preceded by an unconditional jump. Similarly, the sequence:

```
        if a < b goto L1
        ...
L1:     goto L2
```

can be replaced by:

```
        if a < b goto L2
        ...
L1:     goto L2
```

Eliminating Unreachable Code

An unlabeled instruction that immediately follows an unconditional jump can possibly be removed, and this operation can be repeated in order to eliminate a sequence of instructions. For debugging purposes, a large program may have within it certain segments that are executed only if a debug variable is one. For example, the source code may be:

```
#define debug 0
...
if (debug)
      {
            print debugging information
      }
```

This if statement is translated in the intermediate code to:

if debug = 1 goto *L*1

goto *L*2

*L*1 : print debugging information

*L*2 :

One of the optimizations is to replace the pair:

if debug = 1 goto *L*1

goto *L*2

within the statements with a single conditional goto statement by negating the condition and changing its target, as shown below:

if debug ≠ 1 goto *L*2

Print debugging information

*L*2 :

Since debug is a constant zero by constant propagation, this code will become:

if 0 ≠ 1 goto *L*2

Print debugging information

*L*2 :

Since 0 ≠ 1 is always true this will become:

goto *L*2

Print debugging information

*L*2 :

Therefore, the statements that print the debugging information are unreachable and can be eliminated, one at a time.

Algebraic Simplifications

If statements like:

$$a = a + 0$$
$$a = a * 1$$

are generated in the code, they can be eliminated, because zero is an additive identity, and one is a multiplicative identity.

Reducing Strength

Certain machine instructions are considered to be cheaper than others. Hence, if we replace expensive operations by equivalent cheaper ones on the target machine, then the efficiency will be better. For example, x^2 is invariable cheaper to implement as $x * x$ than as a call to an exponentiation routine. Similarly, fixed-point multiplication or division by a power of two is cheaper to implement as a shift.

Using Machine Idioms

The target machine may have hardware instructions to implement certain specific operations efficiently. Detecting situations that permit the use of these instructions can reduce execution time significantly. For example, some machines have auto-increment and auto-decrement addressing modes. Using these modes can greatly improve the quality of the code when pushing or popping a stack. These modes can also be used for implementing statements like $a = a + 1$.

EXERCISE

1. Consider the source code:

   x = y + z
   p = z + q + y

   Explain how commutativity and associativity can be used to generate more efficient code from the DAG of this source code.
2. Consider an expression x – y + z, it can be translated into:

   (1) t1 = x – y
   t2 = t1 + z

   or

   (2) t1 = x + y
   t2 = t1 – z

   The value of the expression computed on a given target machine depends on which of these codes is generated. Comment
3. Generate code for the following basic block using **gencode** algorithm.

   t1 = b + c
   t2 = d * e
   t3 = t2 * t1
   x = t3 * f

   Assuming that two registers are available.

12 LEX AND YACC

Lex

12.1 INTRODUCTION

Lex *(a Lexical Analyzer Generator)* is one of the compiler writing tools, that is used to generate a lexical analyzer or scanner from the description of tokens of the programming language to be implemented. And this description is required as regular expressions. Therefore Lex is a scanner generator used to generate a scanner automatically from the description of tokens as regular expressions.

Input to the Lex is text file containing regular expressions along with the actions to be taken by the generated scanner when each regular expression is matched. The output is a file that contains C source code defining the procedure yylex(), which implements DFA corresponding to regular expressions given in the input file, using table driven implementation. The output file is usually called lex.yy.c or lexyy.c, which when compiled and linked to the main program acts as a scanner or lexical analyzer recognizing tokens specified by the regular expressions of the input file.

12.2 FORMAT OF THE LEX INPUT FILE

Lex input file consists of three parts, a collection of definitions, a collection of rules, and a collection of user subroutines. These three sections are separated by %%(double percent sign) that appears on separate lines beginning in the first column as shown below:

{ definition}

%%

{ rules }

%%

(user subroutines }

where the definitions and the user subroutines are often omitted. The second %% is optional, but the first is required to mark the beginning of the rules. The absolute minimum Lex program is thus

%%

(no definitions, no rules) which generates a scanner that copies the input to the output unchanged.

The definition section contains two things:

1. Any C code that we want to be inserted external to any function (i.e., not as a part of any function), is required to be put in this section between delimiters %{ and %}.
2. If we want to use names for regular expressions, then these names are also required to be defined in this section.

The definition of name is required to start on a separate line and in the first column. The definition has a format:

name regular-expression

The rules section contains the rules. Every rule has the following format:

```
regular-expression   {
                         C code to be executed when
                         regular-expression is matched
                     }
```

The last section contains C code for any user defined subroutines that are called in the second section, and not defined elsewhere. One can also put main function in this section, which calls yylex(), if we want to compile lex.yy.c (output of Lex) as standalone program.

12.3 LEX CONVENTIONS FOR REGULAR EXPRESSIONS

1. Lex allows matching of single character or string of characters, simply by writing the characters in sequence. For example the sequence **if** can be written to match the reserved word if.

2. The meta-chars **(, |, +,*** are used in the usual sense. The meta-character? can be used to indicate an optional part. For example the regular expression **(aa | bb) (a | b)*c?** specifies the strings beginning with **aa** or **bb**, and ending with optional **c**. Lex allows meta-characters to be matched as actual chars by surrounding them in quotes. For example **"*"** can be used to match against *. Quotes can also be written around characters that are not meta-characters, where they have no effect. For example **"if"** can also be used to match the reserved word if. We can also use \ instead of quotes, but this works only for single character.
3. For character set write the chars in square brackets. For example [abcd] means any of the a,b,c, and d. For range of characters use - (hyphen). For example [a-z].
4. Inside the square brackets (representing character set) most of the meta-characters lose their special status/meaning and therefore are not required to be quoted. Even hyphen can be written as an ordinary or regular character, if it is listed first. Therefore it is possible to write [-+], instead of ["-"|"="]. Similarly [."?] means any of the three characters namely period, quote, and question mark. But some characters are still meta-characters, even inside brackets. Therefore that are required to be preceded by \, if we want to use them as ordinary/regular characters. For example [\^\\]is used for ^ and \.

Given below is the list of patterns that can be used and how they are interpreted by Lex.

<table>
<tr><th>pattern</th><th>Meaning</th></tr>
<tr><td>a</td><td>character a</td></tr>
<tr><td>"a"</td><td>character a even if a is a meta-character</td></tr>
<tr><td>\a</td><td>character a, when a is meta-character</td></tr>
<tr><td>a*</td><td>zero or more repetitions of a</td></tr>
<tr><td>a+</td><td>one or more repetitions of a</td></tr>
<tr><td>a?</td><td>an optiomal a</td></tr>
<tr><td>a | b</td><td>a or b</td></tr>
<tr><td>(a)</td><td>a itself</td></tr>
<tr><td>[abc]</td><td>any of the characters a,b, or c</td></tr>
<tr><td>[^ab]</td><td>any character except a and b</td></tr>
<tr><td>[a-d]</td><td>range of characters from a to d</td></tr>
<tr><td></td><td>any character except newline</td></tr>
<tr><td>{xyz}</td><td>the regular expression with name xyz</td></tr>
</table>

12.4 AMBIGUITY RESOLUTION

The scanner or lexical analyzer generated by Lex always first match the longest possible substring of the input to a rule. If the longest substring still matches two or more rules, then the scanner picks up the rule listed first in the rules section. If no rule matches any nonempty substring of input, then the default action is carried out which outputs the character or a string not matching to the output.

Given below is the list of internal names used by the Lex along with their use.

Lex Inetrnal Name	Use
lex.yy.c or lexyy.c	Name of the output file containing C source code generated by Lex.
yylex	Name of the scanner routine generated by the Lex.
yytext	Name of the string used for holding the string matched by regular expression.
yyin	Lex input file (default : stdin)
yyout	Lex output file (default : stdout)
input	Buffered input routine of scanner
ECHO	Macro used for default action

12.5 EXAMPLES

EXAMPLE 1: The following is the input to the Lex, specifying the scanner that recognizes the keywords **begin** and **if**, and an identifier, which is defined as any string that starts with letter and followed by letters or digits. The name **test1.l** is the name of file containing this specification.

```
%{
    #include <stdio.h>
%}
LETTER [a-zA-Z]
DIGIT [0-9]
%%
begin   {
             printf("Recognized KEYWORD : %s\n",yytext);
        }
```

```
if          {
                    printf("Recognized KEYWORD : %s\n",yytext);
            }
{LETTER}({LETTER}|{DIGIT})* {
                printf("Recognized ID : %s\n",yytext);
            }
%%
main()
   {
   yylex();
   }
```

The commands to be given to generate the scanner are:

$lex test1.l

$cc lex.yy.c -ll

The scanner generated by Lex can be executed with the following command:

$./a.out < data

where **data** is the name of the file containing the input to be given to scanner generated by Lex.

The contents of the data file is shown below:

```
if
begin
xyz
ogk
```

The output produced for the above input is :

```
Recognized KEYWORD : if
Recognized KEYWORD : begin
Recognized ID : xyz
Recognized ID : ogk
```

EXAMPLE 2: The following is the input to the Lex, specifying the scanner that recognizes the keywords begin and if, and an identifier, which is defined as any string that starts with letter and followed by letters or digits But since specification of identifier is listed before the specification of if and begin, the generated scanner recognizes both begin and if as identifier. The name **test2.l** is the name of file containing this specification.

```
%{
  #include <stdio.h>
%}
LETTER [a-zA-Z]
DIGIT  [0-9]
%%
{LETTER}({LETTER}|{DIGIT})* {
                              printf("Recognized ID : %s\n",yytext);
                              }
begin              {
                   printf("Recognized KEYWORD : %s\n",yytext);
                   }
if                 {
                   printf("Recognized KEYWORD: %s\n",yytext);
                   }
%%
main()
    {
    yylex();
    }
```

The commands to be given to generate the scanner are:

$lex test2.l

$cc lex.yy.c -ll

The scanner generated by Lex can be executed with the following command:

$./a.out < data

where data is the name of the file containing the input to be given to scanner generated by Lex.

The contents of the data file is shown below:

```
if
begin
xyz
ogk
```

The output produced for the above input is :

Recognized ID : if
Recognized ID : begin
Recognized ID : xyz
Recognized ID : ogk

EXAMPLE 3: The following is the input to the Lex, specifying the scanner that recognizes some of the keywords like begin, if, some of the operators, and an identifier, which is defined as any string that starts with letter and followed by letters or digits, and counts the number of identifiers, keywords, and operators encountered in the input given to the scanner. The action taken by the scanner is to increment a counter named key when it recognizes a keyword, increment a counter op, when it encounters an operator, and increment a counter id, when it encounters an identifier. The name **test3.l** is the name of file containing this specification .

```
%{
    int key=0,op=0,id=0;
%}
LETTER [a-zA-Z]
DIGIT  [0-9]
%%
(begin|if|while|do|then|else)   {
                                    key++;
                        }
[-+*/<>=]                  {
                                    op++;
                                        }
(<=|>=|!=)                 {
                            op++;
                        }
[,;\.]                  ;
{LETTER}({LETTER}|{DIGIT})*    { id++;
                               }
%%
main()
{
yylex();
```

```
printf("Number of ID's = %d\t,KEYWORDS = %d\t,OPERATORS =
%d\t",id,key,op);
}
```

The commands to be given to generate the scanner are:

$lex test3.l

$cc lex.yy.c -ll

The scanner generated by Lex can be executed with the following command:

$./a.out < data1

where data is the name of the file containing the input to be given to scanner generated by Lex.

The contents of the data1 file is shown below:

```
if a + b then x+y;
else p /q;
while a <= b do
 x = y + z;
```

The output produced for the above input is :

Number of ID's = 11 ,KEYWORDS = 5 ,OPERATORS = 6

EXAMPLE 4: The following is a Lex specification to generate a scanner that will take a decimal number between 1 to 999 in words and prints its numeric value as output. For example:

Input	**Output**
one hundred ten	110

```
%{
    int value=0;
%}
%%
one|ONE                    { value += 1;}
two|TWO                    {value += 2;}
three|THREE                {value += 3;}
four|FOUR                  {value += 4;}
five|FIVE                  {value += 5;}
six|SIX                    {value += 6;}
seven|SEVEN                {value += 7;}
```

```
eight|EIGHT                      {value += 8;}
nine|NINE                        {value += 9;}
ten|TEN                          {value += 10;}
eleven|ELEVEN                    {value += 11;}
twelve|TWELVE                    {value += 12;}
thirteen|THIRTEEN                {value += 13;}
fourteen|FOURTEEN                {value += 14;}
fifteen|FIFTEEN                  {value += 15;}
sixteen|SIXTEEN                  {value += 16;}
seventeen|SEVENTEEN              {value += 17;}
eighteen|EIGHTEEN                {value += 18;}
nineteen|NINETEEN                {value += 19;}
twenty|TWENTY                    {value += 20;}
thirty|THIRTY                    {value += 30;}
forty|FORTY                      {value += 40;}
fifty|FIFTY                      {value += 50;}
sixty|SIXTY                      {value += 60;}
seventy|SEVENTY                  {value += 70;}
eighty|EIGHTY                    {value += 80;}
ninety|NINETY                    {value += 90;}
hundred|HUNDRED                  {value*=100;}
%%
main()
 {
   yylex();
   printf("The number is %d\n",value);
 }
```

Yacc

12.6 INTRODUCTION

Yacc(*yet another compiler compiler*) is a parser generator, which is a program that takes as its input a specification of the syntax of the programming language, and produces as its output a parse procedure for that language whose name is **yyparse()**. The notation used for preparing this specification is a grammar(CFG). Historically the parser generators were called compiler-compilers, because traditionally all compilation steps were performed as actions included within the parser. But the modern view is to consider the parser as just one of the parts of the compiler. Hence this term is out of date.

Input to Yacc is a specification file usually with **.y** suffix, containing the rules of grammar specifying the structure of the language to be implemented. The output is C source code for the parser, usually in a file **y.tab.c** or **ytab.c** or **<filename>.tab.c,** where **<filename>.y** is input file.

12.7 FORMAT OF SPECIFICATION FILE

{ **definitions** }

%%

(**rules** }

%%

{ **programs** }

The definition section contains information about tokens, data types, and grammar rules. It also includes any C code that must go directly into the output file at its beginning. The declaration section may be empty. Moreover, if the programs section is omitted, the second %% mark may be omitted also; thus, the smallest legal Yacc specification is

%%

The second section contains grammar rules along with actions in the form of C code to be executed when every reduction is done by the parser using associated grammar rule.

The rules section is made up of one or more grammar rules. A grammar rule has the form:

A : BODY ;

A represents a nonterminal name, and **BODY** represents a sequence of zero or more names and literals. The colon and the semicolon are Yacc punctuation. Names may be of arbitrary length, and may be made up of letters, dot " . ", underscore " _ ", and non-initial digits. Upper and lower case letters are distinct. The names used in the body of a grammar rule may represent tokens or nonterminal symbols.

A literal consists of a character enclosed in single quotes. As in C, the backslash "\" is an escape character within literals, and all the C escapes are recognized. Thus

'\n' newline

'\r' return

'\'' single quote ``'''

'\\' backslash ``\''

'\t' tab

'\b' backspace

'\f' form feed

'\xxx' ``xxx'' in octal

For a number of technical reasons, the NUL character ('\0' or 0) should never be used in grammar rules.

If there are several grammar rules with the same left hand side, the vertical bar " | " can be used to avoid rewriting the left hand side. In addition, the semicolon at the end of a rule can be dropped before a vertical bar. Thus the grammar rules

```
A : B C D ;
A : E F ;
A : G ;
```

can be given to Yacc as

```
A : B C D
| E F
| G ;
```

It is not necessary that all grammar rules with the same left side appear together in the grammar rules section, although it makes the input much more readable, and easier to change. If a nonterminal symbol matches the empty string, this can be indicated in the obvious way:

empty : ;

Names representing tokens must be declared; this is most simply done by writing

%token name1 name2 . . .

in the declarations section. Every name not defined in the declarations section is assumed to represent a nonterminal symbol. Every nonterminal symbol must appear on the left side of at least one rule. Of all the nonterminal symbols, one, called the start symbol, has particular importance. The parser is designed to recognize the start symbol; thus, this symbol represents the largest, most general structure described by the grammar rules. By default, the start symbol is taken to be the left hand side of the first grammar rule in the rules section. It is possible, and in fact desirable, to declare the start symbol explicitly in the declarations section using the **%start** declaration:

%start symbol

The third section contains function declarations that may not be available otherwise through #include.

Yacc also permits C style comments to be inserted in the specification file at any point where they do not interfere with the basic format.

12.8 TOKENS RECOGNITION BY YACC

Yacc recognizes the tokens in two ways:

1. Any character inside single quotes in a grammar rule is recognized as itself. Therefore operator tokens like +, –, * can be included directly in the grammar rule.
2. Symbolic tokens are required to be declared in Yacc %token declaration. For example %token NUM, declares symbolic token NUM. To each symbolic token Yacc assigns a numeric value that does not conflict with any character value, by inserting #define statement in output. For example for declaration %token NUM, Yacc inserts #define NUM 257 in output.

12.9 START SYMBOL

By default the non-terminal to the left hand side of the first grammar rule in the rules section is taken as start symbol. But if we want the non-terminal to the left hand side of some other grammar rule to be used as start symbol, then it is required to put %start <non-terminal> in the definition section. Where <non-terminal> is the grammar symbol that we want to use as start symbol.

12.10 PSEDOVARIABLE

In writing the actions we can use Yacc psedovariables. When a grammar rule is recognized, each symbol in the rule possesses a value, which is integer unless changed by programmer, kept on value stack, maintained parallel to the parsing stack. And the values in the value stack may be referred to using a psedovariable that begins with **$. $$** represents the value of the non-terminal on the left-hand side of the grammar rule. **$1,$2,$3**, and so on represent the values of each symbol in succession on right-hand side of the grammar rule.

All the nonterminals get their values through user-supplied actions. That means user-supplied actions are responsible for assigning values to the nonterminals. Tokens can also be assigned values, but this is done during scanning/lexical analysis process. Yacc assumes that the value of the token is available in the variable yylval, which is defined internally by Yacc. Hence yylval must be assigned the required value when the token is recognized by the scanner. For example consider the following grammar rule and associated action:

```
F   :   NUM ' { $$ = $1;}
```

In the above grammar rule and associated action, $1 refers to the value of NUM token, that was assigned by the scanner to the variable yylval, when the token NUM was recognized.

12.11 LEXICAL ANALYSIS

The user must supply a lexical analyzer to read the input stream and communicate tokens (with values, if desired) to the parser. The lexical analyzer is an integer-valued function called **yylex**. The function returns an integer, the token number, representing the kind of token read. If there is a value associated with that token, it should be assigned to the external variable **yylval.**

The parser and the lexical analyzer must agree on these token numbers in order for communication between them to take place. The numbers may be chosen by Yacc, or chosen by the user. In either case, the "# define" mechanism of C is used to allow the lexical analyzer to return these numbers symbolically.

As mentioned above, the token numbers may be chosen by Yacc or by the user. In the default situation, the numbers are chosen by Yacc. The default token number for a literal character is the numerical value of the character in the local character set. Other names are assigned token numbers starting at 257.

To assign a token number to a token (including literals), the first appearance of the token name or literal in the declarations section can be immediately followed by a nonnegative integer. This integer is taken to be the token number of the name or literal. Names and literals not defined by this mechanism retain their default definition. It is important that all token numbers be distinct.

For historical reasons, the endmarker must have token number 0 or negative. This token number cannot be redefined by the user; thus, all lexical analyzers should be prepared to return 0 or negative as a token number upon reaching the end of their input.

A very useful tool for constructing lexical analyzers is the Lex program. These lexical analyzers are designed to work in close harmony with Yacc parsers. Lex can be easily used to produce quite complicated lexical analyzers, but there remain some languages (such as FORTRAN) which do not fit any theoretical framework, and whose lexical analyzers must be crafted by hand. The name of the file generated by Lex (**lex.yy.c**) then can be included in Yacc specifications as shown in the example given below:

12.12 EXAMPLE

Given below is specification of what constitutes expressions in typical programming language. And the actions for evaluating the expression.

```
%token NUM
%start S
%%

S : E {printf("The value of  expression is %d\n",$1);}
;
E:E'+'T   {$$=$1+$3;}
;
E:T       {$$=$1;}
;
T:T'*'F  {$$=$1*$3;}
;
T:F {$$=$1;}
;
```

```
F:NUM        {$$=$1}
;
%%
#include "lex.yy.c"
main()
{
  return(yyparse());
}
```

The name of the file used for the specification given above is test.y
The lex.yy.c is generated using Lex from the specification given below:

```
DIGIT [0-9]
%%
{DIGIT}+    { yylval = atoi(yytext);
              return(NUM);
            }
[ \t] ;     /*to skip whitespace characters */
.  return(yytext[0]);    /*to return any char other than digits and whitespace
                           as it is like +, and * operator*/
```

Using the above Yacc file when the parser is generated with following command:

$yacc test.y

$cc y.tab.c -ll -ly

When the generated parser is executed gives following result:

Input : 2 + 3 *5

Output : The value of expression is 17

12.13 YACC OPTIONS

1. When we want to make Yacc specific definitions available to other files, then we can use **-d** option to generate a header file named **y.tab.h. yatb.h** by the Yacc, which can be included in any other file that needs the Yacc specific definitions.
2. **-v (verbose)** option can be used to produce a file named as **y.output**, which contains the textual description of the LALR(1) parsing table to be used by the parser, giving information about the conflicts if any. Therefore

it is advisable to run Yacc with this option on grammar rules alone, before associating actions with them, and before adding auxiliary procedures to the specification, to make sure that Yacc generated parser performs as expected. The starting state is numbered as **0**. For example the statement **$accept : .S $end** corresponds to an item **S' → .S, $** augmentation nonterminal is given name **$accept** by Yacc, and end of input psedo-token is explicitly named **$end.**

For example for the specification given below in a file **test.y** the **y.output** file generated when -v option is used is shown below:

test.y file

```
%token NUM
%start S
%%

S : E {printf("The value of  expression is %d\n",$1);}
;
E:E'+'T   {$$=$1+$3;}
;
E:T       {$$=$1;}
;
T:T'*'F   {$$=$1*$3;}
;
T:F {$$=$1;}
;
F:NUM          {$$=$1}
;
%%
#include "lex.yy.c"
main()
{
   return(yyparse());
}
```

y.output file

```
    0  $accept : S $end

    1  S : E

    2  E : E '+' T
    3    | T

    4  T : T '*' F
    5    | F

    6  F : NUM

state 0
    $accept : . S $end  (0)

    NUM  shift 1
    .  error

    S  goto 2
    E  goto 3
    T  goto 4
    F  goto 5

state 1
    F : NUM .  (6)

    .  reduce 6

state 2
    $accept : S . $end  (0)

    $end  accept

state 3
    S : E .  (1)
    E : E . '+' T  (2)

    '+'  shift 6
    $end  reduce 1
```

```
state 4
    E : T .  (3)
    T : T . '*' F  (4)

    '*'  shift 7
    $end  reduce 3
    '+'  reduce 3

state 5
    T : F .  (5)

    .  reduce 5

state 6
    E : E '+' . T  (2)

    NUM  shift 1
    .  error

    T  goto 8
    F  goto 5

state 7
    T : T '*' . F  (4)

    NUM  shift 1
    .  error

    F  goto 9

state 8
    E : E '+' T .  (2)
    T : T . '*' F  (4)

    '*'  shift 7
    $end  reduce 2
    '+'  reduce 2

state 9
    T : T '*' F .  (4)

    .  reduce 4
```

5 terminals, 5 nonterminals
7 grammar rules, 10 states

There are no conflicts because the grammar is unambiguous. But when we use ambiguous grammar for specifying the expressions as shown below:

```
%token NUM
%start E
%%

E:E'+'E  {$$=$1+$3;}
| E'*'E  {$$=$1*43;}
|NUM     {$$=$1}
;

%%
#include "lex.yy.c"
main()
{
    return(yyparse());
}
```

y.output file

```
    0 $accept : E $end

    1 E : E '+' E
    2   | E '*' E
    3   | NUM

state 0
    $accept : . E $end (0)

    NUM shift 1
      error

    E goto 2
```

```
state 1
    E : NUM .  (3)

    . reduce 3

state 2
    $accept : E . $end  (0)
    E : E . '+' E  (1)
    E : E . '*' E  (2)

    $end  accept
    '+'  shift 3
    '*'  shift 4
    . error

state 3
    E : E '+' . E  (1)

    NUM  shift 1
    . error

    E  goto 5

state 4
    E : E '*' . E  (2)

    NUM  shift 1
    . error

    E  goto 6

5: shift/reduce conflict (shift 3, reduce 1) on '+'
5: shift/reduce conflict (shift 4, reduce 1) on '*'
state 5
    E : E . '+' E  (1)
    E : E '+' E .  (1)
    E : E . '*' E  (2)
```

```
'+'  shift 3
'*'  shift 4
$end  reduce 1

6: shift/reduce conflict (shift 3, reduce 2) on '+'
6: shift/reduce conflict (shift 4, reduce 2) on '*'
state 6
    E : E . '+' E  (1)
    E : E . '*' E  (2)
    E : E '*' E .  (2)

    '+'  shift 3
    '*'  shift 4
    $end  reduce 2

State 5 contains 2 shift/reduce conflicts.
State 6 contains 2 shift/reduce conflicts.

5 terminals, 2 nonterminals
4 grammar rules, 7 states
```

Yacc uses the following default disambiguating rules for resolving the conflicts:

1. In case of shift-reduce conflict, Yacc prefers shift action.
2. In case of reduce-reduce conflict, Yacc prefers reduction by grammar rule listed first in the specification file.

In addition to the above disambiguating rules, there exists mechanisms for specifying operator precedence and associativity separately for the grammar that is ambiguous. For this it is required to put the following lines, in the definition section of input specification:

%left '+', '-'

%left '*'

To specify that + and – have same precedence and are left associative, whereas * is also left associative but is having higher precedence than + and The reason for this is declaration of * is listed after the declaration of

+ and –. We can use **%right** to specify right associativity, and **%noassoc** means that repeated operators are not allowed at the same level.

12.14 ARBITRARY VALUE TYPES IN YACC

Values referred to by psedovariables like $$, $1 etc. are by default integer. Many a times we need the type of values in the value stack to be of some other type like float, char * etc. For this it is required to include redefinition of the value type of Yacc psedovariables in the specification file. This data type is always defined in Yacc by using C preprocessor symbol YYSTYPE. Redefining this symbol appropriately changes the type of Yacc value stack. For example if we put #define YYSTYPE char * inside %{ and %}, then it changes the type of values in value stack to character pointer.

Example:

/ This is Yacc specification for converting an expression into an eqivalent postfix representation. Here YYSTYPE is redefined as character pointer because we want the values of the grammar symbols to be of string type*/*

```
%{  #define YYSTYPE char*
%}
%token NUM
%token ID
%start S
%%
S : E {printf("The equivalent postfix expression is %s\n",$1);}
;
E:E'+'T { $$=(char *)calloc(strlen($1)+strlen($3)+1,sizeof(char));
    strcat($$,$1);
    strcat($$,$3);
    strcat($$,"+");
    }
;
E:T      {$$=$1;}
;
T:T'*'F   {$$=(char *)calloc(strlen($1)+strlen($3)+1,sizeof(char));
```

```
    strcat($$,$1);
    strcat($$,$3);
    strcat($$,"*");
    }
;
T:F {$$=$1;}
;
F:NUM {$$=$1;}
| ID {$$=$1;}
;
%%
#include "lex.yy.c"
/*extern YYSTYPE yylval;*/

main()
{
    return(yyparse());
}
```

The lex.yy.c is generated from the following specification using Lex:

```
DIGIT [0-9]
ID [a-zA-Z][a-zA-Z0-9]*
%%
{DIGIT}+    { yylval=(char *)calloc(yyleng,sizeof(char));
        strcpy(yylval,yytext);
        return(NUM);}
{ID}    {
        yylval=(char *)calloc(yyleng,sizeof(char));
        strcpy(yylval,yytext);
        return(ID);
        }
[ \t] ;                 /*to skip whitespace characters */
    return(yytext[0]);  /*to return any char other than digits and whitespac
                        as it is like +, and * operator*/
```

when the generated parser is executes we get the following results:

Input : a + b * c * d + e * f

Output : The equivalent postfix expression is abc*d*+ef*+

In a more complicated situation, we require different type of values for different grammar symbols. For example in the grammar shown below:

E E operator E

operator | - | * | /

We require character type value with operator nonterminal whereas with nonterminal E we require floating point number as its value. To deal with such a situation it is required to define YYSTYPE to be union of double and char. This can be done in two ways. One way is to define the union directly in Yacc definition using %union declaration and telling the Yacc what type of value in the union to return for which nonterminal using %type directive in the Yacc definition section as follows:

```
%union    {
              double value;
               char op;
          }
%type <value> E
%type <operator> op
```

The second way is to define a new data type in a separate include file and then define YYSTYPE to be of this type

Example:

```
%token NUM
%start S
%union {
    double value;
    char op;
    }
%type <value> E T F NUM
%type <op> op1 op2
%%
S:E    { printf("The value of Expression is %lf : \n",$1);}
```

```
E:E op1 T {
        switch($2)
        {
        case '+' : {$$=$1+$3;break;}
        case '-' : {$$=$1-$3;break;}
        }
    }
| T     {
            $$ = $1;
        }
;
T:T op2 F {
            switch($2)
            {
            case '*' : {$$=$1*$3;break;}
            case '/' : {$$=$1/$3;break;}
            }
        }
| F         {
                $$ = $1;
            }
;
F: NUM          {
                $$=$1;
            }
;
op1 :'+'    {
                $$= '+';
            }
| '-'       {
                $$ = '-';
            }
;
op2 : '*'   {
                $$ = '*';
            }
```

```
| '/'       {
                  $$ = '/';
            }
;
%%
#include "lex.yy.c"
main()
{
   return(yyparse());
}
```

The lex.yy.c file is generated from the following specification using Lex.

```
DIGIT [0-9]
%%
{DIGIT}+       { yylval.value = atof(yytext);
                 return(NUM);
          }
[ \t] ;/*to skip whitespace characters */
   return(yytext[0]);/*to return any char other than digits and whitespace
                          as it is like +, and * operator*/
```

When the generated parser is executed we get the following results:

Input : 2 + 3 * 4 - 5 / 2 + 4 * 2 - 1

Output : The value of Expression is 18.500000

12.15 TRACING THE EXECUTION OF PARSER

It is possible to get the trace of execution of the parser generated by Yacc, when the generated parser is executed . This gives the description of the parsing stack, and the actions carried out by the parser for a given input, telling when it goes for shift, and when it carries out the reduction. For this it is required to put the line **#define YYDEBUG 1** at the beginning of the Yacc specification file, just after #includes. And by setting the Yacc integer variable to 1 by adding the lines:

extern int yydebug;

yydebug = 1;

to the beginning of main function. (refer to the example given below).

Example:

```
%{ #define YYDEBUG 1 %}
%token NUM
%start S
%%

S:E       { printf("The value of Expression is %d : \n",$1);}
E:E'+'E   {$$=$1+$3;}
| E'*'E   {$$=$1*$3;}
|NUM      {$$=$1;}
;

%%
#include "lex.yy.c"
main()
{
    extern int yydebug;
    yydebug = 1;
    return(yyparse());
}
```

The lex.yy.c is generated from the following specification using Lex:

```
DIGIT  [0-9]
%%
{DIGIT}+      { yylval = atoi(yytext);
                return(NUM);
        }
[ \t] ;/*to skip whitespace characters */
   return(yytext[0]);/*to return any char other than digits and whitespace
                        as it is like +, and * operator*/
```

Trace of the execution of the parser generated for input 2 + 3 *4

```
yydebug: state 0, reading 257 (NUM)
yydebug: state 0, shifting to state 1
yydebug: state 1, reducing by rule 4 (E : NUM)
yydebug: after reduction, shifting from state 0 to state 3
yydebug: state 3, reading 43 ('+')
yydebug: state 3, shifting to state 4
yydebug: state 4, reading 257 (NUM)
yydebug: state 4, shifting to state 1
yydebug: state 1, reducing by rule 4 (E : NUM)
yydebug: after reduction, shifting from state 4 to state 6
yydebug: state 6, reading 42 ('*')
yydebug: state 6, shifting to state 5
yydebug: state 5, reading 257 (NUM)
yydebug: state 5, shifting to state 1
yydebug: state 1, reducing by rule 4 (E : NUM)
yydebug: after reduction, shifting from state 5 to state 7
yydebug: state 7, reading 0 (end-of-file)
yydebug: state 7, reducing by rule 3 (E : E '*' E)
yydebug: after reduction, shifting from state 4 to state 6
yydebug: state 6, reducing by rule 2 (E : E '+' E)
yydebug: after reduction, shifting from state 0 to state 3
yydebug: state 3, reducing by rule 1 (S : E)
The value of Expression is 14 :
yydebug: after reduction, shifting from state 0 to state 2
```

EXERCISE

1. Write Lex specification to generate a lexical analyzer that will capitalize all the identifier names in a given program.
2. Write Yacc specification to generate a parser that translates an expression containing numbers as operands ento a syntax tree. For example:

Input	**Output**
2 + 3 * 5	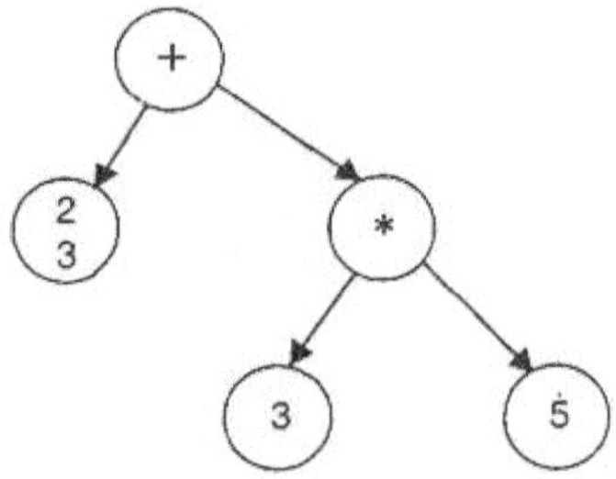

Also give the corresponding Lex specification that generates a lexical analyzer for the above parser.

3. Write Yacc specification to enter type attribute of the identifier into symbol table. Implement your symbol table as a table whose each entry contains two fields one for the name of the identifier and other for the type. Also give the corresponding Lex specification that generates lexical analyzer to be used by the above parser.
4. Write Yacc specification to generate a parser that translates an expression containing numbers as operands into three address code. For example:

Input	**Output**
a + b * c	#1 = b * c
	#2 = a + #1 where #1 and #2 are temporaries.

13 EXERCISES

The exercises that follow are designed to provide further examples of the concepts covered in this book. Their purpose is to put these concepts to work in practical contexts that will enable you, as a programmer, to better and more-efficiently use algorithms when designing your compiler.

EXERCISE 13.1: Construct the regular expression that corresponds to the state transition diagram shown in Figure 13.1.

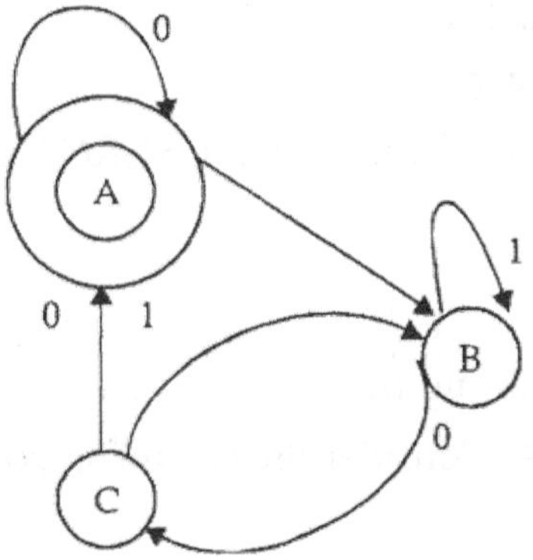

FIGURE 13.1 State transition diagram.

EXERCISE 13.2: Prove that regular sets are closed under intersection. Present a method for constructing a DFA with an intersection of two regular sets.

EXERCISE 13.3: Transform the following NFA into an optimal/minimal state DFA.

	0	1	∈
A	*A, C*	*B*	*D*
B	*B*	*D*	*C*
C	*C*	*A, C*	*D*
D	*D*	*A*	–

EXERCISE 13.4: Obtain the canonical collection of sets of LR(1) items for the following grammar:

$S \rightarrow SA \mid Ba$

$A \rightarrow Ab \mid \epsilon$

$B \rightarrow aA \mid c$

EXERCISE 13.5: Construct an LR(1) parsing table for the following grammar:

$T \rightarrow$ int

$L \rightarrow L$, id | id

EXERCISE 13.6: Construct an LALR(1) parsing table for the following grammar:

$D \rightarrow L : T$

$L \rightarrow L$, id | id

$T \rightarrow$ integer

EXERCISE 13.7: Construct an SLR(1) parsing table for the following grammar:

$S \rightarrow A)$

$S \rightarrow A, P \mid (P, P$

$P \rightarrow$ {num, num}

EXERCISE 13.8: Consider the following code fragment. Generate the three-address-code for it.

```
if a < b then
     while c > d do
          x = x + y
else
do
          p = p + q
     while e <= f
```

EXERCISE 13.9: Consider the following code fragment. Generate the three-address code for it.

```
for (i = 1; i <= 10; i++)
    if a < b then x = y + z
```

EXERCISE 13.10: Consider the following code fragment. Generate the three-address-code for it.

```
switch a + b
   {
        case 1: x = x + 1
        case 2: y = y + 2
        case 3: z = z + 3
        default: c = c -1
   }
```

EXERCISE 13.11: Write the syntax-directed translations to go along with the LR parser for the following:

$S \to AE$

$S \to DS$ while

$D \to$ do

EXERCISE 13.12: Write the syntax-directed translations to go along with the LR parser for the following:

$L \to$ elist

elist $\to$ elist[E] | [E]

$E \to E + T \mid T$

$T \to T * F \mid F$

$F \to$ id

EXERCISE 13.13: There are syntactic errors in the following constructs. For each of these constructs, find out which of the input's next tokens will be detected as an error by the LR parser.

1. while $a = b$ do $x = y + z$
2. $a + b = c$
3. $a *+ b + c$

EXERCISE 13.14: Comment on whether the following statements are true or false:

1. Given a finite automata $M(Q, \Sigma, \delta, q_0, F)$ that accepts $L(M)$, the automata $M_1(Q, \Sigma, \delta, q_0, (Q - F))$ accepts $L(M)$, where $L(M)$ is complement of $L(M)$. If M is an optimal or minimal state automata, then M_1 is also a minimal state automata.
2. Every subset of a regular set is also a regular set.
3. In a top-down backtracking parser, the order in which various alternatives are tried may affect the language accepted by the parser.
4. An LR parser detects an error when the symbol coming next in the input is not a valid continuation of the prefix of the input seen by the parser.
5. Grammar ambiguity necessarily implies ambiguity in the language generated by that grammar.
6. Every name is added to the symbol table during the lexical analysis phase irrespective of the semantic role played by each name.
7. Given a grammar with no useless symbols, but containing unit productions, if the unit productions are eliminated from the grammar, then it is possible that some of the grammar symbols in the resulting grammar may become useless.
8. In any nonambiguous grammar without useless symbols, the handle of a given right-sentential form is unique.

OBJECTIVE TYPE QUESTIONS

TRUE/FALSE TYPE QUESTIONS

1. Every name has an l-value, namely the location/locations reserved for its value.
2. The r-value of an expression with operator is the value produced by applying the operators.
3. The constant 5 has a r-value but no l-value.
4. If p is a pointer, its r-value is the location to which p points to. And its l-value is the location in which the value of p itself is stored.
5. The scope of a name is the portion of the program over which it may be used.
6. The structure of a source language has a strong effect on the number of passes of the compiler.
7. If a language allows the declaration of a name to occur after uses of that name, then the compiler of a language requires at least two passes to generate code easily.
8. A multi-pass compiler can be made to use less space than a single pass compiler.
9. A multi-pass compiler is slower than a single pass compiler.
10. A cross compiler is a compiler running on one machine and producing object code for another machine.
11. Back-patching technique is used to merge phases of a compiler into one pass.

12. The purpose of splitting the analysis of the source program into two phases, lexical analysis and syntax analysis is to simplify the overall design of compiler.
13. It is easier to specify the structure of tokens than the syntactic structure of source program.
14. A non deterministic finite automata is more powerful than a deterministic finite automata.
15. A deterministic finite automata equivalent to a given non deterministic finite automata always has less number of states than the number of states of non deterministic finite automata.
16. Every finite set is a regular set.
17. Every infinite language is non regular.
18. Every subset of a regular set is regular.
19. Regular sets are closed under intersection.
20. Given a context free grammar G it is possible to have a string w in L(G) having two leftmost derivations but only one rightmost derivation.
21. A grammar symbol X is useless if it does not derive to any string of terminals.
22. Every regular grammar is a context free grammar.
23. If for every w in L(G) there exists exactly one leftmost and equivalently exactly one rightmost derivation then the grammar G is unambiguous.
24. Top-down parsing is an attempt to find leftmost derivations for an input string.
25. No left-recursive grammar can be LL(1).
26. Every LL(1) grammar is SLR(1) also.
27. If a grammar G is SLR(1) then it is definitely LALR(1).
28. Every unambiguous grammar belong to the class of either SLR, CLR or LALR.
29. There are context free grammars that not LR.
30. Syntax directed translation is one of the methods of associating meaning with languages.
31. Syntax directed definitions is an extension of context free grammar.
32. Every S-attributed definition is L-attributed definition.
33. Synthesized attributes have a desirable property that they can be evaluated during a single bottom up traversal of a parse tree.
34. The advantage of a top down parser is that semantic actions can be called in the middle of the productions.

35. LL and LR parsers have the valid prefix property.
36. The advantage of using a parser with valid prefix property is that, it limits the amount of erroneous output it passes to subsequent phases of the compiler.
37. For detecting an error a compiler is required to scan some tokens ahead of the point of occurrence of an error.
38. The syntactic errors are those errors that are detected in the lexical or syntactic analysis phase by the compiler.
39. Static scope rules define the scope of a name in terms of syntactic structure of program.
40. When the language uses dynamic scope rules. The region of program over which a name is valid can vary during program execution.
41. If a procedure is non-recursive, then there exists only one activation of procedure at any instance of time.
42. The size of all fields in the activation record can be determined at compile time.
43. In control flow representation the value of a boolean expression is represented by a position in three address code.
44. Loop unrolling involves replicating the body of the loop to reduce the number of tests required to be carried out, if the number of iterations are constant.
45. Loop jamming involves merging the bodies of the two loops if the two loops have same number of iterations and uses the same indices.
46. One of the conditions required to be satisfied for making loop jamming to be legal is : No quantity is computed by the second loop at the iteration i, if it is computed by the first loop at iteration $j \geq i$.
47. Peephole optimization is an effective technique for locally improving the target code.
48. In peephole optimization a short sequence of target code instructions are examined and replacement of it by faster sequence is made whenever possible.
49. It is possible to make use of algebraic properties like commutativity and associativity of operands to possibly reduce the register requirement.
50. A lexical analyzer often need to scan many characters beyond the next token to determine the next token.
51. A finite automata with n states accepts a finite set L. Then the longest string in L can not have length greater than $n - 1$.

MULTIPLE CHOICE TYPE QUESTIONS

1. If w is a string and $|w| = n$ (*i.e.* length of w is n) then the number of prefixes of w are:
   (*a*) n (*b*) $n + 1$
   (*c*) n^2 (*d*) none of the above.
2. The number of subsequences of a string w of length n are:
   (*a*) n (*b*) n^2
   (*c*) 2^n (*d*) none of the above.
3. The regular expression $(a \mid b)^*abb$ denotes:
   (*a*) all possible combinations of *a*'s and *b*'s
   (*b*) set of all strings ending with *abb*
   (*c*) set of all strings starting with *a* and ending with *abb*
   (*d*) none of the above.
4. If a NFA with has n states then the maximum number of states the equivalent DFA can have are:
   (*a*) n^2 (*b*) n
   (*c*) 2^n (*d*) none of the above.
5. Given below are the regular expressions:
   (*i*) $(a \mid b)^*$ (*ii*) $(a^*b^*)^*$ (*iii*) $(ab)^*$
   which of them are equivalent:
   (*a*) (*i*) only (*b*) (*i*) and (*ii*) only
   (*c*) (*i*), (*ii*) and (*iii*) (*d*) (*ii*) and (*iii*) only.
6. Given two DFA's M_1 and M_2,. They are equivalent if:
   (*a*) M_1 and M_2 has the same number of states
   (*b*) M_1 and M_2 has the same number of final states
   (*c*) M_1 and M_2 accepts the same language, *i.e.* $L(M_1) = L(M_2)$
   (*d*) None of the above.
7. Given a finite automata $M = (Q, \Sigma, \delta, q_0, F)$. If δ maps $Q \times \Sigma$ to 2^Q then:
   (*a*) M is a DFA (*b*) M is NFA
   (*c*) M is NFA with $\in$-moves (*d*) None of the above.
8. Given a grammar $G = (V, T, P, S)$ and if every production in P is of the form $A \to \propto$, where A is in V and $\propto$ is in $(V \cup T)^*$ then G is:
   (*a*) Context sensitive grammar (*b*) Unrestricted grammar
   (*c*) Regular grammar (*d*) Context free grammar.

9. If G is a left linear grammar then G is:
   (*a*) A regular grammar (*b*) A context free grammar
   (*c*) A context sensitive grammar (*d*) All the above.
10. Which of the following phase of compilation process is an optional phase:
    (*a*) Lexical analysis phase (*b*) Syntax analysis phase
    (*c*) Code optimization phase (*d*) Code generation phase.
11. A compiler running on computers with small memory would normally be:
    (*a*) a multi-pass compiler
    (*b*) single pass compiler
    (*c*) a compiler with less number of phases
    (*d*) none of the above.
12. Which of the following are the aspects of the high level languages:
    (*a*) Ease of understanding (*b*) Naturalness
    (*c*) Portability (*d*) All the above
13. Which of the following expressions have no l-value:
    (*a*) $a[i + 1]$ (*b*) a
    (*c*) 3 (*d*) $*a$.
14. If the called subprogram does not encounter any exception during its execution. Then which of the two parameter passing mechanisms will produce same result:
    (*a*) call by value and call by reference
    (*b*) call by reference and call by value result
    (*c*) call by value and call by name
    (*d*) call by reference and call by name.
15. Which of the following conflicts can not arise in LR parsing:
    (*a*) shift-reduce (*b*) reduce-reduce
    (*c*) shift-shift (*d*) none of the above.
16. If a grammar is LALR(1) then it is necessarily:
    (*a*) SLR(1) (*b*) CLR(1)/LR(1)
    (*c*) LL(1) (*d*) None of the above.
17. If all operators are binary. Then a string of operators and operands is a postfix expression if and only if:
    (*a*) every nonempty prefix has fewer operators than operands
    (*b*) every nonempty prefix has equal number of operators and operands

(*c*) every nonempty prefix has more operators than operands
(*d*) none of the above.

18. An annotated parse tree is :
(*a*) a parse tree with attribute values shown at the parse tree nodes
(*b*) a parse tree with values of only some attributes shown at parse tree nodes
(*c*) a parse tree without attribute values shown at pare tree nodes
(*d*) none of the above.

19. A synthesized attribute is an attribute whose value at a parse tree node depends on:
(*a*) attributes at the siblings only
(*b*) attributes at parent node only
(*c*) attributes at children nodes only
(*d*) none of the above.

20. An inherited attribute is the one whose initial value at a parse tree node is defined in terms of:
(*a*) attributes at the parent and/or siblings of that node
(*b*) attributes at children nodes only
(*c*) attributes at both children nodes and parent and/or siblings of that node
(*d*) none of the above.

21. Which of the following is not true about dynamic type checking.
(*a*) type checking is done during the execution
(*b*) it increases the cost of execution
(*c*) all the type errors are detected
(*d*) none of the above.

22. A garbage is :
(*a*) unallocated storage
(*b*) allocated storage with all access paths to it destroyed
(*c*) allocated storage
(*d*) un-initialized storage.

23. A dangling reference is :
(*a*) pointer pointing to storage which is freed
(*b*) pointer pointing to nothing
(*c*) pointer pointing to storage which is still in use
(*d*) pointer pointing to un-initialized storage.

24. Consider the statement $I = 1$:, here colon is used in place of semicolon. This error is detected by the compiler in :
    (*a*) lexical analysis phase
    (*b*) syntax analysis phase
    (*c*) code optimization phase
    (*d*) code generation phase.
25. The error of missing right parentheses in the statement : $xyz(a, 2^*(3 + b)$ is detected in:
    (*a*) lexical analysis phase
    (*b*) syntax analysis phase
    (*c*) code generation phase
    (*d*) none of the above.
26. So called 90-10 rule states that:
    (*a*) 90% of the time is spent on 10% of the code
    (*b*) 10% of the time is spent on 90% of the code
    (*c*) 90% of the time is spent on 90% of the code
    (*d*) none of the above.
27. A basic block is:
    (*a*) a block of non consecutive statements
    (*b*) a block of consecutive statements which may be entered only at the beginning and when entered are executed in sequence without halt or possibility of branch except at the end.
    (*c*) a block of statements whose last statement is always a conditional jump.
    (*d*) a block of statements whose last statement is always a conditional jump.
28. A pictorial representation of the value computed by each statement in the basic block is:
    (*a*) tree
    (*b*) DAG
    (*c*) Graph
    (*d*) None of the above.
29. Constant folding means:
    (*a*) replacing expressions by their values, if the value can be computed at compile time
    (*b*) replacing an operand by constant
    (*c*) ignoring the constant
    (*d*) none of the above.
30. A block kills an expression x op y iff:
    (*a*) it assigns x or y and does not subsequently re-compute x or y
    (*b*) it assigns to both x and y
    (*c*) does not assign to either x or y
    (*d*) none of the above.

31. A block B generates an expression *x* op *y* iff:
   (*a*) it assigns to either *x* or *y*
   (*b*) it assigns to both *x* and *y*
   (*c*) it evaluates *x* op *y* and does not subsequently redefine *x* or *y*
   (*d*) none of the above.
32. A variable *x* is said to be live at a point *p* if and only if:
   (*a*) value of *x* at *p* could be used along some path in the flow graph starting at point *p*
   (*b*) *x* is assigned at point *p*
   (*c*) *x* is not assigned at point *p*
   (*d*) none of the above.
33. Which of the following is not a loop optimization:
   (*a*) Induction variable elimination (*b*) Loop unrolling
   (*c*) Loop jamming (*d*) None of the above.
34. Which of the following is not a peephole optimization:
   (*a*) removal of unreachable code
   (*b*) elimination of multiple jumps
   (*c*) elimination of loop invariant computation
   (*d*) none of the above.
35. LR grammar is a:
   (*a*) Context free grammar (*b*) Context sensitive grammar
   (*c*) Regular grammar (*d*) None of the above.
36. Which of the following is an equivalence relation
   (*a*) A relation "is perpendicular to" defined on the set of straight lines in a plane
   (*b*) a relation "is congruent to" on set of all triangles in a plane
   (*c*) a relation "*a* is divisor of *b*" for *a* and *b* in *N*(Where *N* is set of all natural numbers).
   (*d*) "brother" relation on a set of persons.
37. LEX is a:
   (*a*) lexical analyzer generator (*b*) A parser generator
   (*c*) Code generator - generator (*d*) None of the above.
38. YACC is a:
   (*a*) lexical analyzer generator (*b*) parser generator
   (*c*) semantic analyzer (*d*) none of the above.

39. The output of a preprocessor is:
   (*a*) absolute machine language program
   (*b*) relocatable machine language program
   (*c*) assembly language program
   (*d*) a high level language program.
40. DAG representation of a basic block allows:
   (*a*) automatic detection of local common sub-expressions
   (*b*) automatic detection of induction variables
   (*c*) automatic detection of loop invariant
   (*d*) none of the above.
41. Given a string abc, the string ac is a:
   (*a*) subsequence of *abc* (*b*) sub-string of *abc*
   (*c*) prefix of *abc* (*d*) suffix of *abc*.
42. The intersection of a regular language and a context free language is
   (*a*) always a regular language
   (*b*) always a context free language
   (*c*) always a context sensitive language
   (*d*) none of the above.
43. If I is a set of valid items for a viable prefix γ. Then GOTO(*I*, *X*) is a set of items that are valid for the viable prefix:
   (*a*) γX (*b*) γ
   (*c*) prefix of γ (*d*) none of the above.
44. A flow graph *G* is reducible if and only if we can partition the edges into two disjoint groups, forward edges and back edges with the following properties:
   (*i*) The forward edges forming an a-cyclic graph in which every node can be reached from the initial node of *G*
   (*ii*) The back edges consists only of edges whose heads dominates tails.
   (*a*) both (*i*) and (*ii*) are true (*b*) only (*i*) is true
   (*c*) only (*ii*) is true (*d*) none of the above.
45. The advantage of using parser with valid prefix property is that:
   (*a*) it detects an error where it has actually occurred
   (*b*) it reports an error as possible
   (*c*) it detects an error much earlier than its occurrence
   (*d*) none of the above.

46. In a block-structured language if procedure A calls procedure B having the nesting depths N_A and N_B respectively. Then which of the following is true:

(*a*) $N_B - N_A \leq 1$ (*b*) $N_B - N_A \geq 1$
(*c*) $N_B - N_A < 1$ (*d*) none of the above.

47. What is true about $\in$-closure(q), where q is a state of a finite automata.

(*a*) it can be empty (*b*) it contains at least q
(*c*) it is an infinite set (*d*) none of the above.

48. If $G = (V, T, P, S)$ is a context free grammar. Then $L(G)$ will be infinite if and only if:

(*a*) at least one production in P is recursive
(*b*) No production is recursive
(*c*) All productions are recursive
(*d*) None of the above.

49. A left recursive grammar :

(*a*) cannot be LL(1) (*b*) cannot be LR(1)
(*c*) is an ambiguous grammar (*d*) none of the above.

50. Input to the LEX is:

(*a*) context free grammar (*b*) regular expressions
(*c*) output of the preprocessor (*d*) none of the above.

51. Given a grammar $G = (V, T, P, S)$. If S does not derive to any w in T^* then $L(G)$ is an:

(*a*) an empty set (*b*) a finite set
(*c*) an infinite set (*d*) none of the above.

52. If there exists exactly one production deriving every non terminal in a context free grammar. Then $L(G)$ is :

(*a*) a finite set
(*b*) an infinite set
(*c*) a set containing only one string
(*d*) none of the above.

SHORT ANSWER TYPE QUESTIONS

1. A two dimensional array a having 10 rows and 20 columns is stored in a column-major form, with 2 bytes per element and base address is 100. What is the l-value of a[5,2]? Assume that lower bound for each of the dimensions to be 1.

2. Given a string of length n. How many subsequences we can form using n.
3. What is the language accepted by the finite automata having the transition diagram given below:

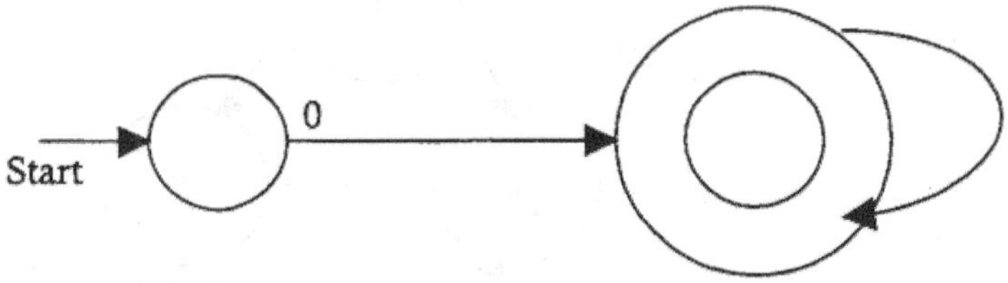

4. What is the language accepted by the finite automata whose transition diagram is given below:

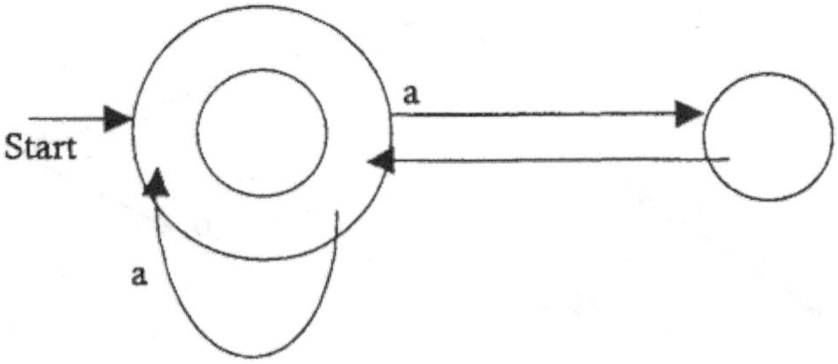

5. If $A \to \alpha$ is a production of a context free grammar and $|\alpha| = n$. Then how many items can be generated using $A \to \alpha$.
6. Given a grammar:

   $E \to E + T \mid T$

   $T \to T * F \mid F$

   $F \to id$

   Which is a set of valid items for a viable prefix $E+$.
7. Consider the following grammar:

   $S \to AaAB \mid BbBa$

   $A \to \in$

   $B \to \in$

   Is the grammar LL(1)?
8. Write quadruples for the expression: $(a + b) * (c + d) - (a + b + c)$.
9. Write triples for the expression: $(a + b) * (c + d) - (a + b + c)$.
10. Construct DAG for the following code:

    $a = a + b$

    $e = a + d + e.$

11. In a flow graph given below: what are the dominators of the node 3.

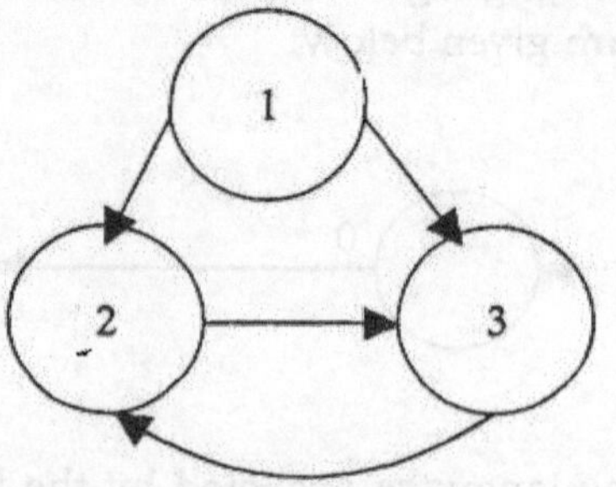

12. What is the register requirement of the tree given below:

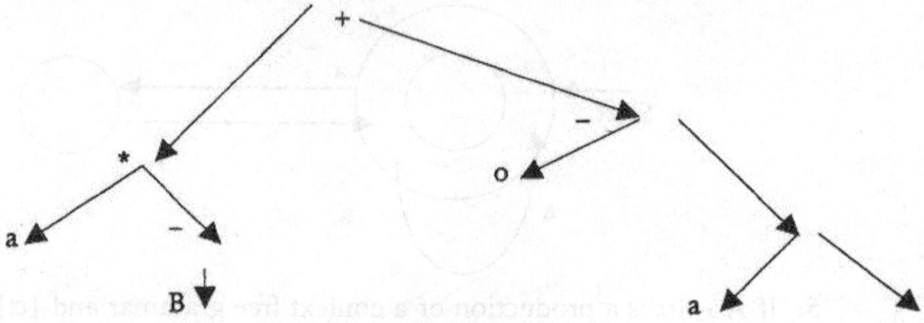

13. A relation R on the set of integers defined as :
    $R = \{ (a, b) \mid a - b \text{ is even integer}\}$
    Show that R is equivalence.
14. For the grammar having productions:
    $$A \rightarrow (A)A \mid \in$$
    Compute FIRST and FOLLOW set of A.
15. Is the following grammar LL(1)
    $$S \rightarrow aSa \mid \in.$$

ANSWERS

TRUE/FALSE TYPE QUESTIONS

1. True	2. True	3. True	4. True	5. True
6. True	7. True	8. True	9. True	10. True
11. True	12. True	13. True	14. False	15. False

16. True	17. False	18. False	19. True	20. False
21. True	22. True	23. True	24. True	25. True
26. False	27. True	28. False	29. True	30. True
31. True	32. True	33. True	34. True	35. True
36. True	37. True	38. True	39. True	40. True
41. True	42. True	43. True	44. True	45. True
46. True	47. True	48. True	49. True	50. True
51. True				

MULTIPLE CHOICE QUESTIONS

1. (*b*)	2. (*c*)	3. (*b*)	4. (*c*)	5. (*b*)
6. (*c*)	7. (*b*)	8. (*d*)	9. (*d*)	10. (*c*)
11. (*a*)	12. (*d*)	13. (*c*)	14. (*b*)	15. (*c*)
16. (*b*)	17. (*a*)	18. (*a*)	19. (*c*)	20. (*a*)
21. (*c*)	22. (*b*)	23. (*a*)	24. (*b*)	25. (*b*)
26. (*a*)	27. (*b*)	28. (*b*)	29. (*a*)	30. (*a*)
31. (*c*)	32. (*a*)	33. (*d*)	34. (*c*)	35. (*a*)
36. (*b*)	37. (*a*)	38. (*b*)	39. (*d*)	40. (*a*)
41. (*a*)	42. (*b*)	43. (*a*)	44. (*a*)	45. (*b*)
46. (*a*)	47. (*b*)	48. (*a*)	49. (*a*)	50. (*b*)
51. (*a*)	52. (*c*).			

SHORT ANSWER TYPE QUESTIONS

1. 128
2. 2^n.
3. All the strings of binary digits whose integer value is an integer power of 2. *i.e.* binary representation of 2^i for $i \geq 0$.
4. All the strings of $a^{'s}$ and $b^{'s}$, having every occurrence of b preceded by at least one a.
5. $n + 1$.
6. $\{ E \rightarrow E + . T$

   $T \rightarrow . T * F$

   $T \rightarrow . F$

   $F \rightarrow . id$

   $\}$

7. Yes the grammar is LL(1).
8.

+	a	b	t_1
+	c	d	t_2
+	a	b	t_3
+	t_3	c	t_4
×	t_1	t_2	t_5
−	t_5	t_4	t_6

Where t_1, t_2, t_3, t_4, t_5, and t_6 are compiler generated temporaries.

9.

(1)	+	a	b
(2)	+	c	d
(3)	+	a	b
(4)	+	(3)	c
(5)	×	(1)	(2)
(6)	−	(5)	(4)

10.

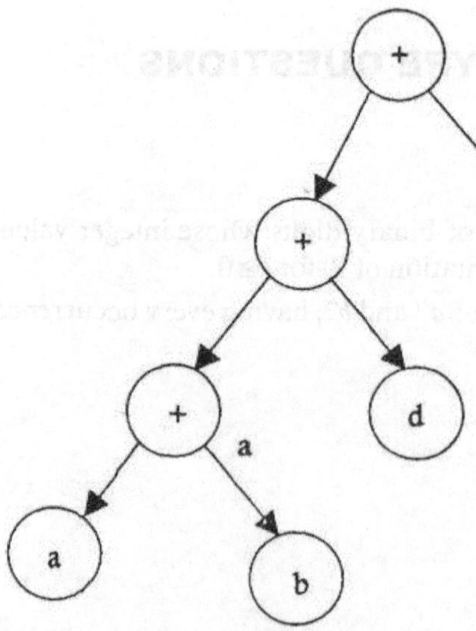

11. node 1 only.
12. 3
13. For every integer a since $a - a = 0$, which is even therefore R is reflexive.
    For every pair of integers (a, b) if $a - b$ is even then $b - a$ is always even hence R is symmetric.
    For every (a, b) and (b, c) if $a - b$ is even integer and $b - c$ is also an integer, then $a - c$ is always an integer, hence R is transitive also. Therefore R is an equivalence relation.
14. FIRST(A) = { (, ∈ }
    FOLLOW(A) + {)}
15. No the grammar is not LL(1).

INDEX

F

M

N

O

P